The 1968 London
to Sydney Marathon

For Patrick

Thank you for your help
and enthusiasm!

Robert Connor

The 1968 London to Sydney Marathon

A History of the 10,000 Mile Endurance Rally

ROBERT CONNOR

McFarland & Company, Inc., Publishers

Jefferson, North Carolina

ISBN (print) 978-0-7864-9586-3
ISBN (ebook) 978-1-4766-2084-8

LIBRARY OF CONGRESS CATALOGUING DATA ARE AVAILABLE

British Library cataloguing data are available

On the cover: *clockwise from top left* Lucien Bianchi and Jean-Claude Ogier
in their Citroën between Numeralla and Hindmarsh, Australia, just before
disaster struck (courtesy of Bruce Thomas); the crowds on Westminster
Bridge, London, as the rally began (courtesy of Mike Wood); No. 47 MGB
checks in at the Hindmarsh Station checkpoint (courtesy of Bruce Thomas);
BMC 1800 factory cars (courtesy of Mike Wood)

Back cover image: the author at the wheel of no. 53 in 2012. The Rambler
American was the sole U.S.–entered car in the 1968 marathon.

Printed in the United States of America

*McFarland & Company, Inc., Publishers
Box 611, Jefferson, North Carolina 28640
www.mcfarlandpub.com*

For Vera who started it,
Rob who believed in it,
and Martin and Pen
who helped in so many ways

Acknowledgments

In addition to all those men and women who welcomed me into their lives and shared their stories, I am indebted to Graham Anderson, Richard Ashton, Bonnie Carlson-Green, Colin Cleaver, Les Dalton, Beverley Doyle, Rob Ford, John and Jeanette Hindmarsh, Rob Howell, Susan Jamieson, Tracy Johansson, Simon Maxwell, the New South Wales State Library, David J. North, Bryan Peebles, Alhazmi Shea, Kim Smith, Bernard Stevens, Stephen Theiler, Bruce Thomas, Time Inc. UK, Craig Watson, Frank and Elaine Wrenick, and especially Martin Proudlock and Max Stahl.

Contents

Contents

Preface

From when I began to crawl, the way to my heart was to give me a toy car—a shiny Matchbox, Corgi or Dinky model—and, as I got older, my obsession with miniature motor vehicles grew with me. I remember that for Christmas 1968, thinking I should have other interests, my father bought me a train set. Unfortunately for him, the set included an automobile-carrier, a beautiful, gray double-decker railroad wagon, which held five tiny plastic vehicles produced by Tri-ang, under their brand name Minix. I can still remember what kinds of cars they were. I was ecstatic to have these perfect, plastic renderings of a Vauxhall Viva, Morris 1100, Austin 1800, Hillman Minx and best of all, an Austin A60 Cambridge. Despite my father's best intentions, I was soon staging scenes of cars stalled on the railroad crossing as a locomotive bore down, drivers stuck in miniature traffic jams, desperate not to miss the train, fender-benders in the station car park and so on.

In the summer of 1969, in a clever attempt to keep me occupied on a long train journey home from a vacation in Cornwall, my mother ran into a shop at the Euston railroad station in London and bought me a toy car. In doing so, she introduced me for the very first time to the existence of Australia, kangaroos and the 1968 London to Sydney Marathon endurance rally. This toy, this magnificent blue and white marvel, was a model of the car that won the Marathon. It had rally decals to fix to the car, it had removable wheels called "Golden Jacks," it had a tool kit and extra wheels and tires on the roof and, best of all, it had a "roo bar." I can remember sitting on the train and gazing at the rally car, the plastic kangaroo and the illustrations of the Australian outback on the box. What was this London to Sydney Marathon? How could a car, in which my friend's father took us to school, drive all the way to the other side of the world and win? And what exactly was a "roo bar"?

The London to Sydney Marathon would be the motorsports competition of a lifetime. Not since the first decade of the twentieth century had there been such an enormous spectacle of motoring endurance. Two hundred and forty three men and 12 women would drive in competition along a 10,000-mile route from London in England to Sydney in Australia. Ninety-eight cars carrying crews from 19 different nations would hurtle through 10 countries before tackling the vast expanse of the Australian outback—the bull dust, the heat, the danger and the "giant" kangaroos. For every finely tuned, professionally-prepared rally car, there would be a barely-more-than-standard family sedan or station wagon. For every experienced international rally or racing driver, there would be many enthusiastic amateurs without any experience of endurance motorsports, some without even the experience of driving on the "wrong" side of the highway.

Who were these spear-carriers, these enthusiastic novices who saw their hope of getting to Sydney realized or worse, saw their dreams disappear on a roadside in India or a ravine in Turkey? Who were these determined men and women who coaxed their tortured, malfunctioning cars across mountain ranges and international borders, through the death-defying throngs that lined the highways of Pakistan and India and across the desolate, dusty plains of the Australian outback? What brought them to that bright, wintery November day in London, their cars laden to the roof with extra parts, extra tires, maps, route notes, food rations, extra clothes and, in one case, even an umbrella?

I didn't set out to write a book about the 1968 London to Sydney Marathon. Four years ago, I was idly searching the internet for other Marathon model cars and came across images of a crashed Citroën DS21, its Marathon number clearly visible on the twisted and crumpled bodywork. Intrigued, I began to look for further references and eventually came to the conclusion that, although much was written about the Marathon in 1968 and 1969, this mammoth feat of endurance motorsports had seemingly disappeared into the mists of time. Certainly when I spoke to friends and colleagues, I realized very few had even heard of the Marathon and they certainly hadn't known that huge numbers of ordinary members of the public had followed events in their newspapers, watched the competitors set off from a South London stadium and lined the roads out of the city and down through the Kent countryside to Dover. My initial research revealed a surprising mix of vehicles that had taken part in the event. It also showed that among the professional rally drivers and factory-backed cars was a substantial number of privately entered automobiles. Some were hardly what might have been considered as suitable choices for driving such a long way—a 1930 Bentley, a little MG Midget and a pair of tiny Dutch DAF 55s. I noted that a few competitors had written published accounts of their experiences, but these books were long out of print and copies were extremely difficult to find. I found myself disappearing down the warren of rabbit-holes that is the internet, setting off a chain-reaction, which eventually led me to tracking down, meeting and interviewing more than 60 of those who competed in this unprecedented transcontinental motorsports event, or played a part in its organization. My own personal "marathon to chase the Marathon" has taken me around England and over to Ireland, France, the United States and twice to Australia, where I was repeatedly afforded the opportunity to sit and listen to these pioneering men and women, some of whom were professional rally drivers and navigators, but most of whom were ordinary people who allowed the spirit of adventure to take them on a 10,000-mile drive all the way to the other side of the world. Some were chasing victory, but most were just determined to make it, determined that their chosen vehicle would survive the rigors of the Iranian desert, the mountain passes of Afghanistan and the endless wilderness of central Australia.

These are some of their stories as well as the story of the Marathon itself, from an idea chanced upon during a boozy lunch between friends in the summer of 1967, through to the last car to cross the finishing line in Sydney in December 1968. In addition to the many interviews I was given, I have drawn from the extensive international press coverage which the Marathon generated in England, France, India and Australia. A small number of competitors were motoring or motorsports journalists who provided daily copy for their editors as they bounced and skidded their way across the world. As a result, regular reports and updates appeared in both dedicated automotive publications and daily newspapers. I have also drawn from some of the films that were contemporarily made about the Marathon and the small number of books written by some of those who competed, tattered second-hand copies of which I was eventually able to track down.

Unless indicated, all quotations are from the transcriptions of interviews I undertook with competitors and organizers. Any monetary values are as they were in 1968, as are any references to names of countries and places.

Three of the six cars that were prepared for the Marathon by the British Motor Corporation (BMC) Competitions Department were officially entered by its new management company British Leyland. However, because the network of service and support for the route across Europe and Asia was organized by the BMC Competitions Department and by BMC Australia between Perth and Sydney, for the purposes of narrative consistency, "BMC GB" is referred to throughout the book.

Introduction

In Great Britain, there is wall-to-wall coverage of soccer in both broadcast and print media. Other sports are often focused upon such as cricket, rugby or tennis, but rarely do we get the chance to watch or read about rally racing, even the World Rally Association Championships. Rally fans have to make quite an effort to capture the spectacle of cars hurtling along forest tracks or across desert landscapes, cars skidding and sliding through tightly packed crowds of spectators, all craning to catch a glimpse of a rally-prepared Peugeot, Ford or Mitsubishi. In the 1960s and 1970s it was a different story—national and international championship rallying was a frequent presence on British and European television, with images of Ford Escorts, Triumph TR7s and SAABs blasting through the English Kilder Forest or over the French Alps. However, during the mid–1980s, a combination of increasingly powerful, specially designed rally cars and the growing numbers of dedicated and passionate spectators crowding the roadsides probably led to a number of shocking fatalities across the European rally circuit and perhaps a gradual decline in media interest. Today, if you want to watch coverage of the World Rally Championships, you have to hunt through the various sports channels on cable or satellite television in the hope of catching the occasional 60 minutes of coverage.

Things could not have been more different in 1968. November 24 saw 98 cars, 243 men and 12 women gather at the Crystal Palace Stadium in South London, England, to embark on what was billed to be the greatest, longest, most challenging competitive motoring event ever seen. The British *Daily Express* and Australian *Sydney Telegraph* newspapers had been promoting and building the event up for months, a spectacular feat of driving skill and human endurance that would see crews of two, three and four people from many nations attempt to drive 10,000 miles across 11 countries in ten days, all chasing a range of individual and team trophies and cash prizes at the finish line in Sydney, Australia. Remarkably, alongside many professional rally and racing drivers making their final preparations for the grueling drive, there were many amateur competitors, some of whom had never raced or rallied a car in their lives.

The range of cars and competitors was wide with representation from some of the big European automobile manufacturers of the 1960s, which ran competitions or "works" departments, as well as commercially sponsored cars, teams representing the British Army, Navy and Air Force and individual private entries. Eighty thousand people turned out to watch the first car start at 2:00 p.m. and millions more lined the route through the busy streets of London and onwards to the docks at Dover on the English south coast. Interest in the event was enormous, from both media and the general public and not just in Britain. Press coverage throughout the 10,000-mile event was meticulously organized and, as the cars swept through each country, pages of local newspaper copy were printed. Vast crowds gathered at each checkpoint, often leading to the heavy-handed crowd control of local police; the use of batons and truncheons to beat back the excited throngs in Eastern Europe and Asia was widespread and, for many of the teams, passage through urban parts of Pakistan and India became nightmarishly difficult as millions of people crowded forward to catch a glimpse as each car sped past, some even trying to snatch a souvenir off of a vehicle's bodywork. Thousands more would watch the cars tackle the tortuous terrain of the Australian outback, many travelling hundreds of miles just to catch a glimpse of the cars as they arrived at, and quickly departed from, the isolated checkpoints set up in some of the least inhabited parts of the country. This was to be the motorsports event of a lifetime, a rally like no other. This was to be the London to Sydney Marathon.

In common parlance, "marathon" means running, those great 26.2-mile races through famous city streets, highways coned off or closed as a mixture of world-class athletes and costumed fun-runners pound the asphalt in search of glory, or charitable fund-raising, or just simply to achieve the exhilaration of crossing the finish line. The accepted definition of "marathon" references long-distance running, with its roots in the legend of the Greek soldier who carried a message during the Battle of Marathon in 490 BC. The marathon became an integral part of the Olympic movement in 1896 and remains a much anticipated event at every Olympic Games.

While there were two endurance motoring events in 1907 (Paris to Peking) and 1908 (New York to Paris), these were deemed "races," whereby the first car across the line won outright (and for the 1907 winner, a magnum of champagne!), so the idea of an extremely long endurance event, across countries and continents and following rally-specific rules and regulations, was unprecedented before the London to Sydney Marathon. It was promoted as the most challenging motorsports event ever and would be open to anyone with a car and the entrance fee of $1,320, to a maximum of 100 entries. It was open to all nationalities and there would be a reserve list for anyone not making the first 100. Organizers hoped it would attract both manufacturers' motorsports teams and enthusiastic amateurs, and one of the few entry criteria was that all cars had to be two-wheel drive. To encourage international cooperation among national authorities, the event would be promoted as a "marathon," not a "rally," thus allowing flexibility when preparing the route to include public highways.

To understand the context and thinking behind the Marathon, it's worth having a look at the economics of the time. In 1967, Britain was experiencing an economic crisis and there was a prevailing gloom across the country. This led British Prime Minister Harold Wilson to devalue the British pound in the hope that exports would be given a boost. Unfortunately, the devaluation didn't have the desired consequence and Britain saw domestic inflation rise. Worry grew among the British public and the political opposition pounced on the opportunity to exploit the obvious decline to their advantage.

It was during this period of economic anxiety that a meeting occurred, a lunch between a motorsports competitor and a magazine proprietor. Thirty-four-year-old Tommy Sopwith, a former British Saloon Car (sedan) racing driver and his good friend, 35-year-old Jocelyn Stevens, had had an idea—how would it be if a motorsports event was held, an endurance rally, in which cars and drivers would cover thousands of miles across many countries, starting in Britain and finishing in Australia? They took this idea to Sir Max Aitken, chairman of *The Daily Express* newspaper. Could this be a potential boost to flagging British morale? Although Harold Wilson had insisted that devaluation would not reduce the value of "the pound in your pocket," a combination of the derisory responses from both newspapers and the political opposition had fueled anxiety among the public at large. Could something be done, be staged to introduce a bit of exotica, excitement and spectacle to a despondent British public?

Unimaginable today, the idea intrigued Aitken to the point where he saw the opportunity for his newspaper to officially sponsor this intercontinental event, and so, as a result of a lunch between friends, the London to Sydney Marathon was brought into being as the perfect solution to raise spirits, capture imagination and undoubtedly give *Express* newspaper sales a significant and welcome boost. Today it's almost impossible to imagine that such a motorsports event could capture the hearts and minds of millions of people across the world, could cause school geography lessons to be adapted to follow the Marathon's progression through the many different countries, could see school children choosing and tracking individual cars and crews, could lead to the sellout of newspaper Marathon guides, could cause tens of thousands to come together and see the cars off at Crystal Palace in London and a million more lining the route to Dover, or could even produce a complicated board game.

But it did.

1

What's the Big Idea?

The Queen magazine was established in 1861 as a British society publication. In 1958, it was sold to Jocelyn Stevens, who quickly rebranded it simply as *Queen* and refocused its design and content to appeal to a younger readership while still maintaining its core as a society magazine. In 1964, in an attempt to capitalize on *Queen's* younger audience, Jocelyn Stevens financed Britain's first commercial pirate radio station, Radio Caroline. Published every fortnight, *Queen* offered articles, reviews and regular features on fashion, travel, food and wine, film and theatre, books and music, motoring, contemporary news events and the comings and goings of the upper echelons of British society. The editorial team was constantly on the lookout for new themes and features and for the July 5, 1967, edition, Stevens decided to dedicate the magazine to aviation, its front cover featuring a glamorous shot of Miss Constance Fenton at the controls of a Brantly B2B helicopter beneath the banner "Aviation or Flying? Who flys [*sic*] what, where, how and why."[1] A qualified helicopter pilot, Fenton's fashion model features obviously served to emphasize the glamour and sexy sophistication of private flight.

To bring this issue of the magazine to the newspaper stands, Stevens invited his good friend and former racing driver Tommy Sopwith to act as guest editor. Tommy's father invented the First World War fighter plane the Sopwith Camel and, as a qualified pilot himself, Tommy had a large number of contacts in the flying world. In addition to its regular columns and features, the finished magazine contained special articles on learning to fly, the who's who of those with private pilot's licenses, flying for fun versus flying for business and how much it would cost to run a private aircraft.

Extremely pleased with the finished product, Stevens was in the mood for a celebration and, as Tommy recounted, "He took me out for very fully licensed lunch, at the end of which we were talking about what we were going to do next and we decided we were going to run a car race around the world. That was, I think, after the third glass of port, by which time we were going to take over the world as well as run a race around it!"

Their discussion turned to the practicalities of turning their idea into something achievable, which prompted Tommy to suggest approaching Sir Max Aitken, the proprietor of the British *Daily Express* newspaper. Tommy was working for the newspaper at the time and felt it would be something Sir Max might be interested in backing. As he explained, "I had to sell the idea to Max Aitken, which I did, and then distill it into something that would actually work and that's how the London to Sydney Marathon started. From a drunken lunch after a successful Queen's Flight edition of *Queen*. It was just the two of us, absolutely."

The Earl of Snowdon, HRH Princess Margaret and Tommy Sopwith, 1968 (courtesy Tommy Sopwith).

With *The Daily Express* on board, thoughts next turned to the organization of the event—what would need to be in place for such an event to happen? This time Tommy turned to his friend and former motor racing rival Jack Sears. Jack had twice driven to victory in the British Saloon Car Championships, including its inaugural event in 1958 when he and Tommy Sopwith finished with joint-maximum points. The decision was taken to hold a two-handed decider, in which Tommy and Jack would compete in a "best-of-three circuits" race around the track in identical Riley 1.5 cars. Jack was eventually hailed the winner by a hair-splitting margin of 1.6 seconds. In asking Jack to join the Marathon's organizational machine, Tommy recalled that "We nearly killed Jack with this because there was much more work attached to this than I thought and I got him in as an old friend. We'd raced with each other, against each other and he'd driven for me so we had all sorts of associations."

Jack Sears recalled receiving a telephone call from Tommy one day in the fall of 1967. Tommy casually asked what Jack was up to as, by then, Jack had retired from motorsports, as a result of an accident testing a Lotus 40 at the Silverstone racing circuit in Northamptonshire and was now devoting his time to running and managing his farm in the East of England. Without giving anything away, Tommy asked Jack to journey to London as quickly as possible to meet with him and Jocelyn Stevens as they had a proposition to put to him, stressing that it would be easier to explain in person, rather than over the phone. A date was made and Jack, greatly intrigued, was quickly heading towards London, all the while wondering what his friend's idea would be. As Jack explained, "So the main part of the meeting took place before we went out to eat, which was sensible. Jocelyn was there and they said well, this is the proposition, we'll come straight to the point and we'll get down to the detail. We want to have an adventure. It's time this country had an adventure." Jocelyn and Tommy went on to explain that they had obtained backing from Sir Max Aitken at *The Daily Express* and that the idea was to run a race from London in England to Sydney in Australia. Quickly trying to take in what he was hearing, Jack asked how they were planning to get the competing cars to Australia, recalling that Tommy replied, "Well, if you take on the job, Jack, that's for you to sort out!" Tommy and Jocelyn pointed out what they thought might be a route from London to Asia, spinning Tommy's globe to show where they had marked a passage to the Indian Ocean. Jack quickly concluded that he would have to drive the route himself and that there was no way he could do this without assistance. As he recalled, "They said well, at the moment the way things stand is, you will be allocated an office in *The Daily Express* building in Fleet Street, you'll have a car pass so you can park in the underground car park there and you will have a secretary."

Jack Sears is the first to admit that, although he had a hugely successful track record as a rally competitor in the 1950s, driving MGs, Austins and Austin-Healeys for BMC, the British Motor Corporation, he had been out of the rally scene for a long time and, in his own words, he "was a bit out of touch." In order to successfully plan the Marathon he would need expertise and so he thought of Tony Ambrose. Successful British rally driver Tony Ambrose had won the 1965 European Rally Championship with Rauno Aaltonen and Jack considered him to be one of the best rally navigators in the world. He would definitely be the right man to work alongside him. Thus, before dinner that evening, with an acceptable remuneration package agreed and with dry martinis in hand, Tommy, Jocelyn and Jack raised a toast to the London to Sydney Marathon.

Now the real work would start.

2

Planning the Route

There are a number of different accounts of how the Australian *Sydney Telegraph* joined forces with the British *Daily Express* in sponsoring the London to Sydney Marathon. According to *Sydney Telegraph* motoring journalist David McKay, he heard of the race from his friend and rally navigator David Lewin in the autumn of 1967 and immediately "leaped into my car and dashed off to the offices of *The Daily Telegraph* in Sydney to see my Editor in Chief, David McNicoll."[1] In turn, McNicoll spoke with *The Telegraph's* proprietor, Sir Frank Packer, who immediately saw the potential promotional opportunities the event could offer the newspaper. Sir Frank then sent a cable to Max Aitken to propose co-sponsorship. Jack Sears remembers it differently, suggesting that as Max Aitken and Frank Packer had been friends and fellow pilots during the Second World War, Aitken had probably spoken to Packer directly to invite *The Sydney Telegraph* on board. Whatever the means, by the end of 1967 it had been agreed that the *Express* would sponsor the section from London to Asia and the *Telegraph* would back the section across Australia.

With sponsorship agreed, Jack Sears, Tommy Sopwith and Tony Ambrose set about creating an organizational machine to deal with the countless issues and tasks involved in turning a bold and exciting idea into a real event. Uppermost in priority was deciding exactly where the Marathon would go—through where could the route pass between London at the beginning and Sydney at the end? How possible would it be to drive eastwards through the many and different countries that lay between Britain and Australia? What would be the logistics of securing international, cross-border cooperation? An eight man Marathon organizing committee was formed, with Tommy as chair, Jack as secretary and other members including Tony Ambrose, Royal Automobile Club Rally organizer Jack Kemsley, former BMC Competitions Manager Stuart Turner, and Royal Automobile Club Competitions Manager Dean Delamont. Jack Sears was hugely grateful to have Jane Appleby as his secretary to be based at *The Daily Express* office. Appleby had previously been Tommy's secretary while he was running the Cowes Torquay Boat Race and organizing the London Boat Show, both also sponsored by *The Daily Express*. Her knowledge of the internal machinations of the *Daily Express's* offices would prove invaluable.

The absolute priority in planning the route was to ensure that as much of the event as possible should be undertaken over land, only allowing for the necessity of a sea crossing to reach Australia. Close inspection of world maps offered many potential routes, which would in turn minimize the time spent at sea. The most logical route would mean passing down through Burma, to the Malaysian peninsula, with a relatively short sea crossing over to Western

Australia. However, it quickly became apparent that this wasn't going to work; the Malaysian authorities refused to grant entry permits for competitors and the Arab-Israeli war had closed the Suez Canal, thus reducing the number of ships available to Marathon organizers in the Far East with capacity to carry cars and crews to Australia. Tommy even visited Admiral Mountbatten to seek his advice on Burma, recalling that "He said if you were going to ask me to organize for you to go through Burma, forget it! He said 'I can't get through Burma so I certainly can't arrange for you to get through.' He said, and I remember the conversation vividly, he said it would be very easy for me to say 'Look old boy, I'll be in touch and let you know, but I know this is just not going to happen, totally impossible,' so we gave it up as a result of one conversation."

Jocelyn Stevens (left) and Tony Ambrose, 1968 (courtesy Jack Sears).

Eventually, Jack struck upon a solution, negotiating an agreement with the P&O shipping company, which would allow their passenger liner, the SS *Chusan*, to take cars and crews from Bombay across to Fremantle in Western Australia. As Jack explained, "The power of a national newspaper is enormous. Through Max Aitken I had direct contact with the managing director of P&O. We went to have a meeting with him and we asked would P&O be interested in collecting all the cars and drivers out from Bombay and taking them down to Perth? We had to decide how many cars would start the event and we also had to decide how many cars could go on the boat to Perth, so we were waiting for P&O to come back to us and they said they would divert. They'd stopped running to Bombay, they went straight round the Cape of Good Hope to Ceylon— Sri Lanka as it's now known. They said because of the importance of the event and the publicity they would agree to divert the SS *Chusan* to go up to Bombay and pick up the cars and the drivers, but we can only take 70 cars. So we had to decide how many we were going to start." Eventually, it was agreed that 100 cars would form the starting lineup, the organizing committee confident that it would be a miracle if 70 cars managed to get to Bombay.

With this agreement in place, it was up to Jack and his team to calculate the *Chusan's* timetable for passage and then work backwards, calculating the time required to make the European and Asian stages of the Marathon both challenging and achievable. Of course it also added the extra "spice" for competitors in that they would have to arrive in Bombay by a certain date, or they'd literally miss the boat!

Next up was the detailed route itself. Jack and Tony Ambrose knew they had to drive to Bombay themselves and set about looking for additional expertise, someone who understood the complexities of international border crossings and road travel across the countries lying between London and Bombay. That expertise came in the form of Michael Wood-Power, who ran a company operating overland buses between Britain and India. With the team established, on January 22, 1968, Jack, Tony and Michael loaded up a Ford Cortina GT loaned by the Ford Motor Company of Great Britain, which they had fitted with stiffened front and rear springs, and set off to spend four weeks reconnoitering potential routes through Europe and Asia, all the while attempting to ensure that chosen sections balanced the fine line between "challenging" and "impossible." Slowly the route began to take shape, combining relatively fast and easy stages along modern European highways with more daunting mountain stages in Turkey, Iran, Afghanistan and Pakistan, not to mention the miles and miles of unpaved roads through countries where horses and carts were still the preferred means of transport.

Michael had explained how border crossings could take at least two hours, especially in Turkey and all countries beyond, which filled Jack with concern as long delays passing through customs and immigration would potentially jeopardize the swift movement of the Marathon. Somehow, Jack needed to secure the cooperation of each country's authority if he was to prevent long queues of cars at each border crossing. They decided the best approach would be to engage with each country's department of tourism as well as their national automobile clubs or organizations. As he explained, "We decided that there was no point whatsoever in writing to governments or motor clubs before we left. We had business cards with '*Daily Express*' on them and we had the plan that we would arrive at the major cities in each country, but we would never go straight to any offices in the late afternoon when obviously people were tired and wanted to go home. We would always stay the night. We took the view that we would wake up fresh in the morning and we'd arrive at these offices, knock on the door, say who we were and hope somebody would talk to us." Quite a challenge, but once again

the power of an internationally known newspaper, plus the fact that international media organizations would be closely following the Marathon, meant that Jack, Tony and Michael were repeatedly able to secure cooperation and support. For example, at Afghanistan's capital city, they went to the local tourist office and were at first confronted by a receptionist with little English. Using single words and gestures, spokesperson Jack explained what they wanted. The receptionist signaled for them to wait and disappeared, returning five minutes later and beckoning to them to follow her upstairs. She led them to an office in which a man sat, well groomed in a jacket and tie. Jack recalled how the man stood and introduced himself, saying "'Good morning gentleman, my name's Tarzi, what can I do for you?' In perfect English! I couldn't believe it, so we all shook hands and we said 'Well Mr. Tarzi, first of all, congratulations on your excellent English.' 'Well,' he said, 'I went to Oxford for three years.' He was a member of the Royal family. The Royal family was in charge in '68 and he was a

Jack Sears (courtesy Jack Sears).

direct member of the ruling Royal family and he was head of tourism. So he was very interested to hear what we'd got to say and he was all in favor of it. He said 'Oh yes, we'll back you to the hilt.'" Jack also recalled that "Every border control was perfect. That was a miracle, in my view. Even India and Pakistan came up trumps, they were good. Again, it was just a few minutes only and apparently the Indian and West Pakistan border controls suddenly became friends as a result of this event. So that was fascinating."

As the chosen route took shape, it quickly became clear that between London and Bombay, two stretches could be the undoing of many cars: the Lataband Pass in Afghanistan and the Khyber Pass that would take competitors out of Afghanistan and into Pakistan. Both sections offered twisting, rocky mountain roads with perilous drops on either side, definitely a means of separating the professionals from the private entrants. Now mostly referred to as the Kabul-Jalalabad Road or Highway, the narrow Lataband Pass through the Hindu Kush mountain range is considered one of the most dangerous roads in the world. In 1968, it probably had less traffic, which is just as well for unlike today, it wasn't paved in any way. *Autocar* magazine motorsports editor and Marathon competitor Innes Ireland reported that, at a briefing prior to the event, he had been able to watch film footage of the Pass, describing that "the shots of the road, if you could call it such, hacked out of the side of the vertical rock face with drops up to 2,000 feet over the edge, were enough to throw a chill into our very marrow."[2] In fact, such were the potential perils of the Lataband that according to David McKay, Jack and Tony had to abandon their attempt to investigate the Pass as it was blocked by snow and Jack would later ask him to complete the survey during his own reconnaissance of the route in the months leading up to the actual event.

View from the Lataband Pass in Afghanistan, 1968 (courtesy Martin Proudlock).

The Khyber Pass, 1968 (courtesy Martin Proudlock).

Eventually the European and Asian stages were agreed. Marathon cars would pass through ten countries including England and India. From Dover, a ferry would take them across to Calais in France, from where they would drive to Paris and then southwards across into Italy. From there, they would head on into the first Eastern Bloc country, Yugoslavia, followed by Bulgaria, Turkey, across the Bosporus by ferry, on into Iran, then Afghanistan and Pakistan, before arriving in Bombay approximately 7,000 miles later. It's extraordinary to think that not only would the route go across countries and regions that today would represent considerable peril, but the Marathon organizers succeeded in securing such a degree of cooperation between national authorities. As Jack reflected, "You must remember the whole area that the rally cars traversed was peaceful. There were no wars, no Taliban, no horrible things going on in any of those countries. There was peace and quiet."

In 1968 the Soviet Union was very much in existence, its power, influence and political control extending out across many East European countries, which today are members of the European Economic Community, including Yugoslavia and its neighbor Bulgaria. Yet somehow, the spirit of adventure that pervaded the London to Sydney Marathon facilitated the easy passage of competitors and service crews from "West to East," despite the very real existence of the "Cold War," the entrenched distrust between the Soviet Union and Western Europe. Indeed, the eventual line up of competitors gathered at Crystal Palace in November 1968 included four teams from the Soviet Union, backed by the Russian Avtoexport company and driven by proven and successful Soviet rally drivers, at least one of whom—Alexander Ipatenko—was a former military tank driver. The Soviets successfully exported Moskvič cars to Western Europe in the late 1960s, so no doubt the Marathon represented an extremely effective means of promoting their flagship automotive brand. Furthermore, just as today, tensions existed between Pakistan and India, but Jack Sear's extraordinary skills at negotiation and diplomacy won through.

Jack calculated that by allowing the European and Asian stages to be both competitive and achievable, cars would be allowed no more than seven days to reach the Bombay control checkpoint from London. Along the route, they would encounter 11 time controls with maximum time allowances between each. For example, the route between Paris in France, and Turin in Italy would cover 482 miles and would need to be completed by each car in no more than 13 hours and 32 minutes. The longest section from London to Bombay would be between Teheran in Iran and Kabul in Afghanistan—1,481 miles in no more than 23 hours and 33 minutes, with a compulsory six hour rest stop before continuing onwards to the much anticipated Lataband Pass during daylight hours. As long as each car completed each stage within the time allowed, competitors would not receive any penalty points.

The administrative challenges were enormous. Each control point would need to be staffed with Marathon officials capable of timing and logging each car's performance. Some checkpoints would need to be set up within busy, crowded urban areas while allowing ease of access for competing cars, the crews of which might be rushing to log their arrival before speeding onwards to keep within limits or minimize penalty points already incurred. The event's commercial sponsors, including Dunlop and Castrol, and the factory teams were also faced with the challenge of ensuring that provision was made for servicing and repairing cars, or supplying fuel, tires, parts or oil. Amateur competitors faced the even greater challenge of keeping their vehicles going without official backing or support, although help was often at hand, sometimes in unexpected ways.

With the London to Bombay reconnaissance completed, thoughts then turned to Australia. In May 1968, Jack Sears and Tony Ambrose flew to Sydney en route to Perth in Western Australia, where they would begin their exploration of the Australian outback. In Sydney, they were met by Kerry Packer, who treated them to dinner before taking them to meet his father Sir Frank at *The Sydney Telegraph*. Jack and Tony explained their approach to mapping out the Australian sections, and were grateful for the chance to make contact with the Marathon's Australian sponsor. They then boarded a flight to Perth, and as their plane took off for the 3,000-mile trip to the west coast, Jack remembered being in awe of the sheer size of the country.

Upon arrival, their first task was to liaise with local government officials to ensure that all required documentation was understood and ready to be in place for when the Marathon cars and crews arrived on Australian shores. Of particular importance was the question of whether non–Australian competitors would be allowed to sell their cars in Australia, should they choose not to take them back to Europe after the Marathon was over and, if so, what the tax implications would be. In 1968, Australian duty and sales tax on imported cars was very high. According to Grahame Ward, who worked for Australian Marathon competitor Max Winkless, "If I remember correctly, duty was about 57 percent and on top of that was sales tax at 20 percent, which was an awful lot of money you would have to pay when the cars landed." It was vital therefore that the foreign competitors wouldn't be hit by these tariffs as they got ready for the long haul from Perth to Sydney. According to Ward, agreement to waive the tariffs was only reached days before competitors steamed into Fremantle on the West Australian coast.

Once Jack was satisfied that all was in order, he and Tony collected a BMC 1800 and

Top: The Australian outback, 1968. *Bottom:* The Nullarbor Plain, Australia, 1968 (courtesy John Hemsley).

were joined by successful Australian rally driver John McKittrick. They would spend two weeks carefully mapping out the route across the outback, including what quickly became known as "the horror stretch"—a potentially car-shattering trek over unpaved roads and barely visible tracks containing partially sunken rocks, dried up or collapsed riverbeds, and deep and treacherous potholes, often disguised by fine sand or "bull dust." To a speeding driver, these would appear to be nothing but a flat surface stretching out before them. Add to this the rough and winding forest tracks between Victoria and New South Wales, the expected heat of an Australian summer and the alarming tendency for large kangaroos to bound suddenly into the path of a speeding car and it isn't surprising that both the Australian press and competitors firmly believed they would leave the Europeans far behind as soon as tire hit asphalt in Perth.

Again, Jack and his team devised a series of time-controlled stages between Perth and Sydney—20 in total, with the longest being 892 miles between Lake King and Ceduna across the desolate Nullarbor Plain in Southern Australia, to be completed in no more than 14 hours and 52 minutes, and the shortest, although potentially one of the toughest, between Numeralla and Hindmarsh Station, 34 miles to be completed in 42 minutes. Jack recalled how they took about seven or eight days to determine the stages, "detouring and stopping at places. I remember one place, we pulled up and wanted to stay the night. It was fairly basic and it was out in the outback somewhere and we walked in and I was always the spokesman. Turned out to be the proprietor sitting at a table with one or two others. He said 'Hello mate.' I said 'Hello, good evening, we're from England.' 'Oh, you're pommie[3] bastards.' A great introduction! So we said 'You're quite right, we are pommie bastards, there are three of us and we want three beds for the night.'"

In total, Jack allowed three days for competitors to drive approximately 3,000 miles coast to coast. Although the Australian leg was much shorter than the European-Asian route, competitors would discover that it was fraught with unique challenges, obstacles and unexpected variations. Would the Australians have the last laugh?

Among the teams of explorers and navigators painstakingly making notes and maps of the potential hazards, twists and turns to be tackled along the route was a team of men sent by BMC GB's Competitions Department. In 1968, Bill Price was working for BMC and watching as it merged into British Leyland. A few weeks before the Marathon commenced, Bill was given the task of delivering supplies of parts and equipment at strategic points along the route from Paris to Sivas in Turkey. This would allow the BMC 1800s, which the motorsports department was preparing for the Marathon, to receive whatever mechanical support and service they might need as they headed south and east. Once Bill and his co-driver, BMC works mechanic Bob Whittington, had reached Sivas in Turkey, they were then required to reconnoiter two Marathon sections between Sivas and Erzincan, the first special stage of the event. Jack Sears and Tony Ambrose had proposed two alternative routes to be used here, one easier but longer and the other much more difficult but shorter. Bob and Bill were to make detailed notes of both routes and then pass them to the BMC GB Competitions Department to enable them to decide which route they preferred. Finally, from Erzincan to Bombay, they were to serve as a "sweeper" service car, following Marathon competitors and stopping to assist any BMC Team car that they might encounter on the way. Bill Price's story follows.

3

That Bloody 1100!

Bill Price began working as an apprentice for BMC in 1953 and by 1960 was working as assistant to BMC Competitions Manager Marcus Chambers. In 1962, Chambers was replaced by Stuart Turner, who is often credited as being the brains behind the competition successes of the Mini Cooper. The more successful the Cooper became, the more Mini owners wanted to race or rally their own cars, and demand for parts to tune Minis began to grow. This led to the establishment of BMC's Special Tuning Department, which sold parts and prepared customers' cars. As Bill explained, "I was a jack of all trades, probably the best job in the place." He accompanied BMC mechanics on rallies, helping with minor mechanical work and acting as a service team supervisor when required. Stuart Turner was succeeded by Peter Browning in 1967.

Because of his skills and expertise, in 1968 Bill was chosen to reconnoiter part of the London to Sydney Marathon route across Europe and Turkey. Bill explained that "In some ways you'd think that you'd want to send three mechanics and I know that one of the BMC race drivers was mooted as being the driver for the survey car, but then I think I put the pressure on because I thought I'd fancy that drive and I convinced Peter Browning that I ought to go. Anyway, he didn't say no."

It was decided that two cars would be sent ahead of the Marathon to deliver parts and equipment to the various BMC service points set up along the route and then survey two special stage routes in Turkey, passing their findings back to the BMC Competitions Department. Upon completion, one of the cars would then wait for the BMC Team Marathon cars to overtake them, before setting off in pursuit to act as a "sweeper" car, making sure any problems encountered could be addressed as quickly as possible.

On November 15, 1968, Bill Price, Bob Whittington, "Fast Eddie" Burnell and Frank Rudman took their places in two large Vanden Plas 4 Litre R automobiles and set off from Abingdon in Oxfordshire to Southampton on the English south coast and the overnight ferry to La Havre in France. Bill commented that "you could question why we would take a Vanden Plas 4 Litre R. Well of course the Vanden Plas 4 Litre was the luxury version of the Austin Westminster—Rolls-Royce engine and automatic gearbox. BMC had fields of them not being sold and somebody told Stuart Turner that maybe it would be a good idea if you ran a couple of these and showed the public how good they are, thrashing them around the country, but when the mechanics thought we were going to get these bloody automatics, you know what? 'We don't want automatic transmission.' But of course, once they got used to them, they were good."

Bill Price and the Vanden Plas 4 Litre R service vehicles stop for gas in Belgrade, Yugoslavia, November 1968 (courtesy Bill Price).

The cars made good progress across France, down into Italy and across the border into Yugoslavia, where the crew began to notice that, unlike in Britain, steam locomotives were still very much in operation. Their journey brought them to a railroad crossing in a small town beyond Belgrade, so the two cars pulled to the side of the road and out climbed Bill and his crew members, cameras at the ready, oblivious to a "No Photography" sign. Within moments, a soldier appeared and demanded that they hand over their cameras. Next, a police car drew up, the occupants instructing the service crews to get back in their cars and follow them. They had somehow managed to point their cameras in the direction of an army barracks on the other side of the Iron Curtain! With a mounting sense of dread, they waited for the soldier to climb into the police car and then set off in pursuit. Suddenly, Bill remembered something that they had agreed to carry in the car, something that would make an already uncomfortable situation very much worse. Bill had been asked by the British RAF Red Arrows team, who were to compete in the Marathon, to take a Search and Rescue Beacon (S.A.R.B.) all the way to Turkey for them to collect. Bill recalled, "As we were being driven down the road with the police escort, all we could think of was our S.A.R.B. What if they found it? We'd got some sleeping bags in the rear foot-well and as we were driving along, Bob leaned over and shoved this thing under the sleeping bag in the foot-well, thinking that if anybody looked they'd just see a couple of sleeping bags."

They eventually stopped at what appeared to be a private house where Bill and his colleagues were told to surrender their passports and were then taken to a first floor office where, sitting behind a desk, a man in a gray suit regarded them coolly and asked them to explain why they had photographed the military barracks. Bill explained that "Of course we only knew after we were stopped that we were right beside an army barracks. This big wall that ran along with a huge ornamental gateway with doors in it was the entrance into the offices of this barracks. It was right against the railway line. It was only when we departed, looking back at the signs we saw a picture, a very crude bellows-type camera with a big red cross through it and we'd obviously missed the one coming the other way." As calmly as they could, they explained about the Marathon, the job they had, the steam locomotives and how different it was compared to England. All was tense, and Bill imagined Yugoslavian officials conducting a thorough search of their cars, rifling through the sleeping bags in the back of the Vanden Plas. How would they explain the S.A.R.B.? After a moment or two of consideration, to their great relief, the man in the gray suit nodded his satisfaction at their explanation. However, he also insisted that they hand over the camera films, issuing a warning that if they refused, there was no way of knowing how long they would be detained. Understandably, film cartridges were hastily removed and surrendered and the unfortunate BMC service crews were hurried on their way, with a second, even more ominous warning ringing in their ears: "Be warned, you'll be in Bulgaria shortly, don't take any photographs in Bulgaria because if you are found taking photographs, wherever you are, you'll be locked up and it might be for a day, a week, a month, who knows?" A cautious glance confirmed that the S.A.R.B. remained undiscovered under the sleeping bags and so two increasingly grubby Vanden Plas cars hastily departed for the border and Sofia beyond.

In addition to delivering equipment to the various service points along the route, Bill and his co-driver, mechanic Bob Whittington, had been instructed to survey two special stage

BMC GB service mechanic "Fast Eddie" Burnell fixing a coolant leak at the Bolu Pass, Turkey, November 1968 (courtesy Bill Price).

routes that were proposed between Sivas and Erzincan. Back in England, crowds and competitors were beginning to gather at Crystal Palace while in Istanbul, having deposited the last service packs, the two Vanden Plas vehicles began their journey to Sivas.

On the way to Ankara, they witnessed the alarming habit of Turkish truck drivers of aiming their vehicles along the middle of the highway, a grim harbinger of what was to come as the Marathon cars passed through—as Bill said, "You really needed eyes up your backside!" At Sivas, there were to be two routes for the stage, and as Bill recalled, for the works Marathon teams, the shorter southern route would be the obvious choice. Bill and Bob chose to follow the southern route first, which took the heavy car along a wet and muddy track, some sections completely under water. Bill explained that "We drove on very smooth, dirt roads, very wet and the back of the car completely covered in a spray of mud. We literally had to drive through flooded bits of road, over a bridge, which was wooden planks—you had to be a bit careful to make sure the wheels were on the planks. Bob had to get out in his wellies [rubber boots] and move rocks, which were on the road and this is part of the rally route!" On they crawled until, a little more than five miles from where the track rejoined the longer northern route, the Vanden Plas got well and truly stuck in the mud. Try as they might, the big, heavy, automatic car refused to go forward. As they faced the prospect of having to return the way they had come and with their attempts to dig out the car proving increasingly fruitless, suddenly a farm tractor chugged up the track. Despite the fact that the driver had no English and the British explorers spoke no Turkish, the use of a little sign language and a modest cash fee soon had the Vanden Plas hooked up to the back of the tractor. Away they went, only for the tractor itself to begin struggling in the deep mud. The driver pointed at an adjacent field and, following even more hand gestures, the unlikely convoy was back on the move, this time cross-country, passing through a village of what appeared to be little more than mud huts and collecting a group of laughing children who hitched a ride on the car's rear bumper.

The survey work complete, Bill's next job, together with Bob Whittington and fellow mechanic Tommy Eales, was to serve as "sweeper" service support. This meant waiting until the last BMC Team 1800 had left the Turkish town of Erzincan on the Marathon, which was now under way, and then following behind, stopping to offer any assistance to a team car should they come across it on the roadside, all the way to Bombay. Bill recalled how it was agreed that, provided it didn't jeopardize assisting a team car, they could also come to the aid of any other competitor driving a BMC vehicle, should they encounter one. This turned out to be a very fortunate decision as the first car they encountered was the Morris 1100 S driven by Eileen Westley, Jenny Gates and Marion "Minny" Macdonald for *The Sydney Telegraph*, and christened by the Australian press as "The Galloping Tortoise." Bill recalled that, although the car was prepared by BMC Australia, it had come to Britain via the BMC Competitions Department at Abingdon, so one of the BMC mechanics had made a few additional preparations when time permitted.

The sweeper car reached the Teheran checkpoint, where time allowances included a brief opportunity to rest or eat, provided an entrant wasn't running at the time limit for arrival and departure. At Teheran, they encountered the young Australian women who, as Bill remembered, seemed to be "farting around, doing nothing." A quick inspection showed that the Morris 1100 S was in good working order, so Bill suggested that perhaps Eileen, Minny and Jenny should get moving, seeing as they'd already incurred a number of penalty points. The women hurriedly departed, eventually followed by the Vanden Plas sweeper. To begin with, the route followed an asphalt highway, but after 30 miles or so, turned off into the Iranian desert, miles of horrendous track described by Bill as like trying to drive across a giant washboard. The sweeper was making steady if rumbling progress through the desert when, glancing in the rear-view mirror, Bill noticed a set of headlights coming up fast behind. He slowed and pulled over, only to see the 1100 S bounce past and into the night.

On they went, straight through until the morning, marveling at the clear blue skies and camel trails all around. Bill recalled, "We came into this village and there was the bloody 1100!" It had stopped on the roadside and was leaning over slightly. To Bill's experienced eye, it was immediately clear what had happened. "It was obvious, the suspension had collapsed on one side. So we stopped, because you're not going to leave them there, so we had a quick look and of course the bloody hydrolastic pipe where it runs down behind the sub-frame had chafed through on a sharp edge." Solving this problem wasn't going to be straightforward, but there was absolutely no way they could just leave the women there. Fortunately, the sweeper car was carrying a quantity of thick neoprene tubing, so Bill, Bob and Tommy set about cutting and fitting the pipe and pumping up the suspension. With a chorus of thanks, the women quickly took to the road again, leaving the sweepers to pack up and set off behind. However, just a few miles down the road, there was the 1100 S, leaning to one side again! This time the sweepers decided to sacrifice a precious amount of BMC 1800 oil cooler pipe, carried out a second repair and again saw the women on their way. Bill is convinced this repair lasted all the way to Sydney.

Bob Whittington had set up an inventive means of guaranteeing hot meals while on the road. He had built a bracket on the chassis of the Vanden Plas opposite the exhaust manifold, large enough to hold three Heinz snack cans. Five miles along the road and the cans would be beautifully warmed through. Now well into Afghanistan, the sweepers decided to stop for breakfast and retrieve their nicely warmed cans of food from beneath the hood. Bill recalled, "You couldn't hear a thing, there were no birds, no aircraft, nothing, no cars, it was absolutely silent. We were eating our food and having a drink and there was this buzzing noise…. Tom said 'What's that noise?'" They peered up and down the road and eventually saw a set of headlights approaching—it was that bloody 1100 S again, the driver determinedly focused on the road ahead. To this day, Bill still doesn't know how the women somehow managed to get behind them again.

The sweepers didn't just try and help BMC cars, however. Coming into Kandahar, they joined a queue of vehicles waiting to fill up with gas, and were happy to be beckoned to the front; obviously being part of the Marathon had its privileges. A full tank later they were off again, but not much farther along the route, they came upon another Marathon car, the sole Alfa Romeo that had been privately entered by Australian rally drivers Tony Theiler, Stewart McLeod and Jack Lock. No. 39 was jacked up and Theiler, McLeod and Lock were sitting in camping chairs on the roadside, staring forlornly at the Alfa. The sweepers pulled over and asked what the problem was. Bill recalled that the three Australians asked, "Oh, you haven't got a puller on you? The diff has seized and we can't get the flange off the pinion." The sweepers did indeed have a puller, which was duly retrieved from the Vanden Plas, and Tommy set about pulling off the flange. The BMC crew asked if there was anything else they could do, but the Alfa team replied that they were now okay and so the sweepers continued on their way. Bill never did find out what happened to the Alfa team after that. In fact, the Australian crew was unable to repair the differential and had to retire No. 39 from the Marathon.

One mystery that remains to this day for Bill is how they managed to miss one of their BMC Team cars that had broken down in the Iranian desert. As he recalled, the progress of Tony Fall, Mike Wood and Brian Culcheth in No. 4 was halted by a fractured top suspension arm in the middle of nowhere. Help eventually arrived for the BMC 1800, although the delay severely impeded their performance. Experienced though they were, 23 other cars beat them in Sydney.

The sweepers' services weren't needed again all the way to Bombay so, as the bases were already covered in the Australian stages, having met up with the BMC Team competitors and other service crews and having managed to sneak onto the P&O liner taking the cars to Perth to have a look around, it was time for Bill Price to fly home and get on with his day job. Everyone at Abingdon knew what was happening during the Australian section of the Marathon, and although BMC performed extremely well in the end, in Bill's view, "nobody remembers the car that came second. The real achievement is to win, you know, to be number one. Everybody talks about the Hillman Hunter that won the London to Sydney Marathon. Unless they're real rally nuts, no-one would have a bloody clue who came second or third or whatever. I mean, I can't remember who came second and third, to be honest, without looking at the results."

In fact, although the British Rootes Group Hillman Hunter was eventually the winner, of the top five cars at the finish line, two are BMC GB Team 1800s, with Paddy Hopkirk, Tony Nash and Alec Poole coming second by only six minutes.

4

Growing Interest

While the route was being devised during the first part of 1968, in Great Britain work was underway to promote the event and secure the involvement of the agreed number of entrants. Having set the field at no more than 100 cars, the organizing committee decided to leave it up to entrants to choose how many occupants their car would carry. The actual composition of each Marathon team was the subject of much discussion among potential competitors, both professional, factory-backed rally drivers and amateurs alike. On the national and international rally circuit, competitors work as two person teams, driver and co-driver/navigator. However, as the London to Sydney Marathon would be a long distance endurance event, the big question was whether two person teams would be able to remain alert enough to achieve their goal and avoid obstacle, accident or injury. Even the big factory teams wrestled with this question, Marathon competitor and BMC GB Team member Mike Wood recalling that "We had a lot of team discussion as to what we should do crew-wise and it was decided that because we'd got 1800s, we should take three up. As it all turned out, it would have been quite easy to go two up, but we didn't know, you know, you were going into the unknown."

For privately entered teams, the issue of how many to have as a team was even more relevant, especially if they were completely inexperienced in rallying or motorsports, as there would be costs involved. In addition to the required entry fee of $1,320 (plus an additional $300 per head if an entry was made up of more than two people), they would have to fund themselves throughout the journey from London to Sydney to cover costs of food, extra parts, repairs, tires and so on. Logically, the larger the team, the more cost incurred as a car carrying a heavier load would require more fuel and probably take a greater beating. Furthermore, the larger the team, the more people there would be to feed and water. Moskvič eventually decided to field a mixture of two and three man teams so they could study whether having an extra driver over long distances could boost performance.

The Daily Express began announcing the Marathon in late 1967 and invited expressions of interest from potential competitors during the winter of 1967–68. There would be guaranteed places for 100 teams and there would be a reserve list should any of the confirmed entrants pull out before departure day. Top prize would be £10,000 ($24,000), "a pound a mile"[1] as *The Daily Express* stated, to be provided by the *Express*, with runner-up cash prizes totaling $16,800 to be provided by *The Sydney Telegraph*, including individual category awards such as those for the highest placed private entry and highest placed women's team. Interested parties would need to complete an application form and the closing date for individual entries would be June 1, 1968, with the fee included in the application. Team applications, i.e., from auto manufacturers, commercial organizations or the armed forces' motoring associations, could enter one or more teams of three cars of the same make and type, were not required to pay a fee and had a closing date of July 31, 1968. By the closing dates, all 100 places had been booked and there was a large reserve list.

On June 17, 1968, *The Daily Express* published the list of confirmed competitors in alphabetical order, detailing team and individual names, nationality and type of car to be driven. They proudly boasted that applicants represented 14 countries worldwide: Sweden, Great Britain, Australia, West Germany, France, Norway, Italy, France, Russia, India, Ireland, Poland, the United States and Holland. Some entrants were not in a position to confirm the vehicle that they would use, while others arrived at Crystal Palace driving a different car from that originally registered. British bar owner Dennis Cresdee had planned to compete in a privately entered Moskvič for which he had placed an order, but delivery delays from the Soviet Union meant his three man team eventually set off towards Dover in the compact Austin 1300 station wagon he had actually purchased for his business. Elsewhere, some of the manufacturer teams had still to confirm the exact lineup of crew members, naming only one driver at the closing date. However, anyone who found that they had only made the reserve list did not need to be too disappointed, for between June 17 and November 24, the lineup of cars and crews would change radically as, for various reasons, successful applicants dropped out. Spare a thought for the unfortunate Mr. and Mrs. Grensted of Taunton in Somerset, England who

No. 53, a Rambler American entered by Sid Dickson. The only U.S. car in the Marathon, it completed the entire 10,000-mile journey on just one set of spark-plugs! (author's collection).

described themselves in early Marathon press releases as "Mr. and Mrs. Average Motorist" and confessed to having never done any rallying before because they could never find the time. Mr. Grensted calculated that in total he would need $7,200 to cover all expenses, but with a few months to go had only raised $100! As for their vehicle of choice, they were simply intending to take the rear seat out of their Renault 16 and add a couple of additional fuel tanks, extra wheels and tires. Sadly, the Grensteds were not in the starting lineup at Crystal Palace. Elsewhere, it isn't clear why Suresh Ghandi withdrew his Mercedes-Benz between June and November or why Michael Offley decided against taking his Morris Oxford VI station wagon on the road to Sydney.

Even after the official guides and souvenir programs had been printed in readiness for departure day at Crystal Palace, last minute changes meant a few of those on the reserve list had only one or two weeks' notice to get ready to go, and in the final days before November 24, more last minute withdrawals eventually meant not all 100 places could be filled Finally only 98 cars actually set off. However, by the time the cars were ready to ascend the starting ramp, individual competitors hailed from 19 different countries.

Interest was also being shown by some rather more unusual observers. At least one elementary school in England had decided to use the Marathon to teach their pupils about geography and international currencies, turning their classroom into a Marathon headquarters with the route lining the walls. The school children were encouraged to follow the event, keep scorecards and exchange money as competitors crossed international borders.

The box lid from Sid Dickson's well-used Marathon board game (author's collection).

Press interest was not restricted to the countries through which the Marathon would pass. In the United States, *The New York Times*, *The Washington Post* and *The News Journal* all featured articles on the only American entry in the event, a privately entered Rambler American, *The Washington Post* reporting that "Two American Davids from Easton, Md are preparing to take on 99 foreign Goliaths in the longest auto race since the 1908 New York-Siberia-Paris grind."[2] Maryland natives Sidney Dickson and John Saladin would eventually be joined by a CBS cameraman in their attempt to drive their Rambler American all the way from London to Sydney, making a film, which was eventually shown on United States television in early 1970.

During the months leading up to departure, *The Daily Express* newspaper was promoting the Marathon on a daily basis, reveling in the publicity it brought. Coverage in October showed the Australian rally driver "Gelignite" Jack Murray water-skiing on the River Thames past the Houses of Parliament. Known as "Gelignite" for his tendency to throw firecrackers during rallies, Murray was reprimanded by the river police who warned that "If he continued travelling on the water so fast, he might be fined."[3] The competitiveness between British and Australian entries was also being ramped up, with journalist Harold Dvoretsky defiantly stating that "Any Australian within reach of the leaders when cars arrive in Perth—watch out! He's probably the winner."[4]

Just as the *Express* maintained its promotion of the event in Britain, so *The Sydney Telegraph* began to stoke up interest in Australia, publishing profiles of competitors, including British motoring journalist Nick Brittan and his Australian wife Jenny, Irish rally driver Rosemary Smith and their own journalists Eileen Westley and Minny Macdonald. Two days before departure, *The Sydney Telegraph* advertised "The London-to-Sydney Marathon Game." Available for $5.50 from Nock and Kirby stores, the game was designed so that "Each player moves his car, according to a throw of the dice, four miniature cars and two dice being provided."[5] The game was quickly a sellout.

Australia's two major automobile manufacturers, Ford and GMC Holden, submitted their own cars, albeit with rather different attitudes and involvement. Ford Australia had a very successful factory motorsports team, with many competitive drivers and navigators, whereas General Motors in the United States had a strict "no motorsports" policy, which reached all the way to Australian division Holden, British subsidiary Vauxhall and West German division Opel. While Ford of Australia leapt at the chance to enter a three car team, it took *Sydney Telegraph* motoring journalist David McKay until April 1968 to persuade Holden to produce and prepare three cars for the Marathon, and only if McKay took on the responsibility of managing the team and recruiting the best crews. In fact, General Motors Australia even decided not to offer service back-up for the McKay-led team during the Marathon itself, instead only agreeing to alert its dealer network across Australia that they might be called into service, should any struggling Marathon car need assistance. David McKay would have his hands full if he was going to be able to arrange service and repair support across Europe and Asia, undertake a reconnaissance from Bombay to London to assess the route and test a car to identify any modification that might be required for the actual Marathon cars, deal with unexpected changes to his preferred team of crew members during his absence in Europe, secure tire and fuel sponsorship and get himself, his team members and cars from Sydney to London ready for the start. Yet somehow, this is what he did.

Other car manufacturers were also busy undertaking reconnoiters of the Marathon route. Ford GB sent rally drivers John Davenport and Gunnar Palm to survey the route to Bombay in a Ford Cortina Lotus. Ford Competitions Rally Manager Bill Barnett replaced Davenport for the survey run across Australia in a Ford Cortina GT, which damaged its front suspension in the outback. As Graham Robson wrote, "Because the car couldn't steer they could only get back to civilization for repairs by reversing the car for 26 miles."[6] The BMC GB Competitions Department collaborated with its BMC Australia division to survey the European, Asian and Australian routes, while Ford Australia flew rally driver Bruce "Hoddo" Hodgson out to India to pick up the Davenport/Palm Cortina and drive back to London. In the weeks and months before the Marathon began, soon-to-be competitors were crisscrossing the routes in Volvos, Holdens, Fords, BMC 1800s, Hillmans and Simcas. As a result of the reconnaissance missions undertaken by BMC GB and Rootes, there would eventually be three potential routes across Iran, which for BMC would lead to problems on the Marathon itself.

Among those professional teams and private individuals who were expressing interest in the Marathon was a young Irishman who had noticed Ford's newly-launched, compact Escort model and had set about obtaining and preparing one for the 10,000-mile competition. Given that after 1968 the Ford Escort went on to dominate the international rally circuit for over ten years, it's perhaps surprising to realize that the only Escort in competition was privately entered by Jim Gavin. His story follows.

5

The One About the Englishman, the Irishman and the Scotsman

In 1968, during the months leading up to the Marathon, Jim Gavin was asked by a motorsports journalist what extra equipment they we were going to take. "'We had a row about that,' replied Jim. 'Oh?' queried the journalist? 'Well, you see,' said Jim, 'I wanted to carry five gallon drums of Guinness, Maclay wanted it in bottles and Maudling wouldn't go without gin!'"[1]

Until 1964, Jim Gavin had never left his native Ireland where he worked for a chain of garages selling farm tractors and Renault cars. He had also started racing and rallying locally, using a Renault Dauphine Gordini. Frustrated by the dearth of motorsports in Ireland, by chance he was introduced to Chris Lawrence. Based in London, Lawrence had a small business preparing and racing cars and as a result of a telephone call, during which Lawrence confessed he wasn't in a position to pay him, in April 1964 Jim found himself walking down Avenue Road in West London and into a little yard crammed with racing and rally cars. As Jim said, "I gave myself one year in England and then I would come back to Ireland—I was happy as a clam in Ireland, the girls were grand, the cars were grand but there just wasn't enough motorsports. I was trying to decide whether I wanted to go full time or just be happy to mess around." Within weeks he was having the time of his life, accompanying Lawrence to race tracks at Brands Hatch and Snetterton in England and the Le Mans 24 hour race in France. Unfortunately, according to Jim, Lawrence wasn't the most skilled of drivers and a couple of bad crashes contributed towards his company going under only four months later. Jim wasn't ready to go back to Ireland just yet so, in partnership with two other Lawrence company mechanics, he set up a new firm, Super Sport Engines, this time focusing on just one type of car, the recently introduced Ford Cortina GT. Jim knew the rally editor of *The Motoring News*, so hit upon the idea of placing an advertisement for Super Sport Engines, highlighting that they were Cortina GT specialists. It paid off and they were quickly up and running, modifying customers' cars and having a ball.

A couple of years went by until, as Jim explained, "I was in bed one morning with a young lady. We were reading the Sunday papers and she said 'Oh look, there's going to be a car rally from London to Sydney, they're going to call it the London to Sydney Marathon. You've got to do this.'" Straightaway, Jim was on the phone to Henry Taylor, Ford Competitions Manager. Ford was aware of Super Sport Engines and the work they were doing on Cortina GTs, so Jim cut to the chase and asked whether Ford would give them a car for the

Marathon. Taylor groaned—Jim wasn't the first to ask and wouldn't be the last, and Ford was already putting together an official entry. But after thinking for a moment he came up with a proposal. If Jim could get a leading motorsports journalist involved, Ford would give them a car on the understanding that they would be responsible for preparing it, and although Ford might be able to offer some assistance along the 10,000-mile route, their own Marathon teams would always take precedence. In return, Ford would own the car and take it back after the Marathon had finished. It was too good an offer to refuse. Jim got on the phone to his *Motoring News* rally editor friend, Gerry Phillips, who didn't hesitate to say yes, and a quick call back to Taylor meant the deal was done. Sadly, Jim and Gerry hadn't bargained for *The Motoring News*' owner, who declared that motorsports was for gentlemen, not profit-hungry opportunists, and if Gerry went ahead, he'd be looking for another job! Feeling despondent, Jim called Taylor again, expecting the worst, but Taylor explained how they'd now got a journalist on board, Nick Brittan, and not to worry, they'd still be able to provide a car.

Ford's plan was to enter a team of Cortina Lotuses in the Marathon, but Jim had other ideas—as a replacement for its popular but aging Anglia model, Ford had introduced the new Escort in late 1967. What if Jim were to take an Escort on the Marathon? Taylor was intrigued and pointed Jim in the direction of Ford's Brentwood factory where he might be able to get hold of one of the pilot-build cars, pre-production models built for testing and checking prior to mass production. Just $480 later, Super Sport Engines took possession of three 1.1-liter (67.13 cubic inch) Escorts, quickly selling two for profit and putting the proceeds toward preparing the third. All Jim needed now was a co-driver and a little financial help.

As Jim explained, "You couldn't do it by yourself. You had to have somebody else. I reckoned three of us would be able to pay the costs—it would stay my car, but we'd divide the costs three ways." Jim's friend John Maclay was an ideal candidate for sharing the adventure in endurance as he had experience in racing cars and was, as Jim explained, a "daft-as-a-brush Scotsman." John didn't need long to consider and also agreed to share the costs. One evening they met in the Victoria pub off Bayswater in London and began discussing the pros and cons of inviting a third team member. John glanced about the busy pub and his gaze came to rest on Martin Maudling, who was also experienced in track racing. They invited Maudling over for a chat and it wasn't long before they had a third driver. As Jim explained, "That's how we got the $480 each for the entry fee. So we had an Irishman, a Scotsman and an Englishman!"

However, there was still a huge amount to do in order to be ready for departure day on November 24. Jim was under no illusion that they would have a winning chance on the Marathon so he decided on three objectives: to get to Calais, to get on the ship to Perth and to get to Sydney itself, even if that meant finishing last. As an experienced rally driver, Jim knew that trying to drive flat out to Sydney would be too much for a car they were going to have to prepare themselves. Despite Maclay's desire to drive like the racing driver he was, it was agreed that they would quite simply be in it to finish, and so the preparations began. As Jim explained, "We built an engine; we selected a block from Dagenham. We went to the place where they forged the things and the guy was very amused. He promised a thick-walled block, you know because some of them vary. We got a thick-walled cylinder head, we got a crank and we balanced all the con rods and did everything like that. We oversized the bores and put liners in standard size, 1600-cc [97.64 cubic inch], because whether it was stupid or

Jim Gavin poses in front of his Super Sport Engines Ford Escort, London, 1968 (courtesy Jim Gavin).

not, we reckoned if we put a rod through the side we could always shove another liner through the thing. If you put a rod through the side of a block, you were dead. We built the whole car for reliability not for speed."

And so it was that Jim was in charge of the car, Martin became treasurer and record-keeper and John was assigned logistics, sorting out the necessary documentation, maps, route notes and fuel stops. One particular logistic that manifested itself as in need of attention was the issue of John's bladder. The three men had been standing in the pub for a while and Martin noticed that John had gone to the bathroom twice as many times as he and Jim had during the evening. They certainly wouldn't be able to get to Bombay in time for the ship crossing if they had to keep stopping for comfort breaks. Jim recalled that Martin said, "'Leave it with me, I'll work something out.' Now Martin's father was Reggie Maudling, Chancellor of the bloody Exchequer, so Martin had some good connections." The next time the three met, Martin had given the issue some thought, explaining that jet fighter pilots didn't stop for comfort breaks, instead using "a sort of tube business." Martin designed a system to allow them to relieve themselves while on the move, but first they had to test whether it worked in practice. Climbing into John's Daimler SP250, the three set off along a newly opened stretch of highway in West London. A compact sports car, the Daimler offered little room for back seat passengers, so with John protesting all the while, they stopped at another pub for more

Left to right: **Martin Maudling, Jim Gavin and John Maclay with the Super Sport Engines Ford Escort, London, 1968** (courtesy Jim Gavin).

beer and then set off on the journey back to central London. As Jim explained, "There's me facing that way and Martin facing that way, car going that way and John sort of crunching up on the back seat with one hand holding his glasses on, one hand holding the top of the windshield and another hand, where he got that from I don't know, holding this plastic bag. Martin turned round to watch and I'm trying to see in the rear view mirror and 'Oh God' said Martin, 'he's doing it,' and I've looked in the mirror and suddenly realized a truck had pulled out. I hit the brakes hard and Maclay arrived between the two of us. Martin was desperate, me trying to keep one foot on the brake and get around the lorry. The last thing I saw was this plastic bag going across the other carriage way where there was a little lad on a Lambretta, beeping his horn and I'll never know what happened to him. So in the event, we decided that for the Marathon itself, we'd stop if necessary. That was the extent of our physical preparations!"

Throughout the summer and early autumn of 1968, work on the Escort continued. Jim replaced all but the windshield with plastic windows and removed every bit of the interior trim as a way of keeping weight to a minimum, including the carpets. He also struck upon a clever way of coping with dust. They had heard about bull dust, the fine, talcum powder-like dust that coats the Australian outback. To counter this, Jim fitted a pipe so that the carburetor would draw air from inside the car and even put a pair of women's nylon hose across to act as a filter. Jim fitted a more powerful heater motor in the car to pressurize the inside of the

Left to right: **Reginald Maudling, John Maclay, Beryl Maudling, Martin Maudling, Jim Gavin and Tommy "Chuck" Walsh at Crystal Palace, London, November 24, 1968 (courtesy Jim Gavin).**

car, so when they had to drive through the dust, they would keep all the windows shut and run the ventilation fan on full speed. That way they would be able to minimize any dust getting into the car. Although the setup made a huge amount of noise, after the Marathon, when Jim took the engine apart again, he found it was spotless!

The day of the Marathon's departure finally arrived and the Super Sport team found themselves with No. 78 and a bit of a wait until their turn to be flagged away. They spent the time chatting to friends and family and marveling at the huge crowds at Crystal Palace. Then they were called to the starting ramp and suddenly they were off, feeling like they were part of a procession through the center of London, the streets lined with cheering, waving people. Progress went smoothly through France, Italy and Yugoslavia, the team curious about the arrangements of flowers by the roadside on route to Belgrade, finding out later that they were to mark where there had been fatal accidents. This was not a common sight in 1968 England, unlike today. Coping with the chaos at the Belgrade control point, set up on a narrow street that meant incoming and outgoing cars had to maneuver around each other, they headed onwards towards Istanbul and the ferry that would take them across the Bosporus. Today there are bridges across, but in 1968 travelers had to rely on the ferry service, which ran only infrequently at night, so the team were therefore forced to wait for a passage, holing up in a hotel at Yeşilköy Airport. Knowing that there would be a pause in proceedings, Jim had made plans to meet up with Sandy, an ex-girlfriend who had married a Turkish man and was now living in Istanbul. Jim recalled that "John and Martin had a meal and went to bed and I'm waiting for Sandy to arrive. Of course she never did. Anyway days later, we're pulling into the control place in Teheran, the Philips factory. I was standing on the back of the Escort—we'd put two steps and two grab handles in case it needed rocking out [of] the mud or something—and there was Mick Jones, the ace mechanic at Ford. Mick Jones shouts, 'Gavin you bastard. Sandy arrived about 20 minutes after you left. She gave me a pressie [present] for you.' And I still have it, a Turkish "evil eye." She'd told her husband she was going to meet a friend and stay overnight and her husband was reading the local newspaper and read there was a car rally coming through and one of the competitors was a certain Jim Gavin. Turning to his wife, he said you stay right here!"

Leaving Istanbul, the route took the cars to the Turkish towns of Sivas and then Erzincan. Jim recalled that the Sivas to Erzincan stage was like a Royal Automobile Club Rally stage in Scotland, with narrow tracks through forests, and reflected that that this was probably not something the Australian drivers were used to. Thus far, the Escort was doing well—other cars would shoot past, but the team was sticking to their plan to get to Bombay and onto the ship in one piece. They also now got into a rhythm whereby whenever they reached a control, there would be two priorities: car maintenance or rest. Not the frantic "get in, get out" for them, all too aware that time and time again private entries would be going too fast and would therefore go off the road, blow an engine part or hit something. Steadily paced, the Super Sport Escort pressed on through Iran, at which time Martin wrote that "Personal relations remained cordial. Serious altercations were forestalled because all three of us wear glasses and as soon as we had taken them off to punch each other we could no longer see whom we hit."[2] After Iran came Afghanistan and the Lataband Pass. Much discussed, much anticipated, the Lataband was an anticlimax when competitors discovered that since the original reconnoiter of the route, the local authorities had taken the step of grading it, making the going slightly easier. After that were the Khyber Pass and the border into Pakistan.

As Jim explained, "There would be three of us in the car and we said we'd only allow ourselves the minimum amount of clothing and stuff like that—cut the handle off your toothbrush and all that sort of stuff. But when we got to the Khyber Pass, I can't remember which of us was driving, but Maclay said 'go slow, go slow.' We were going up the Pass and we realized what he was looking at—there were regimental plaques on the wall. Maclay instructed us to stop and because we weren't in a particular hurry, we did. John rummaged in his bag and he pulled out a miniature set of bagpipes. John got out of the car and he fired these things up. There's a lot of huffing and puffing and squawking like a dead cat and all that. Then he started walking up and down, slowly playing the bagpipes. John got back into the car and said his great grandfather or his great uncle had been on the retreat from Kabul and that was his regimental plaque. Neither Martin nor I said anything. To this day I could nearly cry when I remember it."

The team eventually arrived in Bombay feeling great, really pleased with the car and their performance—44th place out of 72 surviving entries. Before they'd left London, they had repeatedly heard stories about how rough it was all going to be, so as a precaution Jim had decided to take an extra rear semi-elliptical spring for the Escort's suspension, strapping it across the front of the car to form part of the essential kangaroo bar. They'd arrived at Bombay without needing the heavy item, which turned out to be a stroke of luck. Jim recalls sitting in the hotel bar at Bombay when someone came in, having just arrived on a plane from England. Probably arriving with extra equipment for the Ford GB Team, he looked around the bar and asked if anyone knew Jim Gavin. Finding Jim, he produced a copy of *The Motoring News* and relayed a message from Gerry Phillips that the semi-elliptical spring, so carefully tied on the front of No. 78, was for a Cortina GT and was therefore three inches too long for an Escort! Needless to say, the spring was quickly discarded.

Also during the brief stop at Bombay, Jim recalls sitting drinking beer at the Yacht Club with Bill Barnett from the Ford GB Team, John Maclay, Ford GB Team driver Rosemary Smith and a few others. At this point the cars were safely locked away in *parc fermé*, the secure area used in motorsports to prevent unauthorized access during an event, where they awaited transfer to the ship. Rosemary and her co-driver Lucette Pointet had experienced serious mechanical problems all the way from Iran and Bill Barnett was trying to get the full picture. As Jim recalled, "Bill Barnett is saying to Rosemary, 'Tell me again, what…' and Rosemary was much more interested in talking to Alec Poole or John or someone and she turned to Bill and said, 'Oh Bill, I don't know, but I've only got three of what Roger has four of.' I remember thinking; love it, real Dublin act." Rosemary was referring to the fact that she was running on three cylinders, whereas Roger Clark's Cortina Lotus still had four!

Seventy-two Marathon cars were steam-cleaned in accordance with Australian regulations and then loaded into the hold of the SS*Chusan*, off limits for the entire voyage. Meanwhile, the Super Sport Engines team walked up the gangway and immediately went in search of their steward. A Super Sport Engines customer had given them some advice about stewards, suggesting that as soon as they were on board ship, they should find their steward, introduce themselves and, as Jim said, "Stick a fiver in his pocket, straight off, just to say hello." The men found the steward, who showed them their cabin and, noticing John Maclay was Scottish, asked if they would like a bottle of whisky. Jim recalled that "You couldn't get a drink until you were three miles out. 'Yes,' we said and off he went and got a bottle of whisky. He sat on the bottom bunk and I sat beside him and we poured ourselves a drink and eventually he said, 'I suppose I'd better get back to work'!"

Competitors were faced with nine days at sea, punctuated by a stop at Colombo in Ceylon, and it wasn't long before boredom set in. A small swimming pool, a steady round of backgammon and poker and orders from the bar kept spirits up. Jim explained how, before the Marathon set off, all competitors received a letter from the organizers stating that if they put a suitcase together, these would be waiting for them in their cabins. The letter also included a card to complete, indicating which dinner seating competitors would like and asking for any comments. As Jim recalled, "For comments I wrote, 'I will have been alone, locked up in a tin box with these two fellows for at least seven days and with the good Lord willing, I'll be on the ship. If I am on the ship it will be wonderful if we could have a female dining companion, not necessarily one of the competitors.' Now somewhere way down in Australia, P&O had decided that they'd put a dedicated journalist on the ship to get stories and she was going through these bloody cards." Sitting down for their first meal on the ship, they noticed their table was set with four places. The reason soon presented itself when, to the bemusement of Maclay and Maudling, a young woman walked up to the table and asked which of them was Jim Gavin. This was the journalist and she had seen Jim's card. She joined them for dinner and a friendship was struck.

The voyage was also the only real chance for competitors to get to know each other, and Jim recalled how he also became friendly with Minny Macdonald, co-driver for *The Sydney Telegraph* women's team. In 1968, Minny was writing a column, "The Society Spy," for the

Telegraph women's page and, as Jim explained, "She used to get an awful lot of ideas from me. She'd come and say what do you think of this copy and I'd say it's grand, what about putting in … and so on. I remember we were docking in Perth, we were leaning over the rail of the ship and she said 'I need something to describe this to the newspaper.' I said 'Well, my mother said'—because there were five Irish including Paddy Hopkirk, me, Rosemary Smith from Dublin and Paddy McLintock—'My mother said "it's the greatest thing in Ireland since the Eucharistic Congress of 1933.'" So she wrote that. So there'd be Australian ex-pat Irish reading their *Sydney Telegraph*s and Mrs. Gavin, mother of Jim, says…"

On December 13, the *Chusan* steamed into Fremantle on the western coast of Australia. Cars were unloaded and were required to be inspected by the local authorities to ensure they met state regulations. In Bombay, the Super Sport Engines team had realized that the Escort's shock absorber upright struts were damaged, so Henry Taylor had arranged for replacements to be flown out from England as the Ford's new Escort model hadn't yet been launched in Australia. Once the team departed from the Gloucester Park race track in Perth, a local Ford dealership replaced the struts and serviced the car, probably enjoying working on a not-yet-released new Ford model.

This would be Jim's first visit to Australia. Out of Perth and into the vast expanse of desert and dust and increasingly difficult sections, the Escort was going well through to Marvel Loch, but the next section to Lake King would be brutal. It was here that the team broke the car's oil pan. Jim was behind the wheel and the going was rough. Suddenly there was a thud—the underside of the Escort had made contact with a large rock, causing the oil pan to drop onto the steering rack. It hit one of the con rods, heralded by a loud noise. Peering underneath,

No. 78 receives attention in the Australian outback, December 1968 (courtesy Jim Gavin).

they realized the problem so, improvising with a fence post, they tied the engine mounting back up and with judicious use of bungee ropes, they slammed the hood and carried on, grimacing at the noise. By the time they got into the vast Nullarbor Plain, however, it was clear that the oil pan was coming loose and had now developed a hole. Oil began to leak, a little at first, but more and more as they carried on until they were eventually forced to stop and assess the situation. The pros and cons of including or avoiding the next Marathon checkpoints were discussed. Martin argued that the hole wouldn't get any bigger and they could just continue to add more oil, while Jim countered that the engine crossmember wouldn't survive the punishment and that they should avoid the last two checkpoints and just get on the main highway to Sydney. Listening to the argument, John finally intervened to point out the increasing pool of oil seeping into the ground. They decided to limp on to the next control where they knew Castrol would be on hand. Sure enough, there they were and promptly the team was given a five gallon oil drum. Finding a sump pump from somewhere, the team set to work, removing the nozzle and running the pump from the drum to the engine, between the navigator's legs. Thus, whenever the oil pressure began to drop, whoever was navigating would pump frantically and that was how Jim, John and Martin made it all the way to Warwick Farm, getting their documents stamped by Jack Sears and therefore realizing their main objective—to qualify as finishers. Out of 56 cars to finish, and despite the damaged oil pan, the Super Sport Engines Escort finished in 45th place, just one place down on their performance to Bombay.

Exhausted, having driven many of the final sections in the outback, Jim suggested that John and Martin drive the Escort in the victory parade from Warwick Farm to Hyde Park in central Sydney, saying he'd see them there. Joining them at the park, John and Martin laughed as they explained how much oil they'd used. They had managed to pump in another four gallons, leaving a serious oil slick stretching the entire route, a motorbike cop shouting at them as they went. At Hyde Park, Jim was approached by a local Ford dealer, excited to see his first Escort and in return for a car and enough gasoline for a week, asked whether he could display the car in his showroom. Jim said yes.

In the aftermath, Jim wasn't very impressed with the awards ceremony. "I remember thinking one thing which is rather strange to this day. I thought there was Max Aitken and Frank Packer and a big stage and I remember thinking Packer made too much of a fuss about the three girls in the 1100 S. He kept going on about how our girls did so well—our girls, our girls—and I'm thinking there are a few other people here too, but … oh and Roger Clark, there's a cup for you, and our girls…"

After the Marathon, John, Martin and Jim remained firm friends. Jim and John are in regular contact to this day; Martin Maudling died in 2005.

6

Runners and Riders

Interest in the Marathon grew quickly and, by June 1968, the organizers had their first full lineup of entrants, a mix of factory teams, armed forces teams and private entries. Despite commercial uncertainty and fears of closure or redundancy, the motorsports departments of Rootes and BMC, under its parentage of British Leyland, agreed that the Marathon was too good an opportunity to pass. Although BMC had achieved huge rally success in the 1960s, with the Mini Cooper, they quickly dismissed the idea of entering the little cars in the Marathon. Instead, they turned to their larger BMC 1800 model, which had also achieved some successes in international rallying, most notably the Acropolis Rally in Greece. The 1800's affectionate nickname of the "landcrab" derived from "a casual comment by an Australian journalist who, when taking rally pictures from a helicopter through a telephoto lens, remarked that the cars looked like "land crabs."[1] Both Morris and Austin versions of the car were sold by BMC, and then by British Leyland, but, other than a few minor trim details, they were almost identical and were often referred to simply as "BMC" 1800s. British Leyland decided to enter three cars to be led by Paddy Hopkirk, Rauno Aaltonen and Tony Fall, and prepared a fourth car in partnership with BMC Australia, to be run by Australians Evan Green and "Gelignite" Jack Murray. The BMC Competitions Department also helped prepare two additional 1800s, one car for three Royal Air Force Red Arrows pilots and the other for three British Royal Navy officers. The three British BMC Competitions Team cars were officially entered by British Leyland.

In the 1960s, the Rootes Group had achieved considerable success with its Imp rally car at the hands of Andrew Cowan and Rosemary Smith. However, like the Mini Cooper, it too was dismissed as being too small for the 10,000-mile run to Sydney and instead, Rootes chose to prepare and enter its Hillman Hunter model. During 1968, Rootes met with international representatives from the global automobile manufacturer Chrysler, and, as Andrew Cowan wrote, "It was agreed that Chrysler USA would be approached to enter two Plymouth Barracudas, Chrysler Australia would enter a Falcon [sic] and Simca would also enter."[2] However, by November 1968, only Rootes and Simca remained in the field, with two Rootes Hunters led by Andrew Cowan and British Royal Air Force pilot Flight Lieutenant David Carrington, and three French Simca 1100s led by Simca France's competitions director, Pierre Boucher, plus Bernard Heu and Roger Masson.

Factory teams were also entered by Citroën, DAF, Porsche, Moskvič and Ford in Australia, Britain and West Germany. In addition, although officially sponsored by the Australian Amoco oil company, Volvo in Sweden supplied and prepared a number of vehicles, happy to see their recently launched 140 series of cars enjoy publicity, while also benefiting from being put through the kind of rigorous testing that the Marathon route would offer. In fact, as a result of both pre–Marathon survey journeys undertaken by a number of the Australian Amoco competitors, and the actual Marathon itself, Volvo examined the consequences of thousands of miles travelled across a range of surfaces in their cars and, as a result, modified some of their production processes. Volvo helped prepare four cars, to be led by Australian rally drivers Ken Tubman, Gerry Lister, Max Winkless and Bob Holden. According to Bob Holden, Volvo also carried out some work on a Volvo 145S station wagon, which had been privately entered by British businesswoman Elsie Gadd.

As a result of General Motors' "no motorsports" policy, Holden in Australia was only prepared to provide three cars at basic specification, and that only after months of persuasion. Led by David McKay, Barry Ferguson and Doug Whiteford, the three Holden Monaros were, in fact, sponsored by *The Sydney Daily Telegraph*, which also sponsored a female crew, two of whom were from their women's page editorial team. The young women would drive a Morris 1100 S, manufactured by BMC Australia. A fourth Holden was also entered into the Marathon, an HK series Belmont, sponsored by Maitland Motors, a Holden dealership owned by Jack "Milko" Murray and Bert Madden. They were joined by a hugely experienced rally navigator, John Bryson, for the event.

The Morris 1100 S chosen for the Telegraph women's team already had a profile within the Australian motoring press. In 1967, in an amusing publicity stunt, Evan Green and "Gelignite" Jack Murray had driven the car across Australia from east coast to west in competition with a light aircraft, the only rule being that the 1100 S could drive through the night, but the plane could only fly during daylight hours. The 1100 S only failed to win the race when heavy rain caused delays in Western Australia, and it was nicknamed "The Galloping Tortoise" after Aesop's fable. *The Telegraph* agreed to Eileen Westley's suggestion that she enter this car in the Marathon, and duly tasked her colleague, Marion "Minny" Macdonald, with continuing to write her weekly column, "Society Spy," for the newspaper throughout the event.

According to Nick Brittan, in early 1968, Ford GB's original idea was to enter just two Cortina Lotuses with two-person crews, "one for Eric Jackson and Ken Chambers and the other for us. Jackson and Chambers have a terrific amount of experience of long-haul driving, having driven … around the world in 42 days."[3] In 1967, in a similar publicity stunt to the Australian "tortoise and hare" race, Jackson and Chambers had set off from Cape Town in a Ford Corsair and raced against a passenger liner all the way to Southampton in England— the Corsair won. With their track record of endurance driving and rallying, they were an ideal choice to represent Ford GB in the Marathon. Nick Brittan began his motorsports career competing in go-karts, eventually becoming European champion, before graduating to auto racing, journalism and editing magazines. A clever businessman with an eye for an opportunity, in 1968 he was in the position to be able to contact Ford GB's director of public affairs and quite simply ask for a car.

It wasn't long, however, before the Ford GB Competitions Department revised its approach to the Marathon. Initially, many of the automobile manufacturer works departments had been reticent about the event, probably because it represented an unknown quantity and fell outside the annual motorsports calendar—was it really worth the time and investment required to take it seriously? However, like many of the other companies, Ford GB concluded that it would be an excellent opportunity to have a solid, top-drawer presence in the Marathon, and quickly added four of its finest rally drivers to the Ford works team: Roger Clark, Ove Andersson, Bengt Söderström and Gunnar Palm. Next, Ford invited Irish rally champion and former Rootes factory team driver Rosemary Smith to join the team, and Ireland's Henry Ford and Company was tasked with supplying a Cortina Lotus for her to drive. Ford GB would also find a female co-driver for Rosemary, eventually choosing Frenchwoman Lucette Pointet.

Then, during the spring of 1968, Ford GB received an intriguing inquiry from a serving officer in the British Army. How would it be if Ford provided a car to the British Army Motoring Association, thereby creating a unique partnership? That way, Ford could have two teams of three cars to compete for the Marathon Team Prize; the British *Daily Express* and Australian *Sydney Telegraph* had announced a team prize category, and had specified that a team must consist of three cars and crews. Ford agreed to the request and began arrangements to find a car to give to Captain Jeremy Rawlins of the 4th Royal Tank Regiment, on the understanding that the car would have to be prepared by him and whomever he chose as a crew-mate. Thus, the entry list published in June shows five Ford GB team cars and a Ford of Ireland car, with Captain David Harrison of the Junior Leaders' Regiment joining Rawlins. It wouldn't be too long before Ford discovered that having a couple of serving officers in the team was a very useful thing indeed.

The Ford GB team was set and, very quickly, Roger Clark was tipped to win by bookies across the land as an 8 to 1 favorite, which of course didn't please the Australian crews at all, even though Evan Green and Jack Murray, in the BMC Australia 1800, were tipped at 12 to 1.

Notable by their absence from the event were Peugeot of France and SAAB of Sweden. Peugeot had scored innumerable successes on the rallying circuit, demonstrating the rugged reliability of its 404 model by repeatedly winning East African Safari endurance rallies. In fact, Peugeot had been so successful in raising the profile of the 404 that these cars became commonplace sights on the roads of many African and Arabic countries. By the 1960s, SAAB had developed a top-class rallying pedigree, with victories on the Monte Carlo Rally and successful performances in Africa and Australia, introducing such contemporary champions as Erik Carlsson and Stig Blomqvist. Yet both companies decided not to enter cars in the Marathon, instead concentrating on the official international rally calendar, leaving just two privately entered cars to represent the brands: a Peugeot 404, sponsored by the Irish company Kentredder Tires and led by Irish rally driver John Cotton, and a British-entered SAAB 95 station wagon, crewed by British pair Alister Percy and Jeremy Delmar-Morgan. Perhaps ironically, both cars were in the top 30 finishers at Sydney.

Mercedes had also enjoyed the benefits of a hugely successful presence in a range of motorsports, and especially the Le Mans 24 Hours race. However, after the catastrophic crash at Le Mans in 1955, which caused the death of over 80 spectators, Mercedes withdrew from factory-backed motorsports. They did, however, supply and assist with the preparation of three of the five Mercedes-Benz entries, the big 280 sedans, working with the privately entered teams to prepare the cars at the factory in Stuttgart, Germany, and giving copious amounts of advice, not all of which was taken up, much to the eventual regret of at least one of the teams. Australians Dr. Alec Gorshenin and Ian Bryson were also fortunate to "receive a late offer of help from the Mercedes factory, which included three days of factory preparation before driving to London."[4]

The British Army Royal Green Jackets Porsche 911 T of George Yannaghas and Jack Dill, December 1968 (courtesy Colin Cleaver).

In addition to the British Armed Forces cars being prepared or assisted by BMC GB, Rootes and Ford GB, there were a number of others entered by the different forces' motoring associations. The British Army's 17th/21st Lancers regiment entered a Land Rover, its four-wheel-drive powertrain disabled to meet the Marathon's regulation that only two-wheel-drive cars could compete. The Royal Air Force entered a Ford Cortina GT, led by First Officer Nigel Coleman, while the British Army's Royal Green Jackets regiment fielded a Porsche 911 T. The British Army Motoring Association entered two Rover 2000TCs, led by Major John Hemsley and Major Michael Bailey. Up until just a few days before departure on November 24, the Norwegian Air Force was to run another SAAB, this time a 96 sedan to be driven by jet pilot Major Per Ekholdt, but a last minute withdrawal was one of the reasons why only 98 cars set off, rather than the planned 100.

In the remaining list of entries, cars and crews were as diverse as could be, combining experienced freelance rally drivers with enthusiastic amateurs. The range of chosen vehicles was equally eclectic, and while the most popular cars in competition were Ford's second generation Cortina and BMC's second generation 1800, the starting lineup also included a 1930 Bentley Sports Tourer, a VW bug, a tiny MG Midget, complete with fuel tank on its roof, and an Australian 1965 Ford Fairmont, which had previously won an insurance company competition to fit prototype safety features, such as a padded dashboard and burst-proof door locks.

Many of the Marathon cars were fitted with a kangaroo bar, or "'roo bar," something which, before 1968, was practically unheard of outside Australia, but which, by the spring

The cage-like 'roo bar on No. 59, the Porsche 911S of Terry Hunter and John Davenport, seen at Crystal Palace, London, November 24 (courtesy John Hemsley).

and summer, had fast become a hot topic for anyone considering entering the Marathon. One of the many potential obstacles facing competitors, as they sped across the Australian outback, would be errant kangaroos, known to be completely oblivious to the peril of a speeding car bearing down on them or approaching from left or right. When driving at even 20 or 30 mph, let alone the suggested average outback stage speeds of anything up to 60 mph, colliding with a large kangaroo could prove catastrophic, if not fatal. Even in daylight, the sudden appearance of a startled 'roo was acknowledged as a hazard, but as some of the stages were to be held at night, the risk was amplified. Certainly, many of the Australian Marathon teams did all they could to unsettle their European and American counterparts, with alarming stories of giant kangaroos lurking in the bush, ready to leap out and finish a car's chance of reaching Sydney. Consequently, one of the big issues for teams and competitors was whether to fit a 'roo bar or not. Would it be wise to fit a shield, made from welded bars of steel, across the front of the car to add extra impact protection and safeguard radiators, engines and possibly even occupants? Looking at the final 98 cars gathered at the start of the Marathon, it's apparent that most competitors decided to err on the side of caution, and the degree to which 'roo bars were designed and constructed varies widely. For example, the factory-prepared Porsches were encased in what appeared to be re-fashioned cast iron bed frames. In fact, they were exquisitely constructed 'roo bar cages, designed by Porsche in West Germany, after they had visited Berlin Zoo and literally measured their collection of kangaroos to calculate the exact dimensions required for increased protection of the cars.

As well as working on its own cars, the BMC GB Competitions Team had decided to help prepare a car for three members of the British Royal Air Force Red Arrows display team, under the sponsorship of an international transportation and packing company called Evan Cook. The Red Arrows are a familiar and evocative sight in the skies above Britain, the bright red BAe Hawk jets performing incredibly precise and visually stunning aerial displays above the heads of spectators at air shows, royal pageants and jubilees. They even performed during the London 2012 Olympic opening ceremony, streaming out specially colored vapor trails in their wake as they cut through the skies in perfect symmetry. In 1968, the Red Arrows Team was in its infancy, having only come into existence three years earlier. In 1967 and 1968, if anyone had been fortunate enough to stand, gaze upwards and watch the aeronautical acrobatics on display, they would have been watching, among others, Flight Lieutenants Terry Kingsley, Derek Bell and Peter Evans.

Following is the story of their participation in the Marathon.

7

The Red Arrows

For Flight Lieutenants Terry Kingsley, Derek Bell and Peter Evans, it all started many years before 1968.

In 1956 and 1957, Terry and Derek found themselves serving as Junior Pilots on a Hunter Fighter Squadron in the British RAF. During those years they spent many happy hours struggling to keep various clunkers on the road and they were always looking for the opportunity to get involved in some form of motorsports. In 1962 Terry and Derek, once more in the same unit, often competed in rallies organized by the Royal Air Force Motoring Association. These rallies were run at night on open country roads and, according to Derek, their successes were down to Terry's superb navigational skills and his own mediocre but enthusiastic driving.

In January 1966, Derek joined the Royal Air Force Red Arrows aerobatic display team. Though the Red Arrows were not as well known among the British general public as they are today, it was nevertheless a very high profile job and he met and spent time with people in the kind of positions that wouldn't have been at all accessible in a regular RAF unit. Two of these people were to play a very important part in the lives of Derek and Terry in the very near future. They were Arthur Gibson and Raymond Baxter, the latter a popular figure in Britain in the 1960s and 1970s from his work on BBC Television.

Raymond Baxter specialized in motoring, scientific and aviation TV shows and he also provided the commentary for all Red Arrows displays for the BBC. In order to get the best results, Raymond and his program producers would consult with the Red Arrows team to get the best possible camera angles and make sure they could fully explain what was happening to a television audience. Derek explained that he spent many hours with the BBC, looking at and commenting on the film of their aerobatic displays.

Arthur Gibson was a skilled photographer who ran a company called Images in Industry. He was passionate about aviation and worked with several commercial airlines as well as being closely involved with British Aerospace. The majority of the early films and photographs of the Concorde were shot by Gibson. He started working with the Red Arrows in 1966 and continued to produce some of their most outstanding air-to-air pictures and films over the next few years.

Towards the end of the 1967 season, Terry also joined the Red Arrows team, ready to fly as number seven. The morning that the British *Daily Express* announced their sponsorship of the London to Sydney Marathon, Terry and Derek arrived for work and their first words exchanged were, "Let's have a go!" They promptly sent off for more details and, in Derek's words, "it slowly transpired that this was a heaven sent opportunity for us."

As far as Derek can remember, the first details released by the *Express* were that it was to be an open event, the only restriction being that cars could not be four-wheel-drive. There would be a maximum entry list of 100, no competition licenses were required, there would be a seven day, non-stop drive to Bombay, then there would be a ship crossing to take a maximum of 70 cars from Bombay to Perth and finally there would be a three day, non-stop drive across Australia to Sydney. Cars could carry two, three or four person crews.

However, Derek and Terry had a few problems to overcome—they had no car, they had no money, and they didn't know whether the 1968 Red Arrows Display season would be over by the time the Marathon started or, if it was, whether they would be granted extended leave to take part. Most importantly, they had no idea whether the Royal Air Force would grant them permission to enter the Eastern Bloc countries through which the Marathon would pass. Undeterred, Derek and Terry sent off their entry form and immediately began to address the problems on their list.

In their view, in the 1960s the British Services were very different compared to today. At that time, serving personnel enjoyed a great deal of freedom to engage in adventurous activities under the guise of expedition training. All ranks had the opportunity to be sponsored for all sorts of activities, and funds were available for RAF personnel through the Lord Trenchard RAF Benevolent Fund. Derek and Terry applied to the fund and, along with other RAF teams—the second Rootes Team Hillman Hunter crew and a team entered by Avon/RAF in a Ford Cortina GT—were awarded the entrance money, much to their relief.

Of course, before they could start looking for sponsorship for their entry, they needed to find a car, and this is where Raymond Baxter came to their aid. In 1968, Baxter was also publicity director for BMC in Great Britain, so Derek and Terry wrote to him to see if he could help. They very quickly got a phone call from Baxter's assistant, telling them that Baxter was away on business, but that he promised to be in contact as soon as he returned. Not long afterwards, they got a letter with the unexpected news that the BMC Competitions Department was preparing six cars for the event, one of which would be for them.

As Derek explained, "it is impossible to convey the surprise, the joy, the sense of responsibility and the excitement that this news brought to us. For a start there had been a lot of speculation as to whether the leading rally manufacturers such as BMC, Ford, Rootes, etc., would even enter this event. However, once one was in then obviously the rest had to follow. I don't recall who was first to blink!" Of course, there were caveats attached to the offer—once BMC delivered the prepared car to them, they would effectively be on their own. In addition, they would be responsible for returning the car to BMC in Britain once the Marathon, or their participation in it, was over, whichever came first.

The next step on the road to Sydney was something Derek and Terry will never forget. In the early spring of 1968, the Red Arrows Team was at RAF Manston in Kent and their good friend, photographer Arthur Gibson, was with them taking air-to-air and ground-to-air photographs. Derek decided to ask Arthur if he knew of anyone who might be in a position to help with sponsorship, not an easy subject to raise with a friend. Fortunately, Arthur was very keen on motorsports and had done his fair share of competitive driving. He pointed out that as he knew Derek and Terry well enough, he was convinced that anyone who backed them would get value for their money. They agreed to leave the issue with him and continued on with a busy season, flying three or four displays a week.

Arthur didn't take long to come back to them and he had a proposition. He had a friend who ran a company called Evan Cook, which specialized in international transportation and packing. Evan Cook also had a commercial relationship with an Australian company called Grace Brothers and Arthur explained that his friend at Evan Cook could certainly see the benefits of a car in the Grace Brothers' color of dark green, rallying across the world with the Evan Cook logo displayed. Derek and Terry could of course see the benefit of the $3,600 this would generate!

Once they had the promise of the car from BMC they started to get to know BMC Competitions Manager Peter Browning and all the people in the competition department. They watched their car, a BMC 1800, take shape and took a great interest in the specifications and design changes required to turn a standard production model into a rally car. The London to Sydney Marathon would be non-stop, stretching 10,000 miles around the world, a very new concept that required a great deal of re-assessment in terms of how the teams would support the car—they wouldn't be returning to the rally control center every night to be met by the service teams, nor was it going to be easy to retrieve a car that had broken down. All the extra equipment and personnel would have to be available along the route and then they would need to leapfrog ahead of the cars by aircraft—all very expensive. Derek recalls that during their first meeting with Browning they offered to help with the logistics, but were politely told that BMC had done it all before and knew what they were doing. That was ironic given that an essential part of any aerobatic team is the logistical backup and in the RAF they used Transport Command as for many of the display venues, the Red Arrows Team needed the support of ground crew and extra equipment. Over the years they had developed very close relationships with RAF Transport Command, and Derek and Terry were sure that these contacts would be able to help as there was a constant movement of transport aircraft from the United Kingdom to many parts of the world and often these flights had additional capacity.

Not long after their first meeting with BMC, they received a message from Browning saying how amazed he was at the cost of moving extra parts and equipment to Bombay by air freight and did they think they could assist? They of course agreed and a system was quickly set up whereby BMC had boxes of extra parts labeled, weighed and ready to go. BMC would liaise with operations at RAF Lyneham in Wiltshire each day and if there were any movements going to suitable places with additional capacity then these would be used by BMC. As Derek and Terry explained, this was all done perfectly legally with all the paperwork completely in order. As a result, the RAF saved BMC many thousands of pounds and Browning and the team at Abingdon were very grateful for the help given, a consequence of which would soon become apparent.

As Derek explained, "the airlifting of parts led to a rather amusing incident; well anyway we thought it was funny. The RAF had a very active Motorsports Association (MSA) and a number of their members were very competent and experienced rally drivers. The MSA had struck a deal with Rootes, who were preparing two Hillman Hunters for the Marathon, one of which would be crewed by the MSA. In exchange for this car, the RAF would help Rootes with the logistics in the same way as we were helping BMC." Derek continued to explain that "We now move to some far distant airfield—I think it was Teheran—and a Rootes man and a BMC man are waiting for an aircraft to arrive loaded with parts for each. The doors open and out comes a succession of boxes all labeled BMC. The man from Rootes was less than pleased, especially as it turned out that the couple of boxes that were labeled

Rootes contained the wrong bits. This episode was flashed back to the UK, where a Senior Officer in the Ministry of Defense had a bit of a hissy fit and wanted to know what was going on. Terry, who was our nominal team leader, was called to account for this. He explained what we were doing, reassured the Senior Officer that all was legal and asked how the MSA decided what should go where etc. The Senior Officer replied that they had a committee who looked after everything. Terry retorted that there were only three of us! No more was heard, but the incident did sour our relations with the MSA, who disowned us. In their own words, they and only they, were the official representatives of the RAF."

The BMC Competitions team had decided that their entrants would consist of three-man crews, so Derek and Terry were very happy when Peter Evans agreed to join them. Peter had also joined the Red Arrows in 1966 and was a keen motorcyclist who had competed in the Isle of Man TT races.

As the summer of 1968 moved on so did the Red Arrows team's preparations. Their relationship with BMC matured as they were slowly offered more and more help and were eventually invited to a day's testing in Bagshot, Surrey. For Derek, Terry and Peter, this was a revelation. The BMC engineers took a car and ran it for miles over the kind of terrain that they could never imagine a car would survive. The engineers ran the car until something broke and then redesigned the part so that it was stronger and more resilient. Terry, Derek and Peter were given a couple of laps with an engineer to give them an idea of required speeds, before being allowed to go out unsupervised. Lap after lap their times slowly improved and they even began to get close to the engineers' performance. All went well until one of the three got a bit too enthusiastic and ended up with the car on its roof. Fortunately, this didn't seem to faze anyone and the upturned car was back testing again the next day. It did, however, change the odds on whether the Red Arrows team would even get as far as Dover.

Their efforts started to pay off and a particular perk was an offer from the British School of Motoring to take their High Performance Course. Consequently, they spent two days using both track and skidpad and normal roads, learning how to get from point to point quickly but safely. They didn't disgrace themselves on the course, which can't be said for the night they borrowed Peter Browning's personal BMC 1800. The idea was for Derek, Terry and Peter to get some experience driving an 1800, even if as a standard production 1800, the car was quite different from the rally-prepared versions. As Derek explained, "I managed to disgrace myself by having a head on mishap with a Ford Zephyr. All very embarrassing, but at least we learned how very strong the 1800 was!"

Eventually, the eve of the Marathon arrived. Saturday, November 23, 1968, was the day for scrutinizing, during which both car and necessary documentation were examined to ensure all requirements were met. The Red Arrows weren't the only ones to be nervous, as anything not meeting requirements and regulations would mean exclusion from the Marathon. However, all was well and the car went into *parc fermé*, the secure area used in motorsports to prevent unauthorized access. Derek, Terry and Peter spent a restless night wondering what on earth the next four weeks would bring.

The day of departure dawned, and Derek recalled having to wait patiently for their call to the starting ramp as they had drawn No. 64. They spent the time chatting to friends and family who had come to see them off or wandering around the paddock to assess the competition. Derek decided that while there were a lot of very impressive machines in the event, none were any better prepared than their 1800.

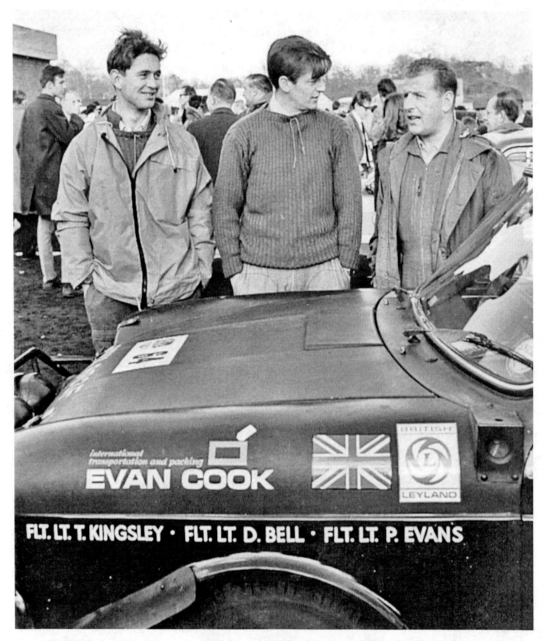

The Red Arrows: *(left to right)* Flight Lt. Peter Evans, Flight Lt. Derek Bell and Flight Lt. Terry Kingsley, Crystal Palace, London, November 24 (courtesy Derek Bell).

The team had decided that their main objective was just to get the car and themselves to Sydney, so they had to be in the top 70 cars to reach Bombay as that was the maximum number of cars the P&O passenger liner could carry on the voyage to Perth. The team recalled that they had no expectations of winning, but did believe that if they didn't wreck the car, kept up a reasonable speed and didn't get lost, they would finish somewhere near the middle of the field. They also aimed to arrive at each control with time to spare, but as it turned out, they only twice had enough time for even an hour or two of sleep. As Derek said, "Even then there was the dreaded thought of oversleeping and missing our start time."

The first part of the trip to Dover took their 1800 through London, the whole way thronged with spectators. There were crowds everywhere, slowing them down to a crawl. Eventually they reached the main highway southwards towards Dover. Their pre-start nerves had eased and they were beginning to enjoy themselves, when suddenly they noticed a large black Citroën in their mirror, with Arthur Gibson leaning out the window taking photographs. He accompanied No. 64 all the way to Dover, where the team arrived with time to spare. As Derek pointed out, they had already "confounded the doubters who reckoned we wouldn't make it this far. Who could blame them?"

All BMC Team cars were using "tulip" route books for the Marathon, a navigational tool first developed for the Tulip Rally in Holland in the late 1940s. As Derek explained, "a tulip gives a rally crew an overhead view of an intersection or place to execute an instruction. You enter the tulip from the bulb—usually at the bottom of the tulip—and exit the tulip at the arrow. Provided that the person who did the survey has done a good job and provided that the state of the roads hasn't changed, this is a very good way of getting from A to B." They felt very lucky to be provided with the tulip route books from Marathon sponsor Castrol and from BMC.

No. 64 progressed from Paris into Turkey without incident, but as expected, the first special stage in Turkey proved more challenging. The team carefully measured an amount of gas and poured it into the tank to ensure they weren't carrying any unnecessary weight and set off in the dark and the rain with Evans driving. All went well until someone checked the gauge and anxiously realized that they wouldn't have enough fuel for the section. Did they have a leak? Was the engine suddenly using a lot more fuel than normal? Had they made a miscalculation on the fuel required or put in less than they thought? The reason remained a mystery, but luckily they found a little gas station in the middle of nowhere. Relief quickly turned to concern, however, as the 1800's finely tuned engine did not like the quality of the gas. As the rain got heavier, the night got darker and the team tried harder, Evans came hurtling down a slope and could see some taillights directly ahead. Assuming this was another competitor, he headed towards them, but too late realized the lights belonged to a car sitting in the middle of a muddy field, having left the road on a sharp turn. The Red Arrows did the same, bouncing over a ditch and past the stranded car. Evans somehow managed to keep the momentum going in the mud and quickly spotted a gate, escaping back onto the road. The muddy field would eventually resemble a secondhand car lot before the stage was over.

Having escaped the quagmire, the 1800 then developed a puncture, the team's first opportunity to put their well-rehearsed wheel-changing routine to the test, not so easy on a wet, bitterly cold night in Turkey on a very narrow road with rally cars rushing by every few minutes. Morale was low as they checked into the control at Erzincan, suffering 67 penalty points, especially when they realized that some of the professionals had only lost one or two minutes.

Onwards to Teheran and again the 1800 progressed smoothly, but the team knew the remaining journey to Bombay would be much more difficult. After Teheran, there was a choice of routes, but as BMC had chosen the southern one into the desert, the Red Arrows decided to follow suit. The first section was mountainous on single track dirt roads with endless hairpins above frightening dropoffs. Then, once out of the hills, the desert began, long stretches of badly corrugated track, the corrugations hidden by sand, setting up alarming vibrations, which shook the car continuously. The team explained that the most effective way of driving in these conditions is to maintain a speed which matches the frequency of the bumps, thus reducing the effect. The Arrows tried normal speeds, slower speeds and, eventually, as fast as possible, yet still the vibrations were so bad that they feared something would break. Derek recalled that he was close to tears at the frustration of having to punish the 1800 so much.

Thanks to all the testing and the subsequent strengthening done at Abingdon, however, the car held together. Only the battery did not, which meant that once the alternator revolutions dropped below a certain point, the ignition would fail, the engine would stop and it wouldn't start again. The only solution was to keep the idling revs up and make sure they didn't stall. In this fashion, they eventually came to the end of the desert and crossed into Afghanistan, very late and facing nearly 500 miles to the Kabul control, along the Russian-American highway, built during World War II.

The team was now pretty tired, but needed to average around 80 mph. Bell reached for the pills they had been given by the Aeromedical people at the Royal Aircraft Establishment at Farnborough. Referred to as "wakey-wakey" pills, the medication had been developed to keep crews awake on long range flights. Bell took the recommended dose and on they went. The highway had been closed to local traffic, and although it was still strewn with the various mules, donkeys and camels that had a tendency to wander into the road, in Derek's view, this was the fastest drive of his life and they got to the Kabul control just within the allotted time period. A compulsory rest period meant the team could catch up on much needed sleep.

They would need all the rest they could get as after Kabul came the much anticipated Lataband Pass, miles of rough, narrow, flint road peppered with hair-raising turns and lined with sheer rock walls on one side and huge dropoffs on the other as it snaked down to the next control at Sarobi. Derek explained that to make matters worse, the authorities had graded the road, which had made the surface even more treacherous as now it would be like driving on ball bearings. Again, the Marathon organizers had planned an alternate route here, one that would avoid the pass but also incur penalty points. As Derek recalled, "Peter Browning was not at all keen on us taking his precious 1800 down there and suggested that we take the alternative route and accept the subsequent penalty points. No thank you!" So, crawling out of bed in time to be ready for the early morning departure, they were faced with freezing darkness and a dead battery. Cars could not be worked on in the *parc fermé*, which meant having to push the lifeless 1800 clear before enlisting the help of a few Afghans to get the car started. Into the pass with Kingsley at the wheel, by driving carefully and steadily, they made it to Sarobi without mishap. Derek remembered that along the pass, "we passed the official RAF Motorsports Hillman Hunter, No. 45, at the side of the road, but it was too dangerous to stop and help."

With the Lataband behind them, the Arrows relaxed a little and drove across the Khyber Pass under a sunlit blue sky, only regretting that none of them had thought to bring a camera. Apart from the need to watch for suicidal truck drivers, meandering ox carts and crowd-lined streets in the various towns and villages through which they sped, the run to New Delhi passed without incident. Even the border between Pakistan and India was crossed without hitch, as Derek recalled: "The border was wide open for the long cavalcade, the first time in three years. One official of the New Delhi Motor Club was even quoted as saying that the

London Sydney Marathon had done more for Indian-Pakistan relations in one year than the UN in the previous ten!"

The final stretch to Bombay was over 880 miles, often in heavy, slow-moving traffic, but nothing had prepared the Arrows for the roadside receptions as they approached the outskirts of the city. Thousands of excited onlookers beat the 1800 with their hands or with sticks as they passed and Derek recalled how it all felt quite intimidating as it could so easily have turned nasty. The slow progress meant they found themselves nose-to-tail with No. 29, Bruce Hodgson's Australian Ford Falcon, the front doors open as a way of pushing the crowds apart to let them through!

The Arrows made the Bombay control with plenty of time before *parc fermé*, but on realizing that the 1800 needed work, exhaustion kicked in. Struggling not to fall asleep, they knew they were last in the pecking order for receiving attention by the busy BMC service crews. As Derek stated, "Alec Poole, Paddy Hopkirk's co-driver, took pity on us and had the jobs done in no time. We will be forever grateful for his help." At Bombay, the Arrows had amassed 94 penalty points, which put them in 32nd position out of a total of 72 survivors. With a wry smile they realized that the RAF MSA Hunter was lying 53rd.

Derek found the ship crossing to Perth rather boring after the adrenaline rush and lack of sleep from the previous seven days. At the time, all he wanted to do was rest and get on with the Australian outback crossing, spending much of the voyage sleeping, eating, lying on the sun deck or reading, resisting the onboard parties and all-night card games. As he regretfully recalled, "a great shame really because there were a lot of very interesting people on the boat and it would have been a good time to make new friends and good contacts for the future."

He did, however, have time to reflect on all the good luck with which the Arrows had been blessed during the preceding few months and to think about all the people who had helped them make possible their Marathon adventure, above all Sheila Bell, his wife. He said that "For the last three years she had looked after this lodger husband who came and went twice a week and who was always preoccupied with some problem or other. She never complained and always made life easy for me and our daughter. I guess she longed for the day it would all end. Sometimes I think she is still waiting."

Eventually the ship arrived at the port of Fremantle and the BMC crews were welcomed by the local BMC motoring club. Derek recalled that some had even driven from Sydney to greet them and proved invaluable to their forthcoming efforts. The route through Australia had been reconnoitered and several of the more difficult stages had even been filmed—Derek remembers some these as being a real eye opener.

As the running order now reflected entrants' overall position, the Arrows found themselves chasing the front runners. From London to Bombay the cars were running in their numerical order and as No. 64 in a field of 98, they had found themselves in the middle of the pack, often with faster cars and drivers behind them, trying to overtake. From Perth to the next control at Youanmi, the going was good for the 1800 and the Arrows even managed to get the BMC service crews to complete any service and repair work not possible in Bombay. Derek recalled that while Youanmi was little more than a crossroads in the middle of nowhere in 1968, as they approached the town they were puzzled by how it appeared all lit up and it was only as they got closer that they realized the light was coming from a makeshift campsite, overflowing with tents, caravans, camper vans and excited spectators who had driven miles to see the Marathon pass by and offer refreshments straight from the "barbie," the Australian word for barbecue.

Things started to get a little tougher after the Marvel Loch control, with miles of almost invisible track in the dust. The team stuck to the route book instruction to follow the rabbit-proof fence for the specified number of miles, at all times trying to stay within the allotted time allowances. All three Arrows shared the driving across the outback, making sure that each got as much sleep as possible. They were all beginning to get tired, which may have caused their biggest penalty when, between the Brookside and Omeo controls, in the mountain fog with numerous tracks running off left and right, the team took a wrong turn. As Derek recalled, "the one big problem with navigating on tulip route books is that it's only when the next turn or intersection does not appear on time that it dawns on the navigator that something is wrong." The error cost them 46 minutes, but at the Murrindal checkpoint they received some encouraging news from Peter Browning, who suggested that they could take it easy from now on as they were doing well enough to help British Leyland win the official team prize.

Feeling invigorated, they pressed on, carefully negotiating the narrow mountain road between Murrindal and Ingebryra and trying to keep their speed up to Numeralla, focused on the simple fact that one error now could put paid to all their hard work. The 1800 continued to perform well along the narrow, rough tracks on the way to Hindmarsh Station, which would be the last difficult stage of the outback section; after that, things should become easier for the last 200-mile run to Sydney and Warwick Farm. However, the Arrows hadn't

No. 64 at Warwick Farm Raceway after the Red Arrows team had stopped on the way in to get the 1800 cleaned, December 17 (courtesy Derek Bell).

bargained for the continued presence of the New South Wales police, who pulled them over for speeding. Irritated but undaunted, Kingsley had the honor of driving the final section and so the Red Arrows rolled into Warwick Farm, 19th out of 56 finishers and the third-best BMC 1800 after Paddy Hopkirk and Rauno Aaltonen. Like Ford GB, the BMC Competitions team had fielded two teams, which meant that Terry, Peter and Derek were highest placed car in their team. They also beat the RAF MSA team and were the highest placed official Armed Forces entry.

In the aftermath, the team recalled quite a party in Sydney as well as doing a spot of PR work for their happy Australian sponsors Grace Brothers. They also got to spend a day relaxing on the river at the home of "Gelignite" Jack Murray, who, with Evan Green and George Shepheard, had driven the BMC Australia 1800. However, all good things had to come to an end and after three days, together with the RAF Hillman Hunter, the dark green 1800 was loaded into a Hercules transport plane and the Arrows took their seats for the long, noisy flight home.

Reflecting on what the Marathon meant to him, Derek Bell said, "We enjoyed all the rush and tumble of preparing for the event. We had the unforgettable experience of driving such a well-prepared car among some of the quickest drivers in the world, along some of the worst roads in the world, across some of the most beautiful countries in the world, and coming out of the other side in one piece. We spent the best part of a month living in each other's pockets and came out with strong friendships, which have endured to this day."

8

Off with a Bang!

In June 1968, the British *Daily Express* published the list of teams that had paid their entrance fee and made the final 100. Looking down the lineup of cars, crews and team names or backers, it's clear that many didn't make Crystal Palace five months later, while many of the eventual starters didn't make the June list: 11 cars and crews were gone by November, to the relief of those waiting in reserve. Furthermore, a number of those, who were waved off by Miss World, ended up behind the wheel of a car other than that listed in June. First off the starting ramp in November 1968 were Bill Bengry, Arthur Brick and John Preddy, driving a Ford Cortina GT, yet, according to the June list, Bengry's car was to be a Renault. The Goulden family, including the youngest competitor at 18 years old, must have decided that a Jaguar E-Type wasn't the best choice for a bone crunching, 10,000-mile drive across the world as they eventually competed in a much more practical Triumph 2000 sedan.

Even up to two days before departure, the list of competitors continued to change. At the last moment French entrant Marie Patoux withdrew, which led to a frantic search for a replacement; then two other entrants withdrew and officials simply ran out of time to organize substitute teams. As a result, rather than the agreed 100 cars, 98 vehicles began the Marathon. Being given just a few days' notice to be ready to start their engines would undoubtedly have been too little, too late for those still on the reserve list, while the reasons why Patoux, Per Ekholdt and Ian Large threw in the towel at the last moment remains unknown. In addition, while just 12 women eventually competed in the Marathon, originally there were to have been 15 at the starting line. Once again, their reasons for withdrawal are unknown.

So, preparations for the Marathon continued throughout the summer of 1968. For motorsports departments and private individuals alike, work was underway to prepare cars for the journey. *The Daily Express* reported that, by the time each car arrived at Crystal Palace on November 24, it would have cost each entrant approximately $18,000 to be ready, an enormous sum. Even though their primary focus was ensuring that their cars were tough enough for the long distance event, the big motorsports teams of Ford and BMC still found the time and generosity to offer advice and support to many of those amateurs who had selected a Cortina, BMC 1800 or MG for the Marathon. BMC at Abingdon assisted Jean Denton and Tom Boyce with their *Nova* magazine-sponsored MGB, and Anthony Wilson with his 1800, while Ford was generous with its time in offering advice to Duncan Bray, who, together with Peter Sugden and Simon Sladen, were hard at work getting their ex-rally Cortina ready. Such generosity of spirit would be seen again and again on the road to Warwick Farm, with the factory service teams coming to the aid of many a struggling amateur driving one of their products.

The Ford Cortina Lotus of Rosemary Smith and Lucette Pointet on scrutinizing day at Crystal Palace, November 23 (courtesy John Hemsley).

According to Marathon organizing committee member Jack Kemsley, South London's Crystal Palace stadium had been chosen for a number of reasons, including that "regular race meetings were held there and it had good parking facilities and was well served by public transport."[1] Also, being a Royal Automobile Club steward at most of the race meetings there, Kemsley had a good working relationship with the Greater London Council, which administered the stadium, something which proved useful as after much discussion, he managed to persuade them that unless measures were taken, the crowds would certainly swarm the track as competitors attempted to complete a circuit before exiting into the London streets.

The weekend of November 23–24 finally arrived, and all cars and crews were expected at Crystal Palace on the Saturday for scrutinizing. Organizers checked each car and each team's paperwork against Marathon regulations to ensure a level playing field was in place. This was the first time participants would be able to size up the competition and get a glimpse of their fellow competitors while vehicles were thoroughly inspected in turn and, as each vehicle passed its inspection, a mark was painted on its bodywork. By late Saturday, 98 cars were ready to go and crews retired for their last night's sleep before the journey began. There were, of course, a few mishaps during this time. On the Friday before the Marathon, the Volvo entered by John Tallis suffered accident damage at the hands of his teammate, former Citroën works driver and Monte Carlo Rally winner Paul Coltelloni, so Tallis was faced with a race against the clock to carry out the necessary repairs in time for starters' orders. Car No. 1's Bill Bengry was in bed early on the Saturday night trying to recover from flu, while Gerry Lister's Amoco team Volvo developed a fuel leak on the way back from scrutinizing, which meant hurried repairs only 16 hours before departure. In No. 39, Australian Stewart McLeod would have to stop the privately entered Alfa Romeo en route to the stadium to buy food rations for the journey!

At last, Sunday, November 24 dawned with the milky winter sunlight so common in England. The crowds had queued overnight to get their first glimpse of the cars and crews and the public car park was overflowing, *The Daily Express* having sold thousands of parking tickets a week before. The Crystal Palace stadium and its surroundings were awash with excited spectators, mingling with competitors' friends and families. Interest in the event was so great that local police struggled to cope as traffic backed up for six miles around the stadium. Some competitors even had to fight their way into the park, using their air horns to clear the crowds at the entrance. In the competitors' enclosure, spectators gathered around each gleaming machine, as crews carried out last minute checks, some struggling to attach the adhesive entry numbers and other sponsorship decals. The heavily laden 1930 Bentley Tourer, for example, appeared to offer little space on its bodywork panels for Keith Schellenberg to smooth down the large "No. 84" that his car and crew had been allotted. Ordinary members of the public mixed with well-known faces, all craning to get a look at this car and that. British Member of Parliament, and former Chancellor of the Exchequer, Reginald Maudling was there to see his son Martin off in the single Ford Escort of the Marathon. Popular movie actor Terry-Thomas probably felt a little nervous as his team got ready to go in their Ford Cortina 1600E. Cigarette clamped between his teeth, he ran a few paces after the Cortina as it was flagged away down the ramp.

The view from the starting ramp, Crystal Palace, London, November 24 (courtesy Simon Sladen).

There was a spirit of carnival at Crystal Palace. The program announced "'Before The Rally' Demonstrations and Entertainments!"[2] and the crowds were treated to the spectacle of seeing 1968 Formula One World champion Graham Hill drive his winning Lotus 49 around the stadium, and then return to steer "Chitty Chitty Bang Bang" around the circuit, pursued by Graham's wife, Betty, at the wheel of "The Truly Scrumptious," Chitty's automotive costar from the hugely successful film. A parade of vintage cars, organized by Lord Montague of Beaulieu, and a hovercraft display added to the atmosphere. Competitors gathered in the marquee for a final briefing from event steward, chief police constable and motor racing enthusiast John Gott, and Marathon instigators Tommy Sopwith and Sir Max Aitken, who warned crews that the Marathon had attracted the attention of police in every country along the route—any accidents or incidents might well land a driver in an overseas jail! "Gelignite" Jack Murray let off his customary firecracker to mark the end of the briefing and competitors made their way back to the enclosure to begin the wait. Cars would be flagged off at one minute intervals, starting at 2:00 p.m., with the order of departure previously agreed by lottery. This meant that, for many, the clock would slowly tick through the afternoon before their number came up, leading to varying degrees of boredom, restlessness and nervous apprehension. Innes Ireland worried that his Mercedes-Benz was too heavy, but couldn't think of anything to remove, while poor Jenny Gates, *The Sydney Telegraph* team member in No. 41, recalled being physically sick as her departure time approached. Attending to the last minute checks on their privately entered SAAB 95 station wagon, Jeremy Delmar-Morgan was aware he had never driven the SAAB before. His co-driver, Alister Percy, recalled that "Jem had had little familiarization with the car and I remember him asking me on the ramp where bottom gear was. Joke—I think!" In one of the two blue and white Hillman Hunters, Andrew Cowan was concerned that, as they had been awarded No. 75, it meant an hour and 15 minutes to wait after the first car had departed.

Then, as the minute hand edged towards 2:00 p.m., Car No. 1, the Ford Cortina GT, driven by Bill Bengry, Arthur Brick and John Preddy, was led to the starting ramp by one of the team of young women who had been tasked with carrying the national flag of each entry. Bengry, a garage owner and experienced rally driver, had already received a civic sendoff by the mayor of Leominster in his Herefordshire hometown, and had been amused at all the press interest in the fact that his team would be first away. At 2:00 p.m., Desmond Plummer, the leader of the Greater London Council, dropped the starter's flag and, led by one of the tiny Royal Automobile Club's blue and white Austin A35 vans, Bengry released the clutch, pressed the gas pedal and rolled down the ramp to complete a circuit of the stadium before heading out into the south London streets and away. The 1968 London to Sydney Marathon had begun.

Throughout the afternoon, car after car was led to the starting ramp and, to the sound of cheering crowds, was waved away by either Desmond Plummer or the newly crowned Miss World, Australian Penny Plummer, stylish in her fur hat and happily granting good luck kisses to a few competitors. Australian competitor Brian Lawler was driving No. 6, a 1965 Ford Fairmont XP, accompanied by *Sydney Sun-Herald* motoring journalist Clyde Hodgins as navigator and Don Waite as co-driver. Brian explained that, once they left the starting ramp, they were required to do a lap of the Crystal Palace circuit before heading out into the South London streets. When it came to his turn in No. 6, Brian recalled that "I went off, up onto the ramp. Bang and we did a lap of Crystal Palace. I can still remember this, I said 'Navigator tell

Under starter's orders—No. 10, the Royal Green Jackets' Porsche 911T of George Yannaghas and Jack Dill, November 24 (courtesy Mike Bailey).

No. 44 Rover 2000TC and No. 46 Simca 1100 wait their turn to start, November 24 (courtesy Mike Bailey).

me where do we go?' The navigator said straight ahead and I thought shit, I've seen this happen because I'm going straight at the wall of people, and I look as far as I can see and they're all lined up. Missed a copper [*police officer*] by about this much! I said 'Well, that's not bad—first instruction, the wrong one!'"

When No. 17, the British Royal Navy–entered BMC 1800, was summoned to start, Penny Plummer handed crew member Commander Philip Stearns a letter from the Lord Mayor of London, to be presented to the commissioner of citizens in Sydney. Penny leaned forward and kissed Stearns for good luck and Stearns promptly stalled the car! Behind the wheel of No. 43, one of the Amoco Volvos, Gerry Lister roared away, forgetting in all the excitement that Australian filmmaker Rob McAuley was hanging onto to the trunk with one hand, filming their departure. American Sid Dickson gunned No. 53 down the ramp with CBS camera man Jerry Sims standing head and shoulders out of the red, white and blue Rambler American's "gun turret," a reinforced hole cut through the roof, his camera capturing the moment. The four-car Russian Moskvič team departed at different intervals, but regrouped outside the stadium, having agreed in advance to travel, as much as possible, in convoy. No. 37, the little Austin 1300 station wagon entered by Dennis Cresdee, with Johnstone Syer and Bob Freeborough, was so heavily laden that it needed a helping push up the ramp, and the crowds must have marveled at No. 52, the tiny red MG Midget of John Sprinzel and Roy Fidler, with its enormous, roof-mounted fuel tank, and No. 11's elaborate, vertical tailpipe running up the side of the Swiss-entered Renault 16TS's windshield. However, probably the loudest cheer was saved for Keith Schellenberg, Norman Barclay and Patrick Lindsay as they waited for the countdown, before waving to the crowds and heading off in their 1930 Bentley Sports Tourer.

Towards the end of the field was No. 90. In their Ford Cortina Lotus, Captain David Harrison and Lieutenant Martin Proudlock were patiently waiting for their number to come up. Alternately chatting to fellow Ford team member Rosemary Smith, who, in No. 93, was parked next to them, or with family members and friends who had gathered to see them away, they had already been treated to an impromptu sendoff by their regiment's trumpeters—Martin recalled that none of the other armed forces teams received such a rousing salute from their regiments—but they were now more than ready to get going. David was already experienced in rally driving, having started competing with the British Army Motoring Association years earlier, but Martin was a complete novice and was there only because original co-driver Captain Jeremy Rawlins had been forced to withdraw after receiving a new posting earlier in the year.

9

Add Lightness, Go Faster

On the afternoon of November 24, 1968, waiting for the signal to approach the Crystal Palace starting ramp and the beginning of the 10,000-mile drive to the other side of the world, 25-year-old Lieutenant Martin Proudlock knew that a twist of fate had secured his seat beside his friend and fellow officer, 28-year-old Captain David Harrison. Assigned No. 90, they were forced to sit and wait as 89 preceding cars were flagged away, excitement and a few nerves quickly turning into boredom and impatience. All the work they had done, the hours spent painstakingly converting their Cortina from a domestic rally car to a machine capable of withstanding the hammering it would endure in the coming days, now lay behind them. For months they had spent every moment of their free time working on the car while still serving as officers of the Junior Leaders' Regiment of the Royal Artillery. They had stripped the car down and practically rebuilt it, replacing the engine, transmission, shock absorbers and back axle, strengthening the body shell, fitting a larger fuel tank, upgrading the wiring and redesigning the cabin to accommodate every need during the ten day drive to Sydney. They were now ready to take their place in the Ford GB Team, alongside professional rally drivers Roger Clark, Ove Andersson, Bengt Söderström, Gunnar Palm, Eric Jackson, Ken Chambers, Rosemary Smith and Lucette Pointet. Yet the previous 12 months had seen Proudlock gain, then lose, then regain his place in the team.

One lunchtime in November 1967, Martin was sitting in the bar at the officers' mess at Bramcote Barracks in Warwickshire, England, where the Junior Leaders' Regiment of the Royal Artillery was based. As he recalls, "David came in and said there's going to be a rally from London to Australia and do you fancy doing it? So I said yes, absolutely, because my father—a recently retired Brigadier—had twice crossed the Sahara, so you only get a chance once in a lifetime to do something 'wacky races.'" David mischievously added that "Martin had never rallied at all, but he was a good mate, he'd be all right and I reckoned that we could hack it together without too many problems. I would have to do it with someone I got on with, absolutely, so it all went downhill from there!"

By February 1968, David was busy investigating the logistics of obtaining a suitable car and approached the British Army Motoring Association (BAMA) to ask whether they would be interested in fielding an official team. Throughout the 20th century, and even today, the various British armed forces have used a wide range of recruitment tactics in their collective attempts to maintain personnel levels across generations. One tactic has been to offer applicants the opportunity to undertake activities such as skiing, parachuting, flying helicopters, scuba-diving or the chance to be a Red Arrow. Driving was also among their promoted activities and, as the various forces have trained personnel to expertly operate different kinds of vehicular transport, by natural progression the idea of bringing military driving skills into the world of competitive motorsports has led to a history of armed forces personnel becoming associated with rallying. David was aware that a number of other serving officers were also expressing interest in the Marathon, including Major Freddie Preston and Captain Jeremy Rawlins, so he began corresponding with them in the hope that a coordinated approach might secure BAMA backing. Eventually, while BAMA agreed to back a two car team in the Marathon, Captain Rawlins had hit upon a different idea. What if Ford GB would be interested in having an army presence in their Marathon team? He dispatched a letter to Ford Competitions Department manager Henry Taylor and in April 1968, Ford replied to say they were indeed willing to lend a car to the Army, with all necessary information and parts in order that it could be competitive as long as Rawlins was able to organize his own service schedule for the actual event. Rawlins quickly contacted David to say that a car had been obtained and did he want to team up? As Martin recalled, "David went up to this meeting in London, having said 'Look, my car's broken down at the train station, can I drive yours?' He came back and said 'Well, good news and some bad news.' He said 'The good news is, I'm in and the bad news is—you're out!'" As David added, "That was a hard decision because I had to more or less say, there and then, right, I'll do it with this other guy."

David and Jeremy set about fundraising to cover the cost of their Marathon entry. The fine detail of the partnership between Ford and the Army was yet to be finalized and while they had the promise of a car, it wouldn't be made available until late July and would then need extensive modifications to be undertaken by Rawlins and Harrison. Then in June, Rawlins received notification that he was to be posted abroad and therefore would have to withdraw. As Martin recalled, "Jeremy Rawlins said to Dave, 'I've got to drop out.' So David said, 'Right.' At that point we went down to Ford and David said to Henry Taylor, 'Look, you know Jeremy has got to drop out, all frightfully sad and all the rest of it, but do you mind if Martin comes instead?'" David went on, "And what is more, this is what we can do for you. And they were really good, weren't they, they were just charming!"

What they could do for Ford was to organize military training exercises for the entire Ford GB Marathon team, first at the Bramcote barracks and then in the Welsh mountains, to put them through their paces on a range of survival exercises, first in the gym and the pool and then outside. So, in early November 1968, with the exception of Jenny Brittan and Lucette Pointet, the Ford GB Marathon team found themselves under the instruction of Captain Harrison and Lieutenant Proudlock, hiking over mountains, sleeping under canvas, climbing ropes and learning how to survive a capsized canoe! As Roger Clark was reported to say, "After those four days, the Marathon should be a rest cure—we hope!"[1] Needless to say, the resultant newspaper coverage provided some welcome PR to both the Army and the Ford Marathon effort.

David explained that "the car Ford gave us in 1968 had been prepared for the RAC Rally, which was nothing like the way they were preparing the cars for the Marathon. We took everything off it, gave it all back to Ford, and they gave us some more stuff. There were the big items, but then there were all the little bits and pieces. We took advice from them and they would say 'Well, you need some of these and you'll need some of those,' and they came off the racks, as opposed to be being invoiced, at no cost."

Adopting the two mottos "belt and braces" and "add lightness, go faster," David and

Lieutenant Martin Proudlock (left) and Captain David Harrison with their Ford Cortina Lotus at Bramcote Barracks, England, 1968 (courtesy Martin Proudlock).

Martin were able to juggle their army duties and a limited budget to transform their car into a machine that would be able to compete in the Marathon, but not without the occasional oversight. During one visit to the Ford Competition Department's HQ, Henry Taylor asked a key question. As Martin explained, "all of a sudden, we were sitting there one day in Henry's office and Henry asked us what we were doing about tires. We looked at each other and thought, doesn't the car come with any? And we said 'Well, we hadn't thought about it.' So he put a call out to his secretary and said get me Jack at Goodyear. Jack comes on the line and Henry says 'You know you're doing us five sets of tires for the Marathon? Can you make that six? Good lad!' Puts the phone down and tells us we're on Goodyears!"

During the week before the Marathon began, David and Martin took the Cortina on a visit to an elementary school in Wath-on-Dearne in South Yorkshire. The school was using the Marathon to teach a class of ten-year-olds about geography and foreign currency, and each child had chosen a Marathon entry to support. For Lynn Cadman and Elizabeth Holtom, the visit by David and Martin was especially exciting as the schoolgirls had selected them as the team to watch. They even presented the two men with good luck charms, two little rubber toys that David and Martin attached to the car's dash panel switches, and which were still there when they got to Sydney.

Finally, David and Martin found themselves at Crystal Palace, waiting to be called to the starting ramp. Taking its place behind the privately entered Cortina driven by Robin

Capt. David Harrison (left) and Lt. Martin Proudlock flanked by the trumpeters of the Junior Leaders' Regiment of the Royal Artillery, Crystal Palace, November 24 (courtesy Martin Proudlock).

Clark and Martin Pearson, No. 90 eased forward and waited for the flag to fall. Before organizers could act, their regimental trumpeters dashed forward and, flanking the car, saluted them away. Out into the packed London streets, David recalled "being waved to by a policeman to go faster the wrong way down the bus lane over Westminster Bridge—very satisfying!" They made steady, uneventful progress down to Dover and then across to France aboard the ferry *The Maid of Kent*, on board which David remembers "we had the first of what turned out to be a series of arguments with waiters all along the route to Sydney!"

No. 90 covered the first 1,000 miles to Yugoslavia without mishap, other than a slight oil leak from the transmission, and at 6:00 a.m. on the morning of November 25, arrived at the Belgrade checkpoint with more than eight hours in hand. The Cortina was in fine shape so David and Martin handed it over to the local Ford dealer for a wash and check over and retired to the Hotel Metropole to get some rest and refreshment or as David explained, "a large capitalist lunch!" After a moment of panic when the Ford dealer couldn't find their car keys, David and Martin pressed on towards Bulgaria, amused at the sight of the Russian Moskvič team, all four cars travelling together, their crews enjoying the fact that the Russian car company had set up service points and support vehicles at regular intervals all the way through both Eastern Bloc countries.

Across the border into Turkey and now the going became rather more challenging. David recalls that while there was virtually no motorsports in Turkey, every truck driver seemed to think of themselves as a racing driver. The highway was littered with wrecked trucks and at one point they passed No. 5, the Australian Chrysler Valiant Safari station wagon, its driver's side completely ripped away. They continued cautiously to Sivas, the next time control, after which they knew things would get much more difficult as the route followed rough, slippery, unpaved mountain roads on the way to Erzincan. David remembers how a sharp, right-hand turn immediately after a humpback bridge almost had the Cortina leaving the road and only hard braking followed by even harder acceleration kept them on track, unlike 16 or so other Marathon cars that ended up skidding around a muddy field trying to find a way back out again. David also recalled vainly trying to keep up with his Ford teammate Rosemary Smith, who had caught and passed them. He explained that "I tried to keep up. She was so neat and tidy and fast. All I got was some broken lights from her stones and the realization that professionals were different." At the Erzincan time control, No. 90 had picked up its first penalty points, such were the difficult conditions over the Turkish mountains, but ahead lay the 916-mile stage across the border into Iran and the city of Teheran.

No. 90 was now entering the third time zone of the Marathon route, but as the entire Marathon's timings were set to British Standard Time, David and Martin kept one wristwatch set to local time with another remaining at British time. Progress to Teheran was made without difficulty and they enjoyed watching the dawn break over Mount Ararat, but the final route into the city was fraught with danger. As David explained, "The traffic volume was enormous and everyone drove with little regard to lanes, or directions." However, even though they had now covered 3,600 miles, the Cortina remained in excellent condition. In Teheran, David and Martin seized the opportunity to shower and eat, which was just as well because the next stretch required competitors to cover almost 1,600 miles in 23 hours, across the border into Afghanistan to the city of Kabul and much of it over unpaved roads and tracks.

Herat in Afghanistan, November 1968 (courtesy John Hemsley).

David reflected how all the work they had done preparing the car now seemed worthwhile as in the 750 miles to the border, nothing came loose and nothing broke. The crossing into Afghanistan was, according to David, "a masterpiece of diplomacy. At the end of a red carpet sat Marathon officials and the heads of Afghani Customs and Immigration and all this in a tent in the middle of the desert, more than 60 miles from the nearest village!" Another 100 miles beyond the border lay Herat, where Ford had a plane waiting, together with a service crew. As Martin recalled, "we picked up the Ford plane at Herat airfield. Roger and Ove had gone, but we arrived at 10 or 11 in the morning and we found the airfield and we went on board. I suppose a mechanic looked at the car and topped it up with fuel, I don't know, but we went on board and Bill Barnett was there and said to have a sandwich and a cup of coffee." However, Bill had more than refreshment on his mind. Teammates Rosemary and Lucette were ahead of Martin and David now and had already passed through Herat, stopping to complain that their Cortina, No. 93, had developed a bad misfire and was probably suffering from a burned-out piston. If they could get to Kabul, Ford would be able to undertake temporary repairs, but until then No. 93 could come to a permanent halt at any time, not something anyone was willing to entertain—having two women stranded in the wilds of Afghanistan needed to be avoided at all costs. Bill instructed David and Martin to head off and, if possible, provide any assistance to Rosemary and Lucette to get them to Kabul. As Martin explained, "we said yes, not realizing it was anything like as serious as it was. We found her down the road and Rosemary had just poured the last pint of oil in and she said this thing isn't going to make it, so we said okay and we towed them. It's a wild, wild country, even in those days, so if you left two women on their own they wouldn't have survived, simple as that. So that's what we did, we hitched up a tow rope and away we went. Now if you were caught towing you'd have been thrown out so we got to the point on the hill where you could look down at Kabul, gave her our last bit of oil, unhitched the tow rope and said right, off you go, sort of pushed her down the hill and left her to it!" Martin suspects this was probably the longest tow in history, although, true or not, in rescuing their teammates, David and Martin lost three and a half hours getting to Kabul. Exhausted, they collapsed into bed at the Hotel Spinzar, taking full advantage of what remained of the compulsory six hour stop before tackling the dreaded Lataband Pass.

Describing the pass, David recalled that "The road—and that flatters it—twisted its way up the sides of the gorges and plunged down again. Coming around corners into the blinding sunshine and the dust of the car ahead, knowing there was an unprotected drop only yards away, was an unforgettable experience. Martin managed to take photographs while hanging out of the navigator's seat, claiming the pace notes were too difficult to read!" Martin recounted that "We nearly went off Kabul to Sarobi on full left lock, 3,000 feet down. We had route notes, but David and I didn't know where they started and we took one look and threw them in the back of the car and I took photographs. It was like driving on marbles and David went left lock and we slid on. Afterwards, we said to Roger Clark, this is what had happened and he said if you go off forward, you're going too slowly. If you go off backwards, you're going too quickly. I said, 'What about if you go off sideways?' 'Oh,' he said, 'you've just over-cooked it.' Typical bloody Roger Clark!" However, despite the dust and stones flying everywhere, No. 90 only lost 14 minutes and was quicker to Sarobi than many of the more favored entries.

The route from Sarobi took them down to the beginning of the Khyber Pass and the

Cortina Lotuses No. 93 and No. 90 side by side at Crystal Palace; 4,000 miles later Harrison and Proudlock in No. 90 would come to the aid of Smith and Pointet in No. 93 (courtesy Martin Proudlock).

border into Pakistan. Across Pakistan and into India, despite the absence of motorized traffic, the roads were heaving with people. Five million spectators thronged the roadside, all apparently determined to touch the car as it passed by. As David recalled, people "sat on the bonnet [hood], roof and boot [trunk], hung on the door handles and occasionally even put their toes under the wheels!" Eventually clearing the hoards, they reached New Delhi in good time and grabbed some sleep before the last leg to Bombay, a hot, sticky 780-mile drive, again dogged by more huge crowds along the highways. During their run through India, Martin recalled an incident involving their daily ration boxes. As he explained, "At the end of each 24 hours we threw away what remained and opened another pack. In each pack was a small tube of suntan cream, which we used on our arms. I remember in India throwing one out of the window and saw a small boy run out into the road and thinking it must have been good, sucked the last remains out of the tube!" Finally, with six hours in hand, they reached Bombay and used the time to have the car serviced and thoroughly cleaned inside and out. Having rested up, David and Martin returned to the car knowing they had 15 minutes in hand to make the short hop to the Bombay time control. However, starting the engine resulted in a loud screech—the alternator had seized. Ford mechanics swooped and repaired the offending item, but after being in Bombay for six hours they were ultimately 21 minutes late to the control.

Of the nine day ship crossing to Perth, David and Martin mostly recall the slippery stewards who, unless they were satisfactorily tipped, took their time taking orders in the bar, and

No. 90 gets a steam-clean in Bombay, India, December 3, 1968 (courtesy Martin Proudlock).

Lt. Martin Proudlock at Gloucester Park trotting track, Perth, Australia, December 14 (courtesy Martin Proudlock).

Martin reflected how they were also fairly absent minded when it came to coming back with his change after paying for drinks! Fortunately for them, they were good sailors as for the first few days, the sea was extremely rough. Eventually, December 13 dawned bright and clear and the ship berthed at Fremantle on the West Australian coast. After having the Cortina thoroughly inspected by the local police, in line with Western Australia state regulations, they joined the convoy of Marathon cars and headed north to Perth and the start of the Australian section.

On the first 340-mile stretch from Perth, David and Martin witnessed their first kangaroo, quickly followed by a second. Unlike the first, however, the second 'roo was less willing to get out of the way. As David explained, "we did the first three movements of a square dance with it and ended up hitting it on our front right-hand side. There was a thump, some flying glass and a 'roo with a headache!" Quickly departing, the 'roo in one direction, the Cortina in another, they were able to inspect the damage at the first time control at Youanmi. To their relief it was superficial, so they sped off towards Marvel Loch, the next checkpoint. They knew the going would be fast and rough, and although the time interval between cars was now increased to three minutes to allow for the ceaseless clouds of dust, they were still caught up in the wake of another car, which meant they were forced to keep to 50 mph, visibility reduced to almost non-existent. Overtaking was for the brave or foolhardy as in addition to thick, swirling dust clouds, the rocky track was lined on either side with scrub and trees. As David explained, "our second mishap in Australia occurred here. We came to a left-hander, not marked on our notes, and ran off into the scrub on the right. Inspecting the damage, we found the left hand side, from the door backwards, was flattened." However, despite broken side mirrors, they were able to get the car back on the road and made it to the control with only a four minute penalty.

A challenging but uneventful 120-mile charge to Lake King followed and then came the long haul across the Nullarbor—900 miles to be completed in 15 hours through a mix of blue gum trees, scrub land and dirt roads. As David explained, "At times we wondered if it would ever end. Dodging the potholes became more difficult. On the dirt surface the car threw up considerable quantities of dust, a lot of which found its way into the car." However, they made it to the Ceduna time control with an hour and a half in hand and were thrilled to realize they had averaged 70 mph throughout the stage. At Ceduna, Ford ordered them to make up as much time as possible on the fast asphalt highways to Quorn to allow for their car to have a major service. As they arrived at Port Augusta, however, they were confronted with the sight of Ford mechanics working flat out, replacing Roger Clark's cylinder head. David reflected that Ford teammates Eric Jackson and Ken Chambers had arrived earlier and had sacrificed their engine to keep Roger in the running. "It was a race against time as Roger was still in the lead at that point. If we had been only a few minutes earlier, we could have been the donor car." As it was, although Jackson and Chambers had been performing extremely well and had been consistently threatening the top ten, Henry Taylor decided to keep Clark going at their expense.

No. 90 pressed onwards, David and Martin only too aware that they could so easily have seen their Marathon unceremoniously come to an end at Port Augusta. Two short stages followed, the first relatively easy, but between Moralana Creek and Brachina Gorge, they all but crashed out permanently. Coming out of a turn, Martin misjudged the angle and they ran off the road at 45 mph, the Cortina crunching into a ditch, resulting in fairly extensive damage.

No. 90 runs off the road between Moralana Creek and Brachina Gorge, December 16 (courtesy Martin Proudlock).

A front wheel had been pushed back into the bulkhead, which had in turn misaligned the gas pedal. On top of that, the starter motor was smashed and damage to the driver's side meant the door wouldn't close properly. As David recalled, "despite being tightly strapped in, which must have saved a few broken bones, the steering wheel was bent down. Our only personal injury was bruised knuckles as we had both hit the battery master switch between the seats." Fortunately the Brachina Gorge control was only five miles away so David set off on foot to get help. Martin recalls that No. 11, the Swiss-entered Renault 16, stopped to help tow the Cortina out of the ditch, by which time David was back with a dozen helpers. Attaching a rope between the Cortina's front suspension and a Toyota Land Cruiser they had flagged down, they were able to pull it forward and after a quick inspection to make sure everything was as realigned as possible, No. 90 was off again, battered and bruised and paying the price with a two and a half hour time penalty.

Now they were faced with what the route notes described as possibly the worst section in Australia, 210 miles of heat and rutted track. The sand and dust were relentless and to make matters worse, the damage to the driver's door meant the window wouldn't close completely. When David and Martin eventually emerged from the Cortina at the Mingary time control, they more resembled chimney sweeps, with bull dust covering them from scalp to toe.

After Mingary, they were into New South Wales, and although there were still more than 1,000 miles to go, they knew that if they could keep the car going, they would finish the

No. 90 finishes in 30th place. Warwick Farm Raceway, Sydney, December 17 (courtesy Martin Proudlock).

Marathon at Warwick Farm in Sydney. Ever mindful of the state police who were determined to ensure that competitors stuck rigidly to the legal speed limits, they pressed on, trying not to concentrate too hard on the slight knocking sound coming from the engine. Keeping an anxious eye on the oil pressure gauge, they set 4,000 RPM as the Cortina's limit and passing out of New South Wales and into Victoria, they began the climb up and up into the Australian Alps, a seemingly never ending series of turns, undulating up and down with sheer dropoffs to left and right. David and Martin knew that as long as they got to Sydney within 12 hours of the target time, they wouldn't be classified as a non-finisher. Not even the first and only puncture of the entire journey just before the last time control at Nowra was going to stop them getting to Sydney and finally, after 10,000 punishing miles, No. 90 drove into the Warwick Farm Raceway at 6:30 p.m. on December 17 with 623 penalty points. They were classified with a final position of 30th out of 56 finishers and were the second Ford GB Team car home.

Amid the resultant celebrations, the victory parade to Sydney's Hyde Park and the awards ceremony, it struck David and Martin that they hadn't given any thought to how they were going to get home to England! As Martin explained, "We never thought about how to get home. Someone told us the RAF was flying a Hercules back and would we like to go on it, so we said yes. It wasn't sorted before the event, it was when we got to Sydney, we just didn't think about it!" And so, exactly one month after it had all begun, on Christmas Eve 1968, Captain David Harrison and Lieutenant Martin Proudlock landed back in England.

As for their car, Martin explained that "Ford had done so much, but Roger hadn't won

No. 90's final resting place in Sydney, December 18 (courtesy Martin Proudlock).

when he might have done. Ken and Eric had gone out and only three of the six cars finished. We were rather left on our own and when we finished at Hyde Park, I guess Bill Barnett said get the car around to Smiths Garage and by the way, would you take Rosemary's car as well, because she's off doing television interviews. So we went back into the park and there's a big group of people around the cars. David jumped in and drove ours and inside we carried extra keys under the bonnet. There's this big crowd of people standing around Rosemary's car so I went up and said excuse me, opened up the latches, lifted the bonnet, removed the key, closed the bonnet and said I bet you wish you knew that had been there! Then we parked both cars up and that was the last we saw of them." David added, "sadly, after all the hard driving we did with her, we had to abandon the car in a car park behind the hotel. I wonder what happened to it. Car CTC 23E, where are you?"

Today, despite living in different countries, David and Martin remain the best of friends and even competed in the 25th Anniversary London to Sydney Marathon in 1993, for which they also prepared and drove a Ford Cortina Lotus.

10

Bound for Belgrade

Within yards of Crystal Palace the British police were struggling to keep competitors moving. Many Londoners had driven down to catch a glimpse of the Marathon cars as they made their way north, and the resultant heavy traffic as well as the thousands of eager spectators lining the sidewalks forced competitors to a snail's pace. The official route was taking them deeper into the heart of London. In fact, in the first hour only six miles were covered, such was the public interest. Captain Hans Hamilton, crew member of the British Royal Navy–entered BMC 1800, later remarked that "the crowd appeared bigger than the 1953 Coronation crowds through which he had also driven."[1]

The official route would take the cars northwards from Crystal Palace, over the Thames at Vauxhall Bridge, past the Houses of Parliament, around Parliament Square and then southwards again, past Big Ben and across Westminster Bridge. Press photographers were stationed opposite Parliament and at the south side of the bridge, capturing each approaching Marathon car against some of London's famous landmarks. Despite the parade-like atmosphere, the police were determined to make sure that the crews obeyed the road rules. Innes Ireland, Michael Taylor and Andrew Hedges in their Mercedes and Peter Capelin, Antony Pargeter and Tim Baker in their Cortina were reprimanded for using their air horns, while Ford GB team members Eric Jackson and Ken Chambers were lucky not to attract police attention or incur damage when, as Jackson wrote, passing the Houses of Parliament "there was an almighty bang. The car went up in the air and banged down onto the road again. Ken had decided to run into one the traffic refuges [islands]."[2] The Swiss team of Axel Béguin, Fritz Reust and P. Gratzer only traveled for 20 minutes in their Renault 16TS when they realized they'd mislaid their road book, the vital document to be presented at each checkpoint. Béguin begged a ride with a passing motorcyclist and raced back to Crystal Palace but couldn't find the book. On returning to the Blick Racing team–backed Renault, he was relieved to learn that Reust and Gratzer had found the book underneath one of the seats.

As competitors left London, they had their first opportunity to drive at speed on the highway to Dover on the Kent coast and the awaiting ferry. With a million people lining the 70-mile run, the traffic police stopped No. 59 for speeding, the uniformed officer noting that the car was a Porsche and attempting to speak to the occupants in very limited German. British drivers Terry Hunter and John Davenport politely attempted to reply in their own limited German, until the police officer saw the joke. Not far from the Dover ferry port, DAF team member David van Lennep gave in to the call of nature and, oblivious to a crowd of chuckling journalists, pulled the little DAF 55 over and quickly relieved himself by the roadside!

Although Dover wasn't a time control point, organizers had used the port stop to help competitors get some experience of how booking in and out would work all along the route, and early arrivals took full advantage of the time available before the *Maid of Kent* ferry departed for Calais in France. Clever pre-event favorites Clark and Andersson filled their Cortina Lotus's gas tank and went into the town of Dover to get something to eat. John Smailes wrote, "By the time the other crews were thinking about refueling and eating, the two European wizards were soundly asleep in a cabin 'bought' from a ferry steward...."[3] Michael Taylor of No. 26, the big Mercedes 280SE, had also found a steward and secured two cabins for himself and his co-drivers, complete with room service and a bottle of wine. Arthur Brick in No. 1 found time to meet up with his wife Irene and their young boys and go for a walk before bidding them farewell—it would be a month until he saw them again. Berwyn Williams, leader of the Welsh team in No. 21, a BMC 1800, ran into a local motorists' accessory shop to pick up a few last minute items, only to be asked to pay for a pair of Vauxhall Ventora windscreen wiper blades that a fellow competitor had taken from the shop without paying. He recognized the competitor so agreed to pay for the blades. Catching up with the non-payer, Williams was assured that he would be reimbursed later on the ferry. Williams suspected he'd get the brush-off and sure enough, he never did get paid. Williams later saw a severely damaged Vauxhall Ventora in a field at the side of a Yugoslavian motorway and wondered whether this was the one with the unpaid-for wiper blades!

As the *Maid of Kent* maneuvered its way out of Dover Harbor for the 90-minute crossing, competitors grabbed the opportunity to find somewhere to sit in the passenger lounges, or queued to change money into different currencies. This would be the last time that competitors would be able to spend time together before Bombay and while many struck up conversations, others were able to find an empty couch or two and, burying themselves beneath coats and jackets, tried to sleep, ready for the run to Paris and beyond.

In Calais, local officials proudly held a reception for the competitors, although few took up the offer of finest French *canapés* and champagne, instead waiting until the business of off-loading the cars was completed before setting off from the ferry port in the same order they had departed Crystal Palace. During the crossing, competitors had been advised that the French police had decided not to allow the Marathon to use the *autoroute* or freeway towards Paris, which would mean a hasty revision to navigation plans as now, competitors would be expected to travel on smaller roads all the way to the first time control at Le Bourget Airport, approximately 13 miles from the center of Paris itself and with a time allowance of four hours and 32 minutes to cover the 177-mile route. A number of competitors duly disappeared into the French fog to try and find their way eastwards along narrow roads and through small villages and it wasn't long before cars became hopelessly lost, drivers having to rely on their navigators who wrestled with maps, trying to make sense of the almost invisible French countryside and, for some, trying to drive on the right hand side of the road instead of their usual left. To make matters even worse, the three women in No. 33 realized there was a problem with their car's main fuel tank and were forced to contend with the fog while also anxiously searching for a gas station to keep the auxiliary tank topped up. In No. 28, a Mercedes 280SL, Australian medical doctor Alec Gorshenin was anxiously braving the fog, all the while aware that his car had developed a fuel leak, while the big Mercedes-Benz sedan of Taylor, Ireland and Hedges was suffering from alternator problems, forcing them to fall in behind a French motorist and follow him for almost 150 miles, conserving the car's battery

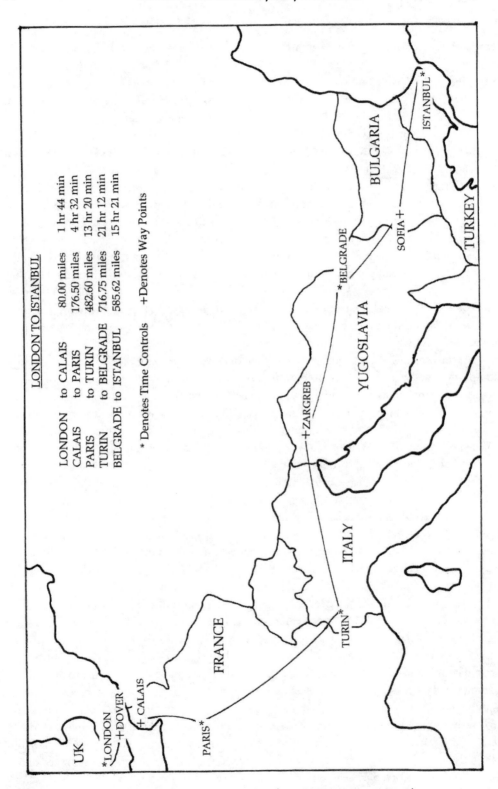

The route from London to Istanbul (map by Martin Proudlock).

by only using parking lights. In No. 36, things were little better. David McKay had been a key mover in leading the effort to both obtain three Australian Holdens from GM Australia and select the nine man team. After all that, to then be late to the first time control just didn't bear thinking about, yet there they were, the Monaro stopped on the roadside while David Liddle and George Reynolds pored over a map, with forward visibility down to little more than 30 or 40 yards. They were lucky to eventually reach the Le Bourget time control with only four minutes to spare. A few others were not so fortunate as the challenging mix of thick fog and frantic map reading meant that the British, four-women Volvo station wagon team in No. 33, two British competitors in the No. 77 BMC 1800 and No. 41, the Australian women's team, all incurred penalty points. In a manner typical of the time, British motoring journalist Hamish Cardno dismissed the women in the 1100 S, suggesting that "they must have stopped to see a fashion show"![4]

Regardless of reason, all those who were late, or who had made it by a whisker, were stunned to discover that, despite the warning issued by the French police, many competitors had merely shrugged, removed their Marathon numbers at the first opportunity and sped off along the forbidden *autoroute* anyway, which was why Lieutenant Jack Dill and George Yannaghas brought their Porsche successfully to the Le Bourget checkpoint in two hours, while McKay and others needed the full time allowed.

At the Paris time control, crews had their first real experience of rushing to get their road books stamped. Each Marathon entrant carried a road book, a document containing details about the car, names and photographs of its crew members, the ideal time of arrival for every control point and a space to record the actual arrival time. As a car arrived, a crew member would dash to a Marathon official sitting at a makeshift desk and obtain formal confirmation of their time; every minute late meant a penalty point. There would be no bonus points for arriving before the target time, but at some controls, an early arrival meant the chance to rest or carry out any needed repairs and maintenance. For one Marathon crew, an early arrival meant a chance for an Australian competitor to catch up with a European relative. No. 43, the Amoco Volvo 144S of André Welinski and Gerry Lister was met by Welinski's grandmother, who had brought a champagne picnic to share with her grandson and Lister. Poor Gerry was in no mood to enjoy the contents of the hamper, however, as he had been struggling with stomach problems all the way from London. It wouldn't be until Turin that he would be able to rush to the nearest pharmacy and obtain some medication.

After Le Bourget, the next control was in Turin in northern Italy, a 482-mile stretch along what would mostly be fast highways and freeways. First, however, competitors would need to get themselves on and around the Parisian *peripherique*, the beltway that circles the French capital. Marathon organizers had arranged for a police presence to help drivers negotiate the various detours and one-way systems that led to the beltway, which to this day remains notorious for its complexities and challenges for map-readers. They failed to appear, however, leaving crews to rely on their own navigation skills, and while some were familiar with the intricacies of the urban Parisian road networks, others struggled. Ford GB team members Nick and Jenny Brittan, a well-travelled married couple, needed a number of attempts to clear the labyrinth of roads, which were busy, despite it being the middle of the night, and No. 41, "The Galloping Tortoise," wasted an hour searching for the *peripherique*. No. 41's team leader Eileen Westley wrote that "four lovely young Frenchman in a Mercedes … led us all the way out of Paris and on to the Marathon route to Turin."[5] In contrast, having stuck to the French dictate that the main freeway be avoided from Calais to Paris, Innes Ireland and his team decided not to be stung a second time and instead sought out the *Autoroute de Sud* (South Highway) and were quickly out of the capital city.

Although competitors continued to be hampered by fog as they moved southwards, the much-discussed warnings of snow failed to materialize and the going was relatively easy all the way to the French-Italian border. The actual crossing would take cars through the seven mile Mont Blanc tunnel from Chamonix in France to Courmayeur in the Italian Aosta Valley. Each car paid the toll and emerged into bright Italian sunshine, spirits being lifted after the foggy, curving, alpine approach roads on the French side. As each car appeared from the tunnel, they were faced with border control, and all the relevant documents—passports, visas and official Marathon paperwork—were carefully presented to the border guards at the Franco-Italian barrier gates. Crews also hastily covered up the numbers adhered to their cars as the Italian authorities had agreed for the Marathon to pass through only if each entrant camouflaged its Marathon status, the fear being that should ordinary Italian motorists spot a car flaunting its official number as it sped along the *autostradas* or freeways of the country, they would forget all else and set off in pursuit in an attempt to join in! The fact that, even with numbers concealed, all of the Marathon cars were highly conspicuous with sponsorship decals, 'roo bars, extra lights and heavily laden luggage racks rather negated any effect of this rule, however.

Once across the border, the Marathon route took competitors the 100 miles to Turin,

Maj. Mike Bailey prepares to cover up his Marathon number before heading from France into Italy on November 25. Behind is No. 86, the BMW 2000 of Forsyth, Uniacke and Rich. Its number is already concealed (courtesy Mike Bailey).

No. 18, a Mark I Ford Cortina with its number concealed, at the AGIP Motel in Milan, November 25 (author's collection).

first descending along fast, sweeping mountain roads and then onto the *autostrada* to the Italian time control. Excited to be driving in good weather and stunning scenery, a number of competitors grabbed the chance to show off and cars began jostling and chasing each other, to the irritation of others. This was a marathon, not a race, there were still thousands of miles to go and there would be no prize for the first to Turin.

The Italian time control was set up alongside a motel on the freeway, one of the Italian AGIP chain of hotels, which stood at an intersection on the Milan/Avrea *autostrada*, and the first arrivals found themselves with hours to spare. Many competitors had pre-booked rooms so they could shower, sleep in a real bed for a few hours, refuel their cars and have some food before continuing on. The fast road from Paris to Turin obviously benefited the high-performance entrants as the first cars through the control were the powerful, rear-engine Porsches of Hunter and Davenport and the experienced Polish drivers Sobiesław Zasada and Marek Wachowski. Others, however, were beginning to experience problems—perhaps most surprisingly, one of meticulously prepared Ford GB team Cortina Lotuses. Driven by rally veterans Bengt Söderström and Gunnar Palm, No. 38 had begun to struggle across France and by the time it limped through the tunnel, it was clear that they needed help if they were to get to Turin. Fellow team members Roger Clark and Ove Andersson gallantly came to the rescue when, as Palm wrote, "they put a pillow between the cars … and we were pushed all the way to Milan."[6] In Turin, a broken timing chain tensioner was diagnosed, but a replacement part wasn't immediately available. The team eventually spotted a local Cortina Lotus sitting in a used car lot and, at a hugely inflated cost, stripped the donor car of its tensioner, although not without angry words aimed at the opportunistic garage proprietor. Ford GB arranged for a mechanic to be flown to Turin to fit the part, costing Palm and Söderström many hours, which they could only recover by averaging over 80 mph to the next control, fingers crossed that they wouldn't encounter an Italian highway patrol!

Other entrants also experienced their first mechanical woes before Turin. No. 47, the compact gold colored MGB of Tom Boyce and Jean Denton, lost power to its windshield wipers, starter motor and overdrive, the latter being effectively a fifth gear in the MG's transmission, a common feature today but not so in 1968. From there on, the MG had to continue with just its standard four-speed manual box. Elsewhere, Alec Gorshenin's Mercedes 280SL needed a repair to its gas pedal linkage and No. 85, a privately entered Cortina Lotus that had been modified with fuel injectors, began to experience water pump failure. However, despite the undoubted frustration and anxiety caused by these problems so early in the event, only one car actually incurred penalty points at Turin as more transmission problems caused one of the Soviet Moskvič vehicles to arrive 28 minutes late.

The AGIP motel was a flurry of activity with competitors checking in or checking out, the maid service working at full speed to prepare rooms for their next occupants. Crews surrendered their passports as part of the check-in process, collecting them again as they settled their bill, but in the confusion, French competitor Robert Neyret discovered that his passport had been mistakenly given to another competitor, long-since departed. Anxious hours followed as, without this essential document, Neyret and co-driver Jacques Terramorsi would be disqualified. Somehow, word came that the passport had been left at the Yugoslavian border control, so with tremendous relief and one or two carefully chosen words directed at the AGIP reception staff, off they dashed towards Belgrade.

All Marathon cars were soon heading eastwards across Northern Italy, the biggest cheers saved for No. 22, the red Lancia Fulvia 1.3HF of Italian racing driver and former Ferrari team member Giancarlo Baghetti and his co-driver Giorgio Bassi. Relaxed behind the wheel as he sped across his native land, Baghetti was unknowingly cruising towards calamity as the field moved closer to Eastern Europe and beyond.

The route progressed past Milan, Venice and Trieste, following the freeway that contained the occasional toll booth. No. 1, the Cortina first away from Crystal Palace, almost crashed out at one toll gate as, with John Preddy at the wheel, a momentary distraction saw the Ford bear down on the queuing traffic at 60 mph. Only some very skilled braking and steering prevented a six-car pileup. With all three occupants now very wide awake, the Cortina eased through the toll and continued towards the border control, where thousands of spectators gathered to watch the cars enter Yugoslavia, witnessing Neyret's reunion with his passport and Innes Ireland hopping about in his sleeping bag, so determined was he not to surrender it before his allocated rest time in the back of the Mercedes was up!

On the way to Ljubljana, the weather worsened again and cars were once more plunged into the fog, the temperature plummeting. Rain and sleet followed, drivers resisting the urge to turn up their heaters to prevent themselves from dozing off as the miles flashed by. Those hours between two and four in the morning would pose the greatest risk of accidents caused by a sudden, drowsy lack of focus, and this was probably the cause of the first real casualty of the Marathon. On the highway between Zagreb and Belgrade, No. 67, a British Vauxhall

The Italians' favorite—No. 22, the Lancia Fulvia 1.3HF—at Crystal Palace. Misery was to strike Giancarlo Baghetti and Giorgio Bassi over 4,000 miles later (author's collection).

Ventora crewed by Cecil Woodley, Steven Green and Dick Cullingford was making steady progress through the night when Woodley, eyes fixed on the road ahead, took a last drag of his cigarette and flicked the butt out of his open window. The Ventora had been fitted with curved, Perspex wind protectors, which allowed the window to remain open while sheltering the driver from the wind. The spent cigarette was caught by the trailing slipstream and flew back through the open, rear passenger window. With the rear occupant asleep, Woodley leant back to try and locate the glowing cigarette end, but in doing so, lost control of the car. The Ventora shot off the side of the highway and rolled, coming to rest on its roof in a pool of mud. Woodley, Green and Cullingford managed to climb out of the wreckage, Woodley obviously in pain, but they were quickly joined by Amoco Volvo team Gerry Lister and André Welinski who had been immediately behind the Vauxhall. Noticing that fuel was leaking from the upturned car, they quickly shut down the engine and then managed to turn the car back onto its wheels. It was obviously completely wrecked, but even worse, Woodley was injured and needed help. At first he refused to leave his stricken car, but he was eventually persuaded to accept a lift to Belgrade, where he was flown back to England with a broken collar bone—but not before he gave an interview to one of the many film crews, during which he sheepishly explained that his car had fallen victim to a high speed tire blowout!

Two cars were now out of the Marathon, the wrecked Ventora and No. 16, a British BMC 1800 that had broken down beyond repair in the time allowed. No. 85 struggled into the Belgrade time control after it had closed, Peter Harper trying valiantly to prevent the fuel-injected Cortina Lotus from succumbing to a failing water pump as it incurred the maxim penalty of 1,440 points.

Central Belgrade was in chaos as each car carefully negotiated its way through the gray, gloomy Eastern Bloc city. Most drivers had arrived with hours to spare so first made their way to the Hotel Metropole, only a few yards from the time control, where they were able to get food and rest, despite the atmosphere of daunting authoritarianism within. Competitors either tended to any urgent issues with their cars or gathered in the Metropole's bar, discussing progress thus far and lamenting the end of experienced rally driver Harper's effort. All felt safe in the knowledge that a short hop across the road to the time control would leave them with plenty of time to relax, while outside, large crowds gathered to look at the Marathon cars as they were washed or checked over—*Sydney Telegraph* editor-in-chief David McNicoll was even present, playing to the cameras as he washed "The Galloping Tortoise" down. Unfortunately, the Yugoslavian Autoclub had inexplicably set up the time control down a narrow, cobblestoned street, which not only served general traffic but also a two-lane tram track. To compound matters, central Belgrade was teaming with lunchtime congestion as pedestrians and vehicles clogged up the streets, and the local police were rapidly losing control of the situation. The time control quickly became a chaotic scene as Marathon cars were forced to enter and leave the side street from the same point. What should have been a brief, 500 yard journey became a 30 minute slog, forcing some cars to make the allowed time with only minutes to spare. Finally, with tempers and nerves frayed, the last cars had their road books stamped and began the 606-mile drive to Turkey and the western city of Istanbul. Of the 95 cars leaving Belgrade, three teams had picked up penalty points for lateness at the control: the Porsche driven by Dill and Yannaghas, actor Terry-Thomas' Cortina 1600E and No. 15, a privately entered Cortina GT driven by Geoffrey Franklin and Kim Brassington, who undoubtedly must have sped away cursing over having been one minute late at the control.

Ahead lay Turkey and the first real challenges for the Marathon teams, not least for No. 35, the Mercedes-Benz 280SE driven by Bobby Buchanan-Michaelson, David Seigle-Morris and Max Stahl.

11

The Curse of the Mercedes-Benz Radiators (Part One)

Forty-three-year-old British property developer Robert "Bobby" Buchanan-Michaelson had decided to enter a Mercedes-Benz 280SE in the London to Sydney Marathon, which he purchased direct from the Mercedes factory in Stuttgart. As well as being a successful and wealthy businessman, employing a cook, a butler, a maid and a chauffeur, Bobby had also competed in the *Tour de Spa* touring car race and, according to Max Stahl, was an accomplished sportsman. Bobby had already been able to recruit 43-year-old former British rally driver David Seigle-Morris into the team, a shrewd decision as David had previously driven for the Standard Triumph rally team, the BMC works team and the Ford works team, during which he had competed in the Monte Carlo Rally, the *Coupes des Alpes* and the extremely tough Liege-Sofia-Liege Rally. Now all they needed was a third member of the team.

Bobby initially approached former Formula One racing driver Stirling Moss, but he declined, citing a lack of availability. Bobby then sought advice from BMC team rally driver Paddy Hopkirk, who strongly advised finding an Australian who had experience in both driving and navigating. Hopkirk suggested Max Stahl, whom he'd previously met at the Bathurst Touring Car Championships in New South Wales, Australia. The invitation to join came via BMC and Max happily accepted. In 1968 Max Stahl was editor of the Australian *Racing Car News* magazine and had considerable touring car racing and rally experience, having competed in a number of New South Wales state rally championships as well as the 1967 Caledonian Safari rally. An accomplished motoring journalist, he also hosted a half hour motoring radio show in Sydney.

In a letter dated October 22, 1968, Bobby wrote to welcome Max on board and advised him to get to London not later than five days before the start of the Marathon. In the meantime, work would continue preparing the Mercedes, strengthening the suspension, fitting an oil pan guard and having a carpenter build in a storage box in place of a full width rear seat. In addition, as with the Mercedes entered by British motorsports journalist Innes Ireland, Bobby arranged for a 'roo bar to be fitted, having discovered that the dimensions of a front bumper from a British Bedford TK truck corresponded exactly with those of the Mercedes. Thus, the chrome bumpers were removed from the car and replaced with a set from a donor Bedford. Instantly, the car had frontal protection, a heavy steel shield reaching almost up to the iconic, grille-mounted Mercedes star.

In mid–November, Max flew out to London, making stopovers in San Francisco and

New York, where he met up with *Racing Car News* journalist and fellow Australian Marathon competitor John Bryson for a night out in Manhattan. Max recalled the shock of seeing so many pornographic movie houses and book shops on 42nd Street and remarked how surprised he was that so many late model cars were scratched, dented and unwashed as if nobody took any pride in owning an automobile.

In London, Max was met at the airport by Bobby, having been advised that he could recognize him as Bobby would be carrying a copy of *Playboy* under his arm. There followed a week of socializing in some of London's best restaurants and nightclubs, combined with receiving training from the local Mercedes dealer's mechanics for all five of the Marathon's Mercedes crews. Max had never met Bobby before and recalls getting an insight into what it is to be a very wealthy man. As he explained, "We did a bit of socializing before the event and there was a restaurant, a pretty fancy place, and there were about 12 or 14 of us and the bill came to something like £190 [$450], which was a bloody fair amount of money in 1968. I nearly died—you could buy a bloody house for that—and he tipped them £200 [$475] at the restaurant. Then we moved on to Annabel's the nightclub, wound our way downstairs. Halfway down there is a bar. I still remember this, we bought a few drinks and then we carried on downstairs and more supper and so on. When we were leaving, Bobby ducked into the bar to settle the account. We're waiting up there and you hear some voices, raised voices down below, all this sort of thing. What's going on? What's keeping Bobby? Anyway, finally he came up and I can't remember whether he told us what had happened or we later found out from other people, but he was querying an orange juice that was on the bill that wasn't properly accounted for, which was probably about nine pence!"

Max Stahl poses with a Mercedes-Benz (courtesy Max Stahl).

The Mercedes training was designed to address any item that might need repair during the 10,000-mile drive. As reported by Max, "unfortunately, they forgot to give us training on changing the head gasket, an item that would have proved extremely valuable for most of us later on. It was also unfortunate that we didn't check the mountings of the radiators."[1]

Departure day finally arrived and, bearing No. 35, just after 2:30 p.m. the red Mercedes-Benz left the starting ramp, with Bobby waving a gnarled plastic hand out of the window and shouting that his inoculations hadn't worked. They were at last on their way and, like most of the Marathon cars, the Benz made smooth progress across to France, down to Italy, over to Yugoslavia and through Bulgaria to Turkey and the Bosporus, beyond which lay Istanbul and then what would be the first real test, the special stage from Sivas to Erzincan. They knew they would need to be alert and focused, but the car was going extremely well and all three were prepared for the rough stuff.

Out of Sivas the first 30 miles or so were dry and dusty, but soon after the road turned to wet mud. Increased concentration was needed, yet with David at the wheel and after miles of trouble-free motoring, the Mercedes encountered a humpback bridge, followed by a sharp right turn, which was to cause havoc for a number of Marathon cars. As the big Benz crested the bridge at speed, David vainly attempted to brake the car into the turn. Steering and brakes on full lock and watched by the forlorn crew of a Cortina that had done something similar, the Mercedes careered off the road, crunched over some large rocks and came to a halt. Max leapt out to inspect the damage and was relieved to find none that he could see, so moments later No. 35 was back on the road, although David noticed a slight heaviness in the Mercedes' steering. Ten miles further on, another sharp turn called for a quick deceleration but suddenly there was no transmission—the linkage had come free. Once again No. 35 rolled to a halt. Crawling under the car in the cold, wet mud, Max concluded that the damage would need to be repaired from inside the car, which meant completely removing the transmission tunnel cover, costing the team 45 minutes and the increasing frustration of seeing more and more competitors hurtle past.

Back on the road, they focused on getting to the Erzincan time control and the awaiting service crew who would be able to check the car over. They continued on, irritated that they had now lost so much time, but resigned to the fact that there was nothing to be done. Then, with only 70 miles to go, even through their crash helmets, they began to hear a buzzing sound. Deciding to adopt the "if you ignore it, it will go away" approach, they continued, but the noise grew louder until suddenly the Mercedes lost power and came to a stop. Clambering out to check under the hood, to their dismay they discovered that the radiator had become dislodged and fallen back into the fan. All the water had drained away and the motor was consequently blown. Because the radiator in the Mercedes sedans was only fixed on two slides and not bolted to anything solid, the previous impact over the rocks had loosened it. No. 35 wouldn't be the only Benz to suffer in this way, but, for now, at eleven o'clock at night with the temperature dropping and most of the other competitors way ahead of them, they were stuck fast deep in the middle of Turkish nowhere. What were they going to do?

The answer came in the shape of No. 78, the Ford Escort crewed by Jim Gavin, John Maclay and Martin Maudling, who had adopted the philosophy of slow and steady, rather than going at full speed. Quickly flagging them down, Bobby explained the situation and they agreed to take him to Erzincan. As Max recalled, crammed into the little Ford, "Bobby drank all their brandy. Jim tells everybody that!" Left behind with the car, there was little David and Max could do, until along came a troop of Turkish soldiers returning to camp. Despite the language barrier, the problem was explained and as Max recalled, "We conversed and managed to organize some help from them. They said 'Yes, you stay here, we're going back to camp now, we'll come straight back with a truck and a tow rope and we'll take you wherever,' which they did, so there we are being towed up the road, totally illegal of course, breaking the rules of the rally, but it didn't matter, we had to get to bloody Erzincan, which we did, and to find Bobby."

Meanwhile, Bobby had located a mechanic at Erzincan, had bundled him into a taxi and was hurtling back to the stranded Mercedes, meeting the unlikely convoy after about eight miles. The mechanic hastily repaired the radiator allowing No. 35 to limp into the time control, eight hours late and incurring 480 points, the Mercedes' head gasket blown. There was no choice but to replace it, so as Max explained, "I set to in the workshop that Bobby had organized. I pulled the head off and everything and I got to a point where I ran out of mechanical knowledge and I just couldn't go any further. So, Bobby grabbed one of the leading mechanics from the Ford team who was busy at the time, but he said 'Okay, for a few dollars, as soon as I've finished the job here I'll come and do it.' He finished taking it apart and installed a new head gasket and got it all running and I watched him and took note of what he was doing." Much later, Max's notes were to come in useful in a completely unexpected way on the road to Sydney.

The work took over four hours to finish, which meant they were now 17 hours behind. Eight hundred and sixty-six miles of road over the Turkish mountains and across the border into Iran lay ahead, with a time allowance of 22 hours. Their average speed would need to be at least 80 mph if they were to avoid incurring more penalty points.

Despite being hindered by a loose heater hose, which meant having to repeatedly stop and add more water until Max worked out the cause, they made extremely good time and eventually found themselves on the approach to Teheran with 45 minutes before the time control closed. They knew they could make it and quickly joined the morning rush-hour traffic until suddenly they realized their route notes had taken them in the wrong direction. Desperately calling upon the help of a passing taxi, they were guided to the control, but to no avail—the time control had closed just five minutes before, an automatic penalty of 1,440 points.

A change of tires and the Mercedes was on its way again, for the almost 1,500-mile slog across into Afghanistan and the next checkpoint at Kabul. Increasingly anxious that they would again arrive too late, with David at the wheel, they quickly covered the first 150 miles when disaster struck yet again. Overtaking a car in the dark at 70 mph, David was suddenly confronted by two cows ambling across the road. The Mercedes struck one of the cows and sustained damage to a fender, the hood and worst of all, the radiator. Needless to say, the cow fared even worse, but luckily help was again at hand as a passing motorist stopped and led them to a local mechanic, but not before giving them a warning. As Max recalled, "He said 'you'd better get away from here because the man who owns the cow will want to kill you.'" An anxious three hours of repair work followed before they were on their way again.

Despite a close shave with a ditch in Shīrvān, which caused the radiator to move again, and the mislaying of David's exit visa for Afghanistan, No. 35 continued on to Herat, Max aware that they needed to find someone to further repair the radiator. However, according to Max, Bobby decided against journeying into Herat itself and instead continued on towards Kandahar, 300 miles to the southeast, stopping every 40 miles to replenish the radiator. After about 150 miles, catastrophe finally struck when the damaged radiator stopped retaining fluid altogether. Max recounted, "We kept on going and I went to sleep, nothing I could do. I finally woke up. 'Where are we? How's it going, Bobby?' 'Wonderful, yeah, it's going fine.' 'How's the temperature gauge?' 'It's all right, it's all right, dead cold.' 'Oh great, stop.' 'Why, what's the matter?' I said the only reason it's cold is because there's no bloody water to heat it up. Well, you've never seen an engine like this, it was spitting and cracking, it was blue. Anyway, we had to wait several hours for it to cool, we had some water, but you couldn't put it in and so waited a few hours and of course you're looking around there, it was the middle of Afghanistan!"

They finally got the car started and decided to turn back to the small town of Farahrud through which they had passed about 13 miles before, nursing the car along in the hope of finding mechanical help. Drawing up at a large Russian-built hotel, all three finally accepted that it was all over. With another head gasket destroyed, for Max Stahl, Bobby Buchanan-Michaelson and David Seigle-Morris the London to Sydney Marathon was run. The Mercedes was beyond repair.

As they stood there, letting the sad realization sink in, a Land Rover drew up and out stepped Tim O'Brien and Tazeena Firth, a British couple who were traveling overland from Bombay back to London. O'Brien and Firth had driven out to Bombay from London two months previously and had had their own adventure in Afghanistan when they struck a chain stretched across the Russian-American highway and rolled the Land Rover. Uninjured, Tim was able to find a phone and call the Kabul Hotel, but because the line was down to the local British authorities, the hotel put him through to the United States C.I.A. station chief in Kabul who arranged recovery. Now on the return journey, they happily offered to take the team to Herat, where they might at least be able to work out what to do about the stricken Benz, and so a few hours later, exhausted and resigned to their fate, Max, Bobby and David

Afghanistan—800 miles of mostly wilderness and desert (courtesy John Hemsley).

checked into the Herat Hotel. A decent night's sleep was in order, for the next day hard decisions would need to be made as to how they would rescue No. 35 from the Afghan wilderness and bring it back to Herat in the hope that the local Mercedes dealership would be able to at least get it running again.

Awaking refreshed, Bobby decided he would fly to Kabul, leaving the others to try and rescue the car. Vainly they attempted to find a vehicle that could tow the Mercedes back, until finally the driver of a jeep agreed to assist, provided that financial compensation was made. Once money had changed hands, the three set off, only to return within an hour as the jeep's fuel pump had expired. Finally abandoning hope of ever rescuing the Benz, they then received word from Bobby that there was a flight from Herat to Bombay via New Delhi. Yet, as they began to check out of the hotel, the manager politely pointed out that there were no flights from Herat to New Delhi! This left them with no option but to spend another night at the hotel and then find overland transport to Kabul in the morning. The following day, another message from Bobby advised that plane tickets were ready and waiting at Kabul to get them to Bombay, but first they needed to find a ride out of Herat.

Once again money changed hands and at last they climbed into an ancient Russian Volga taxi and set off. Five minutes later, the Volga ground to a halt—the fan belt had come off. The driver disappeared under the hood, tightened the generator, refitted the belt, slammed the hood and set off again, the first of countless stops along the 750-mile journey as first the oil pan needed attending to, then the differential and so on. Finally, after freewheeling down a mountain because the Volga had run out of gas, it deposited them at the Spinzar Hotel in Kabul, both men desperate for a few hours' sleep before their plane would take off later that day. However, a message was waiting at the hotel desk, an urgent message to call the British Embassy. Max dialed the number and was eventually advised that his exit visa had expired and that a new one would take days to issue. There followed a panicked dash to organize the essential document, before finally going to collect their plane tickets.

Was everything finally falling into place? No it wasn't as they then discovered that all flights had been cancelled due to the weather. All they could do was wait for the conditions to improve, which at last they did. After three and a half days in Afghanistan, Max and David were on their way to Bombay, arriving just 15 hours before the ship embarked for Perth.

Their Marathon adventure, however, was not over yet.

12

A Valiant Effort

Eighty-eight of the 96 cars still in the running remained free from penalty points as the field sped off on the 585-mile run through Bulgaria and on to the next control at Istanbul in Turkey. The route took competitors through agricultural landscapes, shepherds gazing on as car after car sped by. Progress towards the border into Bulgaria was uneventful for the most part, although 100 miles on from Belgrade, the Amoco Volvo 144S driven by Australians Max Winkless and John Keran was forced to pull over when it started trailing ominous plumes of blue smoke in its wake. The Repco-supplied cylinder head had developed a fault that would put Winkless and Keran 26 hours behind the field before they were able to resume their journey.

At the Yugoslav-Bulgarian border, spectators jostled with Marathon officials and police officers, determined to see the Marathon cars and present gifts of food to their amused occupants. As a result of Jack Sears' careful preparations, negotiating the border control was again swift and efficient and soon the cars had left the paved roads of Yugoslavia and were rumbling over cobblestoned streets before ascending Bulgaria's Dragoman Pass and passing south of the Bulgarian capital of Sofia. Weather conditions began to deteriorate as the Turkish border approached with strong winds and rain forcing drivers to increase their concentration even more. As windshield wipers fought the deluge, the Marathon crossed into Turkey and headed for the checkpoint located near Istanbul's Yeşilköy Airport. Those fortunate enough to have booked hotel accommodations grabbed the opportunity to catch up on sleep until the ferry service recommenced the following morning. At Istanbul, only two cars failed to reach the control before it closed—the incapacitated Volvo of Winkless and Keran and No. 85, David Pollard and Peter Harper's Cortina, not yet officially retired but still languishing in Belgrade.

As soon as the Bosporus ferries began running the following morning, so began the logistics of awaiting and boarding one of the small craft that in 1968 crossed back and forth across the strait that formed the gateway between Europe and Asia. Because the ferries were not big enough to carry the entire field, some competitors were required to wait until their turn arrived, but eventually everyone was away and off towards Ankara, Turkey's capital city, and the more than 540-mile trek to the next checkpoint in the Turkish town of Sivas. Everyone had been warned about the potential dangers caused by truck drivers paying scant regard to lane control this side of the Bosporus, but few were expecting the added obstacle of stone throwing—groups of children standing at the roadside, competing in the sport of seeing who could actually hit a Marathon car with a rock.

One of the first cars to drive off the ferry and accelerate away was No. 5, the large Aus-

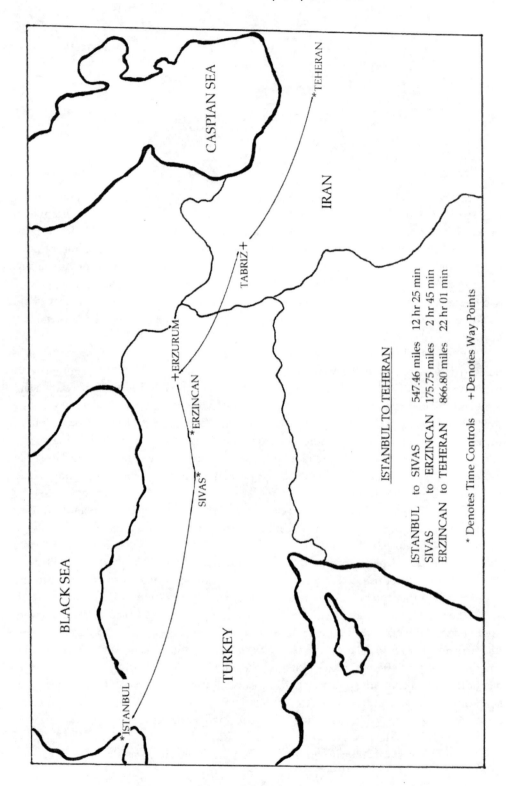

The route from Istanbul to Teheran (map by Martin Proudlock).

tralian Chrysler Valiant Safari station wagon, one of the very few Marathon vehicles carrying a team of four. Experienced British racing drivers Peter Sargent and Peter Lumsden were up front, while snoozing in the back were Redge Lewis and John Fenton. Sargent and Lumsden had previously raced at Le Mans in the early 1960s and Sargent had stirred controversy when in 1961 he acquired a newly-launched Jaguar E-Type. As he recounted, "I actually got my E-Type before Henley's in Piccadilly got their demonstrator and I found out many years later that this caused a hell of a bloody row. I mean I got it and then we started tearing it to pieces and doing things to it."

In considering what car to use for the Marathon, they had struck upon the idea of writing to Chrysler Australia and asking them for a car to use, relying on the hope that the potential publicity for the company would be an attractive proposition. Chrysler Australia had decided not to officially enter a car in the event, yet agreed to the request and shipped a brand new Valiant Safari to England, assured that the team would undertake the necessary preparations and expenditure to get the car in endurance rally condition. Splitting all costs equally, the team called upon garage owner Toney Cox in Birmingham, who transformed the large family wagon into something capable of being driven all the way back to Australia. Sporting a full length, heavy-duty luggage rack and integral front bumper and 'roo bar, the white Valiant even sported a high-visibility orange stripe along its flanks. With the possible exceptions of the 17th/21st Lancers' Land Rover and the Bentley Sport Tourer, it was the largest car in the event and probably one of the heaviest.

After a slight panic, when they were still getting used to navigating on the way to Le Bourget, progress for the Valiant had been steady and trouble-free. However, after only five miles from the ferry, Sargent closed down on a slow moving private car on a very wide stretch of road. With other competitors close on his tail, he decided the best option was to try and overtake, always a tricky move when at the wheel of a right-hand drive car on the right-hand side of a two-lane road. Lumsden recalled that he was dozing in what is often referred to as the "suicide seat" as Sargent began to make his maneuver, edging the Valiant out into the center of the two lanes. As Sargent recalled, "There was a lorry coming towards us. He had bags of room to pull over, I only needed another foot, but he didn't budge at all. I think it was a day's sport and of course we'd been warned about this. I don't know whether they still do it, but they certainly used to back then." The oncoming truck ripped off the entire left-hand side of the Chrysler, showering Lumsden and John Fenton with glass. Lumsden explained how the truck "did a first class job and he made our wagon four inches narrower the whole way down, so the front door, front wheel and the rest of the bodywork was four inches narrower. And he never stopped." In his Marathon report, Max Stahl wrote that "the lorry travelled on sideways for a couple of hundred yards, narrowly missing four or five following Marathon cars, before tipping off the side of the road."[1] Out of the Marathon, Lumsden and Sargent were briefly detained by the police before all four returned to London, leaving the car in Turkey. As Lumsden recalled, "after we crashed it, we were told that it would be a taxi within in a week in Istanbul!"

Turkish trucks were also causing havoc elsewhere, with Australian rally driver Barry Ferguson twice having to use every bit of his experience to prevent his *Sydney Telegraph*–sponsored Holden Monaro from being hit, once when he too pulled out to overtake and as Max Stahl wrote, "The truck suddenly turned left with no signal whatsoever, so Barry, throwing everything onto the brakes and going back a gear, began the turn with him, gunned the

No. 5, the ill-fated Chrysler Valiant Safari, and its crew, John Fenton, Peter Lumsden, Redge Lewis and Peter Sargent (courtesy Peter Lumsden).

big Holden and just slipped past on the wrong side of the road."[2] Almost immediately, he was confronted by two more trucks coming towards him, one overtaking the other. Only complete concentration and a nifty bit of off-road driving prevented yet another truck-related catastrophe.

If unpredictable truck drivers weren't enough for competitors to contend with, they also had to deal with children throwing rocks at them. No. 86, a BMW 2000 driven by Robbie Uniacke, Colin Forsyth and James Rich, lost side and rear windows as a rock smashed its way through the car, while the only Japanese crew in the Marathon, Yojiro Terada, Kazuhiko Mitsumoto and Nobuo Koga in No. 95, a British Vauxhall Viva GT, were over two hours late to the Sivas control when another airborne rock completely destroyed their windshield and they struggled to find a replacement.

More drama awaited a few other competitors on the road from Ankara, in one case from a much unexpected source. British pair Nick and Jenny Brittan were part of the Ford GB team and had been progressing well in their factory-prepared Cortina Lotus. They had settled into "a very comfortable rhythm of two and a half hour shifts. Working this way we found that during each off period there would be time to relax, eat a little, spend a little time chatting and take about one and a half hours sleep."[3] However, about 160 miles from the Sivas control, travelling at 80 miles an hour on a straight stretch of road, they were suddenly confronted with a galloping horse heading directly across their path. Nick, at the wheel with Jenny asleep, slammed on the brakes in a vain attempt to avoid collision. With so little warning, the Cortina struck the horse, sending it crashing into the windshield and over the top of the car, killing it outright. Fearful of the consequences of causing the death of someone's horse in a remote part of eastern Turkey, they rapidly removed the remains of the broken windshield before driving onwards as quickly as they could, making full use of the driving goggles Ford had fortuitously provided!

Elsewhere, another British Ford was in trouble. The Cortina 1600E sponsored by Hollywood actor Terry-Thomas was negotiating the Bolu Pass in darkness when it left the road and, to the horror of Antony Pargeter, Peter Capelin and Tim Baker, tipped over the edge, landing on its nose 20 feet below. Five hours later, the morning light revealed how lucky they had been as beyond the ledge was a much greater drop of 100 feet. They were able to climb out of the upended Cortina via the rear window, which had fallen out, and managed to call on a truck to heave the Ford back onto the road. Shaken but resolute, the car surprisingly undamaged, they continued on to Sivas.

After the relatively easy going journey to Istanbul, the Marathon was now beginning to test competitors. By the time the last car clocked in at the time control, three cars had dropped out, plus a fourth, the Harper-Pollard Cortina, which was now officially retired. In addition to the ill-fated Valiant, the little Austin 1300 station wagon of Dennis Cresdee, Johnstone Syer and Bob Freeborough came to a permanent halt in Yozgat, 140 miles from the control, when an engine bearing seized, and, to many competitors' surprise, the expert pairing of Swedish rally drivers Bengt Söderström and Gunnar Palm were forced to quit when their Ford GB team Cortina Lotus developed a serious piston failure, a portentous sign of what was to come for the British Competitions Team Fords. Three more cars now found themselves with penalty points, having arrived late at the control—in addition to the Vauxhall Viva GT being delayed by a smashed windshield, a damaged oil line at Istanbul meant 223 points for the Bentley Sport Tourer and the British Army Land Rover picked up 38 points.

Conditions at the Sivas control were difficult with mud and poor lighting hindering attempts to carry out repairs and maintenance, while curious and excited onlookers pushed forward to inspect the cars and crews. Andrew Cowan wrote, "When we arrived at Sivas ... everything was rather tense as most of the drivers realized this was one of the crucial points in the rally."[4] Söderström and Palm donated their windshield to the Brittans who called upon teammates Captain Harrison and Lieutenant Proudlock to help them fit the screen to their car. *Sydney Telegraph* team members Barry Ferguson, Doug Chivas and Dave Johnson called upon teammate David Liddle to help sort out a fuel starvation problem in No. 76, their Holden Monaro. Meanwhile, having had their paperwork checked and stamped, No. 65 team member Graham White took the opportunity to find somewhere to relieve himself and somehow, in the dark, fell into an inspection pit and sustained an injury, which turned out to be much more serious than he and his co-drivers David Dunnell and John Jeffcoat first thought.

13

The Curse of the Mercedes-Benz Radiators (Part Two)

Bombay gave Max Stahl and David Seigle-Morris the opportunity to reunite with Bobby Buchanan-Michaelson as well as catch up with the progress and the positions of the remaining Marathon competitors. However, all three had to contend with the fact that as they were now disqualified from the event, rules and regulations meant they had to pay for passage on the P&O liner, the SS *Chusan*. As stated by Max, "One of the things I complained about was the stupid idea that if you arrived at Bombay with an incomplete entry, you had to pay again to get on the bloody ship. I still can't figure that out, really can't."

Once aboard, they set about unwinding and enjoying shipboard life, at least to begin with. Nick Brittan recorded that Bobby had made arrangement to have a suitable wardrobe of the latest men's fashions to wear on the voyage, appearing each evening in one of a selection of frilly-fronted shirts and velvet suits. As is the custom on board passenger ships, travelers are often invited to dine with the captain, but as Brittan wrote, when the invitation came to Bobby, "he refused on the grounds that he hadn't paid £600 [$1,400] for a ticket to be forced to eat with the crew!"[1] However, Max pointed out that this was an old joke and Bobby had in fact happily accepted more than one invitation to eat with the master of the *Chusan*.

Being an Australian motorsports journalist, Max found plenty of time to interview all of his Marathon compatriots during the trip and hear their adventures on the road from London to Bombay. Moving from dining room to bar and bar to lounge, he also had time to join the poker games that were up and running. As he recalled, "I wasn't very good at poker, so I was losing my money there. I dived up to the pontoon [blackjack] tables and won it back again, so that was quite all right!"

At the port of Fremantle, the team was amused to find that even they were being treated as celebrities by the Australian newspaper and broadcast media, all eager to find out what they planned to do now they were on Australian soil. In fact, during the sea voyage, they had decided to find a suitable car and follow the Marathon across the outback. Settling on a used Ford Falcon with a V-8 motor, they paid the dealer and christened the car "No. thirty-five-and-a-half." Keen to show solidarity with their fellow Mercedes competitors, they decided to load the Falcon with relevant extra parts and take on the role of service vehicle for No. 26, another Mercedes-Benz 280SE being crewed by Innes Ireland and British racing drivers Andrew Hedges and Michael Taylor, which had also been fitted with a front bumper surround from a Bedford truck.

The Marathon recommenced from Perth and headed for the first control at the tiny homestead of Youanmi to the north, while the V-8 Falcon set off east for Lake King, the third control of the route. Keeping a steady pace, they were able to see the remaining cars into the checkpoint and then begin their job of bringing up the rear in case No. 26 needed assistance across the great Nullarbor Plain towards the next checkpoint over 890 miles away at Ceduna. Along the way, they came across the third Mercedes-Benz 280SE in the Marathon, No. 62, driven by Australian trucking company owner Des Praznovsky with fellow Australians Stan Zovko and Ian Inglis. The hood was up and Max, Bobby and David quickly learned that the Mercedes had plunged headlong into a crater in the road and as a result had also dislodged the radiator and driven it into the fan. Promising to instruct a Mercedes service team at Ceduna to come out to them, they went on through Norseman and onto the fast paved road to Eucla. With Eucla behind them, and just as the sun began to set on the second day of the three-day route to Sydney, there by the roadside, hood up, was No. 26.

The Mercedes of Ireland, Hedges and Taylor had been just 96 points down at Lake King and had in fact come off the ship with just 50 points, placed 18th overall out of the 72 survivors that had departed from Perth. The crew was determined to at least maintain their position, but a couple of punctures had led to further penalty points at the Marvel Loch and Lake King controls. On the road to Ceduna, with Taylor at the wheel, Ireland was able to calculate that all being well, they would make the time control with plenty of time to spare. All, however, would not be well.

Half an hour after Lake King, the Benz began to catch up with one of the Marathon Volvos that was leaving a thick dust cloud in its wake. In such situations, the choice is either to reduce speed and therefore reduce the intensity of the dust trail, or go for broke and get past the car in front. Taylor chose the latter and began to ease past the Volvo, too slowly for Ireland's liking. Taylor shifted the manual transmission down into third gear and the speed seemed to increase, but, glancing at the car's temperature gauge, Ireland was alarmed to discover that whereas the needle should have been pointing vertically upwards, it was in fact nowhere to be seen. Suddenly, Taylor noticed that the big Mercedes was losing power and with the temperature gauge off the scale, there was no choice but to pull the car over and stop. Nervously opening the hood, the reason for the loss of power was quickly revealed. Ireland wrote that "I found myself staring in horror at the last drops of water trickling from our radiator and making little puddles in the sand...."[2] Just like No. 35 and No. 62, the radiator had become dislodged and had been forced back into the fan. Yet again, a Marathon Benz was stranded on the side of the road with a blown head gasket.

The Falcon pulled over in front of the broken Mercedes and Max, Bobby and David climbed out to see what the problem was. Max recalled that the conversation went like this: "'Okay, what's the matter fellas?' 'The bloody head gasket!' 'Oh, right, I'll be able to help there.' So I pitched in—smarty pants! Innes had hardly dismantled anything and didn't know how to go any further. I pitched in and we got it all together again, ready to start, but it wouldn't bloody start—nothing! We checked everything that we thought of but it wouldn't start." Despite having all the necessary parts with them and despite Max calling on his careful observation of how to take the head off and replace the gasket back in Turkey, the Mercedes refused to fire. With little else they could do, the Falcon crew bade farewell to the utterly despondent No. 26 team and took their leave, promising to send a Mercedes service mechanic back to them as soon as they reached Ceduna. Stopping to use a telephone near Eucla, they called ahead to Ceduna and discovered that the Mercedes mechanics had been working non-stop on a few of the other Marathon cars, but were now on their way to rescue No. 26.

According to Max, the actual cause of the Ireland Mercedes' failure was that all the engine's tappets had closed up and they required a special tool to correct them. When the mechanic finally reached them, it took another eight hours to carry out the repairs, by which time Ireland, Hedges and Taylor knew they were out of the running. So, instead of continuing along the remaining Marathon route, they drove directly to Sydney. For the former No. 35 team, the remainder of the event passed almost without incident, save for hitting a kangaroo somewhere on the road to Sydney.

All that was left for Max was to bid farewell to his co-drivers Bobby Buchanan-Michaelson and David Seigle-Morris. Travelling 10,000 miles with two men you have barely met beforehand wasn't always easy and straightforward, but, for the most part, the competitors in No. 35 worked as hard as possible to be a team. Not always easy, as Max pointed out, and the fact that Bobby badgered him for weeks about recouping the cost of the Falcon purchased in Perth didn't exactly lend itself to a happy conclusion, but, as Max said, "I was one of the luckiest blokes in the whole thing having Bobby as a sponsor, being invited by him on the recommendation of Paddy Hopkirk, and it was good—no expense spared. We had a bit of a clash of personality because we were totally different people. He was a very good organizer and he wanted everything done his way and that was fine, but I was a bit of an organizer too, bit of a rebel and if I thought what he was doing wasn't quite the right way to do it, I'd say so but, even so, it still went all right."

The only Mercedes-Benz sedan that didn't experience a problem with its radiator and fan during the Marathon was No. 32, the 280S of Fred Barker, David Dollar and Johnnie Lewis. This may have been because, when they became aware of what had happened to No. 26 and No. 35, they used wire to further secure their radiator to its mountings. Even though they hit a kangaroo, the radiator remained in place all the way to Sydney.

As for the fate of No. 35, according to Max, Bobby eventually arranged for it to be shipped back to the Mercedes factory in Germany where it was rebuilt before being bought by Andrew Taylor. Taylor entered the Benz in the 1974 London-Sahara-Munich World Cup Rally and ended up wrapping it around a tree on a stage in the South of France.

14

Goodbye Bentley Tourer

Competitors were now faced with the Marathon's first special stage. The challenges and obstacles they had previously endured would be nothing compared to the difficult section that would take them to Erzincan in northeastern Turkey. A choice of routes had been designed by the organizers, but conditions had deteriorated to the degree that the shorter, more difficult southern route was discounted, even by the professional teams. David McKay wrote regular columns for *The Daily Express* and *The Sydney Telegraph* during the Marathon and reported in *The Daily Express* that "most drivers have been hesitant whether to take this route. Today the problem was solved. Rain has completely washed out the southern road and we have all been forced to take the northern route."[1] Only a few days before, BMC's Bill Price had found the southern stage impassable, and although Rootes team competitors Andrew Cowan and Colin Malkin initially considered going south, they chose instead to take the northern route through the mountains, accepting the potential time penalty consequences. To underline how bad the southern route had become, running 17 hours behind the rest of the field after their Repco cylinder head had failed in eastern Yugoslavia, Max Winkless and John Keran reached Sivas and decided to follow it as it would reduce their time deficit. It eventually cost them an hour when they got completely stuck in the mud.

First away from Sivas was the Bill Bengry Cortina, but 51-year-old Australian rally veteran Harry Firth, otherwise known as "The Fox," had been notified of a shortcut out of the town by his Ford Australia team, and ten minutes later, when it was his turn to depart, he floored the gas pedal of No. 2, his Ford Falcon XT GT, and one mile later was looming large in Bengry's rearview mirror. McKay wrote that he had "always had an abhorrence of holding anyone up ... it is beholden on the pursued to move over."[2] Bengry duly let the Falcon pass him and no one caught Firth all the way to Erzincan. Yet there would be another Ford that would achieve the fastest time over the 187-mile track and therefore take the lead on points all the way to Bombay.

The first 40 miles were rough, but dry and dusty, competitors trying to take full advantage before things turned to mud. The section allowed two hours and 45 minutes, which meant an average speed of 68 mph. However, achieving this in the increasingly wet and treacherous conditions would lead to many a calamity before the section was over.

In No. 32, a Mercedes sedan, Captain Johnnie Lewis took the wheel for this, the first special section of the Marathon, and both he and his co-drivers experienced their first taste of driving a real rally stage. Captain Fred Barker recalled how they were progressing steadily when Jenny Tudor-Owen passed them in No. 33, the Volvo station wagon. From that point

No. 1, the Ford Cortina GT of Bill Bengry, Arthur Brick and John Preddy, departs Crystal Palace, November 24 (author's collection).

on Lewis put his foot down, causing not a little nervousness for Barker and teammate Captain David Dollar—none of them had ever driven a special rally stage before. No. 32 lost 60 points at Erzincan, compared to Tudor-Owen's 62.

The pressure competitors had put on their vehicles became evident now and a number of cars began to develop brake problems. No. 26, another of the big Mercedes, suffered a complete loss of brakes, albeit temporarily, forcing driver Innes Ireland to rely on every bit of his experience. "My only way of slowing up," he wrote, "was to put the car sideways and it wasn't possible to judge … the severity of the corner."[3] Behind the wheel of No. 43, Gerry Lister was also dealing with a lack of brakes in his Volvo, and the *Sydney Telegraph* Holden of Barry Ferguson lost a rear brake lining, forcing him to reduce speed. Of the four Porsche 911s competing, No. 55, driven by Terry Hunter, No. 58, driven by Polish rally ace Sobiesław Zasada, and No. 59, driven by Kenyan rally driver Edgar Herrmann, all lost their brakes. The British *Autosport* magazine reported that they "All broke identical brake pipe unions and Zasada and Hunter both had to drive about 100 miles with no form of braking whatsoever."[4]

Mechanical problems weren't the only challenges facing drivers, however, as a number of competitors discovered to their cost. The stage was punctuated with small bridges, often appearing fairly innocuous until a speeding car passed the apex to discover a sharp turn immediately afterwards. About 70 miles into the section, one innocent-looking humpback bridge managed to temporarily defeat at least ten cars as, hurtling over the bridge, some even airborne, drivers had no time to brake as the track twisted sharply to the right. Car after car

No. 91, the Holden HK series Belmont (author's collection).

careened into a muddy field, getting bogged down, with one or two even suffering damage to undercarriages. Among the casualties here were Max Stahl's Mercedes, Peter Capelin's Cortina 1600E, No. 9, a Cortina Lotus crewed by Freddy Bombelli and Tom Belsø, and the Dutch National Team DAF 55 of David van Lennep and Peter Hissink, which damaged its oil pan and had to be towed back to the Sivas control for repairs, costing them the maximum 1,440 points for missing the Erzincan checkpoint before it closed. From there onwards, the tiny, "belt-driven" DAF would struggle to arrive at almost every other control on time and would eventually be the last-place car at Warwick Farm with a total of 13,790 points, but at least they made it.

Another bridge was to cause problems for two BMC 1800s, No. 17, the Royal Navy car, and No. 21, the car crewed by Welshmen Berwyn Williams, Martin Thomas and Barry Hughes. It would also test the patience of a few competitors immediately behind when, at different times, both BMCs skidded on a two-plank bridge, got jammed and almost completely blocked the way. Anxious not to be held up, those competitors immediately behind the stricken Royal Navy 1800 tried to squeeze past, including the Holden Monaro of David McKay, George Reynolds and David Liddle. Liddle recalled that McKay was impatient to get by so he tried to get to the edge of the bridge and, in doing so, sheared the Holden's wheel nuts on one side. Once free of the bridge, the Monaro continued until the wheel fell off. Fortunately, they were carrying extras, but, stopping to refit the wheel, they were forced to lose valuable points. Another car that eased past the Royal Navy team was the Innes Ireland Mercedes, causing Ireland to complain that he lost a precious minute as a result!

Sponsored by Welsh car dealership Hillcrest Motors, No. 21 had been making satisfactory progress, although at Istanbul, the fact that they allowed mechanics to fix a leaking exhaust manifold, rather than undertaking the repair themselves, would have consequences for the Welsh team hundreds of miles later. Driving onto the Turkish two-plank bridge, the 1800's wheels also slipped off the planks. Eventually help arrived in the form of a bus full of Turks on their way to work. Barry Hughes broke open one of the cartons of Marlboro cigarettes that they carried for just such an incident and began to distribute them to the bus passengers and, as a result, the team was soon lifted back onto the road. At the Erzincan checkpoint, the two 1800s picked up 73 and 84 points respectively, while Ireland incurred 38 and McKay 66.

The drama experienced by the two 1800 crews was nothing compared to the life-threatening incident that befell British driver Doug Morris, however, who was competing with David Walker and Brian Jones in No. 40, a Vauxhall Ventora. This was not only to affect the Ventora crew, but, as a consequence of their taking the time to stop and assist, it would also have ramifications for the Australian team of John Bryson, Jack "Milko" Murray and Bert Madden in No. 91, their Holden Belmont.

No. 40 had stopped on the roadside and the crew had jacked up the Ventora so Doug Morris could get underneath to inspect and repair the differential guard, which had wrapped itself around the rear universal joint. As he worked, the jack slipped and the Vauxhall collapsed, trapping Doug's head between the car and the ground. As John Bryson explained, "With three extra people the car was quickly lifted. Five of us looked at each other as we had not thought of how to get Doug from under the car." Once he was freed, it was obvious that Doug needed urgent medical attention, but where to take him? John recalled, "We had two choices—return five kilometers [3 miles] to a Turkish Army first aid post or go on for 55 kilometers [34 miles] to another." Understandably, they decided to go back the way they had come, but this meant driving into oncoming Marathon traffic and they had already overtaken at least thirty cars on the stage before they stopped to help the Ventora crew. They set off and, as John explained, "One of these came around a corner, lights blazing, well and truly on the wrong side of the road. Jack had to 'go bush' and we missed the Cortina by bumping down a table drain." This damaged the Holden's differential housing, the consequence of which Bryson, Madden and Murray would discover later in Iran. Astonishingly, although Morris sustained a skull fracture, after receiving medical assistance, he decided to continue and eventually No. 40 made it to Sydney in 52nd place.

Keith Schellenberg, Patrick Lindsay and Norman Barclay were still in the running in the 1930 Bentley Sport Tourer, having braved the cold, the wind and the rain in their virtually open-top car. Fascinated crowds continued to gather round the vintage Bentley at each control point and, at the Sivas checkpoint, the Bentley was going strong despite having incurred 223 penalty points after leaving late from Istanbul when an oil pipe needed repairing. However, with Lindsay at the wheel, the Bentley left the road on the way to Erzincan and slipped into a ravine, landing on its side. Schellenberg and Barclay emerged unscathed, but Lindsay broke his collarbone. Lindsay promptly arranged for a private plane to take him back to England and, with one man down, the Bentley team was forced to retire from the Marathon.

At the Erzincan control, David Dunnell was also contemplating the end of the road, after co-driver Graham White had fallen into an inspection pit back in Sivas and as a result had seriously damaged a kidney. In the milling crowd, Dunnell and Schellenberg struck up a conversation that would lead to a completely different adventure on the road to Bombay and, for Dunnell, a very different endurance drive back to London.

15

Peeing in the Dark

David Dunnell was introduced to the world of motorsports by his stepfather, John Bolster, the former racing driver, *Autosport* magazine journalist, BBC radio and television motorsports commentator and builder of one-off racing cars or "specials." With his distinctive moustache, tweed jacket and ever-present deerstalker hat, Bolster was a celebrity among motorsports fans in 1950s Britain. David recalled how "He went motor racing all the time and invariably we'd go with him, or clean his cars, so I caught the bug that way."

David began racing competitively in a Mini in 1962 and quickly became friends with fellow competitive driver Graham White. In 1968, another friend of David's, John Jeffcoat, was working for Hy-Mac, a construction equipment firm, and, as David explained, "He just turned up one day and said 'So you want to do the London Sydney?' I said 'Yes I'd love to.' He said 'Okay, if the governor says yes.' Hy-Mac-backed the whole thing, didn't cost us a penny!" Graham was an obvious choice as third team member, so the three set about finding a suitable car to prepare for the event, choosing a BMC 1800, described by David as "Tough cars, well-tried, the engine was pretty bullet-proof. In fact the whole car was built like a tank." Next, with the financial backing of Hy-Mac, they took the car to Janspeed, the performance engineering firm, who proceeded to strip the car and rebuild it, strengthening the chassis and bodywork. Like a number of BMC products in the 1960s, the BMC 1800 was notable for its hydrolastic suspension set up whereby the traditional configuration of springs and shock absorbers commonly used in cars of the time was rejected in favor of fluid-filled displacers connecting the front and rear wheels on each side of the car. Over time and with ordinary road use, this suspension system would require pumping up as part of a car's regular servicing, but, for a car that was going to take on the thousands of miles of rough roads and tracks across Asia and Australia, often traveling at high speeds, any competitor might need to consider packing a pump among their stock of extra equipment. As David explained, "We had a pump so we could pump it up and down, which was useful when it eventually collapsed. That was one of the problems of course, not having the proper fluid."

While Janspeed worked on the car, David, Graham and John decided they would benefit from some kind of bonding exercise to help them face the rigors of spending days and days together within the confines of a car. In order to familiarize themselves with the driving characteristics of their chosen vehicle, they rented another 1800, set off from the south of England, and headed off for Scotland. David recalled that they went "Non-stop, just stopped for fuel, nothing else, eating on the go, to make sure we got on all right, which we knew we would. John was so funny, all he did was crack jokes and he wasn't a driver. Graham and I did the

John Jeffcoat, Graham White and David Dunnell with their BMC 1800, November 1968 (courtesy David Dunnell).

driving, John did some, but he was mostly navigating. I was the only one who was mechanically skilled. They didn't know where the engine was!"

Eventually they were ready and, drawn as No. 65, they set off from Crystal Palace, David enjoying the spectacle of thousands of people screaming, shouting and taking photographs. Noticing the *Sydney Telegraph* Morris 1100 S, another car with BMC's hydrolastic suspension, it struck him that it had very little visible Marathon preparation and that there seemed to be more wheels on its roof than on the car itself. Through the people-lined London streets, on the road down to Dover and into mainland Europe, the bright yellow 1800 behaved impeccably and by the time No. 65 reached the second Turkish time control at Sivas, the Hy-Mac team was still free of any penalty points.

With time in hand, while John and David made sure their road book was stamped, Graham took the opportunity to find a suitable place to answer a call of nature. In the dark, cold and muddy conditions, he walked off behind the time-control, which was in a garage, and failed to see an inspection pit. The ground opened up and he fell, hitting its base hard. The pain was severe and once he was extricated, the team concluded he had probably broken a rib. With only minimal medical services on hand at Sivas, it was decided that the best thing to do would be to carry on to Erzincan and seek assistance there, so, with Graham and John in the back of the 1800, David set off on the 175-mile run.

David Dunnell stands before No. 65 at Crystal Palace, November 24 (courtesy David Dunnell).

It was quickly obvious that something was very wrong with Graham as he began to cry out in pain. David would have to drive as fast as he possibly could and, as he remembered, "Every time I went hounding over some bump, he'd be screaming, he was in a huge amount of pain. We didn't know how serious it was when he first did it, we just thought, oh he'll get over it. He's just broken a rib or something. Then, after a while, we realized it was getting bad. It was a nightmare."

After a grueling couple of hours, the yellow 1800 arrived at Erzincan and David was directed to the local hospital where Graham was quickly admitted, joining the injured Doug Morris from the Vauxhall Ventora team. Eventually the doctors diagnosed kidney damage, which required emergency treatment and a period of recovery before Graham would be allowed home. No. 65 would not be continuing in the Marathon and so thoughts turned to what John and David should do next.

The answer came in the form of Keith Schellenberg, who was also in Erzincan with his team member Norman Barclay. Having seen the injured Patrick Lindsay off on a plane back to England, they had begun to resign themselves to the fact that the old Bentley would have to be left at the bottom of the ravine back on the track to Sivas. Listening to this tale of woe, David struck upon an idea—at the hospital, an officer from the Turkish Army had wanted a photograph with the two injured Marathon competitors and had seen it as his responsibility to make sure both Graham and Doug received the best possible care. Couldn't they call upon him to help recover the Bentley? As David recalled, "John and I rushed along with Schellenberg to see this chap back at these bloody great barracks. The bloke said yes and he got out

No. 84, the 1930 Bentley Sport Tourer, at Crystal Palace, November 24 (author's collection).

tank recovery vehicles, so off we went—a great convoy of vehicles, all armed!" Upon returning to the crash site, they discovered that the car was being guarded by a group of locals who at first refused to step down, despite the military presence. Eventually, after a tense standoff, during which David recalled that shots were definitely fired, the group beat a hasty retreat and the Bentley was hauled back up the bank and onto the road. To their surprise, apart from a broken windshield and a couple of bent fenders, there was very little damage. David fashioned a makeshift windshield and pulled the fenders free from the front wheels and Keith started the engine. It ran, so the party returned to Erzincan to consider their next move. A call to Hy-Mac gave them their answer—why not continue to Bombay anyway? Perhaps they might be allowed to continue on to Australia? After all, the 1800 was still in excellent condition so, after conferring, it was agreed that John would remain with Graham and make sure he was successfully transferred back to Britain while Norman, Keith and David would carry on to Bombay.

Before the Marathon began, David had stocked up on Benzedrine to help keep them awake when they were driving so, with a dose of the drug administered, Norman set off at the wheel of the Bentley with David and Keith following in the 1800. David ensured that he didn't travel too close to the Bentley's tail, just in case the effects of the medication wore off and he found himself dozing at the wheel. The next stop would be Teheran, capital city of Iran, some 860 miles away, but it wasn't long before the Bentley was in trouble again as, rounding a corner, David found the vintage car slumped at the side of the road with a wheel missing. A quick search located the missing item and its stub-axle in a field nearby, so they quickly retrieved them, carried out repairs as best they could and fitted the Bentley's extra wheel. In this fashion, they finally arrived at the now disbanded checkpoint at the Philips factory in Teheran where they were able to call upon a team of mechanics who painstakingly welded the stub-axle, refitted the bearings and got the old car ready for the next leg of the journey into Afghanistan.

David recalled that the Bentley's brakes weren't very effective and, as they would now be driving into the mountains, they devised a means of ensuring that the car would always be able to stop. As David explained, "Whenever we came to a hill, to slow it down, we put the 1800 in front and used that as a brake!" Continuing to use their pace notes, they decided to try and keep up a steady 80 or 90 mph in the hope that they might catch the field ahead of them. On they went out of the mountains and into the desert, both cars experiencing the effects of corrugation, the intermittent ridging caused by traffic over sandy roads and tracks. Travelling in convoy along the desert track at speed led them to decide that it would be wise to keep a good distance between the two cars, the Bentley in front and the 1800 bringing up the rear. After a while, David noticed that, in the distance, something was wrong. He recalled that "Keith was driving the Bentley, Norman was asleep in the back of the 1800 and some way ahead, I saw the Bentley stopped with two or three people around it. So I woke Norman up and said there's some problem up ahead. Something just worried me a bit so we stopped and it was dark. We rolled the car up reasonably close and walked up." As they approached, David was thankful that John had included a pistol in the gear they had loaded into the 1800, even if he hadn't thought to tell them of this until they had arrived at the Le Bourget control. Standing next to the Bentley was a man brandishing a rifle and demanding that Keith hand over his diesel. As David recalled, Keith was sitting in the Bentley saying "But my good man,

The Bentley on the way to Bombay—it nearly made it under its own power (courtesy David Dunnell).

The Hy-Mac BMC 1800 and the Bentley in Afghanistan (courtesy David Dunnell).

this isn't a diesel car!" David and Norman carefully approached the two men from behind, one of whom was now waving a container in the air and continuing to demand that it be filled with diesel. David raised the pistol, fired a shot into the air and the two men fled into the desert. Understandably, the Bentley and the 1800 were very quickly on their way again.

Eventually, the Bentley stopped running as they drove through India, which meant that, while the 1800 arrived at Bombay under its own power, the older car made its entrance into the city on the back of a truck. With both cars secured at a local garage, David and Keith quickly received confirmation that No. 65 and No. 84 had officially been disqualified from the Marathon. While Keith made arrangements for the Bentley to be shipped back to Britain, David began to hatch another plan. What if he could try and break the record for the fastest solo drive from Bombay back to London? Another call to Hy-Mac and the plan was set. All that was needed now was for the 1800 to be checked over and serviced, so David approached the proprietor of the garage where they had parked both cars. Could he do the work? Yes, he could, although he would need to move the 1800 to another of his sites, and would David like to go duck hunting with him while the BMC was being made ready? Thus, while his car was being worked on, David found himself hunting ducks in Nashik, approximately 100 miles to the north east of Bombay. As he said, "None of this was part of the plan!"

With the 1800 finally ready for the long, lonely drive back to London and pausing only to receive a blessing from a local holy man who gave him some water from the Ganges to drink, on December 14, David took some more of his dwindling supply of Benzedrine and, with a sendoff from the Indian Automobile Association, began the drive home, accompanied for the first 100 miles or so by a member of the Indian press. Despite the best efforts of the

Indian mechanics, however, on the way to the Pakistan border, the 1800's hydrolastic suspension collapsed. Fortunately, Janspeed had suggested that they carry an additional unit, so David quickly jacked the car up and set about fitting the replacement, using water to fill the system's pipes in the absence of any hydrolastic fluid. As David recalled, "I had the car on the jack with a wheel off and suddenly, a very nasty looking bloke appeared out of the jungle with a bloody great long knife. I quietly got the pistol and laid it down and he suddenly backed off, but I think without the gun I would have been in trouble, because he was about to rob me blind!"

David set off again and finally reached the border with Pakistan, only to discover that the goodwill shown during the Marathon itself had suddenly evaporated. David could get out of India quite easily, but the Pakistani border guard was not going to let him enter his country based on the documentation David presented, pointing out that he was going the wrong way. Stopping himself from picking up the table, at which the border guard was sitting, and dropping it on his head, David returned to the Indian border guards, who immediately went into action, securing the car and bundling him onto a train, complete with an escort, to the closest town where David could organize a new visa. As David explained, "When I got back, the Indians were all smiling. They said this bloke had been sacked, he was in trouble and they just let me drive through and off I went."

David's determination to beat the record spurred him on as he bounced and wrestled the 1800 back along the Marathon route through Pakistan and Afghanistan, despite the fact that the paperwork he had been given to allow competitors to obtain fuel along the way was now being rejected at some gas stations. Where necessary, he either relied on the money the Indian garage owner had lent him or the hope that a Marathon car that had unexpectedly reappeared days after competitors had passed through, albeit going in the opposite direction, might persuade those he encountered to provide assistance. On the way to Iran, however, a new problem loomed. As David recalled, even though the Marathon's international infrastructure had begun to disappear, his progress thus far was "all pretty straightforward, until I ran out of Benzedrine."

In Teheran, where he was again able to call upon mechanical assistance to carry out repairs and maintenance on the 1800, David was also somehow able to obtain a quantity of substitute medication, possibly Dexedrine. However, a combination of his growing exhaustion and the possible side effects of this new medication caused severe headaches. News of his endeavor was beginning to spread along the route, and eventually he was stopped by the Iranian police, who told him he needed to sleep. David agreed, if only to appease them, and was then on his way again towards the Turkish border, the weather conditions deteriorating until they too became an obstacle. David recalled that "The borders were shut because of the weather. The roads were iced up, but I told them I'd prepared for this, I can do it and they let me go through." It wouldn't take long before the reason for the border closure became obvious.

In pitch darkness it was impossible to see the sheets of ice covering the road ahead and David suddenly found himself skidding wildly and plowing 20 feet down a bank. He explained how he came to a stop, remembering that "All I could see down below me were all these lights and I was airborne and the car ended on a ledge. It was cold, very cold—every time you touched any metal you stuck to it. So I started the old girl up and charged like mad to get up this bank and she got up to the top and she rocked and hung there." Leaving the car in gear, he got out and climbed onto the 'roo bar, rocking up and down until the front wheels caught and the 1800 lurched forward. To this day, he believes this probably saved his life as otherwise he would have frozen to death.

By now the 1800 was more than a little worse for wear—one headlight was out and the tailpipe was hanging off. Perhaps because of this, or because the yellow Marathon car still displayed its "No. 65," at the toll station in Italy he was refused permission to join the *autostrada*. David retired to a safe distance and consulted his map, noticing that up ahead there was a road that ran parallel to the freeway. He followed this for a while until the toll booths were out of sight and then crashed through the dividing fence, bumped onto the freeway and floored the gas pedal.

A call to Hy-Mac in Paris confirmed that they had booked passage on one of the British Air Ferries' flights from Le Touquet to Lydd airport in England. David recalled that by the time he got to Paris, the 1800 was really struggling, running on only three cylinders, and finally, as he maneuvered the car up the ramp into the belly of the Carvair aircraft, it ran out of gas. At last, on December 24, with a welcome from friends who had dashed to Lydd to meet him, David and his battered BMC 1800 arrived back on British soil. Solo, he had driven the 7,000-mile route in ten days, which David believes beat the previous record of 12 days, although he wasn't able to verify this.

Reflecting on his achievement, David recalled that "The main thing was your eyes got tired, so I had bottles and bottles of Optrex. I got that in Bombay, I had gallons of it and of course I couldn't take my hands off the wheel so I was taking it and just tipping it on the floor. The whole car was just rotten inside, all the carpets and all my clothes where I'd spilled it were rotten. Apparently the car stunk. Friends afterwards said the car stunk like a sewer, but bless its heart, that car saved my life. She kept going in various situations I got into. I just never wanted to stop. The fun of getting home and meeting everyone gave you that boost and they led me all the way to London. We went in convoy and I was still going as fast as I could."

Jean Denton and Tom Boyce's MGB prior to being fully kitted out for the Marathon (author's collection).

The Renault 16TS of Swiss team Reust, Gratzer and Béguin on scrutinizing day, November 23 (courtesy Mike Wood).

BMC 1800s—three for BMC GB, one for BMC Australia and one for the Red Arrows Team, November 1968 (courtesy Mike Wood).

No. 5 shows off its 'roo bar—the Chrysler Valiant Safari of Peter Lumsden, Peter Sargent, Redge Lewis and John Fenton at Crystal Palace, London, November 23, 1968 (courtesy Peter Lumsden).

The Denton/Boyce MGB on scrutineering day at Crystal Palace, November 23 (courtesy Mike Wood).

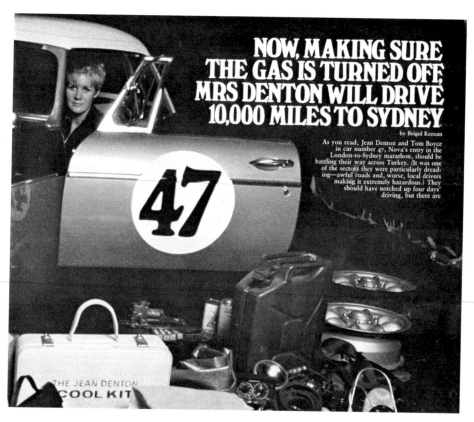

NOW, MAKING SURE THE GAS IS TURNED OFF, MRS DENTON WILL DRIVE 10,000 MILES TO SYDNEY

by Brigid Keenan

As you read, Jean Denton and Tom Boyce in car number 47, Nova's entry in the London-to-Sydney marathon, should be battling their way across Turkey. (It was one of the sectors they were particularly dreading—awful roads and, worse, local drivers making it extremely hazardous.) They should have notched up four days' driving, but there are

Jean Denton and MGB fashion shoot for the December 1968 issue of *NOVA* magazine (©Time Inc. [UK] Ltd).

The crowds on Westminster Bridge, London, on November 24 (courtesy Mike Wood).

Jenny and Nick Brittan drive the No. 50 Cortina Lotus to the starting line at Crystal Palace, November 24 (author's collection).

No. 97, the Ford Falcon XT GT of Reg Lunn, Clive Tippett and Jack Hall, at Crystal Palace, November 24 (author's collection).

Behind the No. 81 Cortina Lotus, the only Indian Marathon team of Wadia, Tarmaster and Kaka, at Crystal Palace, November 24 (courtesy Simon Sladen).

No. 4 BMC 1800 at Crystal Palace, November 24 (author's collection).

Waiting to begin. No. 82, the Ford Cortina Lotus of Duncan Bray, Simon Sladen and Peter Sugden, at Crystal Palace, November 24 (courtesy Simon Sladen).

No. 43, the Volvo 144S of Gerry Lister and André Welinski (author's collection).

No. 41, the Morris 1100S of Eileen Westley, Minny Macdonald and Jenny Gates, at Crystal Palace, London, November 24 (author's collection).

British Army Motoring Association Ford Zephyr 4 Marathon service vehicle in France, November 25 (courtesy John Hemsley).

The Triumph 2000 of British father-and-sons team Frank, Barry and Geoffrey Goulden. Partly seen at left is the Vauxhall Viva GT crewed by the Japanese team of Nobuo Koga, Yojiro Terada and Kazuhiko Mitsumoto (courtesy Mike Wood).

The consequence of hitting a bus in Teheran (courtesy Bob Holden).

Stuck in the mud—Bob Whittington poses for the camera while local farmers attach a tow rope to the stricken Vanden Plas. Between Sivas and Erzincan, Turkey, November 1968 (courtesy Bill Price).

Problems with the No. 44 Rover's de Dion suspension begin (courtesy Mike Bailey).

No. 72, the Ford Cortina Lotus of Ernie McMillen, John L'Amie and Ian Drysdale (courtesy Mike Wood).

The roadside crowds in India (courtesy John Hemsley).

Bombay *parc fermé. Foreground:* No. 28 Mercedes Benz 280SL and No. 5 Porsche 911S. *Rear, from left:* No. 100 Simca 1100; No. 33 Volvo 145S; No. 90 Ford Cortina Lotus; No. 86 BMW 2000 (out of competition but allowed to continue); No. 44 Rover 2000TC; No. 18 Ford Cortina (courtesy Mike Wood).

No. 78, the Super Sport Engines Ford Escort, covered in garlands in the *parc fermé* in Bombay, India, December 1968 (courtesy Mike Wood).

The "Galloping Tortoise" in Bombay, India (courtesy Mike Wood).

Bruce "Hoddo" Hodgson and Doug Rutherford heading for Hindmarsh Station (courtesy Bruce Thomas).

The Marathon "marching girls," Gloucester Park trotting track, Perth, December 14 (courtesy Mike Wood).

The Red Arrows' BMC 1800 coming into the Hindmarsh Station control in Australia, December 17 (courtesy Bruce Thomas).

Major Freddie Preston repairs the damaged radiator during "The Horror Stretch" (courtesy Mike Bailey).

Roy Fidler awaits the correct part for the stricken Midget (courtesy Mike Wood).

No. 53, the Rambler American, at the Hindmarsh Station control, December 17. Jerry Sims walks behind in his crash hat, John Saladin stands through the turret and Sid Dickson is at the wheel (courtesy Bruce Thomas).

Rosemary Smith tries to get No. 93 pushed up a hill in New South Wales, Australia (courtesy Bruce Thomas).

The winning Hillman Hunter with Brian Coyle, Andrew Cowan and Colin Malkin at Warwick Farm Raceway, New South Wales, December 18 (courtesy Mike Wood).

16

A Peykan by Any Other Name

With the Marathon favorites, Ford GB team members Roger Clark and Ove Andersson, now in the lead and the field down to 90 cars, competitors contemplated the next section of the Marathon. It would be nearly 870 miles combining mountain passes, Mount Ararat clearly visible in the distance, and long deserted stretches of fast road with the potential hazard of straying camels all the way to Teheran. Organizers had allowed 22 hours for crews to arrive at the Iranian time-control, which was located at the city's Philips factory. Beyond Teheran lay a choice of two routes, one running up into the eastern ranges of the Elburs Mountains and the Kopet Dag, the other shorter route skirting the northern fringes of the Kavir Desert, although BMC GB had also calculated a third, quicker desert route, which would lead to problems for two of their cars. The routes then met near Mashhad before crossing the border with Afghanistan to Herat and finally the eastern city of Kabul via Kandahar. For many of the professional crews, the run to Teheran was relatively easy after the rigors of the previous stage, but for some, the long, relentless drive would be fraught with problems, disruption and calamity. For two more entrants, it would see the end of their dream.

At the Erzincan checkpoint, Clarke and Andersson had been fastest, only six minutes off of the target time, followed by the Ford Germany team of Gilbert Staepelaere and Simo Lampinen in their Ford 20MRS at 14 minutes and the French Citroën pairing of Lucien Bianchi and Jean-Claude Ogier, only 16 minutes down. The closest Australian team was Harry Firth, Graham Hoinville and Gary Chapman in their Falcon XT GT, but it was clear that European drivers had stolen the march thus far. Just a few penalty points separated the remainder of the top ten, however, so there could be absolutely no easing off as car after car set off on the 300-mile slog to the Iranian border at Barzargan. Almost immediately, competitors were forced to endure sudden snow storms and freezing cold as the road began to climb ever higher, elevating 8,000 feet above sea level. The improved road conditions across the border into Iran seemed a long way off for Nick and Jenny Brittan when a faulty alternator forced them to return to Erzincan after only 35 miles. Back up and running, but now two hours behind, they were to suffer further misfortune when a tire blew out, sending the Cortina into a ditch. A passing truck stopped to pull them out, but the jolt popped out their only recently replaced windshield and once again the husband-and-wife team found themselves driving with goggles, this time all the way to Tabriz.

Mishaps befell a few other competitors on this final Turkish section, in two instances leading to retirement. Maryland natives Sid Dickson and John Saladin, with the CBS camera man Jerry Sims, had arrived at Erzincan more than two and a half hours down on the target

The only U.S. Marathon team—John Saladin, Jerry Sims and Sid Dickson with their Rambler American (author's collection).

time in their red, white and blue Rambler American. On the way to the Turkish town of Erzurum, a momentary indecision at a junction saw the American team drive straight into the side of a house. As Sid explained, "Now they tricked us, it was at night. It was on a mountain section in Turkey, where the road ran along a river. So there's a river there and there's a bridge and wherever there's a bridge on the river, there's a village—half the village here, half the village there. Well, they had turned the lights off in the village on the other side of the river and it was night time. Maybe we weren't reading the road book just right. The bridge was a right-angle bridge and I missed the bridge, sailed off and ran into this stone house!" The car was stuck fast, but as the three men climbed out to inspect the damage, they noticed a group of people running towards them. As Sid recalled, "So Jerry whips out a revolver. 'Jerry, that's one of the rules, we weren't going to carry firearms, remember?' We're having this argument while the guys are running at us. He says, 'Yeah, I know I agreed to it, but I thought I'm going to carry it anyway.' I said, 'Jerry you don't even know if they're hostile, put the thing away until we figure out whether they're hostile! I mean you shoot two or three of them, you know what they're going to do!' So he says, all right, he stuck it in his pocket just as they got to us." Fortunately for the Americans, the group of men were only too happy to help out, and after a few moments of pushing and pulling, the Rambler was on its way again.

No. 15 was not so lucky—the privately entered series one Cortina GT of Australian

Geoffrey Franklin and his co-driver Kim Brassington suffered a blown engine in the Turkish mountains, and, as *Autosport* reported, "The crew was stuck with no money, either for a new engine or for the fare home."[1] Another car was out of the Marathon.

Australian former Victorian Trials champion Reg Lunn had decided to enter the Marathon in a Ford Falcon XT GT, accompanied by fellow Australians Clive Tippett and Jack Hall. Sponsored by the Australian firm Lunwin Products, No. 97 had lost 33 minutes at Erzincan, but disaster was to strike before the border control into Iran, which according to Ford Australia team member Bruce Hodgson could have been avoided. Months before the Marathon, Bruce had discovered a potential weakness in the Ford Falcon's transmission while driving his own XR series car. Stripping the gearbox down, he worked out how it could be fixed, so when he bumped into Lunn in London during the weeks leading up to the Marathon, he brought the modification to his attention. According to Bruce, Lunn dismissed the suggestion, which is possibly why, as No. 97 raced towards Tabriz, it suddenly developed a serious problem with its transmission. A message was sent on to the Teheran control where Ford Australia team Competitions Manager John Gowland arranged for a replacement unit to be sent back along the route to the sidelined Falcon. However, according to John Smailes, Lunn "fitted it to their Falcon GT on the spot, but the box was fitted with the wrong ratios, limiting the drivers to a valve bouncing 65 mph top speed."[2] No. 97 eventually made it to Teheran, but the damage was done: Lunn, Tippett and Hall were out of the Marathon.

The remainder of the field pressed on, many of them relieved to be finally out of Turkey and onto the fast road that would take them southeast through Tabriz and towards Teheran. After the icy weather in the Turkish mountains, the descent into Iran and warmer conditions was very welcome, although Arthur Brick in No. 1 reported that as they were driving east, the sun made visibility difficult.

Hour after hour of relatively fast road quickly turned to monotony and competitors were thankful when, on the approaches to Teheran, police motorbikes appeared and escorted each to the checkpoint on the other side of the city. Marathon control and servicing facilities at Teheran were extensive, with the different automobile companies' motorsports teams lined up to attend to their official entrants. As Jack Kemsley noted, "there were thousands around the control, which was easily the best equipped and most efficiently controlled in the whole trip."[3] Teheran was of particular benefit to the Rootes team cars of Andrew Cowan and Flight Lieutenant David Carrington.

In 1967, the Iran Khodro factory had begun assembling Hillman Hunters under license from Rootes and marketing them in Iran with the brand name Peykan. As arranged, before arriving at the control, Cowan and Carrington were intercepted by Iran Khodro personnel who then led the Marathon Hunters to the factory for servicing and any other work that the crews identified as needed. Other than general servicing and a few minor modifications required by Cowan, however, both Hillmans were in excellent working order, much to the disappointment of the Peykan mechanics who were primed to take the cars apart and put them back together again if necessary. The Rootes Marathon crews were treated like heroes by Iran Khodro, who provided food and washing and rest facilities for the crews while they set to work to do what little was required. As they were also looking after the three Simca 1100s in the event, they were at least consoled by that fact that one of the Simcas required welding to its muffler.

Other competitors were also well served at Teheran. Although Mercedes had decided not to officially enter cars in the Marathon, it had arranged for a service presence along the 10,000-mile route, using local Mercedes agents and mechanics. For the Holden cars, arrangements had been made for assistance using a local American automobile importer that was also taking care of the Marathon Citroëns. Their knowledge of Chevrolet vehicles was gratefully received by Barry Ferguson, Doug Chivas and Dave Johnson as their General Motors Holden Monaro required a complete brake reconstruction. At the Philips factory control site, Ford and BMC had set up their own service centers, prioritizing their official entries, but happy to assist any privately entered Cortina or BMC 1800 if time allowed. The sole Indian team, headed by Bomsi Wadia, took full advantage of the Ford facilities, having a new valve fitted to his privately entered Cortina Lotus, although they were eventually delayed at Teheran for two days trying to solve the problem of why the Cortina's timing was out. Indian newspapers and Marathon enthusiasts were to be bitterly disappointed when Wadia finally drove into Bombay to discover that the ship had sailed.

As competitors prepared to depart Teheran, the positions of the leading cars were little changed. Clark and Andersson remained in the lead, still followed by Staepelaere and Lampinen, then Bianchi and Ogier, all factory motorsports team drivers. Highest placed independent entry was No. 39, the Australian Alfa Romeo 1750 Berlina, backed by Addison Motors of Adelaide and crewed by experienced rally men Tony Theiler, Stewart McLeod and Jack Lock. In advance of the Marathon, Theiler had taken the car to the Alfa Romeo factory in Italy for final preparations, and en route to London had caused chaos on the ferry between France and England when he placed a ship-to-shore call to his family back in Australia, block-

No. 54 and No. 3 stop for fuel in Iran (courtesy John Hemsley).

ing the ship's radio and preventing it from communicating its approach to the port, leaving it sailing in circles in the English Channel!

With police escorts racing ahead of the first cars away, the next section began, the majority choosing to follow the mountain route. The Rootes GB cars had decided to take the faster but more isolated southern route, while BMC opted for a third route, a shortcut they had identified during their many reconnoiters a few months before. None of these passages would be risk-free, not least because gasoline quality along the way was not guaranteed. The Burmah-Castrol oil and fuel company was originally responsible for supplying gasoline at designated sites along the road to Kabul, but the required export permit to allow fuel supplies to be delivered from Pakistan had not arrived. At the last minute the Iranian National Oil Company was given the task of supplying fuel, sending trucks on ahead of the Marathon and dropping drums of gasoline off. However, the trucks were late setting off, which meant there was a serious possibility that Marathon cars would beat the fuel train to Kabul. *The Sydney Daily Telegraph* reported a Burmah-Castrol representative saying "we shall not uncross our fingers until we hear a lorry has reached Kabul."[4] Rootes and BMC had also made arrangements for fuel to be available along the alternative routes.

As well as Nick and Jenny Brittan, among those anxiously awaiting the start of this, the longest section of the Marathon and the task of arriving as close as possible to the allowable time of 23 hours and 30 minutes was the only other male and female pair in the event. Tom Boyce and Jean Denton were competing in No. 47, the gold-colored, fixed-head MGB.

17

More Than Just the Mechanic

Canadian Tom Boyce didn't really want to participate in motor racing in England. Having already achieved a master's degree in plasma-physics at the University of Toronto, he relocated to Britain in 1961 when he was offered a fellowship to study for a doctorate at Imperial College, London. He had previously rallied in Canada, mostly as part of the university rally club scene, and had been able to gain a useful amount of experience competing on wintry Canadian roads, but, by the time he was settled on Imperial, his attention was devoted exclusively to combustion kinetics and pollution control. As he explained, "I didn't really want to get involved because I didn't really want to get diverted from my primary purpose, which was to get a Ph.D."

Studying alongside Tom at Imperial was Tony Denton, who, with his wife Jean, had grown increasingly interested in motorsports. A busy PR professional, Jean Denton had discovered the thrill of motor racing in 1963 and had quickly started competing, racing a Mini before going on to purchase Scottish racing driver Jackie Stewart's Formula Three Cooper. Tom recalled that, as a result of a visit to her orthodontist one day, she had struck up a conversation. Tom explained that "Her dentist was into rallying and he learned from Jean that she was interested in motor racing. He suggested that she try and do some rallying." When she mentioned this to Tony, however, he pointed out that he wasn't really a suitable candidate to be her navigator as he had a tendency to be physically sick when riding in the passenger seat. Tony remembered that Tom was a keen MG enthusiast, however, having arranged for his MGA to be shipped over from Canada, so the Dentons suggested that he join Jean in club rallies, which they proceeded to do for the next year, learning as they went along.

Jean also continued track racing, growing frustrated with the performance of her 850-cc (52 cubic inch) Mini, and although she graduated to the larger 1-liter (61 cubic inch) version, it was Tom who suggested she consider an MG. He also suggested that, rather than approaching an independent mechanic, he could help prepare an MG for Jean to race, explaining that "You're not going to get the best, no matter who does the work for you; they will always keep that bit back." In Tom's view, he would be able to get as much as possible from an MG's 1.8-liter (110 cubic inch) engine and began to show Jean how to achieve maximum performance. With Tom's expert mechanical knowledge, it isn't surprising that Jean went on to become women's racing champion, winning the British Women Racing Drivers Club Embassy Award driving an MGB in 1966, although the modifications that Tom had made to the MG were subsequently prohibited for the next season. As a consequence, Tom decided to supercharge the MG by increasing the density of air supplied to its engine, which in turn increased combustion and overall power. With the MG now up to 140 horsepower, they entered Jean in the next competition class up and she triumphed for a second time in 1967.

With her profile raised as a result of her racing successes in an MG and Tom's great mechanical expertise with the MG's engine, plus their improved knowledge of rally rules and regulations, it was inevitable that, being PR-savvy, Jean would notice the London to Sydney Marathon. Why not enter an MG with Tom? The Dentons paid the entrance fee and Jean quickly set about using her professional network to secure sponsorship for the event.

Among the fashionable magazines of "swinging sixties" Britain, *Nova* marketed itself as a new kind of magazine for a new kind of woman. First published in 1965, *Nova* had an illustrious editorial team, including art editor Harry Peccinotti and fashion editor Molly Parkin. Jean approached *Nova*, who agreed to sponsor them, capitalizing on the publicity by running two features on Jean and the MG in their November and December 1968 editions, complete with photographs of Tom and Jean working out at the gym and modeling rally outfits designed by Hylan Booker. As the magazine states, "For the cooler part of the trip (to Bombay) Hylan Booker designed three soft Viyella shirts each (orange, yellow and camel for Jean; black, camel and orange for Tom) ... The Nova embroidery on the jackets and shirts was done specially for us by Jacoby's."[1] Tom recalled that "There was a great big hustle going on in the studio down in Chelsea and a great discussion going on. Jean came over and I said 'What the hell is that all about?' Jean said that 'They're discussing whether you'd let them put makeup on you.' I said 'Do you think it's really appropriate?' It was a whole new world."

It is no coincidence, however, that the magazine's glossy articles focused mostly on Jean. Tom recalled that "Any reference to me—the car and what I was building—was deleted in any publicity that Jean had. She edited stuff out in articles, simply because she didn't want people to realize that, if it wasn't for me, she wouldn't have got there. That's why I didn't object, I mean, that was the main reason I was involved, because I was the only one that could give her some sort of guarantee of being able to get there and not just put the car together, but to drive it as well." In short, Tom knew very well that this was a woman competing in a male-dominated sport and it was therefore important that Jean appeared front and center throughout. To her credit, however, in one of the *Nova* articles Jean is quoted as saying that "I can play my part in technical operations, but he's the expert—and he's the one who'll lift it out of ditches."[2]

While Jean pursued other sponsorship opportunities, eventually securing additional backing from Air India and the vodka company Smirnoff, Tom was hard at work transforming the MGB into one that would withstand the punishment it would have to endure. The first thing he did was obtain a brand new car from the factory at Abingdon in Oxfordshire, specifying to MG's chief engineer Sid Enever that all the seams needed to be double-welded. The car was supplied with full trim, but without suspension in the main chassis, as Tom had very specific ideas about how the car needed to be adapted. He explained that "I supplemented it with hydrolastic suspension, so we had infinitely variable spring rates on the front and the rear. This allowed the car's handling to stay the same, no matter what the loading was. It also meant that, across these corrugated sections, you still retained control, no matter how rough the road was." Tom also fitted a heavy-duty air filter to counter the much-reported dust that would be a constant hazard across the Australian outback. Unlike those preparing a number of other Marathon cars, he decided against lowering the motor's compression, concluding that the standard setting could cope with any low octane gasoline they might be forced to

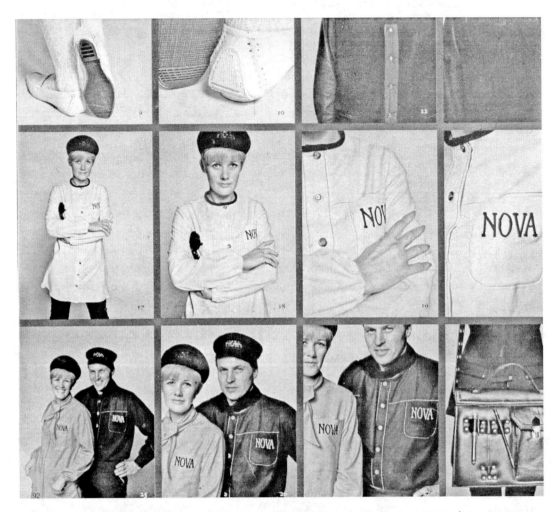

Tom Boyce and Jean Denton pose for the December 1968 issue of *Nova* magazine (©Time Inc. [UK] Ltd).

use. Provided they were light on the gas pedal, the motor wouldn't be forced to work too hard and the pistons wouldn't be damaged.

Tom did all the work in a garage beneath his mews apartment in London's West Kensington. The apartment was owned by fellow Marathon entrant Peter Lumsden, who was chair of Imperial College's student motor club. Tom recalled that he had "no idea he [Lumsden] was going to enter the Marathon. He didn't let me know until I stumbled upon the fact that he was also in it!" Tom also fitted double fuel tanks to the car and helped with the design and construction of a customized seat with an aluminum frame and webbing, which reclined to allow the passenger to sleep. He explained that they consulted with the London School of Hygiene and General Health to determine the optimum position for sleeping while still being able to return the seat upright for navigating.

Before the Marathon itself, Tom and Jean decided to enter an overseas rally to gain experience, competing in the first *Rallye de Montagne*, or Rally of Lebanon. Tom recalled one point on the 620-mile course where they were confronted by a group of locals insisting they buy drugs off them. "We got them on one side of the mountain and we said no, no, we don't want them. We got around the other side and there they were up top. They started rolling boulders down at us. We got out of there in a hurry!"

November 23, 1968, the day before departure, saw Tom struggling with a problem. The Halda Speedpilot navigating clock, an item of equipment being used by all competitors, wasn't working correctly. Designed to compute time and distance in relation to a pre-selected average speed requirement, the clock needed to be in full working order. Tom recalled that this is the reason his memory of departure day at Crystal Palace is so vague—he had been up all the previous night fixing the Halda.

At 2:40 p.m. on Sunday, November 24, Jean eased the gold-painted MGB down the Crystal Palace starting ramp and drove away through London, out onto the A20 road and down to Dover and the ferry to France. At the ferry port, they collected two Mauser handguns, a .22 and 9mm. As Tom explained, "We were advised to carry our own firearms. Some of Jean's contacts had come over one evening while we were building up the car and they happened to mention it was going to be quite an adventure and by the way, you'd better equip yourselves with firearms, make sure you do have something. We did it legally, Jean took care of that. She did a lot of the donkey work, bits and pieces of organizing, that was her forte and she organized gun permits, not that we could carry them in England in those days, they were very tight on firearms." Fortunately for both of them, they never had cause to put the guns to the test.

Once in France, Tom took his turn behind the wheel and they began their well-practiced routine of driving four hours on and four hours off. On the drive south towards the time control at Turin, however, he noticed that a number of auxiliary systems weren't working and, worst of all, the MG's overdrive wasn't kicking in.

A common modification in the 1960s, the overdrive mechanism enabled a car to cruise at sustained speed with reduced engine revolutions per minute (RPM). Reduced RPM meant better fuel economy and reduced engine wear, extremely useful for a car that had to cover 7,000 miles in seven days, often running on less than premium quality gasoline. Trying to identify the cause would take more time than the pair had and while Tom was able to fix some of the auxiliary systems, the overdrive remained inoperable. Press reports at the time described how "the starter motor had packed up and she [Jean] and her partner Tom Boyce were having to push start the car,"[3] or "The Mrs. Denton/Boyce Nova MGB broke its overdrive solenoid, so they have big troubles."[4]

The reality was somewhat different, however, as Tom explained: "It was another one of the false stories put out by Jean. What actually happened was that Tony did some last minute work at the garage. He took it apart to check, make sure everything was working and he overlooked reconnecting the overdrive switch. So we were sunk from beginning to end, no overdrive!" Tom wasn't to discover this until a week later, on board the SS *Chusan* bound for Perth with Jean and Tony, who had joined his wife for the voyage.

Another hindrance for the *Nova* team was the fact that when Jean wasn't driving, she suffered constantly with car sickness. Jean wrote that "My disability became so well known that as soon as I wound down the window and hung out my head, the car behind backed off immediately!"[5] Tom recalled how "That's where John Hemsley came in because when we were on the boat going from Bombay down to Fremantle, John suggested some medication, a prescription that the army used and so we got that and it was this huge damn pill. We went back to John and said 'no way anybody can … what do you do, dissolve it or what?' He said 'oh, that's what they use for the horses!'"

Other than Jean breaking a tooth, progress to Bombay was achieved mostly without incident. Tom described how, up until the Istanbul control point, "We didn't have any [of] what could be interpreted as hostile incidents, but after we left that control, from there on we had to be careful, traveling in groups because the local youths took to throwing stones at us, so you didn't take the lead. A lot of it was at night and very rickety bridges, excuses for bridges, just planks on a trestle and greasy and muddy, really hazardous as hell." He also recalled being fascinated by the local tribesmen in Afghanistan, remembering, "It was quite amusing when we left Kabul and saw them all lying on their sides, in the hills all around, with their guns next to them, chewing betel nut, watching the rally cars going by. We were in a totally different world here, we don't want to stop." Leaving Kabul, however, the MG's oil pan guard made contact with the pavement, forcing Tom to stop and carry out repairs.

Tom also explained how he did most of the driving during the more challenging sections towards India, because he simply had more experience, but when the MG encountered the huge throngs of excited onlookers in India he began to struggle, which was when Jean came into her own. Tom recalled, "You had to point and put your foot down and hope you didn't hit anybody. I found that very difficult to do and Jean put up with this for a couple of hours until she finally said 'Let me drive' and she just put her foot down and God help you, here I come! She just drove at them and she was not going to be stopped, she was that determined."

After stopping in New Delhi to change tires at the Dunlop service area, where Tom recalled they had ornamental carpets and a polished brass drip tray for when the car was

Jean Denton and Freddie Preston (center) look very happy to see Fremantle after the nine-day voyage aboard the SS *Chusan* (courtesy Mike Bailey).

jacked up, the MGB arrived at the Bombay control having accumulated 319 penalty points, making Jean the highest placed woman in the field. Any satisfaction she was able to derive from this was countered, however, as the damaged tooth she had suffered was causing considerable discomfort. Tom recalled how they were adopted by a local businessman who had come down to watch the competitors and service teams working on the cars before moving them into the *parc fermé*. "He turned up and bought me a couple of beers. We got talking and he befriended us. He got little things, took us out shopping in a local market. He had a local Indian batman running around for him. He did what he could to help." The man directed Jean to a dentist, who repaired the damaged tooth and promptly refused payment as she was a Marathon competitor.

Jean wasn't very impressed by the SS *Chusan*, despite being reunited with her husband Tony. "If you didn't feel hungry at the regulation time there was very little prospect of getting anything to eat in between,"[6] she wrote. Coupled with sea sickness, Jean saw the ocean crossing as the real horror stretch of the Marathon.

Upon arrival at Fremantle, Australian broadcast and media journalists were eager to get their scoops from competitors and Jean certainly grasped the opportunity for more PR, giving interviews for most of the day. Meanwhile, Tom enjoyed the enthusiastic welcome provided by the MG Car Club, a parade of MGs glinting in the Western Australian sun, ready to escort No. 47 to Winterbottom's service center in Perth. It wouldn't be long before Jean and Tom would be expressing their gratitude to the club.

The gold MGB departed in 49th position from the Gloucester Park stadium in Perth, 23 places ahead of the final car to speed around the circuit and exit towards the first time control. Jean and Tom made good time to the Youanmi checkpoint and then set off on the next stage to Marvel Loch, but two punctures and a malfunctioning fuel pump meant the MG lost more time. Tom fitted a replacement pump at Lake King and away they sped to tackle the 890-mile section across the Nullarbor Plain, where the bull dust awaited.

Much had been made of the fine dust that could fill a crater and make it appear flat, so an unsuspecting driver, believing the road ahead was even, would suddenly crash over, or worse, into, a deep hole. Tom recalled how "We went into this one hole and immediately the engine mounts broke at the front and the engine surged forward as we hit the edge of this hole. The car went down and the engine went up. The fan hit the header tank and, because it comes over the radiator, the fan bent and it made a perfect cut, a perfect hole in the radiator." Tom tried everything, attempting to plug the hole and even bypass the entire coolant system, but the damage was too great. They needed a new radiator and the next town was at least 100 miles away. All they could do was flag down another Marathon car and ask that they report their plight when they reached Norseman.

Before the Marathon, the MG Car Club in England had contacted the club's Western Australia chapter, suggesting that members be on hand to assist No. 47. The club mobilized, organizing a network of support across the country so that on each section, Australian club members monitored the MGB's progress and staffed each of the checkpoints. Now, as they waited anxiously at Norseman, the message was delivered and, as MG Car Club member Richard Ashton wrote, "At the toss of a coin, which I lost, my radiator was sacrificed to the cause and quickly removed from my car. Away we went; about six suddenly MG Car Club radiator experts were sandwiched into two cars, complete with a dripping radiator, a toolbox and water."[7] Meanwhile, Tom and Jean were crawling along the track, stopping every few miles

No. 47 awaits departure from the Gloucester Park trotting track in Perth, December 14 (courtesy Colin Cleaver).

No. 47 checks in at the Hindmarsh Station checkpoint, December 17 (courtesy Bruce Thomas).

to let the engine cool down. When they noticed a car coming towards them in the distance, they were astonished to see it was an MGB. With one replacement radiator supplied and fitted, Tom and Jean were on their way again. As Tom remarked, "They came to our rescue. They were marvelous." No. 47 continued on to the next two controls, but at Moralana, Tom took the time to repair the engine mounts and get the motor back in place again. They then opted to miss the next control at Brachina, take the maximum penalty points on the chin and press on to Mingary and each subsequent checkpoint thereafter. In this fashion, they made it to the Warwick Farm Raceway in Sydney, their overall place improved to 42nd out of 54 finishers.

On completing their 10,000-mile adventure across the globe, Jean wrote, "Everyone tells me that to get here in a sports car with only two drivers is quite some achievement and one of the nicest things is how the other drivers congratulate us on doing this."[8] Tom recalled that "BMC was totally at a loss to explain why we were there. As far as they were concerned, we shouldn't have been. Just ignorance of what could be done and what our capabilities were. They didn't know the vehicle either, like I did, because I built the damn thing. That's why we had the necessary bits and pieces that we did, why we had the spare parts to give away!"

The Boyce/Denton team attracted a degree of media attention in Sydney but, as there were 41 cars placed higher, two of which included women competitors, Tom observed that "Jean again got some coverage, but they weren't interested in me, I was only the driver and mechanic, co-pilot. I was hardly the mechanic, chum, but I had to go along with it. It's history and that was it. I still have no regrets. That's life."

Jean Denton died in 2000, aged 65. Dr. Tom Boyce remained a sharp, profoundly intelligent man into his early eighties and was both astonished and thrilled to learn that the MGB had been rediscovered, languishing in a breaker's yard (or junkyard), in 2015. The car is now in the ownership of the British MGB Register and Tom was able to provide further insight and explanation of his engineering prowess to the team of enthusiasts who, as this book goes to press, are undertaking a meticulous restoration of the car. Tom died in his sleep in August 2015, aged 84. In the 1968 London to Sydney Marathon, he was definitely more than just the mechanic.

18

All Along the King's Highway

Not far into the nearly 1,600-mile trek to the Afghan capital city, three Fords were in trouble during the easier mountain section, the first having not even left Teheran's city limits. The first car to experience Teheran's driving conditions at their worst was the privately entered Ford Cortina Lotus of young British trio Duncan Bray, Peter Sugden and Simon Sladen. Having covered only a few miles from the control, the team became the victims of a double-decker bus driver who failed to give way to the Cortina, smashing the front end. Forced to return to Teheran for repairs, they suffered an 18 hour delay and a taste of the Iranian legal system for Sladen.

Until the Teheran control, No. 23's four-man, Anglo-Australian crew had been making steady, trouble-free progress in the Marathon's only Ford Corsair, a privately entered 2000E model, picking up 101 penalty points by the time they departed for the next control at Kabul. However, only 50 miles into the section they were involved in a collision, which meant an introduction to Iranian law enforcement. A second accident 50 miles further on caused the red Corsair to roll, coming to rest on its roof and narrowly missing a deep drop-off at the roadside. Once the car was recovered to the town of Amol, Australians Keith Dwyer and Ian Mackelden decided to fly on to Bombay, while British pair Peter Wilson and D. Maxwell agreed to make arrangements to drive the battered Corsair back home to England. Taking a taxi back to Teheran, the four men encountered the third Ford in serious trouble.

Nick and Jenny Brittan had already had more than their fair share of misfortune as they drove away from Iran's capital city. A collision with a horse, needing to be towed out of a ditch, the loss of their windshield, not once, but twice, and a faulty alternator had all contributed to their 1,572 penalty points. Now, on an icy mountain road approaching the small city of Abali, Nick began to negotiate a corner and the Cortina went into a skid, barreling into the side of a large truck laboring up the hill in the opposite direction. The impact spun the Ford around until it came to rest with enormous front end damage. The Brittans emerged from the wreckage uninjured, but it was obvious the Cortina had been fatally hit. As other Marathon cars skidded and swerved to avoid the wreckage, a taxi appeared carrying the Corsair's crew back to Teheran. Keith Dwyer gallantly swapped places with Jenny and remained with Nick to sort out recovery of the car, which ironically was eventually towed to Abali by the truck it had hit. Nine hours later, with the smashed Ford back in Teheran, Nick and Jenny booked onto a flight to Bombay, but not before running the gauntlet of Iranian bureaucracy to retrieve the passports they had been required to surrender to the Abali police.

Joining the beaten-up Corsair in the police compound in Amol was No. 91, the Australian

Holden HK Belmont crewed by Jack "Milko" Murray, Bert Madden and John Bryson. During their dash to get Doug Morris back to Sivas for medical treatment they had been forced to contend with oncoming competitors' cars, and a close encounter with a Cortina had damaged the Holden's axle and differential. Initially unaware of the severity of the damage, they pressed on until the axle eventually broke in Iran. The team was towed to Amol and deposited in the compound, their savior telling the police chief, "These are my friends, for them, do the utmost." As it was 2:00 a.m., the police chief took them to a local hotel and left them to get some sleep. The following morning at 6:00 a.m., Bert set to work on the car and, as John recalled, "Our host is having breakfast in his house and more or less forced to offer us hospitality. He mentioned that he had been given his position with the help of his father-in-law who was one of the Shah's ministers." Leaving Jack to his breakfast, the police chief beckoned John upstairs. John felt compelled to comply and was taken to the man's bedroom, remembering it as "Twenty-foot square, a polished timber floor with white walls and ceiling. It is furnished with a double bed, bedside locker and a ply wardrobe." The chief invited John to sit, observing that he was "a long way from home." John did as he was told as he was beginning to realize that he was indeed a very long way from home. His discomfort grew further when the chief announced that "Women are disgusting, are they not my boy?" John's imagination went into overdrive as the police chief walked over to the wardrobe and retrieved something wrapped in red silk. The man set the bundle down and said, "This is my collection of *Playboy* centerfolds, I am missing these dates." They were able to post the missing editions from Delhi, but it took a long time for John to stop feeling anxious! With more than a little relief, the Holden team finally managed to get the Belmont repaired and carried on over the mountains to Mashhad, although the delay cost them 4,320 points at the Kabul checkpoint. There would be more axle problems before they got to Bombay.

On the shortcut route through the desert, BMC team competitors weren't having it all their own way either. Brian Culcheth, driver in No. 4, explained that choosing this third route was a mistake made by BMC's reconnaissance team, and if he had "looked at that road first off, I would have said let's look at something else. The washboard was hundreds of miles and you have to try and get up onto a plain on it so you're not trying to stay on top of it, missing one and hitting the next one at speed, but you can't do that all the time. So that was a bit of a setback for us." The first BMC team 1800 to fall afoul of the desert conditions was No. 61, crewed by Finn Rauno Aaltonen and British pair Henry Liddon and Paul Easter. As they attempted to achieve the right harmonic across the corrugations, their car banged down hard on a ridge and damaged the front suspension. They lost time as they used their front-mounted winch to wire up the suspension and then continued on until they caught up with their fellow team members Culcheth, Tony Fall and Mike Wood, who had also hit a sand-drift with much more dramatic consequences. Aaltonen told them he would send someone back to help and sure enough, as Mike Wood explained, "a Hillman, very similar to the one that won the event, with some quite wealthy Iranians who had been watching came back to us and I think they must have spoken some English. So, we'll go back to the next village and they'll mend it." It was agreed that Tony and Mike would accompany the Iranian men, leaving Brian with the car. Mike recalled that "Prior to the event, it had been recommended that you perhaps should take firearms with you, so I bought a brand new Beretta .22 pistol, lovely thing, took this with us—you can't believe it—so when we left Brian in the car, we left him with the gun and said save the last bullet for yourself!"

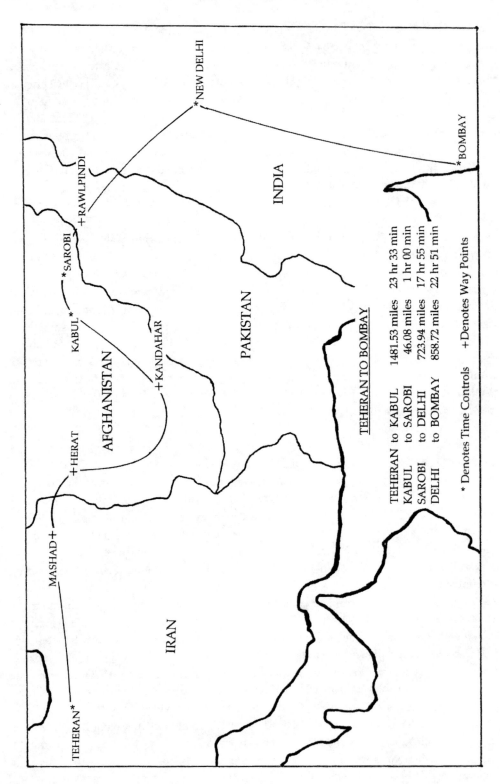

TEHERAN TO BOMBAY			
TEHERAN	to KABUL	1481.53 miles	23 hr 33 min
KABUL	to SAROBI	46.08 miles	1 hr 00 min
SAROBI	to DELHI	723.94 miles	17 hr 55 min
DELHI	to BOMBAY	858.72 miles	22 hr 51 min

* Denotes Time Controls   + Denotes Way Points

The route from Teheran to Bombay (map by Martin Proudlock).

Rootes had decided to follow the proposed southern route. As Andrew Cowan wrote, at the Teheran control "we were approached by Paul Easter and Henry Liddon ... they wanted to know which way we had decided to go.... We were being equally cagey with them and we were not going to reveal all the information we had. Eventually ... we admitted we were taking the northern route and so they said they were going north.... In fact, they took their third route and we took the southern route; gamesmanship at its best."[1]

Again, things were not straightforward for the Rootes Team as No. 45, the RAF Hunter of Carrington, King and Jones, also broke their front suspension on the desert track. Limping back to control, they met the Cowan Hunter, which was being tailed out of Teheran by an Iran Khodro Peykan loaded with extra equipment. The RAF Hunter was repaired in two hours and back on its way. Rootes had made arrangements for fuel to be available on the desert route, but the drivers of the truck sent ahead to supply gasoline had neglected to mark out the site with Rootes banners, leading to a very anxious 50 miles for Cowan, Colin Malkin and Brian Coyle as they searched in vain for the desperately needed gasoline.

As the rest of the competitors headed for the mountains, the John Davenport–Terry Hunter Porsche suffered a second brake line failure. Hastily repairing it, they pressed on, but out of the mountains and into the desert roads near Mashhad, the rear-engine car needed oil and lots of it. As Davenport wrote, "We borrowed oil from everyone and I reckon that in reaching Kabul from Mashhad ... we must have used nearly 16 gallons...."[2] Although they did manage to nurse the ailing Porsche to the Kabul control, the damage was done and they were forced to withdraw.

Another car in trouble was No. 21, the Welsh BMC 1800. On the road from Mashhad to the Afghan border post, everything went wrong. Driving across a section of road that had been partially washed away, the 1800's oil pan guard crunched against rocks. Berwyn Williams drove on but the car was losing power and the engine began to sound very unhealthy. Stopping to investigate, they discovered that the oil pan had cracked and precious oil was draining away. Berwyn, Martin Thomas and Barry Hughes realized that trying to continue would mean serious engine damage and all they could do was ask a passing competitor to take a message to the next service point. Eventually, a small convoy of Iranian army vehicles arrived and towed them to the next village, Torbat Jām, very close to the Afghanistan border. An inspection underneath the car revealed the reason for the cracked oil pan: back in Istanbul, when mechanics had repaired the leaking exhaust they had incorrectly refitted the oil pan guard. Williams removed the engine and dismantled the transmission unit to find his worst fears confirmed. The 1800's crankshaft was beyond repair and in this isolated region of Iran, locating replacement parts for a BMC 1800 appeared to be an impossible challenge.

A telephone call to the BMC dealer in Teheran was abandoned when the line kept breaking up, but then Williams had an idea. Didn't the British RAF have observation posts in Northern Iran? Somehow he made contact and explained the problem. The RAF immediately contacted the BMC Competitions Department in Abingdon who in turn contacted the BMC dealer in Teheran to see if they had a crankshaft in stock, which they did. With the help of the U.S. Army, Williams was able to catch a flight back to Teheran. Although he was able to pick up the replacement part, fly back to Mashhad, jump in an awaiting U.S. Army jeep and return to repair the 1800, the time delay was just too great. Before Berwyn, Martin and Barry made it to Bombay, they quite simply ran out of time and the ship sailed without them.

In Mashhad, Marathon cars were once more on the same route and headed for the border

Rosemary Smith (at the wheel) and Lucette Pointet were plagued with mechanical problems from Iran all the way to Sydney (courtesy Bruce Thomas).

crossing into Afghanistan, approximately ten miles from the small Iranian city of Taybad. Rumors and fears that there would be delays at the border control proved unfounded and competitors were astonished to see a red carpet leading to Afghan customs officials wearing uniforms and medals, sitting at tables along the roadside. There were even money exchange facilities. Mr. Tarzi, Jack Sears' friend at the Afghan tourism department, had been true to his word!

Throughout the morning of November 29, with the exception of the few cars that were running late, Marathon teams passed from Iran to Afghanistan. The first 80 miles on Afghan soil took competitors to Herat, where Ford GB had set up a service point at the airport. Ford GB competitors were therefore able to take advantage of facilities aboard Ford's Gulfstream aircraft to get something to eat or grab some sleep while mechanics checked over their cars. According to John Smailes, at the sight of this setup adjacent to the road, Captain James Hans Hamilton, driver of No. 17, the British Royal Navy BMC 1800, remarked that "they should be driving in bloody dinner jackets!"[3] It would be here that Captain David Harrison and Lieutenant Martin Proudlock were instructed to watch for Rosemary Smith and Lucette Pointet on the road ahead, their Cortina firing on only three pistons.

After Herat, the Marathon followed a 350-mile stretch of concrete road to Kandahar. Constructed by the Soviets and Americans in the 1960s, the road would surprise competitors because it appeared deserted. Days prior to the passage of the Marathon through the country, the King of Afghanistan, Mohammed Zahir Shah, had prohibited domestic traffic from using the two-lane highway and had even decreed that local drivers should not seek fuel for their vehicles until after the Marathon had passed through. Jeremy Delmar-Morgan, British co-driver of No. 56, the only SAAB in the event, recalled that "One of the problems on that road was we were really quite tired so we were hallucinating by that point. You were imagining people leaping out of the darkness at you the entire time and every now and again you came across a bonfire and you thought, oh, it's perfectly all right, it's at the side of the road, but other times you thought, oh God it's not, it's in the middle of the bloody road! And of course it was people who were using the tar to burn and keep themselves warm. They were literally sitting on the edge of the road or the middle of the road, with the tarmac alight, keeping themselves warm!"

For most competitors, the drive towards Kandahar was long, relatively fast and easy going, although obstacles and challenges awaited a few. Max Stahl, Bobby Buchanan-Michaelson and David Seigle-Morris began to realize their Mercedes was going no further while Harrison and Proudlock came to the aid of Rosemary and Lucette. In No. 44, the British Army Motoring Association duo Major Mike Bailey and Major Freddie Preston struck upon an ingenious if hair-raising solution to their Rover 2000TC's damaged rear suspension. While stopping to put gas in their red Lancia Fulvia, Italians Giancarlo Baghetti and Giorgio Bassi rushed to get back on the road and in doing so left behind a vital part of their paperwork. They resumed the 500-mile stretch past Kandahar and onwards to Kabul, oblivious to the fate that awaited them. Australians Ken Tubman and Jack Forrest encountered more juvenile rock-throwing, losing a headlamp from their Volvo, while in another Australian Volvo, Lister and Welinski had a high-speed blowout. Driving at 100 mph, Gerry recalled that "On the

On the road from Kandahar (courtesy John Hemsley).

Russian concrete road to Kandahar, we suffered ply separation due to heat and blew our right rear tire. This left us with only one spare to get to Kabul. I was worried that the tires may blow before we got to the Dunlop store, which was before the Kabul control, but the crowds were so thick that we couldn't see them and went straight past into the control." Failing to change tires would have consequences for the Amoco-backed Volvo 144S in the section out of Kabul.

The highway ran past Lashkar Gah and Kandahar before taking the Marathon northeast, still on the Russian-American road, for the 350-mile run to the next checkpoint at Kabul. Here, two more teams saw their goal of reaching Sydney collapse. First, the Australian Alfa Romeo lost its differential. Despite the best efforts of Bill Price in the BMC sweeper car, the Alfa eventually made it to New Delhi on the back of a flatbed truck where Theiler, McLeod and Lock found the supply of Alfa Romeo parts severely limited. Left with little they could do, No. 39 was out of the event.

The second crisis befell Germans Dieter Glemser and Martin Braungart, who had hustled their fast Ford 20MRS to an excellent sixth place overall at Teheran. However, despite their skill and determination, a broken camshaft meant too much time was needed to carry out repairs and continue and yet another high-profile factory team car was forced to retire. Elsewhere, No. 42, the unusual British Cortina Savage powered by a Ford Zodiac V-6 engine, began to struggle as a result of failing bearings in its gearbox, forcing the crew to nurse the car along using only its lower gears.

The route to Kabul took surviving cars up into the Hindu Kush mountains before arriving at a service stop where it was so cold that mechanics were forced to heat their supplies of engine oil to enable it to be poured into lubricant-starved engines. Next they descended to the city and the awaiting Marathon officials ready to stamp road books. It was here that Harrison and Proudlock untied the tow rope and waved Smith and Pointet away to coast down the hill. Meanwhile, No. 72, the maroon Cortina Lotus of Ernie McMillen, John L'Amie and Ian Drysdale was struggling with a faulty coil, eventually persuading a couple of tourists to donate theirs at Kabul, who in turn persuaded Davenport and Hunter to provide a replacement from the damaged Porsche. First car at the control was David McKay's Holden, the reward for which was, as *The Daily Express* reported, "a special gift from Sultan Mahmoud Ghazi of four magnificent Afghan coats."[4] Highest placed on points remained the outstanding pairing of Roger Clark and Ove Andersson, having still lost only six minutes throughout. German Gilbert Staepelaere and Finnish Simo Lampinen remained second overall with the Franco-Belgian duo of Jean-Claude Ogier and Lucien Bianchi still in third place. In fact, although ten cars would be officially retired in Kabul, 34 made it without losing any time at all.

It was here that Giancarlo Baghetti, the much favored Italian Formula One racing driver, realized his vital road book was missing as well as his passport. He was forced to turn the Fulvia around and dash back along the 500-mile route to where the documents must have been lost. Upon arrival, Baghetti and his co-driver Giorgio Bassi retrieved what they could, but the road book was gone. They raced back to Kabul, but without the road book, there was no alternative for the organizers but to disqualify the Italian team. It was also here that dreadful news awaited a British competitor, which eclipsed the competition into insignificance. No. 86, the single BMW in the Marathon, was being crewed by the British team of Colin Forsyth, James Rich and Robbie Uniacke. Upon arrival, Uniacke was notified that his wife Sally had

No. 42, the Ford Cortina Savage V-6 of Peter Graham, Leslie Morrish and Michael Woolley, before its transmission bearings perished (courtesy Mike Bailey).

been killed in a road traffic accident back in England. Uniacke immediately flew home, but Forsyth and Rich decided to continue, out of the event but determined to reach Bombay. In fact, the BMW and its remaining crew members were even allowed to board the ship to Perth and drive, out of competition, across to Sydney.

Competitors were now faced with a compulsory rest stop to ensure that the next section, the much-discussed Lataband Pass, could be crossed in daylight. Amid the crowds and resultant chaos, local police were barely able to control the throng and many an anxious moment ensued as service crews or private competitors set to work on cars where time allowed before all vehicles were placed securely in *parc fermé*. Kabul's Hotel Spinzar was packed with Marathon folk trying to relax or sleep or eat, in readiness for the next special stage along the 8,100-foot high mountain pass that connected Kabul and Jalalabad. During the many reconnoiters of the proposed route, the Lataband had been repeatedly cited as the point where competitors would either stand or fall. They were facing 47 miles of tortuous, twisting track carved into the mountainside, sheer rock face on one side, nothing but dizzying dropoffs on the other.

So anticipated was the Lataband section that, during the seven-hour break, Gerry Lister found a taxi driver willing to take him along the route in a bid to survey the challenges to come. As he explained, "I hailed a taxi, a Volga in Kabul and told the driver to take us to Sarobi. He headed for the main highway and I said we wanted to go via the Lataband Pass. He said it was too bad to drive. I then put him in the back and headed down what they called a road at a reasonably brisk speed, which wasn't very easy in a Volga—a dreadful Russian car.

No. 79, the VW of Pat and Tony Downs, made it to Sydney despite losing a fender (courtesy Bruce Thomas).

The poor cab driver was actually screaming in fear and crying a lot. We did not, however, hurt his taxi and we drove back from Sarobi on the main road." Disqualified Ford GB driver Gunnar Palm also explored the Pass, somehow finding a private car and following the route in order to make notes and pass them on to his still competing Ford teammates. However, what had been a treacherous, rocky track a few months previously bore little resemblance now. At the behest of the King, to show the rest of the watching world that Afghan roads weren't all perilous goat trails, the Pass had been graded, ironing out the bumps and boulders!

Last into Kabul were the two brothers, Pat and Tony Downs, in No. 79, the little VW 1200 bug, which was in desperate need of attention. They had smashed the car's oil pan, and although they incurred the maximum penalty points of 1,440, they were able to secure the services of Indemar, a local company serving as import agent for VW plus a range of other makes. Also receiving attention at the Indemar workshop was No. 91, John Bryson's injured Holden Belmont. By the time they reached Kabul, John explained that "The axles had been sharpened to pencil points where they fitted the differential housing." John watched as a mechanic took a sledge hammer to the VW's engine, the Downs brothers looking on in horror until the workshop foreman brushed a hand across his holstered pistol and suggested that the brothers leave the mechanic to his work. Returning to the workshop a few hours later, John recalled that, "The beetle is throbbing with power. The mechanics had welded the magnesium crankcase back together, which I thought some achievement. They upgraded the engine to 1500-cc [91.5 cubic inch] because they did not have the older 1200 parts. The beetle arrived in Sydney and the advertisements screamed 'London to Sydney without a spanner [wrench] on it.' Definitely not a single spanner—lots of them!" John, Bert Madden and Jack "Milko" Murray were able to collect their repaired Belmont and continue, but time spent at the workshop meant they had to miss the Lataband Pass and the Sarobi control and their problems were not yet over.

By the time the Kabul control closed, ten entrants were declared as retired or missing in action and out of the event. Running very late, but determined not to give up, were three young British men who had seen their progress severely hampered by a wayward bus in Teheran, a close encounter with the Iranian police and judicial system and 18 hours of repair work needed to get them going again.

19

We're Not Going Home

In 1969, under its popular brand name Corgi, the British toy company Mettoy produced a model of the Marathon winning Hillman Hunter. Three young British men came very close to seeing Mettoy's marketplace rival Meccano also produce a Marathon model. The toy car would have been produced in rally trim with various decals and, on each of its doors and the hood, the number "82." This would have been a model of the car that was entered by Duncan Bray, Peter Sugden and Simon Sladen. Duncan and Peter were 25 years old and Simon was 23.

Early in 1968, Simon and Peter met up for a drink in a London pub called The Australian. Brandishing a copy of *The Daily Express*, Simon pointed to an article about the newly announced London to Sydney Marathon and told Peter that this was something they just had to do. As Simon recalled, "Everything in England was pretty bloody depressing and, when you're in your early twenties, the idea of getting away and going somewhere else was quite exciting." An amateur racing driver, Peter didn't need any persuasion and immediately thought of his friend Duncan Bray, an excellent mechanic and a fellow racing enthusiast, both sharing a passion for Jaguar XK120s. A meeting was convened between the three and agreement was reached, so they filled in the application form and, together with the entrance fee, sent it off. Initially planning to drive a Triumph 2000 station wagon, they changed their minds when Duncan's step-father pointed out a used rally car for sale in *Autosport* magazine. For $2,000 the three men bought a 1967 Mark II Ford Cortina Lotus with a competition history, the seller claiming it had competed in that year's Tulip Rally. With a rally-prepared car in their possession, half the battle was won, or so they thought.

Minds turned to sponsorship as the men had only a limited budget to work with, so they approached Meccano, which produced Dinky Toys. As Simon recalled, "We went up and had a meeting with them. Dinky was owned by a family called Lines and there were various brothers. I'd never been into what I thought was a smart office and they had Dinky Toys absolutely everywhere. He said 'I think it's absolutely wonderful stuff, we'd love to do it,' to sponsor us completely, and we thought, gosh!" Meccano agreed to bankroll them to the amount of $12,000 with the condition that they be allowed to produce a model of the Cortina Lotus. Handshakes confirmed the deal and then the men contacted Ford GB to see what kind of assistance or support they might be able to offer them. Impressed by the men's agreement with Meccano, Ford GB suggested that Duncan, Simon and Peter approach the Alan Mann Racing Team, which had become a Ford factory team in 1964. On the back of Meccano's generous promise of funds, Alan Mann agreed to prepare the car for the Marathon.

Before taking the Cortina to Alan Mann, the men decided to drive up to Simon's family home in Oxfordshire for the weekend, during which, as Duncan recalled, Simon "took it out one evening to the pub and, going down one of the hills, he lost it, went straight off the road, into the ditch and it was quite badly damaged. Then, of course, you had to leave the car there and the next day, well all the wheels had gone." With tempers slightly frayed, they managed to recover the car to the Alan Mann workshop in the hope that they would be able to include repairs in the plan for preparing the car. Alan Mann began working on the Cortina, but, on inspecting the engine, it was clear that a major rebuild would be required as the former owner had obviously pushed it to the limit during its previous rally existence. To compound matters, as Peter explained, "We got a letter from Dinky Toys saying that there had been a change of management and they had been scrutinizing their expenses and they hadn't a clue who we were or why the previous management had done this or

Peter Sugden, November 24, 1968 (courtesy Simon Sladen).

whether we were even fit to drive. I mean it was quite a rude letter. They withdrew the sponsorship and so we were left high and dry." Fortunately for the men, both Ford and Alan Mann felt this was extremely poor behavior and therefore agreed to continue working on the Cortina.

Once the structural and mechanical work was complete, Duncan and Peter fitted out the interior of the car themselves, removing the rear bench and replacing it with a single seat, fitting a tank for drinking water and three five-gallon jerrycans to hold gasoline. As Simon was the least mechanically minded of the three, he took on the task of obtaining all the necessary international transit documents the men would need, following the guidance notes issued by Jack Sears' office, and trawling through London's cartographical shops to put together a portfolio of maps as a supplement to the official route notes supplied by Castrol. All three men had taken leaves of absence from their jobs and spent September and October putting the final touches to the Cortina, putting together food ration packs, practicing the changing of tires in the dark and trying to get themselves as fit as possible, running in London's Battersea Park and even practicing only sleeping for four hours at a time. Having managed to raise approximately $2,300 each to cover the cost of competing in the Marathon, they were determined to be as prepared as possible. Peter even painted a luminous orange flash along the white Cortina's lower bodywork and trunk edge as he had heard that some of the roads would be treacherous and wanted the car to be as visible as possible. As with most of the cars in the event, the hood was painted black to counter any glare from the sun.

Duncan recalled that he drove the Cortina to Crystal Palace on the morning of departure, meeting Simon and Peter at the stadium. During their 10,000 mile journey, Simon kept an audio-diary, in which he said of their experience at the beginning of the Marathon, "We left Crystal Palace in a blaze of hooting and people waving and cheering all the way out of the stadium and of people all the way through London, all the way down the road to Dover, really incredible, a fantastic sendoff, never seen anything like it. People just waving and cheering, flashing lights, everyone wishing us good luck, small kids, old people, young people, absolutely amazing." At Calais, local dignitaries had arranged a champagne reception for the 98 teams and, while the professional competitors sagely declined the offer of wine and *canapés*, Simon admitted that "We couldn't resist, just a little sip, but we did limit ourselves and went back and had a quiet kip [sleep] in the car."

Simon also acknowledged that having to navigate through the dark, fog-bound country lanes against the clock was certainly something the three were not used to and it all took a while for them to grow accustomed to driving in rally conditions. Their inexperience really manifested itself when, after a straightforward run through France and Italy, they arrived at the Hotel Metropole in Belgrade, checked into their hotel room and slept for five hours, arising to discover that Simon had left their route notes on the roof of the car. They were now missing, but Martin Maudling, competitor in Jim Gavin's Ford Escort, lent them his notes so Peter could copy them out, at least as far as the end of the first special stage in Turkey. Deciding to treat the whole thing as a lesson learned, they checked in at the Yugoslavian time control and set off for Bulgaria and Turkey beyond.

After the Istanbul control, competitors were required to take the small car ferry across the Bosporus and Simon recalled how they sat waiting in the pouring rain and strong winds as the boat's skipper took three attempts to line up the ferry before cars could embark. On the other side, they drove off the ferry into atrocious weather conditions and heavy early morning traffic. It wasn't long before all three men were glancing anxiously out of the car's windows as they passed the wrecked Valiant Safari of Peters Lumsden and Sargent. Near Ankara they spotted groups of children gathered along the roadside, apparently waving as Marathon cars sped by, but as they got closer, the children released a hail of rocks, which ricocheted off the Cortina, one actually cracking the windshield. Simon recounted how they passed other cars that had fallen victim to the onslaught, including the Japanese team's Vauxhall Viva GT, which had lost its windshield altogether. A greater challenge was waiting for them, however, on the first special stage between Sivas and Erzincan.

Halfway through the difficult 186-mile section, Duncan was driving and they were happily following No. 93, the Peugeot 404 driven by Irish rally driver John Cotton. Into a village and suddenly a rear wheel completely disengaged and bounced away. The Cortina screeched forward on three wheels, Duncan wrestling the steering wheel and realizing he had no brakes. The road began to descend into a series of corners so Duncan was forced to scrape the car along a wall to slow it down. The Cortina came to a stop and the men climbed out to inspect the damage, Simon recalling that only a generous nip from their brandy flask prevented him from fainting. Duncan explained that with "Ford differentials, the main bearing goes in and holds the rear wheel. It's only a press-fit and it actually pulled out, so as we were going into this corner, we picked up a cobblestone or something and it actually hauled the whole wheel out. The wheel came away with the brake drum, everything came out." The commotion quickly attracted attention from local folk and a crowd began to form, someone running back to retrieve the liberated rear wheel. In the dark and cold, with people pushing and shoving, Peter and Duncan got the car jacked up and the wheel refitted. Closing off the brake line, they were able to continue with braking on only three wheels, but the incident cost 239 points in Erzincan. They immediately sought assistance from the Ford service crew, taking their place alongside two other Cortinas that had also been damaged along the stage. Simon explained that "What had happened was that the little collar which holds all the bearings in onto the half shaft had slipped and the whole damn lot had come out. We hadn't discovered this little collar and consequently, all the way from our accident, all the way to Erzincan, we could only go at about 20 miles an hour and, every 15 or 20 miles, the thing would work its way loose and come out again."

On the way to Teheran the rear wheel again separated from the car and at one point Simon misjudged a U-turn trying to find a gas station and thumped the Cortina into a ditch, but they made the Iranian capital only 18 penalty points down. Straightaway they again sought assistance from Ford's service crew—Ford had agreed to come to the aid of any of their privately entered products throughout the Marathon, but only after factory-backed cars had been attended to. Then it was off on the 1,559-mile grind out of Iran and around Afghanistan to Kabul, but leaving the control point, they first had to get gasoline. At around 4:00 a.m., with Simon at the wheel, they set off through the rain-drenched Teheran streets, all on the lookout for the fuel dump that had been set up for competitors. Simon recalled, "It was a huge big main road with traffic lights and this bus just came straight across. The traffic lights were green, I still remember to this day." A local double-decker bus was on its way from the depot to begin its run through the city, but as it approached the intersection, its driver failed to yield. Simon hit the brakes, but it was too late and the Cortina slammed into the bus. Simon recalled, "We really thought this had to be the end. We were unbelievably depressed. The front end was completely staved in, the cow catcher was all right back, the offside front wheel was all shoved in and the bonnet [hood] was broken, cracked actually, it was a fiberglass bonnet and it really did look an absolute mess." Incredibly, no one was injured, so Duncan caught a ride back to the control point on a passing scooter and the police were summoned, leaving Peter and Simon to inspect the damage and try and prize the twisted metal away from the front wheels.

Thus began a nightmarish brush with the Iranian legal system as Simon was taken away by the police while Peter and Duncan got the smashed Cortina to a local Ford dealership, under the supervision of its owner who had accompanied Duncan back from the control. Simon was held for three hours, during which time the police fortunately determined that the fault lay with the bus driver. Next, Simon was bustled across to the courthouse, along with an interpreter, the bus driver and the bus conductor, where the judge took ten minutes to find the bus driver guilty. His innocence proven, Simon was taken to the Ford garage where the car was being repaired. As Simon explained, "When enough was stripped down, it was the most extraordinary procedure. A lorry [truck] drew up into the garage and they chained the rear of our car to a great big rolled steel joist, which was going vertically up the wall of the garage, and they chained the front of our car to the rear of this lorry and he took up the

No. 82 stops for fuel in Afghanistan (courtesy Simon Sladen).

slack and he charged, it was really quite spectacular. Eventually, after about six or seven of these charges, we managed to stretch the car back into some sort of recognizable shape." Under Duncan's supervision, the Ford mechanics also fixed the collars on the car's rear half shafts and took the cylinder head off, revealing hardly any valve clearance, the problem that was to haunt some of the Ford GB team Cortinas. Eighteen hours after the men had collided with the bus, No. 82 was again ready to get on its way. From that point onwards, the men would never again be able to steer the Cortina in a straight line.

Now hours behind most of the rest of the field, No. 82 made its way out of Iran and into Afghanistan, with Simon and Peter taking turns behind the wheel to allow Duncan to catch up on sleep in the back. Peter recalled, "Going along the Kandahar Highway and I was terrified of that because they'd said that there were these chains across the road and I thought that with our lights, you could easily get decapitated by one of these chains." With Duncan at the wheel, they sped on around Afghanistan until Duncan's exertions at the workshop in Teheran caught up with him. Peter explained that "We were plowing along this amazing road and it was the desert and there were mountains in the distance along both sides. It was really, really cold and Duncs fell asleep and the car veered off the road. We went down about six feet into a kind of a ditch and by some incredible stroke of luck, it didn't roll over." Fortunately, the ditch ran back up onto the road, so the men managed to extricate the Cortina, but all was not well with its suspension. Simon and Duncan spent two hours in the freezing cold repairing the damage while Peter slept in preparation for the drive to Kabul and onwards to Pakistan.

The team was now running so late that at the Pakistan border control on the Khyber

Pass, as Duncan recalled, "We couldn't believe it, we had soldiers and machine guns through the car windows, plenty of chains, and someone was raised from their bed, some officer came out. He said 'What do you want?' 'Well, we want to go through!' All these guns at each window! I'm not sure what the problem was there. The guy went and made a phone call and then said 'Okay, we'll take the chains off, go away,' so we crossed in the middle of the night and apparently, at that point, no one had ever crossed at night because, of course, it's too bloody dangerous, so someone made a decision to get us out of there—we could go and be killed somewhere else!"

Coming towards New Delhi, the Cortina began to misfire badly and the men only just managed to reach the control. Once again the Ford service team was sought out and this time, a faulty distributor was diagnosed. As Duncan explained, "We replaced that and then it ran perfectly. We also replaced the starter motor, which had managed to burn out in the morning trying to start the car. All in all they were really very helpful and for this day's work and about five mechanics, they charged absolutely nothing!" Restored, the team continued on to Bombay, despite the fact that now the clutch was giving up, and were officially recorded as the 72nd car home out of 72 qualifiers, but not before an anxious meeting between Tommy Sopwith and P&O to confirm that the original limit of 70 cars could be waived.

At Fremantle in Australia, No. 82 went through the obligatory inspection by the Australian authorities and, as Duncan explained, "They passed it! They must have thought, get this car out of Perth, out of the area, we don't want it. How on earth? That light was held on with wire!" At the Gloucester Park trotting track at Perth, Duncan, Peter and Simon were in

Simon Sladen and Peter Sugden in South Australia, December 1968 (courtesy Simon Sladen).

No. 82 at the Hindmarsh Station checkpoint (courtesy Bruce Thomas).

the final car to depart and had to suffer the indignity of having a microphone shoved through the window and being asked how it felt to be in last place.

Across the outback, the Cortina's valves really began to deteriorate and, eventually, the clutch completely perished. In addition, because of the extensive damage that had been inflicted on the Ford, one of the rubber blocks that damped the car's roll bar had deteriorated to the point where it repeatedly dislodged so, for 3,000 miles, Duncan was forced to stop again and again and hammer it back in. The team often found that at service points, most of the mechanics had packed up and left by the time they nursed the Ford in but, at Nowra, they found a service crew who located a "civilian" Cortina and stripped it of its master cylinder. At last they had a working clutch to get them to Sydney, but first they had to cope with the New South Wales police. As Duncan recalled, "There was an absolute police blitz on every car coming through. They were so rude and we just didn't understand any of this. We were so angry about it and we were stopped in Cooma and held at the side of the road. It was just so vile. You know—first question, 'Where did you do that, mate?' We said, 'Oh, Teheran.' 'Where's that, Western Australia?' That was the typical bloody response!"

As darkness fell on the Warwick Farm Raceway on December 17, 1968, one tired Ford Cortina Lotus and three tired young British men crossed the finish line. Having started in last place in Perth, they were finally classified as 53rd out of 56 finishers. Of the victory parade the following day, Simon recalled how "56 cars came into the city in this huge great procession. I mean it was ticker tape all the way through the city center, it was absolutely fantastic. We must have been near the end. My wife didn't know anything about cars and she was going somewhere in Sydney, she was working and she went out and couldn't work out why the roads were closed and all these cars—who are all these good looking young men? Most of them are from England. Little did she know that she would marry one of them!"

As the dust settled on the Marathon, all three men came to the conclusion that there was no reason for them to return to England, so they decided to stay on in Sydney, but they would all need to find financial support as soon as possible. Duncan Bray's solution was to find a buyer for the mangled Cortina. As Bob Holden recalled, "Cheeky bugger told me he needed the money to get back home! I never knew that he stayed. I rallied it—that got me started on the Fords." In fact, Bob Holden rebuilt the Cortina and rallied it for two years before selling it back to Duncan, who continued to rally it with Peter Sugden.

Looking back at the time he joined Duncan and Simon and took an ex-rally Cortina Lotus from London to Sydney, Peter Sugden said, "I think the highlight was finishing it. I mean it was a moment. Simon said this bit about going over the brow and seeing Kabul down below and this incredible mountain-scape. That is an image that made an incredible impression because it was dawn and it was a sight we had never seen the like of. The great thing for me with the Marathon was it completely changed my career in a big way and that was an incredible bonus from it. It also ingrained in me a love of car racing that has never gone away and I worked for the rest of my life to make enough money to be able to enjoy racing."

Over the years, Peter, Simon and Duncan remained great friends, even after Peter and Simon eventually returned to England. Duncan Bray died in October 2013, six months after sharing his memories of the 1968 London to Sydney Marathon.

20

A Million Broken Metatarsals

Marathon organizers had allowed one hour for competitors to cover the 47-mile stretch from Kabul to Sarobi, which meant teams would need to achieve an average speed of 47 mph over the treacherous mountain stage.

Some crews had gone to great lengths to reduce the weight of their cars, moving items from the trunk to inside the cabin, while some of the professional teams opted to shed all extra equipment they had been carrying, safe in the knowledge that their extensive network of service crews would be able to replenish supplies at Sarobi. As bleary eyed drivers and navigators returned to *parc fermé* to get ready for departure, David McKay, George Reynolds and David Liddle experienced a moment of high anxiety when their Holden Monaro, which had performed so superbly on the way to Kabul, now refused to start. *Parc fermé* rules prohibited crews from carrying out any kind of remedial work so the Australian team was forced to push the car out of the enclosure before hand-choking the engine into life, not once but three times before they managed to achieve steady idling revs. Filled with nervous relief, McKay gunned the Monaro away from the start, only to overdo a corner leaving the city, bouncing off a curb and damaging the steering.

First away, however, were Bill Bengry and Harry Firth, continuing their tussle of trying to either get or keep ahead of each other and therefore avoid the other car's trailing dust cloud. No. 1 sped away from the control just as the chilly dawn was breaking with the big Australian Ford V-8 engine roaring away 60 seconds later. Bengry's Cortina only just reached the beginning of the Pass before the big Falcon loomed in his mirrors. This was the section many had feared, the section that had defeated some of the earlier reconnaissance teams. This was the Lataband Pass.

Afghani authorities had closed the Pass to all but the Marathon cars and soldiers were stationed at strategic intervals to indicate the direction of travel. As the number of competitors entering the Pass increased, so did the clouds of dust thrown up by cars ahead. American driver Sid Dickson explained that "Whenever you see dust, you mash it. You've gotta get through it. You have to get through it, because every time you get through it, the guy behind you has to do it. That's how you leave people behind you." Innes Ireland wrote that "it was like driving through a real pea soup fog, but the difference was we were driving up to 90 mph with not the slightest idea of what lay ahead."[1]

What lay ahead was mile after mile of rocks, loose stones and unguarded turns. For many of the amateur competitors, it would be like driving on marbles, but for the experienced rally drivers it would be a chance to demonstrate their skill and fearless concentration as they worked hard to keep penalties to a minimum, sliding their vehicles into tight curves and sending showers of stones to either ricochet off vertical rock faces or disappear over the edge into the ravines below. As Andrew Cowan wrote, "Colin [Malkin] was really worried on this section, because I was trying hard and eventually he lay down on the back seat with two cushions over his head and didn't look."[2] The accepted etiquette of allowing quicker cars to pass was now being sorely stretched because as a car overtook, even more dust and debris was thrown up, all but blinding the following driver to the road ahead. Although graded, the road was really little more than a twisting stretch of compressed rubble, which began to play havoc with tires, wheels and shock absorbers as many a competitor discovered.

Gerry Lister and André Welinski were having a great run, although Gerry was only allowing André to get behind the wheel when absolutely necessary! Even though they had experienced a few mishaps thus far, in Kabul, they were running 23rd overall and only 50 points down on the leading car of Clark and Andersson. Having already completed an impromptu reconnaissance of the Pass the night before, Gerry was determined to put this prior knowledge to good use. As he recalled, "We're pounding through this and I'm keeping my fingers crossed for the tires. Something's going to go wrong sooner or later, tire separation with the heat and we blew a tire. I was crazy because I knew the road and we were doing well, so I had to find somewhere so I could jack the car up that wasn't in a foot of bloody sand. I finally did it. I lost probably two or three minutes doing it, so we got into Sarobi and amazingly only lost about 11 or 12 minutes I think. I was really happy."

Not so happy were the British crew members of No. 66. After a determined effort all the way into Afghanistan, Messrs. Buckingham, Lloyd and Hackleton saw their dream come to a shuddering halt on the Lataband when their privately entered Ford Cortina GT ran off the road. Fortunately, no one was injured, and although theirs would be the only retirement on this section, lesser dramas still befell many others, even some of the professional teams.

Ford Australia competitors Bruce Hodgson and Doug Rutherford were lying in sixth place in Kabul and were, in fact, the leading Australian entrants as they entered the Lataband. The Australian Ford Falcons were using speed-nuts to secure the wheels to the studs; steel springs wound around the studs to prevent the drum brake disengaging under stress. Earlier in the competition, No. 29 had had a wheel and tire change, but either the refit had been mishandled or someone had tampered with the speed-nuts at Kabul. As the Falcon hurtled over the Pass, Bruce noticed that the car's handling was becoming increasingly vague. Quickly finding somewhere to stop, he found in a hasty inspection that all of the speed-nuts were missing off one wheel. With the clock ticking, Bruce took a nut off each of the other wheels and completed the remainder of the stage with only three nuts holding each wheel in place. Max Stahl wrote that in Sarobi "a mechanic then pointed out one of the front wheels to Bruce, who saw that all of the stud holes had enlarged to three times their normal diameter!"[3] The emergency stop to remedy the wheel nuts meant that Bruce slipped to 11th place, with three Australian teams now ahead of him on points. Competition between the Australian drivers was definitely heating up.

One of the Australian crews that had moved ahead of Bruce Hodgson was that of Bob Holden and Laurie Graham in their Amoco Volvo 142S. They picked up just nine penalty points over the Lataband to secure tenth place at Sarobi, even though the Volvo's rear shock absorbers had collapsed. Another, Evan Green and "Gelignite" Jack Murray in their BMC Australia 1800, had been determined to make up time over the Pass and, despite the dust and

Service point at Sarobi, Afghanistan, November 30 (courtesy John Hemsley).

debris, had actually passed 13 cars, finally hurtling into the control minus their brakes after a rear pipe split. They incurred only eight points for their efforts. Polish ace Sobiesław Zasada was only five miles out from the control when the red Porsche 911 suffered a puncture. Too close to stop, Zasada kept the Porsche going and arrived at Sarobi on three tires and a rim!

Andrew Cowan's Hillman Hunter was very fast to Sarobi, losing only six minutes, but the other Rootes car was in trouble, sidelined on the Pass with a puncture caused by a faulty wheel spacer and no hub puller. When news of this got to Des O'Dell, Rootes team manager, he set off back to Kabul by means other than the actual route and bribed a police officer to take him into the Pass on his motorbike, but only once every competitor had cleared the section. Repair equipment strapped on tightly, the police motorcycle jolted and bounced all the way over the Pass and into Sarobi without finding the Hunter! It transpired that Rootes team service mechanic Derek Hughes had decided to walk into the Pass from Sarobi, find another police motorcyclist and persuade him to take Hughes to the car so he could carry out temporary repairs to get the RAF team to the control.

Cars continued to careen into Sarobi, some more the worse for wear than others, and the total skill of the professionals soon became evident as, although every car picked up penalty points on this stage and five cars incurred over 200 points, Clark and Andersson, Bianchi and Ogier, and Hopkirk, Nash and Poole were into Sarobi just five minutes after the allotted 47 minute allowance. As a result the Clark/Andersson Cortina Lotus remained out in front, with the German 20MRS of Staepelaere and Lampinen in second place and the Bianchi/Ogier Citroën in third.

After the excitement of the Lataband, the next section would take competitors past Jalalabad, over into Pakistan across the Khyber Pass to Peshawar, across to Lahore via Rawalpindi and then over the border into India and the next control in New Delhi. The route would be over 720 miles on partially paved roads, and after the Khyber Pass, would pose a dangerous combination of people, vehicles and animals, including elephants. Yet, even though the Marathon route notes warned of the conditions to be expected, no one was prepared for the huge numbers of excited Pakistani and Indian spectators awaiting them.

As with the Lataband, the Khyber Pass was closed at night to prevent travelers from encountering bandits, but it was also a relatively easy section along a paved road, affording a number of competitors the opportunity to stop and take photographs or be interviewed by television crews. The entrance to the Pass was marked by the border crossing between Afghanistan and Pakistan and it was soon clear that Marathon organizers and local authorities had worked extremely hard to make sure the competitors could move from one country to the next with ease and not a little style. As Innes Ireland wrote, "The setting was perfect, for it was in a clearing surrounded by trees with a huge gateway through a wall on the far side.... Set out on one side were long tables covered with pure white linen tablecloths and laid with dozens of cups and saucers...."[4]

The hard work and careful diplomacy undertaken months before by Jack Sears and Tommy Sopwith was again in evidence as team after team was offered tea while their documents and passports were processed in record time. Teams were also presented with a bugle-like horn to take with them as a souvenir and then it was up and away over the Pass itself, spectacular views at every turn and the occasional glimpse of ancient fortresses built during the conflicts of previous centuries.

As always on the route between Crystal Palace and Bombay, cars left in their numeric order, so first up into the Pass was the Ford Cortina GT of Bill Bengry, Arthur Brick and John Preddy, escorted by a guard car. As Brick wrote, "When we got over the top we had the leader of the biggest tribe in West Pakistan to ride with us for about 70 miles—right through his tribal area. His people were all lined up on the roadside to see us. He kept on asking me to slow down so that his people could see us—or perhaps see him—because he was just like a king. He had 150 servants and 15,000 odd whom he ruled and they had to give him half their earnings. It was a great honor to have him—but we were quite pleased to see him get out—as we were going much too slowly!"[5] Their attempts to keep ahead of Harry Firth in No. 2 suffered a setback, however, as the Ford's rear brakes failed, forcing them to stop, seal off the brakes and continue on to New Delhi with only the Cortina's front brakes at their disposal.

Towards the back of the field, No. 93 was still struggling. After their adventure on the end of a tow rope in Afghanistan and with only some make-do repairs in Kabul, Rosemary Smith and Lucette Pointet were continuing to nurse the sickly Ford Cortina Lotus along, determined to get to Bombay and hopefully a permanent remedy for the failing engine. Having opted to take an alternative route from Kabul to Sarobi, therefore avoiding the Lataband Pass, they had almost found themselves out of the event when, upon approaching the Sarobi control from a different direction from the other competitors, they were quickly flagged down and told that to do so would mean automatic disqualification. Given the choice of finding a way of entering the control correctly or accepting the maximum penalty points of 1,440 for missing the control altogether, Smith and Pointet chose the latter and carried on towards the border crossing at Torkham. Now onto the Pass, the Cortina was finding the steep inclines almost too much for its damaged pistons so Rosemary hit on an ingenious idea: "As my father

The Khyber Pass as seen from No. 44 (courtesy Mike Bailey).

told me many years before, if a car won't go forward it will always go in reverse, so I turned the car around and I reversed the entire way over the Khyber Pass!"[6]

From the Pass, the route descended to Peshawar and competitors were at first astonished and then alarmed as they began to encounter enormous crowds of onlookers pressing forward beyond the edge of the road, a hazard that would remain all the way across Pakistan and India. In fact a number of competitors recall the route to New Delhi as the least enjoyable of the whole Marathon as they struggled with the crowds, the chaotic traffic and the occasional political procession. David McKay wrote that at one point "we were reduced to walking pace. The engine overheated…. To stall in a mass of hepped-up Pakistanis who crowded around the silent giant in amazement was not very pleasant."[7] To make matters worse, some young Pakistanis took to congregating at the approaches to the many small towns along the route, running into the center of the road as a car approached and hurling sticks and rocks before beating a retreat at the last moment. In this way a number of cars were damaged as they attempted to dodge the missiles at speed, often losing side mirrors or auxiliary lights or receiving a cracked windshield. Near Siālkot, between Rawalpindi and Lahore, the Ireland Mercedes became caught up in a political rally, forcing them to take a detour to bypass the throng of marching people, which meant bouncing along what was little more than a track for three miles before rejoining the road again. Shortly afterwards, they were treated to the spectacle of a private motorist first tailgating them and then speeding past. Initially they thought this was just a local fanatic determined to race them, but they soon realized this was someone who was willing to clear the path ahead, often using death-defying tactics. This he did all the way to Lahore where astonishingly, he peeled off and another impromptu guide took over to lead No. 26 onwards. Unfortunately the second herald was less skilled than his predecessor and eventually collided simultaneously with a truck and an auto rickshaw.

Conditions continued in this chaotic fashion all the way to the border crossing between Pakistan and India. Driving into Lahore, a couple of crews adopted methods of clearing or distracting the crowds, all intent on seizing a souvenir off of a slow moving car. Bruce Hodgson and Doug Rutherford drove through the crowds alternately opening and closing their front doors to serve as great hinged shovels, while Des Praznovsky, Stan Zovko and Ian Inglis took to waving merrily from inside their Mercedes-Benz because if the crowd was waving back they weren't throwing rocks or snatching at windshield wipers! More than one driver experienced the discomforting sensation of bumping a tire over an injudiciously placed and often shoeless foot.

During Jacks Sears' reconnaissance, the logistics of securing swift passage between India and Pakistan had posed a particular challenge. In 1968 tensions between the two nations were as high as they are today. Only three years previously, both nations had entered into armed conflict for five weeks, so security at the border was fierce, often causing crossing times to take many hours. Yet the Marathon had once again caught the imagination of authorities, and so enthusiastic were both Indian and Pakistani officials that a crossing, which only days previously would have taken up to six hours, was achieved for competitors within a minute.

On the Indian side, organizing committee member Jack Kemsley was astounded to discover marquees and armchairs set up at the outpost, writing that "Tables were set out at which three people could sit so that Customs clearance could be handled with a minimum of delay. The boulders surrounding these tables were ... being dusted and painted by a squad of natives."[8] Cross-border cooperation was also very much in evidence; Nick Brittan wrote that "it came as a great shock when there was a power cut on the Pakistani side to find the Indians running a cable across to give them light to work by. Such unprecedented diplomacy achieved more in the name of international motorsports than many an intergovernmental intervention before or since!"[9]

Competitors slipped safely into India and set off on the 280-mile run to New Delhi, via Ferozepur, Ludhiana, Ambala and Karnal, again being forced to try and maintain the suggested average speed of 41 mph while avoiding collision with whatever wandered into the road ahead. Captain David Dollar in Mercedes-Benz No. 32 described the conditions as "Very narrow, built up tarmac strips down the middle with dropped shoulders. Lots of bullock carts and thousands of people in every village and town—it was positively dangerous as to stop would have resulted in being mobbed, albeit in a very friendly way, and keeping going brought the risk of running over someone, usually a child, probably squeezed in front of the car by hundreds pushing from behind. It is true that there was no police sympathy for anyone who was knocked down."

Ambitions were dashed for two more Fords on the run across Pakistan and into India when first the privately entered Cortina Lotus of Indian resident Freddy Bombelli and his Danish co-driver Tom Belsø suffered a blown engine in Pakistan and ended up arriving in Bombay on the back of a truck, courtesy of a complicated but congenial transfer at the border with India, and then No. 34, the Cortina Lotus of British pair Keith Brierley and Dave Skittrall suffered irreparable mechanical failure and could go no further. Both were declared missing in action at New Delhi and awarded maximum penalty points before eventually being formally retired by the time the rest of the field arrived at Bombay. Perhaps saddest of all, however, was the fate that awaited two Australian Amoco Volvo team members as they reached the final 50 miles before the New Delhi control. A runaway Indian Army truck plowed into the front of No. 63 and in one violent moment Bob Holden and Laurie Graham were both out of the event and into a local hospital for treatment of their injuries, receiving help from an unexpected benefactor.

At last, after negotiating motorized and non-motorized vehicles, assorted livestock and what seemed like millions of people, cars began to arrive in India's capital city and the control located by the Hotel Ranjit, but not before they had been forced to endure the almost uncontrollable crowds that lined the last few miles. More cyclists were upended by Marathon cars, first at the hands of the Australian pair Alec Gorshenin and Ian Bryson in their pagoda-roofed Mercedes-Benz 280SL and then by one of the two British Army Motoring Association Rover 2000TCs. Inching through the crowds and followed by the Andrew Cowan Hunter and the SAAB 95 station wagon of Alister Percy and Jeremy Delmar-Morgan, Major John Hemsley slammed on the brakes as both cycle and cyclist landed on the Rover's hood. Lightning-speed reflexes prevented a three-car collision. As the airborne biker appeared uninjured, the three cars continued on their way.

The majority of surviving entrants arrived well within the time allowance, which meant there was no change to the leader board at New Delhi and, once they managed to wrestle their way through the vast throng of people who massed around the hotel, thrilled to see the cars and crews in their city, they got their road books stamped by control officials and immediately headed off on the long journey towards the last stop before Australia.

A few cars needed urgent attention, however, as drivers coaxed them into the busy city— John Bryson, Bert Madden and Jack "Milko" Murray were now seriously considering the possibility that their Holden would go no further. John explained that the repair at Kabul had "got us through to Delhi, struggling to the dealer with the limited slip almost on its last legs as it worked to keep the wheels turning in city traffic." At the Delhi Holden dealership the men spotted "three dark green Monaros parked in a corner. Bert immediately set about liberating a differential, complete from wheel to wheel while we politely visited the Indonesian Ambassador. To say we were pleased when he agreed to let us have the part was an understatement. Just as well he was generous because the unit was fitted to our Holden before he even said yes!" The replacement differential had a different ratio, which meant that the Belmont's automatic transmission now offered vastly increased bottom end power. John commented that "We had the quickest acceleration in downtown Bombay you have ever seen. We made it as the last car on the boat; we made it with three hours to spare!" At Bombay No. 91 was placed 68th out of 72 surviving entrants.

Competition between the three Ford Australia team Falcons remained avid with Harry Firth, Graham Hoinville and Gary Chapman in seventh place at New Delhi, Bruce "Hoddo" Hodgson and Doug Rutherford only five points adrift in tenth place and Ian Vaughan, Bob Forsyth and Jack Ellis only six points behind in 11th place.

21

The Fighting Falcons (Part One)

Graham Hoinville began his motorsports career in 1949 at the wheel of a 1939 Singer Nine roadster and immediately stamped his mark on what would become 20 years of rally and circuit racing success. As he explained, "The first event in which I competed was just a club event, but I came equal first with a well known driver, Peter Damman, who was supported by the Citroën distributors and he ran a big Six Citroën, the six cylinder version of the Light Fifteen. He was a bit of a top rank and I drew with him and people said, 'Jesus!'" Given that Damman went on to win the first touring car race at the Bathurst race track in New South Wales in 1950, this was quite an achievement.

During the 1950s, Hoinville became a regular competitor on Australia's burgeoning rally circuit and it was during this time that he met and became great friends with Harry Firth, who was also to become a hugely successful track and rally driver as well as an expert in preparing racing and rally cars. In 1953, Graham and Harry teamed up for the first time to compete in the Australian Alpine Trial and won the event. The following year they entered the Australian Sun Rally and made it two for two. A motorsports partnership was born, which would last for the next 15 years, culminating in the 1968 London to Sydney Marathon.

By contrast, Ian Vaughan graduated from university in 1965 and immediately joined the Ford Motor Company of Australia as an engineer, with a brief period working for Ford of Britain. While still in school, Ian had begun to enter his own Ford Cortina into rallies with his brother Roger as navigator. A number of successes got him noticed by his employer's motorsports division and, as a result, he found himself joining the motorsports department as a driver. As he explained, "I got into the Ford Team; we were running anything from Cortinas, Falcons. We ran Falcons in the bigger, tougher rallies and the rallies here were pretty tough. I mean they were mud events in winter and dust events in summer and they really were car tests, so the car company was interested in that respect in that it was proving the car. You still had to get a result, you still had to drive fast, but the car was pretty tested, it did a lot for the reputation of the cars here in Australia."

Graham and Harry were already part of the Ford Competitions Team, having joined in 1961. As Graham recalled, "At that stage, '58, '59, we were an absolute pain in the arse to the Ford Rally Team. Ford was managed by the late Les Powell, who was quite a character, and they were running five Ford Anglias in the Victorian Trials and we kept beating them, which got up his skirt no end. We got an approach from Les Powell, who said, would you like to join our team? We said 'oh yeah, what's the incentive?' He said, well, Ford Australia has just introduced the first Ford Falcon,' which was a derivative of the middleweight USA car, redesigned. He said, 'We're taking five Ford Falcons to the East African Safari in Easter 1962. We'd like you to be in that.' You can imagine what the answer was!"

By 1968 Les Powell had been replaced by 26-year-old John Gowland and, as Ford of Australia had decided to enter three Ford Falcon XT GTs in the Marathon, it was Gowland's job to put together the teams that would crew the Falcons over the 10,000-mile event from London back to Sydney. A meeting with Harry and Graham was convened, where they discussed how many to take in each car. As Graham explained, "We'd immediately said we'd take the Falcon because we reckoned the Cortinas weren't capable of doing it. So we had a discussion with the crews and John said, 'Well, what do you two want to do?' Let's get a third bloke."

"I had contact with an Adelaide driver who was a very competent rally driver and navigator called Gary Chapman. We had contact competing against each other and I said I'll try and recruit Gary Chapman as our third member. That was our crew." For the second car, Ian was an ideal choice for Gowland, as was his regular navigator Bob Forsyth. Again the question of taking a third member was considered and this time Gowland selected Jack Ellis. As Ian recalled, "He was a seasoned competitor from Round Australias and East African Safaris, a very good long distance driver, sensible head and knew what a Falcon was, so I was well pleased to have him as my third man." For the third team, John had originally chosen former Victorian rally champion Frank Kilfoyle to drive with his regular navigator, Doug Rutherford, but when Kilfoyle announced that he was unable to compete, John had to find a replacement. What about that driver who had also been busy beating Ford Competitions team cars on events in New South Wales?

The Ford Australia Team. *Left to right:* **Bob Forsyth, Bruce "Hoddo" Hodgson, Gary Chapman (rear), Graham Hoinville, "Miss World" Penny Plummer, Doug Rutherford, John Gowland, Jack Ellis, Harry Firth, Ian Vaughan (courtesy Ian Vaughan).**

Thus, during one such event in 1968, John approached Bruce Hodgson and asked whether he'd be interested in joining the Ford team. Affectionately known as "Hoddo," Bruce didn't need to be asked twice and so was partnered with Doug Rutherford as a two man crew. The three cars were set. As Ian explained, "Bruce is the original bush boy and he made sure that it was absolutely reliable, so you can drive it through a copse of trees, which I did. You know, you run off the road, go through the trees, come out the other side and Bruce designs a car that can do that, so we have good, rough, tough rally preparations and that harks back to the Round Australians and the rallying that was going on."

Once the teams were agreed, John placed Harry in charge of preparing the cars at his garage business in Melbourne, the intention being that the teams would have the opportunity to test the finished Falcons at the Ford proving ground at Geelong, southwest of Melbourne, before they were flown over to London. Unfortunately, Harry's shop fell behind schedule to the point that when the cars arrived at London's Heathrow Airport, not only had none of the teams driven them but they were not quite finished.

As Harry struggled to get the Falcons ready, John turned his thoughts to reconnaissance, first of the Australian route and then the 7,000-mile section between London and Bombay. First he sent Bob Forsyth and Jack Ellis to investigate and notate the route from Sydney to Perth and then, although there was an agreement that Ford of Britain would survey the route to Bombay, after which the route notes would be swapped, John decided that the Ford Australia team needed to complete their own survey. As a result he sent Bruce to meet Bob in New Delhi where they were to pick up the ex-rally Cortina Lotus that Gunnar Palm and John Davenport had used to survey the route from London.

Next, once the remainder of the team arrived in London, he instructed Graham, Ian, Jack, Doug and Gary to pick up two British Ford Zephyrs, get them across to France and then survey the route to Istanbul where they would meet up with Bruce and Bob and return to London in convoy. Harry would also fly to London but would then set up shop and continue working on the Falcons. To give them a target at which to aim, John told them that they were to use the Carvair plane service to fly the Zephyrs over to France on a Monday, two weeks before the Marathon began, and that they were all booked into the Istanbul Hilton on the Wednesday night where they could expect to see Bruce and Bob.

Sure enough, the Zephyr team arrived in Istanbul late on the Wednesday afternoon, having driven non-stop from the French airport, and were reunited with the Cortina crew who had sped all the way from Delhi. The following day the three Fords set off back to France with more than a little incentive. As Graham explained, "Gowland was bloody shrewd and he said, if you can get back to Paris by Saturday night, you can have a night out on the town on Ford, because we were booked on the Carvair at two o'clock at Calais the Sunday afternoon." However, while the Zephyrs were in excellent condition, the Cortina, an ex-rally car, was suffering from the fact that it had already driven 7,000 miles from London to India and was now making the return journey—and Bruce hadn't exactly driven gently across Pakistan, Afghanistan and Iran. "Of course, everyone had to take their turn driving it," Graham recalled. "This was doing penance to drive the Lotus. So we're heading back, this must have been the Friday night, we're trundling across northern Italy, it was a left hand drive car too and Hoddo and I were driving it. Hoddo was sleeping and we're on about three inches of snow on bald rally tires, you see? I'm passing a truck, I think it was a Volvo, and all of a sudden there was a wallump and Hoddo wakes up. He said 'Are you awake?' I said 'I am now—I just touched the front wheel of the Volvo truck overtaking it!'" Despite the tired Cortina almost losing a rear axle in Italy, the Ford convoy made it to Paris in time for a night out in the city, and even though they all woke up to six inches of snow the following morning, the cars were finally loaded onto the Carvair and the team returned to London.

The Falcons were finally ready, and although they had been prepared to a standard specification, the three teams were able to request small variations to suit their driving methods and physical comfort. Ian explained that his car "had the third seat at the center of the back seat, looking through the middle and we had a little toilet in the back. We didn't actually use the toilet; I think we ended up giving it to some Indian beside the road." Bruce changed his spark plugs from carbon wire to solid and asked Harry to make sure that all the Falcons' gears were adapted to ensure oil could circulate adequately; months earlier he had discovered a potential flaw in his private Falcon's transmission and with John Gowland's blessing had worked out that apart from third, the gears needed to be re-machined to allow the flow of lubrication.

When the teams at last had a chance to test the cars, they took them to Ford GB's testing track at Boreham in Essex. By this time the Ford GB team's Cortina Lotuses were already prepared and tested and, despite working under the global Ford banner, national rivalry was stoked up when the British had their first sight of the large Falcons. Graham recalled how Bill Barnett from Ford GB's Competitions Department said "'Oh Jesus, your cars!' He said 'They're big and heavy, aren't they?' I said 'Yes, Bill, but they're strong.' I said 'Look, your Lotuses are all prepared. Do you believe they'll stand 10,000 miles hard driven?' He said 'Oh yes, we do 10,000 miles a season over here.' I said 'On the one engine?' 'Ah shit no, we change

No. 2, the Ford Falcon XT GT of Harry Firth, Graham Hoinville and Gary Chapman, at Crystal Palace, London, November 24 (author's collection).

the engine after every event.'" Graham and Harry had previously rallied a Cortina Lotus for a season in Australia, during which they noticed a reduction in performance. They inspected the exhaust valves and discovered they had almost closed up. By restoring the valve clearances the Ford's performance returned, but, at the Boreham track, Graham wondered how the British Cortina Lotuses would stand up to the relentless drive ahead.

However, thoughts of the British competition soon evaporated as the Australians were faced with a problem of their own. With all the modifications and increased capacity fuel tanks, the Falcons had put on a lot of weight, so when the drivers took the cars out onto the track and drove hard into the first corner, the Falcons' back ends came swinging out wide. How could they compensate the weight to restore the cars' handling? Graham quickly suggested increasing tire pressure and eventually, with 45 psi on the front and 50 at the rear, they achieved the handling they needed, even seeking assurances from Dunlop that the cars could run all the way to Australia on this amount of increased pressure.

Finally, November 24 arrived and in the starting lineup, Graham, Harry and Gary were assigned No. 2, Ian, Jack and Bob No. 26 and Bruce and Doug No. 29. Up front, Harry would go on to spend much of the run to Bombay doing everything he could to get past car No. 1, Bill Bengry's Cortina GT, as they left each time control. As the third car away, it was agreed that Bruce would carry additional axles as the Falcons' rear axles were different lengths. If Bruce passed either car in front, it was also agreed that he would pass the axle parts on. With this arrangement in place, all three cars set off for Dover and France beyond.

Apart from Bruce and Doug having a close shave with a patch of black ice in Paris when they took a wrong turn, the run down to Italy was uneventful for all three Fords. Heading into the Italian Alps, however, things went wrong for Ian. As he explained, "My gearbox started screaming and I thought shit, you've only made it to here and you're out here and how do you get some help on the gearbox? So we were sitting on the side of the road wondering what to do about it, should we go on or what?" As they were still running in sequence, Bruce was behind No. 24 so it wasn't long before he came across Ian, Jack and Bob with their Falcon up on a bank on the side of the road. He pulled over and Ian explained the problem. Bruce immediately knew what had happened and instructed them to run in third gear for an hour to allow the transmission to receive the required lubrication, something that could easily be achieved without losing time as the Falcons were still capable of high speeds in third. Both cars continued on through the Aosta tunnel, which allowed the oil in Ian's transmission to get down into the shaft. Sitting over breakfast at the Milan time control, however, Bruce began to wonder whether Harry had actually done what he had been asked back in London.

Out of Italy and into Yugoslavia, Harry and Bill Bengry were still enjoying their jousting at the front of the field but, with Doug at the wheel so Bruce could take a well-earned nap, No. 29 began to sound unhealthy as a screeching sound from the transmission jolted Bruce awake. He immediately instructed Doug to drop down into third and the noise faded away. No. 29 passed through three more countries before Bruce was able to undertake the necessary remedial work to the Falcon's gears, all the while unconvinced that No. 2 had experienced the same problem.

After miles of paved roads, the Australians finally had the opportunity to put their rally experience to the test on the Turkish stage between Sivas and Erzincan. How would the big Falcons perform against the smaller British and German Fords of Roger Clark and Gilbert Staepelaere on the first rally-proper stretch? Competitiveness between the Australians and

Left to right: **Jack Ellis, Bob Forsyth and Ian Vaughan with their No. 24 Falcon XT GT (courtesy Ian Vaughan).**

the Europeans was fierce—three years earlier BMC rally drivers Paddy Hopkirk and Rauno Aaltonen had gone out to Australia to compete in the Southern Cross Rally, which Harry and Graham had won. Memories had lasted and now the Europeans were determined to show the Australians just who was in charge on this side of the world and the 175-mile special stage in Turkey over narrow mountain tracks sometimes hardly wide enough for a single car would be the perfect place to achieve this.

The stage was certainly a wake-up call for Ian in No. 24, who explained that "Then there was this section, Sivas to Erzincan, which was where we all started to lose points and I was half asleep. We were driving along at the same pace I'd been driving for the last three days and all of a sudden in my mirror was Bruce Hodgson and I thought shit, he's supposed to be two cars back, what's he doing here? I suddenly thought, shit I've been asleep and I lost more points on that section than I should have. Really cost me the position at the end—I wasn't nearly competitive enough on that stage." Bruce and Doug had their own challenge to contend with on this stretch of the competition as earlier in Turkey with Doug at the wheel, No. 29 had hit a large dog that ran into the road. The collision sent the Falcon swerving into a steel stanchion on the roadside, denting a door and smashing all the auxiliary driving lights. The mountain stage to Erzincan would need to be navigated in darkness. Without a full complement of lights, Bruce knew he'd have to be at the top of his game.

Harry and Graham were too far ahead to catch, but as the cars bounced and skidded their way through gravel, mud and snow, Bruce was soon on Ian's tail. At the first opportunity, Ian let him pass, Bruce signaling that Ian should follow him to keep up. As Ian emphasized, "We weren't competing against each other. I was very much the team person; I wanted the team to win the team prize." However, despite the Australian Ford team's best efforts, the Europeans were able to claim victory at Erzincan. In No. 35, a Mercedes-Benz sedan, Australian Max Stahl had had a firsthand demonstration of how the Europeans dealt with tricky forest stages with British driver David Siegle-Morris at the wheel, stating that "At first I thought David was over his head, but soon I began to realize that this was the European style of tackling the loose stuff." At Erzincan, every surviving entrant had lost points, and although two of the three Falcons were in the top ten with Bruce losing 18 minutes, Harry down 20 minutes and Ian 25 minutes, it was British rally driver Roger Clark who had now stamped his authority on the event, losing only six points. As Ian commented, "Roger Clark and the boys are sprinting through the forests in very fast cars in Europe, you know, we couldn't match them for speed and the only way we could do well was with durability." Despite his achievement, Clark was hugely impressed with the way the Australians had handled the comparatively large Falcons through the mountains and made a point of telling Bruce, cementing a friendship that lasted until Clark's death in 1998.

Having seen their teammates beat them to Erzincan, Ian, Jack and Bob knew that they now needed to step up to the plate if they were going to make sure the Falcons had a chance of winning the team prize at Sydney. They had quickly adopted a routine of four-hour rotations between driving, navigating and sleeping, although as acknowledged fastest driver, it was Ian who would take the wheel on the shorter, more difficult sections, the next one being Afghanistan and the Lataband Pass. Similarly, Harry and Bruce had assumed responsibility

Kandahar fuel stop; the men are unidentified (courtesy Ian Vaughan).

as lead drivers in their cars. In this fashion, the Falcons pressed on out of Turkey, across Iran and into Afghanistan, improving or maintaining their positions in the rankings at each checkpoint. At Kabul, the gateway to the next special stage across the Lataband, Bruce was in sixth place, Harry only two points down in seventh and Ian up to 12th. At 4:44 am, Harry blasted away from the control, again hot in pursuit of Bill Bengry, almost but not quite getting ahead of him as the two Fords entered the Pass. Half an hour later it was Ian's turn, followed by Bruce ten minutes after that. Graham recalled, "The Lataband Pass wasn't too bad, it was loose but not big boulders," while Ian recalled "a fair bit of rocks and roughness." Their times to the next checkpoint at Sarobi were impressive, however, with No. 2 dropping only nine points and No. 24 only three points more. Bruce and Doug, however, were forced to make an unscheduled stop in the Pass as their Falcon had shed a number of wheel nuts, forcing them to borrow from the other three wheels and continue to Sarobi with an incomplete set all round. To say the least, Bruce was perplexed as to how these special self-retaining clips could have become dislodged. Whatever the reason, No. 29 had to accept the 18 point time penalty and as a result found itself out of the top ten. Now Harry, Graham and Gary were the leading Australians and the Amoco Volvo 142S of fellow Australians Bob Holden and Laurie Graham had moved ahead of Bruce and Doug. Increasing the pressure still further, Ian was now only one point behind as was another Australian team, *The Sydney Telegraph* Holden Monaro of rivals Barry Ferguson, Doug Chivas and Dave Johnson.

Ahead lay the Khyber Pass, Pakistan, India and, beyond that, 3,000 miles of home territory.

22

Close Shaves and Sacred Cows

On December 1, 1968, the British *Daily Express* reported that "India has opened its heart to the competitors in *The Daily Express* London to Sydney Marathon…. All the way through the cities hysterically enthusiastic people have crowded round the cars, blocked the roads—and even obscured road signs—in their desperate attempts to get near the weary drivers."[1]

For the most part, however, the agitated throngs in India seemed less mischievous, less menacing than those that competitors had encountered in Pakistan, although by their very volume they posed a huge challenge for the increasingly exhausted crews. Adding to the chaos was the perpetual flow of ox carts, bicycles and "sacred" cows that teemed along or across the almost 860-mile route to Bombay on India's west coast. As BMC GB team member Brian Culcheth's hand-written route notes state for the Delhi to Bombay section, "Beware of the cow. He has priority!!" and for John Sprinzel and Roy Fidler in the tiny MG Midget, the quantity of spectators was extraordinary. Sprinzel reported, "If there are 540 million Indians then I would estimate that 20 per cent of them were out to watch … our little Midget was practically torn apart by the eager young crowds."[2]

Seventy-four cars departed the Delhi time control, including No. 8, the Volvo 144S of Max Winkless and John Keran, which had earned over 10,000 penalty points since it broke down and needed major mechanical repairs in Yugoslavia. The car restored, Winkless and Keran had embarked on a high-speed, non-stop 64-hour chase to catch up with the field, determined that the Australian Volvo would be at the dockside ready for loading onto the ship home. The Land Rover of the British Army's 17th/21st Regiment plugged onwards, despite having its four-wheel-drive setup permanently disengaged to comply with regulations. Running on two-wheel-drive only, the heavy off-roader was anything but fast, but, as team leader Lieutenant Gavin Thompson said, "We don't have the speed but we shall arrive in Sydney in good shape while most of these flashy cars will be clapped out junk."[3] Last out of Delhi was the *Sydney Telegraph* women's team in their pink and white Morris 1100 S, which had lost so much time between Teheran and Kabul after troubles with the car's hydrolastic suspension and an incident with a donkey.

The route took competitors south towards Mathura and then on to Agra and Gwalior before turning southwest to Indore and finally the 360-mile run to Bombay. On the approaches to each town, the crowds swelled and countless police officers struggled to maintain control as cars inched past, often using long sticks to beat and physically restrain excited spectators. In Gwalior, one of the three French Simca Motors teams became a casualty. Crewed

The wrecked Simca 1100 of Roger Masson and Jean Py at Gwalior, India, December 1 (author's collection).

by racing driver Roger Masson and his navigator Jean Py, the Simca 1100 had been lying in 52nd place in Delhi, incurring points as a result of delays caused by a burst radiator in Turkey and then a broken CV joint on the Lataband Pass. Speeding at over 80 mph, Masson lost control of the Simca as it approached a railway bridge and smashed into a telephone post. Both Masson and Py were airlifted to the hospital but were later discharged, although the Simca was damaged beyond repair. This was the first of two extremely lucky escapes on the road to Bombay. Next in trouble was No. 96, the privately entered Ford Cortina 1600E of British pair Ronald Rogers and Alec Sheppard. Approaching Agra, a wayward truck forced Rogers to swerve off the road at Sikandra and the Cortina tumbled down a 20-foot bank. When it finally came to rest the Ford's roof was all but completely caved in. Incredibly, Sheppard escaped injury, while Rogers suffered a broken collar bone and the Cortina was totaled.

For many of the competitors the city of Indore was perhaps the most challenging point across India. Reduced to crawling speeds, drivers were forced to edge their cars forward through the crowds in first or second gear. *The Times of India* even reported that a 16-year-old boy had been knocked down by one of the competitors during the struggle to get through the city. David Liddle, mechanic in No. 36, was suddenly confronted by a young girl pushing her bicycle along between the line of cars and the crowds pushing forward. To Liddle's horror, the bicycle toppled and fell under the wheels of the big Monaro. Liddle slowly reversed off the bike and the girl dragged it away. Knowing that to get out of the car would mean being caught up in the mass of people craning forward, all that Liddle could do was keep going. As

Bombay welcome, December 1 (courtesy John Hemsley).

Gerry Lister eased his Volvo along he noticed that those closest to the car were reacting angrily and realized the cause was navigator Welinski's choice of hat. Such was the tension between India and Pakistan that, as Lister recalled, "This was where we removed André's *fez* because he looked like a Pakistani, but our car still took a bit of damage from rocks and other items that were thrown at us. My car still has the chromed rear quarter window trim showing a very large dent made from a piece of rock thrown by a spectator." In contrast to the chaos, No. 33, the heavily-laden Volvo 145S station wagon, and its all-women crew received unexpected and hugely welcome repair services from a local garage owner when they stopped to buy cold drinks in Indore.

At last, on December 1, 1968, the first cars arrived in Bombay and made for the final checkpoint at Ballard's Pier. First to arrive was No. 26, the Mercedes-Benz of Ireland, Taylor and Hedges, quite an achievement given that upon entering Bombay's city limits they had referred to their route notes, read the simple instruction to use a map to find the pier and then panicked because they didn't have a map of Bombay to follow. They were finally forced to stop a passing taxi and ask that the driver lead them to their final destination—and even then they were eight hours early! However, any amusement, relief and excitement would quickly turn to anger before the final car was accounted for.

Throughout the afternoon and into the evening, cars in various states of disrepair cruised or chugged into the city. No. 6, the Australian Ford Fairmont "survival car," arrived within the time limit and driver Brian Lawler found his team in 46th place overall and the Fairmont in desperate need of new shock absorbers. Heading to the service center, he noticed that the Ford Australia team mechanics were hard at work replacing the shocks on the Falcons. Lawler knew that as the Ford Australia Falcons had had a professional servicing team supporting them all the way to India, any discarded shocks would probably have plenty of life left in them. As they would fit the Fairmont, Lawler asked Harry Firth if he could have the ones being removed from No. 2. Firth said yes, but the team mechanics quickly intervened, as

Lawler recalled, claiming that "'We need those.' I said 'What do you need them for?' I said 'You've changed them every bloody chance you got, you put new shocks on.' I said 'We're running with the ones that left Sydney.' He said, 'No.'" Lawler's teammate Clyde Hodgins, a motoring journalist for *The Sun Herald*, was writing a column during the Marathon. Lawler explained that Hodgins "wrote up in the *Sun Herald* the fact that Ford would not give us a loan of their used shock absorbers. Bloody headlines that big, so by the time we got back to Perth, every shock absorber was there!"

In the early hours of December 2, the down-at-heel Cortina Savage crawled into the control, still only able to run in lower gears, while Rosemary Smith's Cortina Lotus clocked in on only three of the Ford's four cylinders. It would be another two days before new pistons and camshaft could be fitted by Ford technicians and, for a while, it was touch and go that Smith and Lucette Pointet would even be able to continue. By late Monday night, the number of cars that had been accounted for was fast approaching 70, 20 more than organizers had predicted, and a new administrative headache began to emerge. The P&O shipping company had emphatically stated that their liner the SS *Chusan* could accommodate no more than 70 cars in its hold. However, there was still a chance that a few more competitors could arrive, especially because once a car had formally checked in it was required to immediately go to *parc fermé* and, for some crews, urgent repairs were needed before their car was rendered off limits. Tommy Sopwith quickly contacted P&O to discuss further options, determined to ensure that as many cars as possible would cross the Indian Ocean.

Overall leaders Clark and Andersson then found themselves with their own problem to solve as somewhere during the previous seven days they had mislaid the Cortina Lotus's registration documents, a prerequisite for being loaded onto the ship (and being allowed off

Bombay, December 2 (courtesy John Hemsley).

again in Australia!). *The Daily Express* led with the headline "Marathon ace may be ruled out" and reported that "A desperate search began last night to get a copy of a car registration book to Bombay. It is needed to save Roger Clark, leader of The Daily Express London to Sydney Marathon, from disqualification."[4] Eventually, Ford GB team manager Henry Taylor cabled to his wife back in England to send out a copy, which arrived by airliner just in time.

For most of the crews it was party time in Bombay as they were invited to receptions, cocktail parties, dinners and award ceremonies. Onboard the docked *Chusan*, Clark and Andersson were awarded the Carreras Guard's Trophy and a prize of $4,285, while in downtown Bombay the India Oil Company presented Elsie Gadd, Jenny Tudor-Owen, Sheila Kemp and Anthea Castell with a prize for being the front-running women's team. The British women were surprised to find themselves benefitting from the much more experienced Smith and Pointet team's mechanical problems and No. 41's delays in Iran. However, when it came to rewarding the best-place private entry, Ireland, Taylor and Hedges were at first dismayed and then furious to learn that the honor had gone to the Anglo-Italian team of John Tallis and Paul Coltelloni for their effort in a Volvo 123GT.

All smiles for the press, Ireland immediately afterwards grabbed the first opportunity to complain to Tommy Sopwith, claiming that as his team had incurred 50 points to Tallis's 57, surely they should have won the award. Tommy recalled that the Benz "was quite clearly a works-supported team, because it was a Mercedes and I was a Mercedes dealer at the time and so I knew the people at the headquarters of Mercedes and this was purely a Mercedes Great Britain thing. I've not changed my mind!" The dispute was finally resolved in Sydney when the award was officially recorded as having been won by the Mercedes team, but by then, nobody cared who had won awards in India!

A different kind of dissatisfaction was reportedly being expressed by other private entries who complained that "According to the conditions and regulations publicized by the sponsors ... the original concept of the London-Bombay run was to be a non-stop marathon, but the works car entrants had several stop-overs where they rested in hotels before proceeding."[5] However wide the gulf was between the professional teams and the dogged amateurs, the number of entrants successfully reaching Bombay in the allowable time included a large number of privately entered cars.

Two late arrivals to the checkpoint brought the final total to 72 cars. Duncan Bray, Simon Sladen and Peter Sugden had managed to get their battered Cortina Lotus all the way from Teheran, despite falling behind the field after their encounter with a bus, and, once the lengthy repairs required in Turkey by No. 69, the little DAF 55 of the Dutch National Team, were completed, David van Lennep and Peter Hissink had soldiered on. Both entrants had amassed almost 11,000 points at Bombay and had an anxious wait to find out whether they would actually get to see their cabins on the *Chusan*. They were relieved to hear that they would, as were Colin Forsyth and James Rich. Marathon regulations stipulated that no car could continue in the event if it lost a team member, which meant that because of third crew member Robbie Uniacke's family tragedy and consequent return to England, Tommy had made the difficult decision to disqualify the BMW 2000. As Tommy explained, "Pressure was brought to bear, which I resisted, and it was not a popular decision. They were excluded. It came to the boil when we were in Bombay and I can remember that that was really controversial because it was the heart on one side and the head on the other." However, as a sympathetic gesture, the BMW was allowed to proceed to Australia out of competition so Forsyth and

Rich could at least be present at the finish. Unfortunately for another team there would be no such sympathy—Italians Baghetti and Bassi had carried on despite losing their road book in Afghanistan, and having gotten to Bombay before the control closed, their hope that they might be allowed to remain in the event was dashed and the ship sailed without the red Lancia aboard.

By December 4, 1968, 72 cars were parked in the dockside *parc fermé* where, in order to meet Australian regulations, they were comprehensively steam-cleaned before each was drained of gasoline and then pushed down to the quay to be loaded by crane into the *Chusan's* hold. Competitors would not have access to their vehicles until tires touched Australian ground at the western port of Fremantle. And so, with sirens wailing and paper streamers showering down on the waving well wishers, the 24,000 ton ocean liner cast off its moorings and 188 surviving contenders set sail, first for Colombo in Ceylon and then onwards to the next phase of the Marathon, the 3,000-mile section across Australia.

23

The Fighting Falcons (Part Two)

Having cruised across the Khyber Pass, the Falcon teams began to get their first taste of the crowds and chaos that would be the hallmark of the run all the way through Pakistan and India. Bruce Hodgson and Doug Rutherford adopted their novel method of clearing the crowds using the Falcon's front doors, while Ian Vaughan was daunted by the long lines of trucks heading along the same road as competitors, describing how "You pull out to pass a line of trucks, 15 trucks in a row, and after a while you get to realize the rules of the road. At the back of the trucks it always said 'please toot' and 'please toot' means it because when you get out there and you're halfway down the line of trucks and something comes down the road—you just toot and a hand would come out of the window and wave you in, makes a little spot for you and then out you go and off you go again."

The disaster that struck Bob Holden and Laurie Graham in their Volvo on the approach to New Delhi meant that Bruce and Doug were now back into the leading ten as they set off on the final section to Bombay and the ship crossing beyond. During this stretch, Bruce took the opportunity to sleep for an hour or two and as he dozed he half-listened as the Falcon thumped over the constant carpet of potholes. It was clear that the Ford's axle bearings were taking a pounding and, even though he had repaired the damage caused by losing the set of clips off the wheel in New Delhi, he decided that at the first opportunity he would make sure the Falcon's axles, front springs and shocks were all replaced in readiness for the haul across Australia. Bruce made sure this was carried out in Bombay, suggesting to Ian that he do likewise. Crucially, Harry Firth opted not to follow suit—when interviewed for the cameras in Bombay, he was asked "What have you got to do to your car No. 2 that's in such a very good place at this stage?" Harry replied, "What have we got to do to it? Nothing. New brake pads, new Dunlops, tighten the fan belt, give it a grease and change the oil."[1]

Following the seven-day voyage across the Indian Ocean, the Ford Falcons were at last back on home ground and the team knew this was their chance to seize the advantage. This was their territory; these were conditions that they knew better than any of the Europeans, the Russians, the Japanese or the Americans. This would be their chance to show the rest of the field what rallying in Australia was all about. As Ian explained, "In Australia I was much more confident, very much back on home ground, and we also sensed on the boat that the other guys were feeling nervous about it. They didn't know how rough Australia was and we told them great stories on the boat, how rough it was."

From Gloucester Park in Perth, cars now departed at three-minute intervals in the order of their ranking, so at 4:00 p.m. on December 14, Clark and Andersson did a circuit of the

Two of the Ford Australia team Ford Falcons at Bombay (courtesy Ian Vaughan).

No. 24 at Gloucester Park in Perth, Australia, December 14 (courtesy Ian Vaughan).

race track and set off for the outback crossing. Five more crews set off before Harry, Graham Hoinville and Gary Chapman sped away as the home crowd cheered for the leading Australian crew. Two more cars departed, including the BMC Australia team of Evan Green, "Gelignite" Jack Murray and George Shepheard, and then it was time for the other two Falcons—first Bruce and Doug, followed three minutes later by Ian, Jack Ellis and Bob Forsyth. All three crews knew they had a real chance of winning the team prize. Better yet, the individual prize was still up for grabs, with only 26 minutes separating Clark and Andersson in the lead from Ian, Jack and Bob in 11th place. Perhaps more than any of the other team members, Ian felt the responsibility that Ford of Australia had given him. The youngest by far, Ian recalled how "I felt a huge responsibility, I sort of felt, you know, I was an employee and my navigator, Bob Forsyth, worked in the assembly plant. It was on my shoulders. I didn't want to let the team down; I had my own personal reputation at stake as well as the company's."

The first 600 miles across the outback were uneventful for all three teams, but on the difficult section between Marvel Loch and Lake King, Bruce encountered something both completely unexpected and utterly infuriating. In motor rallying it was an accepted rule that, except in cases of emergency, service vehicles were not allowed on special stages during a competition. However, as No. 29 barreled along the 120-mile track in the pre-dawn darkness, it came up behind a ute.[2] It was immediately evident that this was a BMC service vehicle bouncing along through the scrub. Bruce had no choice but to slow down, Doug frantically searching for a space to pass on what was little more than a single car track lined on either side by mallee trees, the impenetrable stems making it impossible to find a way through. With his temper rising by the second, Bruce repeatedly bore down on the ute, lights ablaze, but the dust that was being thrown up by the errant vehicle severely hampered his vision. At the worst they knew they were 15 minutes off the target time but eventually the way ahead opened up into wide grassland and the ute pulled to one side, allowing the furious drive of No. 29 to continue unimpeded, finally reaching the tiny settlement of Lake King just seven minutes late. Bruce and Doug immediately put in a complaint, which allegedly led to Ford threatening to use their own service vehicles to police any further infringements. Bruce also realized that the next section, nearly 900 miles across the Nullarbor Plain, might provide an opportunity to get some payback, so he waited until the BMC ute departed, this time well within the rules as this was not classified as a special stage, and then set off in pursuit. Catching up to the ute he then used the sheer grunt of the heavy Ford V-8 to nudge the service vehicle off the road and into the bush!

Meanwhile, No. 2 and No. 24 had each lost only five points at Lake King, placing them seventh and ninth in the running. Ian was really beginning to come into his own now, and he explained that "Across Australia I was pushing it harder and harder. My two co-drivers told me, 'You're pushing it a bit harder, aren't you,' and I said, 'Is that a criticism? Are we going too fast?'"

Looking back, Ian believes that the Marvel Loch to Lake King section was the turning point for him as he plunged along the tunnel-like track, somehow allowing the eight-foot mallee trees on either side to keep forcing the car front and center as he pressed his foot harder on the gas pedal. The team prize constantly in his mind, he was also spurred on by John Gowland who maintained a presence at checkpoints or service stops and kept the team informed of the front runners' performance. In doing so, Ian began to get a picture of which cars and competitors had to be beaten. Back in London it had been clear who the favorites were, the 20 drivers who could win the event, and now it came as little surprise to hear that Clark, Cowan, Staepelaere and Hopkirk were leading the field. As for the Citroën and its Franco-Belgian crew, Ian recounted that "Bianchi, I don't know that I'd heard of. He was a Le Mans driver and various other things. I knew I couldn't catch Bianchi, I knew that from about five stages back, he was solemn and fast, the car seemed to be strong." Ian was also aware of who was catching up across the outback, not least the red Porsche of Zasada and Wachowski. The regular bulletins from Gowland spurred all three Falcons onwards across the desolate miles of the Australian outback.

After enduring the Nullarbor Plain, the next control was at the small coastal town of Ceduna in South Australia. Clark and Andersson were still leading with Harry seventh, Ian ninth and Bruce tenth, but by the time they reached Quorn in the South Australian Flinders Mountain Ranges things were beginning to change. For the first time in the event there was a new leader as Clark and Andersson lost 14 minutes on the relatively easy paved road from Ceduna. The German Ford team of Gilbert Staepelaere and Simo Lampinen were the new front runners, with Bianchi and Ogier in the blue Citroën just one point behind. As Ian recalled, "By that stage, from halfway across Australia, I knew Clark was a writeoff." Would the German Ford 20MRS hold together or go the same way as Clark's Cortina? As the Falcon drivers were being kept updated on events by Gowland, so they were also aware of each other's standing, all three crews determined to improve as they swept out of South Australia. At the tiny village of Gunbar in New South Wales, Bruce was amazed to see droves of people, many from his hometown of Griffith about 50 miles to the east, all there to wave him on.

The route now took the Marathon into the Victorian Alps, where, as Ian explained, "I felt even better and better, you know, I was back in my home country, I'm back where I do skiing. I know these roads, so there was a confidence factor there." At Edi, the final control before the alpine stretch, Harry was lying in sixth position, with Ian in eighth and Bruce in ninth and only nine points separating No. 2 and No. 29. They were now in pole position for the team prize as a wheel problem had cost BMC Australia team members Green, Murray and Shepheard 230 points on the road to Mingary over 600 miles back. Now Ian would throw everything he had at the next five sections over the mountains and down the other side to Numeralla in New South Wales.

Graham Hoinville knew both Ian and Bruce were closing on points and also knew that the 50-year-old Harry Firth was finding night driving difficult. He explained that he "was aware that Harry had a problem with declining night vision. At night he was not competitive. I'd not said a word. As we drove out of Wangaratta to get into the alpine section, Harry said that bugger cameraman discharged a flash in my face, which I think was true, but it affected his eyesight. So we go into the mountains, alpine sections, and we were slow. Harry was not the sort of bloke you could say that to." Meanwhile, all was not well in No. 29 as a navigation error cost precious points for Bruce and Doug when they took a wrong turn near Mount Beauty on the section between Brookside and Omeo and only a locked gate alerted them to the error. As a result, at the Omeo control, Ian was now in sixth place overall with Harry in seventh and Bruce cursing Doug's error in tenth.

There were now just 500 miles to go with five more checkpoints before the finish at Sydney. Gowland was continuing to keep them informed of the performance and standings of other competitors and none of them ignored the magnificent performance that Zasada was achieving in his Porsche. After Omeo the route continued eastwards for approximately

100 miles and then turned northwards over the Snowy Mountains and into New South Wales. A disastrous section for Clark and Andersson meant that at Murrindal Ian was now in fifth position with Harry one minute behind in sixth and Bruce in ninth. The red Porsche was now really threatening, just one point behind Harry and two behind Ian as just before dawn the cars sped on over the Snowy Mountains towards Ingebryra. Perhaps because of tiredness, perhaps because of the lack of daylight, but having incurred penalty points just twice between London and Bombay, Harry lost minutes for the fourth time in Australia on this stretch. Even more significantly, Ian and Bruce did not, but worse was to come for the wily Fox on the penultimate competitive stage before Sydney and the finishing line.

During the relatively short but difficult 35-mile section from Numeralla to the tiny homestead of Hindmarsh Station, No. 2 suffered a mechanical setback. Graham explained, "We did a rear wheel bearing, which seized and let the axle disengage from the diff, so we came to a standstill. Hoddo was half an hour behind us, he had the axles. We just had to sit. We had the car jacked up, we had the axles out. The bearings seized; they're low quality semi-floating axles and when the bearing seizes, it deflects the shrink ring and the axle comes out." At Numeralla they had been in seventh place, but the bearing failure cost them 56 minutes and by the time they rolled into Hindmarsh, No. 2 had slipped to ninth overall while Ian was now in fourth place and Bruce in seventh. There was just one timed section remaining.

On the shock of realizing that Bianchi and Ogier had crashed on the section to Nowra, Ian recalled that "we knew when we passed it on the side of the road, it was in front of us on the road and the accident had happened. I would guess we were ten minutes behind and things were being done to look after the driver when we were there, we didn't feel we had to stop. It was amazing, I only thought what bad luck because you could see the Mini there and what had happened, bloody head-on in the road. Then we started to do our sums and, well, there's the Hillman Hunter and the Austin 1800 and we might get third if we can get this bloody heap doing it. We were shocked, you know, what does this mean, you know, isn't that bad luck, bad management, whatever. But it did destabilize your concentration." As a result of this catastrophe, Ian, Jack and Bob arrived at the Warwick Farm Raceway in third place overall with Bruce and Doug in sixth and Harry, Graham and Gary in eighth. Their performance won the team prize for the Ford Motor Company of Australia and, for Ian, Jack and Bob, the honor of being the highest placed Australians.

In third place: (*from left*) Jack Ellis, Ian Vaughan and Bob Forsyth at Warwick Farm Raceway. December 17 (courtesy Ian Vaughan).

On the highlights of the 1968 London to Sydney Marathon, Ian reflected, "There are two stages I remember as my high points. One was that Lake King section in Australia, where I think I discovered that I could be almost as fast as these Europeans, and there was one of the stages in the Australian Alps when I had the bit between my teeth. I knew what the requirements were, you know, to stay in my position and things were going well. I remember Bob Forsyth telling me, Ian you're going faster and faster and it was sort of, that's good, but because they knew the pressure that was on me and it's the old story with motorsports, you want to press it up to the limit but you certainly can't afford to go beyond."

Bruce "Hoddo" Hodgson, Ian Vaughan and Graham Hoinville continued competing in rallies after 1968 and both Ian and Bruce entered the 25th anniversary London to Sydney Marathon in 1993. In 2011, Graham Hoinville was awarded the Order of Australia Medal by HRH Queen Elizabeth for services to motorsports. Harry Firth passed away in April 2014 just nine days after his 96th birthday.

24

Shenanigans at Sea

In Fremantle, when asked by BBC television reporters how he'd found the nine-day voyage aboard the SS *Chusan*, BMC GB team competitor Paddy Hopkirk said he thought "the sea journey was the best advertisement for air travel ever."[1] Given that they had seen their involvement in the Marathon as a major PR opportunity, P&O were less than pleased as Hopkirk's comment played out on television sets around the world!

For most Marathon competitors, embarkation meant the chance to catch up on sleep after seven days of fitful napping inside a jolting, skidding, rocking rally car. At least one driver was also afflicted with a severe case of "Delhi-belly" as the ocean liner set sail—Australian Alec Gorshenin was particularly laid low by sickness and confined to his cabin for most of the trip. However, apart from recuperation, this was the first time crews could socialize with their rivals, swap stories and find out what had happened elsewhere on the run from London to Bombay. Stewart McLeod, whose Alfa Romeo had broken down beyond repair in Iran, tried without success to sell his detailed Australian route notes, while Australian motorsports journalist and disqualified participant Max Stahl grabbed the opportunity to spend time talking to drivers, navigators and mechanics during the voyage, which in turn allowed him to write his comprehensive account of the Marathon in his magazine *Racing Car News*.

Those wealthy enough to meet the additional cost had arranged for wives and, in Jean Denton's case, husbands to join them on the ship. As preparations for the Marathon had included sending luggage on ahead, fresh clothing awaited crews in their first class cabins. Suitably attired, they were treated to a short stop at Ceylon (now Sri Lanka) and the island country's largest city, Colombo. Ceylon was a scheduled stop for the *Chusan*, which had made the diversion to Bombay as a special arrangement for the Marathon. The ship anchored in the harbor and a flotilla of boats transported passengers to the harbor side where they were greeted by members of the local motoring club who set off in convoys to show competitors the sights of the city. In the evening, the festivities transferred 12 miles down the coast to the Mount Lavinia Hotel where the crews were treated to a Kandyan dance display and dinner overlooking the ocean. As Brittan wrote, "all this from a country that was not even on the Marathon route. The hospitality was tremendous."[2]

Once sleep had been caught up on, apart from the impromptu diversion to Ceylon, what began as a pleasant, relaxing cruise quickly turned to boredom as competitors struggled to find things to keep them occupied. Poker games sprang up and for some, the steady flow of alcoholic beverages soon led to mischief making. P&O operated a two-class system on its ocean liner and it didn't take long for some of the more high-spirited rally men to notice a large contingency of young Australian women traveling in second class on their way home from England for Christmas. Although not exactly segregated by *Titanic*-like gates and chains, it was still not the "done thing" for second class passengers to enter first class or even worse, for the opposite exchange to occur. Regardless, foot traffic between classes began to increase until Captain Ralph Nowell decided to hold a formal event to allow first and second class passengers to come together for drinks, vainly hoping this would diffuse the situation. The ship's open air swimming pool also became a focal point for many and not always during daylight hours. As Graham Hoinville recalled, "There were fun and games in the pool and every so often, a bikini would go over the side of the *Chusan*. Dodging the gate that separated first and second, that became a bit of a sport. I go into the bar to get a drink, I looked out the window and I thought I saw a naked girl go past and I thought ah, it's the grog. Anyway, at that stage Rosemary Smith walks in wearing a

Rosemary Smith onboard the SS *Chusan* (courtesy Mike Wood).

bikini. I said, 'Hello Rosemary.' She said she might have a dip in the pool. I said, 'Well Rosemary, if you go into that pool, I can tell you this. You will lose your bikini.' She said 'Oh well, what will be will be!'" Minny Macdonald, a member of *The Sydney Telegraph* Morris 1100 S team recalled that the British were probably the main instigators of mayhem, saying, "I remember drunken poms constantly took each other's clothes off and threw each other in the pool!"

Elsewhere, a number of the Australian competitors saw an opportunity to unnerve some of their European rivals with tales of what they could expect in the outback. As American competitor Sid Dickson recalled, "'Gelignite' Jack Murray and all of them were trying to scare everybody about Australia, trying to get everybody psyched up so they would screw up." Murray's stories grew increasingly tall as the voyage progressed, regaling those present with warnings of eight-foot kangaroos, deep craters and even worse, the terrifying "bunyip" that could cause havoc for an unsuspecting rally driver negotiating the dusty tracks across Australia. Unbeknownst to some of those listening, Murray's bunyip is actually a fictitious beast deeply woven into the fabric of Aboriginal mythology. Not content with just telling tales after dinner, Murray also organized physical exercise sessions on deck and even turned his attention to one of his favorite water sports. As Gerry Lister recalled, "He arranged that he was going to water ski behind the *Chusan* and he got the timber down below, but somebody woke up

Crowds welcome the Marathon teams at Fremantle, Western Australia, December 13 (courtesy Martin Proudlock).

and said 'Hang on, what if you fall off? It's going to take us a week to turn around!'" Perhaps ironically, for all of his warnings about giant kangaroos and mischievous wombats, in Australia the first car to actually collide with a large marsupial was No. 31, the BMC Australia 1800 driven by Evan Green and "Gelignite" Jack Murray!

As Marathon competitors were sharing the ship's first class facilities with ordinary, fee-paying passengers, it didn't take long for a number of complaints to reach Captain Nowell and it fell to Jack Kemsley to adopt the role of mediator between a concerned master mariner and the rally crews. Joining Nowell for dinner one evening, Kemsley was appraised of the situation and the worrying fact that "many of the lads had already found their way below into tourist class and the bars were overcrowded, making usual service difficult to maintain."[3] In the interest of good public relations Kemsley and David Benson, motoring editor for *The Daily Express*, agreed to meet with Captain Nowell each morning thereafter to try and solve any issues arising, although there was little they could do when three young British men were discovered as stowaways. David Price, Spencer Thornton and Bernard Cairns had been on a hitchhiking trip around the world when they ran out of money in India and decided to sneak onto the SS *Chusan*. All three promised to pay P&O for their fares as soon as they found jobs back in England.

Carousing and fraternizing with 300 young Australian women in second class wasn't to everyone's taste, however, and many other Marathon participants kept a lower profile on the voyage. Hampered by the language barrier, the ten-strong Russian Moskvič team kept themselves to themselves, often to be seen crowded around maps of Australia, carefully studying both route and route notes. For the most part, Sid Dickson abstained from the party scene, explaining that "We didn't want to get sidetracked, we had investment in the race itself and doing well in our performance and resting and staying healthy and staying out of trouble, so we stayed on message." This didn't prevent Sid from becoming the voyage's only casualty, however, as during a game of deck tennis he broke a toe. "We practically knocked a house down in Turkey and I survived that, then go and do a thing like this," he lamented.[4] Whether or not American teammate and CBS camera man Jerry Sims complied with Dickson's doctrine is unknown, but the voyage did afford him the opportunity to get to know British Volvo station wagon crew member Jenny Tudor-Owen. After the Marathon was over, the pair would go on to marry and settle in the United States.

Eventually the liner began to plow its way towards Australia's western coast and competitors spent the remaining time preparing for what was to come, reviewing documents and notes or discussing their plans of attack. On its final approach to the port of Fremantle on December 13, 1968, the *Chusan* was escorted by an assortment of press launches and other private craft, its passengers now eager to disembark. For many, these were their first glimpses of Australia, the December sunshine highlighting an enormous blue sky and sparkling waters. For others, it was quite simply "home," Minny Macdonald writing that "The Australians among us, their faces split by enormous grins, were pressed to the windows…. All morning we have had to restrain ourselves from singing 'Advance Australia Fair.'"[5]

Crowds lined the dockside and harbor buildings, although these seemed minimal after the teeming masses in Pakistan and India, while journalists and television crews got ready to thrust microphones and cameras at the Marathon crews. Max Stahl commented, "Drivers who considered themselves rank amateurs were suddenly thrust into the limelight alongside the established stars."[6] Finally, the gangplanks were lowered and the *Chusan*'s 2,000 passengers began to descend while journalists ascended, determined to seek out a scoop or two. Meanwhile, the Fremantle stevedores began the process of unloading Marathon cars, buoyed up by the fact that an 18-gallon barrel of beer had been presented to them as a gift from the Marathon crews. Whether this was a help or a hindrance is debatable, but once all cars had been crane-lifted over the side of the ship and deposited on the wharf, a number were definitely the worse for wear. Film footage shows the Bianchi/Ogier Citroën bumping against the superstructure of a crane as it's lowered to the ground, and John Smailes wrote that "The entire Australian Ford Falcon team was dented front and rear as the cars crashed against the steel side of the hold."[7]

While competitors entertained or suffered the media on route to the hotels in which they would be staying before the restart of the Marathon the following day, after another round of steam-cleaning police and customs officials began clambering over the newly arrived automobiles, searching for any modifications or defects that might put a car on the wrong side of Western Australian state authorities' acceptance criteria for roadworthiness. Of the 72 cars still in competition, 16 were issued defect notices, which meant varying amounts of repairs or corrective measures would need to be expeditiously carried out if they were to be all present and correct at Perth's Gloucester Park trotting track the next day. The authorities were unhappy with cars having sirens or flashing lights and instructed that these be removed, while other cars would need to have any broken light glass repaired. However, Marathon regulations meant that once they had been scrutinized, all cars needed to enter *parc fermé* until just before it was time to set off on the next section, and although a crew could enter to fix a

No. 1 swings free of the SS *Chusan* at Fremantle (courtesy Colin Cleaver).

defect, for every minute they took, they would be awarded a penalty point. To show that the police meant business, they were also setting up their own control point on the way out of Perth and were expecting every car with a defect notice to report there and evidence the required remedial work. This was the competitors' first taste of how the Australian police would be reacting to the Marathon as it moved across the country.

Once the cars had been cleaned and inspected, the teams set off in a police-escorted, high-speed convoy to drive the 20 miles to Perth. Western Australian speed limits had been repeatedly drummed into competitors' heads with the recurrent message that police would be strict and rigid, a fact that Zasada and Wachowski were reminded of when on the drive up to Perth, they found themselves the first but definitely not the last Marathon entry to be ticketed for speeding by the Australian forces. As the convoy followed the Kwinana freeway, some cars became a little spread out and "a private car was able to cut in. The car travelled with the convoy over the Narrows Bridge and along Riverside Drive, but when the convoy turned left onto Plain Street, the car continued straight on—followed by the last 20 rally cars."[8] The police escorts were forced to chase after them and get them turned around!

The Marathon convoy was expected at the Gloucester Park trotting track so that they could do a lap of honor before the spectators who had been watching horse racing. British competitor Anthea Castell remembered that "We arrived at about 11 o'clock in the evening, after the horse racing had finished, but the problem was that all the spectators left the race course at the same time as the horses. Nobody bothered to stay and watch the rally cars!" Finally, the cars were placed in *parc fermé* at the side of the track.

On December 14, 1968, 25,000 people crowded into Gloucester Park to watch the fes-

Cars and competitors line up at Gloucester Park trotting track, Perth, Western Australia, December 14 (courtesy John Hemsley).

tivities, enjoying the spectacle of 72 multi-colored Marathon cars lining up in an arc around the edge of the oval track in order of their standing. Under a bright sun, competitors milled about, anxiously waiting for the moment when they could open a car door and climb aboard— *parc fermé* rules remained in place until thirty minutes before departure time. As at Crystal Palace 20 days before, spectators were entertained by various displays and demonstrations. Marching bands, judo and fencing presentations and an attempt to break the world record for the longest trampolining attempt were all on offer as cameras clicked and Marathon crews posed for photographs. In the final half hour, Western Australian State Premier David Brand, Federal opposition leader Gough Whitlam and Penny Plummer's successor to the title of Miss Australia, Suzanne McLennan, took their positions to flag the cars away. As the minutes ticked towards 4:00 p.m., six marching girls in bright red miniskirts led the Cortina Lotus of Roger Clark and Ove Andersson to the starting line, and exactly on the hour, Brand waved his flag and leading No. 48 roared off around the track, followed three minutes later by No. 57, the German 20MRS of Staepelaere and Lampinen. The crowds whooped and clapped as Paddy Hopkirk managed a sideways skid around the circuit, but the loudest cries were saved for the leading Australian team of Firth, Hoinville and Chapman. Jack Murray let off his customary stick or two of "Gelignite" as throughout the hot afternoon, cars were flagged away until, over two and half hours after Clark had departed, Duncan Bray floored his crumpled Cortina's gas pedal and No. 82 was gone. The Australian section had begun and ahead lay 3,000 miles of rugged terrain, hazards of flora and fauna, barely visible rutted track, the much-touted "horror stretch" between Marvel Loch and Lake King and worst of all—dust.

Six minutes prior to Bray's last-place departure, the car that took its turn to hurtle around the track before disappearing out into the streets of Perth had defied all the odds to be there at all. Eighteen days previously, 100 miles southeast of Belgrade in Yugoslavia, the Australian two-man team of Max Winkless and John Keran had suffered a potentially catastrophic mechanical failure in their Volvo 144S. Having somehow managed to get the Amoco Oil Company–backed car repaired, they had raced non-stop to catch up with the field in time to qualify for the onward passage to Perth.

25

A Tale of Two Volvos (Part One)

Reflecting on rallying as a motorsport in Australia, Max Winkless explained, "It's always been very light here, always. It's never been a thing, except in the fifties there were the Redex Trials and they were bigger than *Ben-Hur*. I would say the first three Redex Trials were actually bigger than the London [to] Sydney Marathon for the press and unbelievable. I went in five of those, it was great." Max's introduction to rallies came in 1949 when he was working as an interstate truck driver for the Antill Ranger trucking company, the owner of which, Peter Antill, had been competing in motorsports in Australia since before World War II and in 1947 and 1948 had won the Australian Castrol Rally. For the 1949 event, Peter's usual navigator wasn't available so he asked the 21-year-old Max if he could read a map. They went on to win the event and thus began a very successful partnership, despite the fact that Max was constantly plagued with car sickness. They competed in five Round Australia events, of which Max recalled, "In those days, it was as much endurance as anything. Keeping awake, because it would be 36 hours, drive there, drive back again. No support cars, anything like that."

Max was appointed manager for Antill Ranger's New South Wales region in 1952 and three years later became general manager. In the late 1950s, the composition of Antill Ranger evolved until in 1961, it was acquired by a bigger trucking company, Mayne Nickless. Neither Peter nor Max wanted to work for such a large organization so they branched off and set up their own truck sales and servicing company. Four years later, Volvo in Sweden appointed them as licensed importers of Volvo products for New South Wales, Queensland and South Australia and as a result Max began both a commercial and competitive relationship with Volvo cars, which culminated three years later when he became New South Wales Rally Champion in 1968. By now Max was also managing director of Volvo Australia and as well as occasionally competing in events with the managing director of the Amoco Oil Company, he had also established a good working relationship with Volvo personnel in Sweden. Having decided he wanted to compete in the recently announced London to Sydney Marathon in a Volvo, he learned from his co-driver that Amoco had expressed interest in sponsoring Gerry Lister and André Welinski in a Volvo for the Marathon, so Max successfully proposed that they sponsor two cars with him as a driver. Initially deciding to run a two-door 142 model in the Marathon, Volvo Sweden suggested that instead he choose a four-door 144 as the chassis would be much stronger. Eventually, Amoco backed three S-model Volvos, two 144s and a 142. They would also support a fourth 144 to be sponsored by the Western Australian television news station TVW-7.

In the late fifties and early sixties, Volvo had established a successful presence in international rallying and touring car races, scoring class and outright wins across Europe, in Canada and in Australia when in 1964, Gerry Lister scored a class win at the 4 Hour Sandown race in a 122S. However, during the 1966 Acropolis Rally in Greece, two Volvo team mechanics were killed when they were hit by a car and Volvo decided to withdraw from motorsports, although they were still prepared to support private rally drivers. For the 1968 London to Sydney Marathon they provided extensive assistance in preparing the cars for the event. They were also very keen to investigate the effects of endurance rallying on their products. When Max first drove a Volvo from Sydney to Perth to assess its durability and then took a Swedish Volvo engineer from Perth to Darwin, over endless corrugated dirt tracks, the car lost its jacking points and developed a crack across an A-pillar, the part of the car's body that separates the windshield from the front door frames. When Max flew out to Sweden a while later, Volvo was very keen to show him the reasons for the failures of the jacking points and A-pillar and to explain structural modifications they would be incorporating on their assembly line as a result.

Max needed a co-driver for the Marathon and the solution came in the shape of John Keran. Max explained that John "was our best Volvo customer…. I was very nervous about taking him with me because he was noted as being a driver that would either win the rally or not finish. He'd smash, absolutely fearless. That year in 1968 he was the winner of the Southern Cross Rally, which was then an international rally. We had blokes like Hopkirk and Aaltonen, all those guys out here, and he won." They twice crossed Australia by car to test their working relationship as well as their joint reaction to long periods of driving. John's wife was a dietitian and developed a meal plan for the team so they wouldn't have to eat anything offered or provided on the 10,000 mile road from London to Sydney. Mrs. Keran's efforts meant that Max and John "were fantastically fit, really, we were never hungry. We arrived in Bombay and we were as fit as anything. No problem!"

During their recent rally season both John and Max had run Volvos with a cylinder head conversion engineered by Repco, which had previously developed successful Formula One racing engines for World Championship winners Jack Brabham and Danny Hulme. As a result, Max decided that their Marathon Volvo would also have the Repco modification. "At that time, I think the best Volvo tuning kit was about a 130 DIN horsepower," he explained. "Well, the Repco head gave us 160 DIN horsepower, so it was really a going machine." Of the other 140 series sedans in the Marathon, only Jack Forrest and Ken Tubman in the TVW-7 car also opted for the Repco head conversion. Bob Holden and Gerry Lister decided to stick with Volvo's own rally engine.

All four cars were prepared at Volvo's Gothenburg headquarters in Sweden, which allowed the teams the flexibility of specifying what they needed, even if Volvo didn't exactly approve of the Repco conversions. Bob Holden had driven his 142S all the way from Sydney, so Volvo even allowed him to work on his car on site. Once all the cars were ready and the teams had been given the opportunity to test them, they headed off for London and the start of the Marathon. Max and John were drawn as No. 8, so at 2:07 p.m., the safety orange Volvo set off for Dover.

Progress was faultless all the way to Belgrade, not least because from Paris they were able to fall in behind Sobiesław Zasada's fast red Porsche 911 and use him as a guide through the foggy conditions down towards the Italian Alps. However, after only 100 miles of the 605-mile section to the next control at Istanbul, No. 8 ran into problems. Speeding along a fast, concrete, two-lane highway, the Volvo suddenly developed an unhealthy sounding engine noise, which, as Max Stahl wrote, "manifested itself in an extensive blow-up as a piston let go and showered Firth's Falcon GT traveling but a few yards behind with engine oil."[1] Max steered the car to the side of the road and they got out, minds racing to think of what had gone wrong. It was obvious the car would go no further, so while John tried to flag someone down to take him back for help, Max got the car jacked up and slid underneath to inspect the damage. As he explained, "The temperature was zero and I'm lying under there. I thought, being an ex-truck driver, I can get this thing fixed up and get underway again. Not as easy working on a car. I was trying to find out what it was. I knew it was bad because I was driving and there just a little tinkle and a plume of blue smoke out the back and I'm sort of thinking, well, if I can't get this going, God, I should be home with my beautiful wife and four kids, what the hell am I doing?" Their Volvo teammates stopped to offer help, but seeing there wasn't anything they could do, Max hurried them on.

Hours later, another Volvo pulled up and out stepped John. Max knew Volvo didn't have any dealership or service network in Eastern Europe, but just as John had trudged into a gas station back along the road, two Volvo truck service engineers arrived, who had been following the Marathon on the radio and had heard that a Volvo was missing in action. They quickly set about towing the 144S back down the road to the gas station where Max was keen to carry on trying to fix the car as he had realized what the problem was—one of the pistons had shattered. However, the service engineers had a better idea and explained that they could tow them back to Belgrade where they believed they would be able to find additional assistance. Two hours later, Max and John were astonished to find themselves being towed past armed guards and through the gates of the Atomic Energy Commission. Max recalled, "When we got in there it was the best workshop I've ever seen anywhere. Everything was immaculate, the canteen was beautiful and I said to these two guys 'I want the engine out of your motor car.' He said company car, can't touch it!" Max immediately put a call through to Gothenburg and got the all clear to cannibalize the very car that had saved them from the side of the road! Working flat out, they painstakingly removed the donor engine and fitted it to theirs. The Volvo engineers assured them they would get the damaged engine back to Gothenburg for a thorough analysis, but now Max and John had a choice. By their calculations they had lost 26 hours, and although they had a car that ran, instead of the quick 160-horsepower machine they had lost, they now had a standard, single carburetor version with a maximum of only 75-horsepower. They could either quit and get the car to a suitable port for shipping home, or they could take their chances and get to Bombay in time for the ship. What was it to be? On November 26, 1968, John and Max shook hands with their saviors, pulled out of the Atomic Energy Commission lot and took the first sign they could find for Nis and then Pirot beyond. They were going to Bombay and this time it really would have to be non-stop.

Following their route notes, the Volvo progressed without incident until the pair reached Sivas where on the previous day competitors had begun their first special stage, which on paper meant a choice of routes. However, heavy rain had led to the shorter, tougher course being declared impassable, so the field had all scrambled to Erzincan via the longer route. Now, more than 24 hours later, the checkpoint was gone and with no advance warning, John and Max set off on the short section, eager to make up time wherever possible and oblivious to the conditions that awaited. The track got ever muddier until, trying to get the Volvo up a steep incline, the wheels refused to get traction. Skidding and spewing mud, Max recalled an alarming moment when "All of a sudden one of us looked up and there's a whole line of people up on top of the hill watching us. They all came down towards us and they were all standing back and suddenly, one of them—we had a kangaroo painted on the side of the car and they then sort of made sign language. We were brothers—Australia and Turkey. They decided to give us a push." However, no matter how hard they strained, the car just wasn't going to get up the hill. Up on the crest of the rise was a Toyota Land Cruiser, and with more frantic sign-language, they persuaded the owner to hook the Volvo onto a tow rope and drag it up out of the mud.

Stopping only for fuel and bathroom breaks, they pressed onwards, coaxing every last horsepower out of the 144S's shrunken engine. As they were speeding through Teheran, a motorcycle cop coming in the opposite direction shot past, turned around and began to pursue them. Instead of pulling them over for speeding, the Harley-Davidson drew level and the rider beckoned them to follow him. Thus they were given a high-speed police escort through the Iranian capital's busy streets. Across Afghanistan they were still able to take advantage of the empty highway, but racing into Kabul, they were disappointed to find not a single trace of a service crew, which meant they really were on their own with no hope of locating a source of replacement tires—they were still on the studded tires with which they'd left London. Faced with no option, they carried on with grim determination and, as a result of their relentless sprint, they began to catch up with a few of the cars at the back of the field. After incurring 10,080 penalty points by the time they had reached Kabul, from then on they only picked up another 18 points to Bombay. However, they were shocked when they realized the completely wrecked Marathon car they were passing as they roared towards New Delhi was that of teammates Bob Holden and Laurie Graham and it wouldn't be until they got to Bombay that they would be able to learn of their fate.

Of his experience driving through India, Max recalled, "The crowds of people, you just couldn't believe it. I had one woman fall over behind me, like she fell in the wake of the car, and I thought oh shit, should I stop? We'd been warned not to stop and I looked in the rear view mirror and the police are rushing over to help her up and they had bloody sticks and they start whacking into her to get up and she jumps up and off she goes, so yeah it's quite different, it was quite an event." By the time Max Winkless and John Keran drove into Ballard's Pier in Bombay, not only had they made up the time but they even managed to check into the control with fewer points than No. 82, the battered Cortina Lotus of Duncan Bray, Simon Sladen and Peter Sugden, and the Dutch National Team DAF 55 driven by Peter Hissink and David van Lennep. Grahame Ward, an experienced Australian rally driver who was working for Max in 1968, suggested that "Tommy Sopwith and everybody else in Bombay were so thrilled at what Max and John had done that they had to get them on the boat. There wasn't a situation of, no you're 71st and we're only taking 70 cars—you're on the boat! It was just one of those enormous endeavors." On the boat they definitely were, but not before Max contacted the Volvo dealer in Perth and arranged for No. 8's single carburetor to be upgraded with a twin plus a different cylinder head as soon as they touched home ground. As he said, "John and I reckoned we could set some really fast times going through, because we knew the roads pretty well, pick up to the Snowy Mountains and we'd get a bit of publicity." Although they stood at 70th out of 72 competitors when both car and crew boarded the SS *Chusan*, their dogged determination, extraordinary stamina and competitive drive kept them going all the way to Sydney, despite the ruinous amount of penalty points they had amassed.

Once onboard ship, John and Max allowed themselves to give vent to their frustrations at having had such appalling luck, but the voyage to Perth also gave Max the opportunity to catch up on how everyone else had been performing and who the contenders were for the various awards that awaited competitors in Sydney. As a result, he realized that there was a rather interesting and totally unexpected opportunity to generate some excellent publicity for Volvo in Australia. Among the professional and private entrants competing in Volvo cars was the team of four British women in a privately entered 145S station wagon. Of the four, only Jenny Tudor-Owen and Sheila Kemp actually had any motorsports experience. Despite the overloaded wagon suffering from chassis fatigue in India, the Volvo 145S was the front runner for the Ladies' Prize because the obvious favorites, professional rally drivers Rosemary Smith and Lucette Pointet, had suffered mechanical calamities in their works Cortina Lotus and because the completely inexperienced Australian women in their Morris 1100 S had incurred many penalty points. The other women's teams would not be able to make up the time, so all Sheila, Jenny, Anthea and Elsie had to do was get to Warwick Farm in Sydney and they would be triumphant. Max recalled, "We spent quite a bit of time talking to them, giving them our maps and advice on Australia."

In Perth, No. 8 received the improvements Max had arranged in Bombay, including different exhaust extractors. Then it was off and out into the Australian wilderness, but nothing Max and John weren't already familiar with. They knew the route and were at last able to really enjoy themselves, reveling in the increased power the twin carburetors afforded them, passing other Marathon cars and competing as they had wanted to do across Europe and Asia. Motoring across the vast expanse of the Nullarbor Plain, they began to close in on a car ahead and suddenly realized what it was. It was the Volvo 145S station wagon, the British contenders for the women's award. Into and out of a checkpoint, Max and John lost them for a while, but then noticed a car trailing a huge dust cloud over in the distance. The Volvo wagon was obviously heading in the wrong direction. As Max explained, "I said to John, oh we better go and turn them around, so we chased, caught them, turned them around, and we said, 'We'll guide you through a bit.'"

Max recalled that Sheila and Jenny "were really fantastic drivers. We were punching along to keep up with them." Ever interested in Volvo products, back in London on the eve of the Marathon, he had approached Elsie Gadd, No. 33's team leader, and suggested that she made sure the wagon's battery was reinforced in its cradle, otherwise it would eventually fall out. Sure enough, through the Flinders Ranges section of the Marathon, the Volvo women crawled to a halt when the stresses of thousands of miles already traveled caught up with the car's battery. It had finally vibrated lose, fallen into the engine and cracked. Max and John were quickly on the scene and Max's ingenuity came into play. Not for nothing had he been a solo truck driver, hauling rigs across dusty outback roads. "When I was a truck driver, there was nobody there to help me and I used to drive all these roads on my own, and if something broke, you had to fix it or you'd die out there, so I was used to doing those sorts of things, I used to always reckon I could always get home."

Max and John kept No. 8's engine running to charge the alternator and then they took out their battery and cobbled together a makeshift setting for it in the 145S. Both Volvos were back on the move again, and this time they stayed in convoy, Max hell-bent on supporting the women to just keep the wagon going and win the Ladies' Prize. As Max explained, "We were really worried about whether the car would get there or not, because the wheel arches

No. 8 Volvo 1445 between Numeralla and Hindmarsh Station, Australia, December 17 (courtesy Bruce Thomas).

on the back of the wagon were both snapped right through." However, despite the punishing trek over the Victorian Alps and the Snowy Mountains, Jenny and Sheila kept the 145S going and so, with more than a little help from Max and John, they arrived at Warwick Farm and the eager attention of the waiting press. Invited to give television interviews, the women insisted that "Maxie" join them, much to the bemusement of Mrs. Winkless who was there to welcome her husband home. With a final position of 41st out of 56 recorded finishers, Elsie, Jenny, Sheila and Anthea were officially declared the winners of the Ladies' Prize and the $480 that came with it. Despite their 26-hour setback, Max and John still managed to beat two other cars home.

Today Max firmly believes that if the Repco cylinder head conversion hadn't failed in Yugoslavia, the Marathon "would have been a piece of cake." Once back in Sydney, however, he learned the cause of the mechanical malfunction from Volvo in Sweden, and wasn't very happy to hear that when the car was being prepared for the event in Gothenburg, "somebody had put a cleaning towel into our sump [oil pan], and when they took it out the filter was all blocked up, and we had a valve seize." On whether this was "cock-up or conspiracy," however, Max Winkless remains tight-lipped.

26

Roo Bars and Bull Dust

Talking to journalists on the eve of beginning the trek across the outback, Roger Clark addressed the issue of potentially being the first car to reach "kangaroo country," stating that "The 'roos have got to find me first. I will wake them up for the rest of the drivers."[1] "Gelignite" Jack Murray's scare stories about the dangers of Australian wildlife did have a grain or two of truth as hitting a 200-pound "big red" at speed could be catastrophic for both a kangaroo and a driver. Another hazard facing the Marathon survivors was bull dust, the fine, talcum powder-like dust that blanketed the terrain, which had the tendency to fill craters and gullies, giving them the appearance of a flat surface on the road ahead. It would be easy for an unsuspecting driver to suddenly crash into a large hole that had been completely disguised by the fine, red bull dust. Disturbing the dust mantle resulted in dense trailing clouds, reducing visibility to practically non-existent, so with the exception of front-running Clark and Andersson, crews would be faced with very tough conditions from now on.

The section from Perth to Youanmi was 340 miles with an allowance of seven hours to get there. Heading out of Gloucester Park, a number of crews calculated that the generous provision of time meant they would be able to attend to much-needed repairs and servicing before embarking on the final 3,000 miles to Sydney. The four-woman Volvo 145S team needed to have the windshield replaced as did the little red MG Midget. The Cortina Savage of British trio Peter Graham, Leslie Morrish and Michael Wooley had been running in second gear since Kabul, meaning they had made it to Bombay and out of Fremantle at little more than 36 mph. A replacement part had been flown in from London, so the powerful Cortina was at last able to run at full speed. Winkless and Keran upgraded their Volvo's replacement engine, while the axle-blighted Holden Belmont and the collapsing Morris 1100 S received attention, all three Australian crews opting to bypass Youanmi and instead head east to the second control at the tiny settlement of Marvel Loch. With 10,098, 8,657 and 6,154 points respectively, they all accepted that another 1,440 penalty points for missing a control was a price they could pay.

Two cars were in trouble only 25 miles out of Perth when they were "chased by a shire traffic inspector with his siren blaring. The cars—No. 56 a British-entered SAAB, driven by A. Percy and No. 58, a Porsche, driven by Polish driver S. Zasada were both stopped by the traffic inspector and apparently cautioned."[2] However, police were also on hand to hold back the crowds as drivers sped out of the city, even warning some local drivers to move their own cars out of the way.

Once a thriving gold mine, in 1968 Youanmi was all but deserted after the mine closed

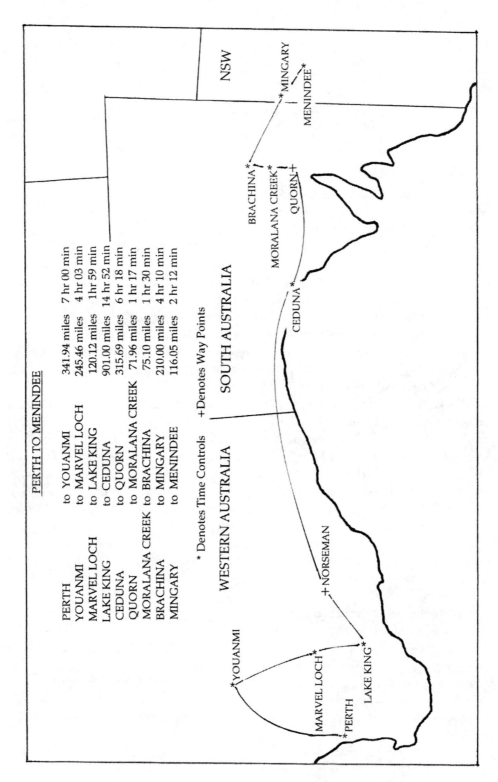

PERTH TO MENINDEE			
PERTH	to YOUANMI	341.94 miles	7 hr 00 min
YOUANMI	to MARVEL LOCH	245.46 miles	4 hr 03 min
MARVEL LOCH	to LAKE KING	120.12 miles	1hr 59 min
LAKE KING	to CEDUNA	901.00 miles	14 hr 52 min
CEDUNA	to QUORN	315.69 miles	6 hr 18 min
QUORN	to MORALANA CREEK	71.96 miles	1 hr 17 min
MORALANA CREEK	to BRACHINA	75.10 miles	1 hr 30 min
BRACHINA	to MINGARY	210.00 miles	4 hr 10 min
MINGARY	to MENINDEE	116.05 miles	2 hr 12 min

* Denotes Time Controls   + Denotes Way Points

The route from Perth to Menindee (map by Martin Proudlock).

Youanmi, Western Australia (author's collection).

in 1942. As Andrew Cowan wrote, "I remember discussing with Colin Malkin as to how we get ahead of time on this first section and go to a hotel at this place Youanmi and try and get a slap-up meal. Of course, when we got there it was just a wooden signpost and nothing else."[3] The route from Perth was a mixture of paved and gravel roads taking competitors northeast, and while progress was impeded by the closely monitored speed restrictions out of the city, thereafter cars found it easier to achieve the average speed requirement of 49 mph—previous reconnaissance of this section had found that it was possible to arrive at Youanmi in less than four and a half hours. As a result, aside from the three crews that avoided Youanmi altogether, only six cars picked up points, mostly caused by punctures or wrong turns, and positions of the leading ten remained unchanged. The section wasn't completely without incident, however, as some teams had their first encounters with kangaroos, including British Army duo Harrison and Proudlock in their Cortina Lotus, the French Simca of Pierre Boucher and Georges Houel and, most ironically, "Gelignite" Jack Murray and Evan Green—Murray's scare stories had caught up with him! Luckily, all cars only suffered minor damage, although it is unclear what became of the errant marsupials.

After Youanmi, the route turned south to another former gold-mining settlement, the town of Marvel Loch. The section allowed four hours to complete the 245 miles and while organizers concluded this could be a fast run, it wouldn't be as easy as the drive up from Perth, as a few competitors were to discover. The main challenge for all but the leading car was the ever present dust clouds churned up by the cars in front, which seemed to hang in the still air and severely hamper vision. The rigors of over 7,000 miles now traveled began to take their toll on a few cars as well. No. 6, the Australian Ford Fairmont "survival car" driven by track racing veteran Brian Lawler, had made eventful but mostly steady progress thus far. Competing with the less experienced pair of Australian motoring journalist Clyde Hodgins and New South Wales University of Technology faculty member Don Wait had meant that Lawler had done most of the driving to Bombay, and even allowing for the nine-day voyage on the *Chusan*, he was tired. During the section to Marvel Loch, as Lawler explained, "It was about two o'clock in the morning and I'd been driving all day and all night and I thought Jesus, I'm tired. I've got hardly enough energy and the steering was so heavy, this is unreal. I thought bugger, I just can't endure it any longer. I just relaxed and it went straight across the road. I got out and both the front wheels were splayed out like that. I'd been steering on one wheel and the other wheel had been trailing and that was why it was so heavy." A tie-rod end had broken, and although Lawler worked to repair the damage, it cost them six hours, by which time both the Marvel Loch and subsequent Lake King controls were closed. They were out, so they took the most direct route to Sydney to at least be at Warwick Farm at the finish.

Having become embroiled in the dispute over who had won the leading private entrant prize at Bombay, Anglo-Italian pair John Tallis and Paul Coltelloni ran into difficulties when their Volvo 123GT broke an axle, and although BMC Team service member Terry Douglas was able to take the news to the Volvo service crew at Marvel Loch, by the time the mechanics found No. 13 and carried out repairs, too much time was lost and they were forced to retire. La Trobe, Chesson and Warner also ended their attempt to Sydney when a connecting rod severed in their Volvo 122S. A Hong Kong newspaper dramatically reported that the British trio and their car had disappeared, but the truth was that La Trobe was offered an acceptable sum of money for the disabled car, which he accepted. The three then caught a ride back to Perth and took a plane to Sydney. Rather more fortunate was No. 32, the Mercedes Benz 280S of British Army Captains Fred Barker, David Dollar and John Lewis. Driving at 90 mph, the team encountered a kangaroo, and Barker reported that "it pounced straight in front of us. My co-driver had no choice but to hit the kangaroo head on without even going for the brakes."[4] The army trio collected 20 penalty points when they were forced to stop and try to get the Benz's damaged hood to open.

Of the remaining 69 cars, only 21 made it to Marvel Loch within the allowed time, but the leader board remained unchanged with Clark and Andersson still nine points clear of their closest rival. The leading Cortina checked in at the control and roared off into the night for what the Australian newspapers had named "the horror stretch," nearly 120 miles of rocky, narrow, winding track tunneling through mallee scrub that grew right up to the edge of the path and peppered with dust-filled craters. Any competitor that caught up with a car in front would find it almost impossible to overtake, yet organizers were requiring teams to achieve an average of 60 mph. Lying in fourth place overall before this section, Paddy Hopkirk's BMC 1800 broke a tie rod end on this section with just 17 miles to go. Opting to continue with reduced steering, the BMC GB team lost 14 minutes, a penalty that would come back to haunt them during the final stages before Sydney. So tough was the "horror stretch" that only three crews arrived on time: Clark and Andersson, Staepelaere and Lampinen and Bianchi and Ogier. Further down the field, frustrations were being voiced with complaints of slow-moving cars refusing to allow others to pass, and for John Sprinzel and Roy Fidler, the irritation of discovering that the Marvel Loch control officials had made an error in their road book, forcing them to return to have it corrected, only to be met with blank refusal. In their

"The Horror Stretch"—Marvel Loch to Lake King (courtesy Mike Bailey).

Holden Monaro, McKay, Liddle and Reynolds raced to get ahead of the Midget as it started back into the section, wanting to get clear of the less powerful MG and at the same time avoid its dust trail, but Sprinzel beat them onto the red dirt track. Further along the stage, McKay missed a sharp left hand turn and ran into soft sand, adding to their woes and their points. It was also during this stage that Harrison and Proudlock left the road and damaged their Cortina's side panels. Murray, Green and Shepheard were forced to stop and replace a punctured tire, but still managed to improve their final position in the top ten. At Lake King, *Sydney Telegraph* Holden team driver Eddie Perkins reported that "This event has really become a marathon. Neither of the Round Australia Trials was ever like this."[5] Perkins knew what he was talking about—he had twice won the Round Australia Trial rallies.

While other cars were torturing their brakes, tires and suspension along the section, Australian Amoco Volvo team Ken Tubman and Jack Forrest had taken advantage of an earlier reconnaissance and opted to follow a longer, easier and therefore faster route that took them along part of Western Australia's State Barrier Fence, otherwise known as the "rabbit proof fence." Constructed during the first decade of the twentieth century, it was designed to keep rabbits and other pests out of the state's agricultural regions. Forrest and Tubman made impressive time along the fence road, but then found themselves approaching the time control in a different direction from everyone else. To complicate matters further, the final approach meant they were faced with a mass of spectators' cars parked in the road. As Tubman explained, "We crashed about trying to find a way through, but the more we drove, the more blocked we became. In frustration Jack leapt out to guide me backwards, but I didn't see him and ran right into him."[6] Forrest was grazed and badly bruised and what should have been a clever decision led to 16 penalty points and, for Forrest, a very painful remainder of the Marathon.

For the surviving teams, beyond Lake King lay 892 miles of almost treeless wilderness across the Nullarbor Plain and the fear of temperatures reaching 130 degrees. During the morning of December 15, 1968, competitors shot into and then out of the control, eager to get on their way. Among them, lying in 48th place overall, were the four British women in their privately entered Volvo 145S station wagon. Having found themselves with the chance to win the Ladies' Prize at the finish, with support from Max Winkless and John Keran, they were soldiering on, the Volvo's chassis and shell really beginning to show the signs of fatigue. At 21 years old, Anthea Castell was the youngest member of the team.

27

A Tale of Two Volvos (Part Two)

By 1968, Anthea Castell was a veteran of the outback, having already spent 18 months working on sheep and cattle stations in Australia, and, as a result, she had gained experience of "driving for hundreds of miles of dirt tracks, in bull dust, along dry creeks and river beds and had coped with the hazards of night driving with bulls, camels and kangaroos roaming about in the dark." Having returned to England in early 1968, she took a job at H.R. Owens, the London-based prestige car dealership, where she picked up and returned customers' cars for servicing and repairs. So it was that she found herself delivering a car to a customer in North London's affluent Fitzroy Park area of Hampstead. The customer was 47-year-old Elsie Gadd, a successful chartered surveyor and property developer, and as they attended to the business of delivering and receiving the car, Elsie and Anthea began talking. Anthea mentioned that she had been in Australia and suddenly she had Elsie's attention. Here was a young woman who had driven in the outback, had experienced what it was like. Elsie was interested because she had been accepted as an applicant to take part in the London to Sydney Marathon and was in the process of putting together her team. She had already found two women to be lead drivers—Jenny Tudor-Owen and Sheila Kemp were both track racers who regularly competed against Jean Denton—but she also needed a navigator and relief driver. She asked Anthea if she would like to join them and without hesitation, Anthea said yes, even though at that point she knew nothing about the planned event.

As a result, Anthea eventually parted company with H.R. Owen and began to work for Elsie, "learning the rules and regulations, plotting and learning the route, arranging petrol uptakes, tire availability, communicating with Volvo, visas—the paperwork was endless but it was good because I was familiar with all the details by the start date of the Marathon." As she explained, "It was ultimately the lucky case of my being in the right place at the right time. I belonged to a couple of car clubs where I had competed in various trials and done a few laps of Brands Hatch but nothing even close to an international rally."

Elsie had originally planned to use an Australian Chrysler Valiant Safari for the Marathon, but during the summer had decided instead to order a brand new 145S station wagon from Volvo in Sweden. Volvo was also preparing the Australian Amoco cars, so they were willing to offer advice and suggest modifications for the wagon prior to delivery. The 145S was eventually delivered with a 'roo bar, secondary gas tank, oil pan guard and full-length luggage rack for the roof. Volvo also revised the rear seat configuration to add what Anthea described as "a coffin like box in which we took it in turns to sleep. Although this all looked rather unprofessional and attracted a few raised eyebrows amongst the more seasoned rally drivers, it was

Jenny Tudor-Owen (left) and Sheila Kemp at Crystal Palace, London, November 24 (courtesy Anthea Hartley).

a real luxury to be able to stretch out and lay flat for a few hours each day." Despite Volvo's warning that she was adding too much weight to the car, Elsie also ordered four extra wheels and tires to carry on the roof—Volvo even offered to buy them back, but Elsie was insistent, a decision that would have consequences for the team.

On the morning of November 24, despite a minor altercation with a red London double-decker bus, Elsie and Anthea arrived at Crystal Palace where they met up with Jenny and Sheila. Drawn as No. 33 in the running order, Jenny looked at the Volvo and wondered whether she should have been more involved in its preparation. Scheduled to be flagged away at just after 2:30 p.m., Anthea recalled that "There was a lot of hanging around whilst we awaited our turn to start—last minute checks, more photos, farewells from family and friends and of course the press and promoters were grabbing every last opportunity to get their coverage too. Once again, I don't remember much because we were so preoccupied in our preparations. It is strange to look back on the Marathon because at the time I really didn't think it was such a big deal and wondered what all the fuss was about!"

At last, No. 33 was away, out into the congested South London streets and then up and around Parliament Square and Big Ben before turning south toward the coast and the ferry port at Dover. As cars were driven onto the ferry for the crossing to Calais in France, the women had a momentary panic when they discovered their boat ticket was missing. A search of the car revealed nothing, so each emptied their pockets and sure enough, there it was in Elsie's jacket. During the ferry crossing, the Marathon crews were advised that they would not be allowed to take the main highway to Paris as had previously been planned, but instead were required by the French authorities to follow a more complicated cross-country route. While many drivers chose to disregard this instruction, those who complied soon realized that their route notes weren't detailed enough to guide them along the capillaries of minor roads and villages, made worse by heavy fog that shrouded the French countryside. No. 33 was among the cars that wove their way through the darkness, eventually arriving at the Le Bourget checkpoint six min-

Anthea Castell at Crystal Palace, London, November 24 (courtesy Anthea Hartley).

utes late, one of only three cars to pick up penalty points. The fog continued to challenge drivers as they wound their way southwards around Paris, not helped by the absence of a promised police escort, and the women briefly got lost in the warren of back streets before eventually finding the A6 *autoroute*.

The women made steady progress out of France, across Italy and into Yugoslavia. In Belgrade, they were thankful for the opportunity to shower and rest at the Hotel Metropole before setting off toward the next control at Istanbul, arriving in pouring rain and frantically trying to find their service Land Rover amid the bustle of cars, competitors, officials and spectators. As Anthea recalled, "I think Elsie had underestimated, as had I, quite how geared-up the checkpoints would be. There was usually some fuel for sale, along with food and drink and some spare tires."

After the first special stage of the Marathon between Sivas and Erzincan, Anthea told Australian journalist Alan Sawyer, "It was awful…. It was only thanks to Jenny Tudor-Owen who drove the stretch that we got through in one piece."[1] Although the Volvo was more than an hour over the allowed time, Jenny's skill meant they were faster over the difficult mountain track than 40 other competitors, including David MacKay's *Sydney Telegraph* Holden Monaro. Among the female competitors, only the experienced professionals Rosemary Smith and Lucette Pointet were quicker. However, the heavy station wagon had taken a pounding to its standard suspension setup, a first taste of what was to come. Standing at 56th out of a surviving field of 91 cars, they next faced the 915-mile section to Iran's capital, Teheran.

All four women alternated driving and navigating duties, with Jenny and Sheila taking the longest stretches behind the wheel. Out of Turkey and into Iran, however, Jenny, Sheila and Anthea were becoming increasingly concerned about Elsie's relentless car sickness and the fact that she wasn't able to sleep, eat or drink, which meant she was quite simply in no fit state to take her turn at driving. At the Teheran checkpoint, she climbed out of the car to get their papers stamped by the Marathon control officials and suddenly collapsed. Jenny, Sheila and Anthea realized they had a difficult decision to make—unless Elsie's health improved, unless she started eating and drinking, they wouldn't allow her to drive at all. To compound

No. 33 sets off in London, November 24 (courtesy Anthea Hartley).

matters, while the station wagon was being serviced, Volvo mechanics again raised the subject of weight, advising that unless the team shed some of the load, including the roof-mounted extra wheels, there was a danger that the car would snap in two. Anxious that they needed to be prepared for anything, Elsie was at first resistant to taking the advice, but eventually relented and two of the wheels plus the team's empty fuel cans were discarded. This lightened the car, but the damage had already begun as the women would discover.

Ironically, driving across Afghanistan the Volvo suffered its first and only puncture of the entire event. Stopping to change the tire, Anthea recalled how they were "immediately surrounded by curious tribesmen who appeared from nowhere. They squatted on their haunches at a respectful distance and stared at us, rifles across their knees, their faces expressionless." They also took this opportunity to clean out the car and discard any paperwork that was no longer required, including maps and route notes from the previous sections. Anthea recounted that "At Crystal Palace my father had thoughtfully put a huge bar of Cadbury's milk chocolate in the glove box for us, but with the intense heat in Iran and Afghanistan it had melted and everything was covered." She also remembered that "the obsolete maps were hugely popular with the tribesmen who immediately seized them, unsure which way up they should be read. We thought at the time that perhaps they would be used as wallpaper for their homes or sold to local spies for a handsome price!"

No. 33 arrived at the Kabul checkpoint nearly three hours behind schedule and the women seized the opportunity to get cleaned up and rested during what little time they had left of the compulsory halt in proceedings prior to the opening of the Lataband Pass the following morning. The Volvo was now really beginning to show signs of distress, so Jenny took it easy over the Pass, getting the team to the Sarobi control just under an hour down on the allotted time. Immediately, mechanics set to work on the station wagon, removing its rear wheels to replace the shock absorbers, only to discover that the car's rear suspension was severely damaged and even more alarmingly, the rear wheel arches were cracked. Sheila, Jenny and Anthea decided not to tell Elsie as they were worried she would quit the Marathon. Even though the mechanics told them they'd be lucky to get to Bombay, they went ahead and changed the shocks. No. 33 continued on towards the Khyber Pass but this time they kept speeds to a minimum, even though Elsie was urging them to pick up the pace, losing 42 minutes into New Delhi.

Through India, Anthea recalled that "The crowds would push and shove the car. We lost both wing mirrors and had a brick thrown through the windscreen but the police wielded their batons quite effectively and their system of crowd control was pretty effective." They cautiously pressed on but at Gwalior, south of Delhi, they came across the wrecked Simca of Jean Py and Roger Masson. The less injured of the two asked them to get to a first aid station

Inspecting the damage at Sarobi, Afghanistan, November 30 (courtesy Anthea Hartley).

further along the route and ask for help. The Volvo hurried on but at each station the women found that personnel were either unequipped to help or had no English. In the confusion, one group of first aid personnel mistakenly thought Anthea was the injured party as she had taken her turn to rest in the box and it took a few chaotic moments before they stopped trying to wrestle her out of the car. Eventually assurances were given that a car would be sent back to the French crash site.

Trying to balance the need for cautious driving with the fact that they were anxious to get to Bombay in time to qualify for the next leg and a place on the ship was a great challenge for the team, but a little advice from a fellow competitor came in useful. Anthea recalled that they were told "If you are running a bit late and there is another car on your tail, drive with your kerbside wheels on the unsealed track beside the road. The dust that you throw up will prevent the bloke behind you from being able to see properly and unable to overtake!"

Coming into Indore, the Volvo team stopped at a gas station and, as Anthea recalled, "By now the car had almost broken in two. The cracks in the door pillars had extended across the roof and over the wheel arches and the back of the car was, literally, falling off. We had been through 13 shock absorbers, a new set at almost every checkpoint." Pulling over, the team was immediately surrounded by fascinated Indians, but at the instruction of the gas station owner, they disbanded, allowing the women to climb out of the station wagon. Anthea explained that "As luck would have it, he had one of the biggest Mercedes dealerships in the country and had a fully equipped workshop behind the petrol station. We explained about the back of the car falling away from the front and he immediately sprang into action, insisting that we sit down and rest, while his mechanics welded the car back together for us." The women were hugely relieved, although when Anthea went to check on progress, she found one of the mechanics working with his welding torch just inches from the car's reserve fuel line. Anthea recalled that "As though just to please me and to allay my concerns, he agreed to run a cold hose pipe over the fuel line—just as a safety precaution!" The garage proprietor refused any form of payment, happy to have played a part in the Marathon. Welding complete, No. 33 continued on and arrived in good time at Bombay.

Happy to have made it in one piece and pleased to find they were lying 51st out of 72 cars, the four were amazed to learn that they had won the prize for the leading women's team to Bombay. "When we arrived in Bombay we were allocated our accommodation and thankfully sunk into a bath and a change of clothes," Anthea explained. "We were shocked and amazed when there was a knock on the bedroom door and [we] were told to get dressed and ready for a reception at the Taj Mahal Hotel to receive the India Oil Company best performance cup for women. We were whisked off to the reception where we were treated like celebrities—a reception followed by a wonderful meal, speeches, photos and the presentation of a beautiful rose bowl. This was a bolt out of the blue—a good thing I had taken a dress with me! Apparently we had been the first women's team to arrive in Bombay—but only by a wing and a prayer!" A whirlwind of receptions and parties followed, to the point where Anthea believes she had less sleep in Bombay than during the entire drive from London. There was also time for a horse-drawn cart ride through Bombay in the early hours of the morning, which ended in chaos when a wheel fell off and she and fellow traveler Australian filmmaker Rob McAuley had to put it back on again.

Finally, it was time to board the ship for their voyage to Australia, although Anthea recalled that she was "disappointed in the *Chusan*, the boat that was to take us from Bombay to Fremantle. It was an old liner, and although we were travelling in First Class, the accommodation was fairly basic. There were approximately 250 male rally drivers and only nine women. This disparity between the sexes resulted in some minor problems." However, while some of male competitors misbehaved, Anthea decided that as a young woman among so many boisterous and, for the most part, much older rally drivers, she needed to keep her wits about her. "I tried to socialize equally with everyone and was very concerned that I did not acquire an 'unwanted reputation'—I wanted to retain the respect of my fellow competitors and to avoid any problems." During the voyage, Jenny began to get to know American cameraman Jerry Sims, whom she would go on to marry after the Marathon, but Elsie took the opportunity to try and recuperate after the difficult time she had had, occasionally joining the rest of them for dinner. Distressingly for her, however, after seven days of constant car sickness and dehydration, she was then forced to deal with seasickness as well.

Life aboard ship quickly became tiresome, so it was with much excitement that Anthea caught her first glimpse of the Western Australian coast, thrilled to be back again so soon. During the sea crossing, Australian Volvo competitor and Volvo dealer Max Winkless had realized that if the women could get to Sydney, they would win the Ladies' Prize as the other two female teams had accumulated too many penalty points to be able to catch up. Thus he hatched a plan, which in part involved Amoco offering their support to the Volvo wagon team. In exchange, the women would participate in promotion of Amoco fuel once they got to Sydney. Sheila, Jenny and Anthea had already brought Elsie up to speed on the state of the car and she finally agreed to offload some more of the equipment they were carrying. She was, however, less happy that Volvo and Amoco were prepared to increase their support, protesting that it wasn't necessary. Looking back, Anthea felt some sympathy for their team leader, saying that she could "appreciate Elsie's frustration at having Volvo and Amoco involved. So far we had managed reasonably well under our own steam as an amateur entry and she wanted it to stay that way. However, having got this far, the rest of the team was reluctant to refuse the help from Volvo because it would probably mean the difference between finishing and not finishing."

At 5:20 p.m. on December 14, 1968, No. 33 was led to the starting line, this time with Elsie at the wheel. After a circuit of the track, the team headed straight to a local Volvo garage where the station wagon was rewelded for the second time as well as receiving new shock absorbers, manifold, carburetors and radiator. The mechanics worked for an hour and a half to restore the car back to better health, which left five and a half hours to complete the 350 miles up to the first control at Youanmi. Back on the road, the transformation was incredible and they quickly discovered that the Volvo was once more capable of 95 mph. With no time to lose, the difficult decision was made to relieve Elsie of driving duties—from here on Elsie wouldn't get back behind the wheel all the way to Sydney—and with Anthea in the driving seat, the team got to Youanmi with ten minutes to spare.

After Youanmi, the route headed south to the next control at the tiny settlement of Marvel Loch before taking competitors along the 120-mile special stage to Lake King. However, unlike almost all the other cars, Jack Forrest and Ken Tubman had told the women about the alternative route they had discovered, which, although longer, would be easier and therefore quicker. Anthea recalled, "We took a chance and set off along this little used track. I had done plenty of driving in these conditions and was not fazed by the dust." They made it to Lake King, but picked up another 62 points for their trouble.

More repairs for No. 33 in Australia (courtesy Anthea Hartley).

Max and John caught up with them on the long stretch that ran through the southern edge of the Nullarbor Plain and took up their position at the rear all the way to Ceduna where the women arrived without further penalty. The route from Ceduna on the South Australian coast to the township of Quorn took the field via Port Augusta where service crews had set up in readiness for any cars needing attention before they began the extremely tough sections through the Flinders Ranges. No. 33 limped into the Volvo service point and once again, mechanics set about rewelding the car and refitting shock absorbers, which by now were taking the full force caused by the damaged rear suspension.

Between Port Augusta and Moralana Creek, however, conditions for the four women were rapidly deteriorating inside the station wagon. Anthea recalled, "As the cracks in the car started to re-appear, the bull dust came pouring into the vehicle and we were struggling to breathe. My lips were dry and cracked so I put some Vaseline on them, only to discover that the dust stuck to the grease and formed a sort of colored paste all over my face. The atmosphere was so dry that it caused the blood vessels in my nose to crack and I started to suffer from nose bleeds." Then disaster struck, as despite the swirling dust, the women began to notice a burning smell. Pulling over, they clambered out and, as Anthea explained, "When we lifted the bonnet we saw that the battery had bounced off its mounting into the engine and had a hole in it. The fuses had burned out and something was on fire. We grabbed the fire extinguisher from the foot-well of the car and extinguished the fire before it could do too much more damage." This was how Max and John found them, so they quickly went into action, donating their battery and getting the station wagon up and running again. From then on, No. 8 would be right behind No. 33 all the way to Sydney.

Between Port Augusta and Sydney, the Volvo was re-welded five times, but it also developed a hole in its exhaust, leaking noxious fumes into the passenger cabin. With Max and John never too far away, they pressed on, even though the wagon had now sprung leaks at its fuel line joints, so Anthea "plugged them with chewing gum and wrapped them in Elastoplast from our first aid kit." To preserve the splitting station wagon, the Volvo teams conferred and decided that No. 33 would miss the 75-mile section between Moralana Creek and Brachina Gorge, by this time focused on just getting to the finish line rather than avoiding any more points. Despite the constant welding repairs, there was absolutely no guarantee that the Volvo's shell wouldn't just break in two! As Anthea recalled, "Three hundred miles away from Sydney we passed Rosemary Smith stuck on a hill. We couldn't offer to give her a tow because our car was in such a fragile state it would probably have pulled the back off completely."

At long last, having endured the torments of car sickness, dehydration, sea sickness,

No. 33 before Hindmarsh. Australia, December 17 (courtesy Bruce Thomas).

dust, carbon monoxide fumes and a car that was quite literally disintegrating around them, Jenny Tudor-Owen, Sheila Kemp, Anthea Castell and Elsie Gadd rolled into Sydney at 25 mph. Max Winkless arranged for them to stop just short of Warwick Farm where both Volvos were thoroughly cleaned in preparation for their entry into the race track. The women were able to take showers before donning the Amoco shirts and skirts the wily oil company had provided for them to wear. So, at 8:00 in the evening on December 17, 1968, No. 33 drove into Warwick Farm to a champagne welcome and confirmation that the Ladies' Prize was theirs.

By the time the Volvo 145S came to rest at the race track, it was, as Anthea explained, "in a terrible state. We had lost the front bumper and the wing [side] mirrors and several sets of lights. The roof rack had been removed because this lessened the weight and wind resistance, thus improving our top speed by seven mph. The chassis had cracked and the door pillars were split, there were more cracks up the wheel arches and the door sill, and the roof had collapsed under the weight of the tires and was sagging on the inside. The back end of the vehicle had dropped three inches and the whole thing was so twisted that the rear doors would not open and the windows would not close." Amoco and Volvo were extremely keen to reap the benefits of being associated with the winning team and after the reception and awards ceremony was over, Sheila, Jenny and Anthea were quickly off on a series of promotional engagements. Volvo wanted to purchase the station wagon and display it at different dealerships across the state of New South Wales before shipping it back to Gothenburg in Sweden for a detailed analysis. They even offered Elsie to replace it with a brand new 145S. Elsie declined and the day after the reception, she made arrangements for the car to be freighted back to Perth and then shipped back to England. Although she had paid for the women to fly home, once the awards ceremony was over, they never saw Elsie again.

Reflecting on the Marathon, Anthea commented that "It wasn't until I arrived back in the UK that it dawned on me what a great challenge I had experienced and how lucky I was to have been offered the chance to participate in this one off motoring event of a lifetime." Reflecting on her team captain, Anthea pointed out that "She was very upset with us for selling our souls to Amoco and Volvo as she had perceived it and she resented the decision making being taken out of her hands. Being older and wiser now I can understand her point of view, but at that time we were all young and ambitious and had our sights set on crossing the finishing line of the London to Sydney Marathon."

28

Turning on a Dime

Good fortune shone on the surviving Marathon competitors as they sped away from Lake King en route to the southern coastal town of Ceduna almost 900 miles to the east. In this part of Australia, average temperatures usually reached around 130 degrees in December and January but unseasonably cooler conditions prevailed across the vast desert that is the Nullarbor Plain. Crews tried to ignore the sporadic remains of long abandoned cars, their rusting hulks baking in the sun, and instead set their sights on the town of Norseman about 100 miles to the northeast where service crews had gathered to attend to any car that needed preparation for the long drive across the Nullarbor.

The Mercedes-Benz curse now affected No. 62, the 280SE of Australians Desmond Praznovsky, Ian Inglis and Stan Zovko, when it fell victim to a disguised crater and ended up with the fan forced into the radiator. Having to wait for a service crew to reach them with a replacement helped lose them 131 points by the time they checked in at Ceduna. Car No. 1 had also hit this hole hard and, as a result, as Arthur Brick wrote, "bent our back axle very badly. This, in fact, was the turning point in the rally as far as we were concerned. From now on the thing was to finish."[1] Meanwhile, competitors began to arrive at Norseman, to be greeted by the aroma of the bacon and eggs that were being cooked in almost mass production quantities by the only café. Each team either headed straight to a waiting mechanic or, in the case of many private competitors, pulled over and seized the opportunity to carry out their own repairs and maintenance required to see them start the long slog east that would take them out of Western Australia and into its neighboring state, South Australia. Car No. 18 shimmied in with a completely collapsed front suspension, but the British pairing of Mike Greenwood and Dave Aldridge were soon at work on the two-year-old Mark I Cortina—no team of mechanics for them! There was, however, a general acceptance that, provided a works service team had nothing else to do, they would help any independent entrant in need, especially if they were driving a version of the brand they were supporting. Irish private competitors Ernie McMillen, John L'Amie and Ian Drysdale arrived in search of a new fan belt for their maroon Cortina Lotus, which was promptly supplied by a Ford team mechanic. Having had an extremely uneventful run all the way from London and now lying in a very respectable 28th place in the field, British team Alister Percy and Jeremy Delmar-Morgan appeared in their compact SAAB 95 station wagon, which was now missing its front spotlights. On the way to Ceduna, they had briefly become airborne and landed nose-first but had carried on regardless.

Despite seeming endless, the road to Ceduna was at least either paved or graded and therefore invited many a driver to floor the gas pedal. Marathon organizers suggested an average speed of 64 mph during this section, but many of the more powerful cars were really given a chance to open up and run at 90-plus. The miles of boredom were occasionally interrupted by the sudden appearance of small groups of cheering spectators, having apparently popped up from nowhere, there being no obvious villages or homesteads on the maps. These distractions were few and far between, however, and everyone was hugely relieved to finally reach the time control, especially Cowan, Coyle and Malkin, who had had a narrow escape when they hit another disguised crater. As Cowan wrote, "we hit it at over 90 mph. The car leaped ten feet in the air, I'll swear, and I sat in the back seat so that I could see which gum tree we were going to hit."[2] Innes Ireland, Andrew Hedges and Michael Taylor were not so lucky as it was here before Ceduna that they saw their Marathon hopes fade into nothing.

The top ten crews remained more-or-less the same as leaders Clark and Andersson sped off into the night on the next section, a 300-mile-plus belt over mostly paved roads. Another team having an excellent run were teammates Eric Jackson and Ken Chambers, who were only four points down on tenth-place Falcon crew Bruce Hodgson and Doug Rutherford. For now, things were looking encouraging for Ford GB, after the disappointments of Gunnar Palm and Bengt Söderström, Nick and Jenny Brittan and Rosemary Smith and Lucette Pointet, although the British Army team of Captain David Harrison and Lieutenant Martin Proudlock still soldiered on in 35th position. At the next control in the town of Quorn, however, things would take an incredible turn for the worse.

Twenty-six miles before Quorn lies the seaport town of Port Augusta at the top of Spencer Gulf, and it was here that competitors were headed as service centers had been set up so both professional and private competitors alike could stop and get their vehicles ready for the extremely tough coming sections through the Flinders Ranges. The leading cars were expected after midnight and, as the minutes passed, ears were straining to hear the sound of high revs, especially the team managers for Ford GB, Citroën and Ford Germany. Suddenly lights appeared in the distance, approaching fast. Ford GB boss Henry Taylor watched as the first car in was the Citroën, followed moments later by the Ford 20MRS. As the German car was set upon by mechanics, racing to replace front suspension parts, more cars arrived, but not Clark and Andersson. Fifteen minutes after the Citroën had appeared, a Ford GB team Cortina Lotus hurtled into the Ford service area and out climbed Jackson and Chambers, who immediately sought out Taylor. The news wasn't good—they had passed Clark a while back and No. 48 was in trouble, struggling to do more than 50 mph. As Ford mechanics descended on the Jackson and Chambers car, Taylor began the waiting game. At last Clark's car arrived, the engine sounding suspiciously similar to how the Smith and Pointet Cortina had done back in Herat in Afghanistan. A valve had closed and the car was laboring with only three cylinders. Worse still, the Ford service team didn't have a replacement cylinder head at Port Augusta, so Roger Clark and Ove Andersson, the leading competitors for thousands of miles, were suddenly faced with defeat.

For Ford GB, although they had entered six cars into the Marathon, they believed that Roger Clark was their greatest chance for success, and although every Ford GB competitor was "in it to win it," there was also a team hierarchy. As Eric Jackson wrote, "A team is a team and in my experience, it's the team who calls the shots." Henry Taylor looked at the crippled Clark/Andersson car and then looked at the other, healthy Ford GB Cortina Lotus. Jackson wrote that "Henry had to make a decision.... I think he made the wrong one. He turned to

Eric Jackson and Ken Chambers set off from Gloucester Park trotting track in Perth, Australia, December 14 (courtesy Martin Proudlock).

me and said, 'Sorry, old man, but we're going to take the cylinder head off your car and put it in Roger's.' Well, what could we do? We couldn't do anything."[3] Suddenly, after thousands of miles of well-planned and careful driving, during which they had kept up with the top ten throughout, Jackson and Chambers were out.

Once the decision was made, mechanics quickly began to remove the cylinder head from No. 73 and refit it to No. 48. Racing against the clock, Taylor instructed them that without fail, Roger and Ove must be given a minimum of 30 minutes to cover the last 26 miles to the Quorn time control, but as the work continued it was clear that time was simply running out. With less than half an hour to go, the command was given to start the engine. Nothing— the engine turned over but failed to spark. Frantic activity followed while Clark, Andersson, Taylor and a tangle of fascinated spectators held their breath. At last the engine fired and No. 48 shot away into the night, driver and co-driver hell-bent on making the checkpoint on time. It wasn't to be and they picked up 14 points, but they actually managed to complete 26 miles of night-time, snaking track in 16 minutes. They weren't about to give up yet!

Volvo pair Jack Forrest and Ken Tubman had new problems during the drive from Lake King. With the injured Forrest unable to contribute, Tubman was struggling to combine driving with checking the route notes and, as a result, "dropped the Volvo into a pothole at speed. That must have been when I knocked off the brake master cylinder."[4] They tore into Port Augusta without any brakes, but were then forced to continue on to Quorn before the problem could be fixed. In spite of this, unlike nine other cars, they were points-free at the Quorn control. In total, 67 entrants remained in the Marathon, but the Simca 1100 of Pierre Boucher and George Houel was awarded the maximum 1,440 points for failing to appear and was officially retired at the next control. Clark and Andersson had now slipped to third overall at Quorn, with Lampinen and Staepelaere leading in their German Ford 20MRS and Bianchi and Ogier in second place. The next three sections, however, through the Flinders Ranges would probably be the most difficult Australian stages of all.

The Castrol Navigation Notes, as prepared by Ford's Bill Barnett, John Davenport and Gunnar Palm from their reconnaissance prior to the Marathon, described the 72 miles north to the Moralana Creek checkpoint as "One of the less pleasant sections as there is no asphalt and the road is quite rough in places. It is doubtful whether this section is on in the time allowed."[5] Drivers had 77 minutes to complete the stage, which meant an average speed of 56 mph over gravel and dirt with sudden dips and crests, cattle grids, gates that would need to be opened and closed, shallow rivers and creeks and rock-strewn track. It is a testimony to the skill and resolve of the remaining drivers that only 31 cars lost time, but the terrain was tough and shock absorbers were being pushed to the limit—Alister Percy and Jeremy Delmar-Morgan checked in at Moralana without penalty, but they were puzzled that their air-horn had stopped working. Examining the SAAB, they noticed a hole in one of the fenders where a shock had been wrenched loose, taking the air compressor with it. Percy recalled that the driving conditions had been so difficult that they'd failed to notice the difference! It was also here that Jim Gavin's Ford Escort came down hard on a rock and damaged its oil pan, forcing the team to repeatedly feed the car with gallons of oil all the way to Sydney, while British competitor Frank Goulden and his sons Barry and Geoffrey saw their Marathon come to an end when No. 27, their Triumph 2000, could go no further.

The next section to Brachina Gorge on the edge of the Flinders Range National Park was even tougher and navigation notes warned that conditions meant it would be easy to damage a car beyond repair, something that sixth-place Scots Cowan, Malkin and Coyle only just managed to avoid as the Hillman fought its way to Brachina. Cowan had begun to notice that the Hunter's brakes were losing bite and approaching the end of the section, he was confronted with a hairpin. Cowan wrote that "Brian was calmly reading his pace notes to me…, when to my horror the brake pedal went straight to the floor. As I attempted to take the corner at about 70 mph, I shot straight off the road into piles of deep sand."[6] Luckily, there were enough spectators on hand to help get the car back on track and, once checked in, investigation revealed a separated brake line joint. Coincidentally the other Rootes team Hunter also suffered brake problems before Brachina, but the RAF team was able to match Cowan's points-free section.

Bianchi and Ogier were now in the lead as failing shock absorbers hampered Staepelaere and Lampinen, which meant a renewed Clark and Andersson moved into second place. As cars raced into the control, drivers were quickly able to take advantage of service points to have their pummeled vehicles checked over, and stories soon began to emerge of unexpected problems that many competitors had been forced to contend with after leaving Moralana. Enthusiastic local car club members had used colored flags and markers to highlight the best way over some of the most difficult terrain and those few who had previously studied the section were annoyed that this advantage had been eliminated. Others complained of dirty tricks, with one driver reporting that "a young man, acting as interference for a top team had told him the route he was about to take had been blocked."[7] The driver had ignored the warning and had found no such obstruction. Regardless of these additional challenges, all cars covered the section with the exception of Australians Alec Gorshenin and Ian Bryson, who felt a rock smash into their Mercedes 280SL's undercarriage, taking out its transmission.

From Brachina Gorge, Marathon organizers had devised what navigation notes warned would be perhaps the most difficult of all sections, a 210-mile scramble along a barely discernible path covered with boulders, shallow rivers and the ever present dust across the state border between South Australia and New South Wales. The warning proved to be highly appropriate as a number of competitors discovered. After his near-miss on the previous section, soon after leaving Brachina Andrew Cowan misjudged a corner and came to a halt in a gully, the Hunter stranded on a hump. The Scots anxiously tried to find purchase for the rear wheels, but the blue Hillman was going nowhere. Fate intervened in the form of BMC Australia crew Evan Green, "Gelignite" Jack Murray and George Shepheard, whose help in getting the Hunter back on track made a significant contribution to the Marathon's final outcome, not least because out of Brachina, the Australian 1800 and the Scottish Hillman carried 32 points each. The gallant actions by the "Gelignite" crew enabled Cowan to arrive at the next control at Mingary without penalty, but further along the trail No. 31 broke a torsion bar. Although Cowan reciprocated the favor by alerting the BMC service mechanics at Mingary, a breakdown in communication led to inaction by BMC. Beginning to wonder if anyone was going to arrive and rescue the sidelined 1800, the three Australians resorted to carving a message in the sand to attract their own team's service aircraft! By the time they were moving again, having long been a serious contender, they collected 232 points for lateness at the next control, effectively blowing their chances of a prize at Sydney.

John Hemsley, British Army Rover 2000TC driver, remarked that "I was always terribly interested in the psychology of long distance driving when you got really tired and the relationships you have with your co-driver, what used to happen when you got very, very tired. That's when tempers can get very short; it's when you start making mistakes." No. 36 was crewed by a driver, David McKay, a navigator and support driver, George Reynolds and a mechanic, David Liddle. However, during the drive across Europe and Asia it had become apparent that Reynolds didn't want to navigate and felt his driving skills were better than McKay's. Thus it was that, with McKay asleep in the rear of the Holden Monaro, Reynolds was driving as fast as possible because the dust was so deep when he encountered a hard right-hander. A combination of speed and dust defeated Reynolds and, as he wrestled the wheel, the car skidded and flipped over. Unfortunately, although the team had been wearing crash helmets during some of the European and Asian sections, they had relaxed the rules once they were on home soil and, as a result, although McKay and Liddle were unhurt, Reynolds sustained a serious head injury. With the help of a spectator's Land Rover and a length of rope, the Monaro was rolled upright and surprisingly started up first time. The injured Reynolds was placed on the rear seat and the luckless crew raced on to the nearest emergency center at Broken Hill, the road to which went straight through the Mingary control. No. 36 checked in for its final time in the Marathon and immediately continued on so that Reynolds could be hospitalized. Without their third crew member, McKay and Liddle were out, so they chose the most direct route and drove the damaged Holden straight through to Sydney.

The section from Brachina claimed other victims, with the tortuous conditions finally defeating No. 95, the Vauxhall Viva GT of Japanese trio Nobuo Koga, Yojiro Terada and Kazuhiko Mitsumoto and No. 3, the British Royal Air Force Cortina GT. The orange Porsche

911T of the British Royal Green Jackets Jack Dill and George Yannaghas also saw its demise when it lost its front suspension. No. 94, the Citroën DS21 of Anglo-French team Jean-Louis Lemerle, Olivier Turcat and Patrick Vanson saw its hydro-pneumatic suspension collapse. Although the Cortina Lotus of Irish threesome Ernie McMillen, John L'Amie and Ian Drysdale had a rollover, they were able to continue in the competition. All told, at Mingary, 59 cars remained in the running, including two British Armed Forces entrants, which were lying in 33rd and 49th positions respectively. Major John Hemsley and Warrant Officer Frank Webber were competing in No. 54 and No. 44 was crewed by Major Mike Bailey and Major Freddie Preston.

John and Mike had quite a Marathon.

29

A Sleeping Bag to Kandahar

By the time Royal Electrical and Mechanical Engineers (REME) Major Michael Beaton Bailey sat waiting for his Rover 2000TC to be called to the starting ramp at Crystal Palace in November 1968, he was already no stranger to automotive adventure. Three years previously, Mike had climbed into an Amphicar 700 and set off from London's Marble Arch with a fellow serving officer, Captain Peter Tappenden, on the way to the Frankfurt Motor Show in Germany, via the English Channel. Produced from 1961 to 1965, and boasting President Lyndon B. Johnson as a customer, the Amphicar was designed to combine the joys of motoring with those of boat ownership. However, nobody had ever attempted to cross the busy Channel to France before. Two Amphicars entered the water at Dover Harbor on England's south coast and despite encountering a force five wind and large waves, seven hours and twenty minutes later they arrived at Calais, although not before Mike and Peter had been required to attach a tow rope to the other vehicle mid-crossing when its bilge pump became blocked. This degree of *chutzpah* and ingenuity would serve Mike well during the 10,000-mile drive from London to Sydney, even if it didn't actually include driving across the sea.

The British Army Motoring Association (BAMA) was established in 1960 as a means of testing navigation and driving skills both on and off the road. A very early member was John Hemsley, who had done his mandatory military service, or National Service, in 1953 and decided to remain in the Army thereafter. As he explained, the BAMA was "an official organization driving Land Rovers and other vehicles at events. In those days there were about six or seven of us who had international licenses." John initially concentrated on sport cars and track racing, but when he was posted to Africa in the early sixties he was introduced to rallying by East African Safari Rally veteran Arthur Berton. As he explained, "I'd been racing this car and Arthur Berton came up to me and he said, 'Have you ever done any motor rallying?' The racing fraternity tends to look down on rallying and I took that as a grave insult because obviously my style on the track was thoroughly untidy—too much sideways motoring!" Berton was particularly persuasive, however, and John went on to compete in African rallies in a VW bug. Upon returning to England, for a while he joined the Ford GB works team and throughout the 1960s drove for different factory teams in a number of national and international events, including the Monte Carlo Rally, all the while continuing to serve in the army.

Mike Bailey was introduced to rallying in 1960 when, as part of his REME corps training, he was sent to Associated Electrical Industries in Manchester in northwest England. He joined a local motoring club and began entering amateur events until he was posted to Malaya,

No. 54 team: Warrant Officer Frank Webber (left) and Major John Hemsley (courtesy John Hemsley).

where he set up a forces motoring club. Returning to England in 1964 he found himself based in Bordon in Hampshire and quickly joined the BAMA, which was headquartered close by. His first event was the Scottish International Rally, in which he competed in a Land Rover. "I started at the tail end and I finished at the tail end," he recalled. "In the back we had spare wheels and nobody told me you've got to screw these things down because I'd never actually been on a special stage in my life. I had a five-gallon Castrol Oil can loose in the back. When we got to the far end, we stopped, booked ourselves in and I went to the back and there was this spare wheel askew and the oil can had been punctured and everything was covered in Castrol XL—learning experience!" Mike graduated to a Mini Cooper S the following year and eventually got invited to drive for the BMC factory team.

By 1967, Mike had begun competing with Freddie Preston, a Major in the Royal Army Ordnance Corps, while John was entering events with REME Warrant Officer Frank Webber. Both Freddie and John had already driven Rovers in rallies and Rover had a long established partnership with the British Armed Forces, manufacturing and supplying Land Rovers adapted for military use. In 1968, ex-army officer Peter Pender-Cudlip was responsible for Rover's military sales and had built a relationship with the BAMA, so when the London to Sydney Marathon was announced, Pender-Cudlip suggested that Rover's motorsports department consider the possibility of offering two cars to the BAMA, which they did, supplying two 1965 ex-rally Rover 2000TC cars. Rover also seconded David Moss, a member of its

No. 44 gets ready—Major Mike Bailey (left) and Major Freddie Preston (courtesy Mike Bailey).

motorsports team, to the School of Electrical and Mechanical Engineering at Bordon for three months where the cars were to be prepared, advising on all things mechanical and structural while the teams took responsibility for specifying the cockpit setup. Because Major Hemsley was based in Germany at the time, however, he was busy arranging for a BMC 1800 to be prepared for competition and decided to fit the rally driving seat intended for his Rover into the 1800. As a result, a lack of expenses meant that he was forced to keep the original seat in the Rover, which he believes has contributed to him having back pain ever since.

John eventually returned to England, only weeks before the Marathon began, and promptly developed pneumonia. As he explained, "I was not sure that I was going to be a lot of use to anyone on this particular trip. However, there could be no thought of falling out at this stage—too many people had helped us to get this far! The Army helped to finance the project through funds provided by BAMA, the NAAFI [Navy, Army and Air Force Institutes] provided £200 worth of personal clothing and equipment and countless firms and manufacturers had loaned or presented us with every conceivable item that we might need on the journey from brake linings to boiled sweets. Last but not least, a long-suffering Army headquarters had given me permission to be away for the period of this event—it is just possible that they hoped we should not come back!" On November 23, the two teams presented the Rovers at Crystal Palace for scrutiny, where promoters quickly got to work, attaching advertising decals onto the cars, while Mike and John learned their positions in the starting order—Mike and Feddie Preston would be 44th away and John and Frank Webber 54th. Stuffed full of medication, John blearily inspected his car, this being the first time he had actually seen it. As he recalled, "The inside looked rather like an ironmonger's van and I wasn't at all sure where we were both going to fit in." Overall, however, both Rovers definitely looked fit for purpose, complete with 'roo bar and a large array of main and auxiliary lights. Both cars' engines had been detuned to cope with the low octane gasoline that they would undoubtedly have to use across Asia and in the trunks were two additional 15 gallon fuel tanks fitted with high-capacity pumps. The cars' springs had been uprated to provide increased ground clearance and the rear seats had been removed to allow space for carrying extra wheels, water, extra parts and tools. As John reflected, "The one thing I learned fairly early on—and we made this mistake on the Marathon—is the danger if you try to take too many extra parts. Normally the spare you want is not the one you're carrying."

On the day of departure, Mike recalled that on the approach to the Crystal Palace stadium itself, the roads were jammed with cars and people and while everyone was trying to move aside whenever they saw a Marathon car, it took them 30 minutes to cover the last mile. With cars finally parked in the competitors' enclosure, the two teams fought their way through the crowds for a final briefing. As Mike explained, "The tent was just big enough to hold everybody as Sir Max Aitken stood up to make an announcement. As he rose there was a thunderous bang as "Gelignite" Jack Murray let off a firework and simultaneously there was a sound of splintering wood and half a dozen of those assembled collapsed onto the floor in a heap." Cheered on by their families and a number of British Army Generals, Colonels and Majors, at 2:42 pm, Mike and Freddie were called to the starting ramp where they were flagged away one minute later. After 20 minutes it was the turn of John and Frank, but not before John's young daughter insisted that a toy koala presented as a mascot by one of their sponsors should remain in her care for the duration of the event. All competitors were required to complete a circuit of the race track before exiting the stadium and, as John recalled, "I was actually really fueled up on antibiotics and I knew Crystal Palace racing circuit, I had raced there, but I drove round Crystal Palace thinking I was at Brands Hatch, so none of the corners matched. Poor old Frank Webber was distinctly nervous before we ever actually left the starting line at Crystal Palace!" John's and Mike's Marathon had begun.

The BAMA had used its networks to ensure that the Rovers were met by service vehicles at pre-arranged points through Europe and Asia and that, where possible, they would be able to supply 100-octane gasoline, although it wasn't certain whether the service crews would be able to take the fuel across international borders. With

Major Freddie Preston at Crystal Palace, London, November 24 (courtesy Mike Bailey).

BAMA service Land Rover (courtesy John Hemsley).

this support structure in place, both Rovers arrived at the Belgrade control in Yugoslavia without incident and then continued on into Bulgaria, with more than a little trepidation— as serving officers in the British Army, this would be their first time "behind the Iron Curtain." Their reception at the Bulgarian border crossing was uneventful, but once across, Freddie decided to get some gasoline coupons from the exchange point. Mike parked the Rover and, as he explained, "It was very dark. A short stubby man dressed in a dark overcoat which reached down to his ankles and a Kremlin-type trilby hat walked past pretending not to be there. As he turned around I noticed a flash camera hanging around his neck. The same strange feeling I had experienced on the other side of the border returned, a world of secret police, a world of fear." Fortunately, just then, Freddie returned with the coupons and they sped off into the night in search of a gas station.

Both teams were reunited at the Bulgarian capital of Sofia, where the British military attaché had set up an impromptu picnic of soup, chicken and wine for any of the British Armed Forces entrants who wanted to stop. Whether it was the wine, the antibiotics or the gradual acclimatization to competitive conditions, shortly afterwards, as John recalled, "It was a long straight, pitch black and pissing with rain, slashing down. Apparently, according to the car behind, there was a sign, which said 15 kph [9 mph], level crossing. I never saw it and we must have been doing about 90 and we hit this crossing with a most enormous bang. Everything went quiet, like an airplane taking off. Most of the car was going up in the air and all the lights were shining up into the air and I could just see the rain coming down. There was absolute silence for quite an appreciable time. I believe we flew something like 30 yards and when we came down there was an enormous crash on the road. Silence again and then a second crash and it really did settle all the bits and pieces down in the boot [trunk]. From then on I was quite all right actually." In fact the toxic mix of wine, medication and raging pneumonia lasted until Istanbul when, upon leaving the time control, John managed to gun the Rover over the lawn of the Istanbul Hotel, through a hedge and end up straddling the concrete divide on the highway out of the city.

The route across Turkey saw the first of two mishaps to befall John and Frank when before Sivas, as John explained, "clouds of acrid smoke started curling from behind the dashboard and Frank spent most of the time rewiring the electrics every time I threw a switch. We discovered that all the wiring was in one color—red—which caused some consternation. Finally, in the middle of a blinding sleet storm, the windscreen wipers packed up for good. We were to have 1,000 miles of rain and snow and no windscreen wipers until we got to Tehran. We disconnected the motor and operated the windscreen wipers by string led in through the side windows." Then, on the first special stage of the Marathon between Sivas and Erzincan, although Mike and Freddie put in a respectable performance, losing only 39 minutes on the difficult section, a stupid error cost John and Frank dearly. At Sivas, No. 54 was serviced, even though John didn't think it was really necessary. As he explained, "There was a service crew there and you know when these guys are traveling hundreds, thousands of miles to get to the back of beyond, you've got to let them do something, they're all so enthusiastic. They started looking at everything, checking everything up. They're all enthusiastic because they haven't seen the inside of the car before and this guy left his pliers, a pair of pliers on the top of the radiator, slammed the bonnet [hood] down, off we went." Leaving the control, John got the Rover up to 5,000 revs and suddenly there was a bang—the pliers had fallen into the fan, which promptly punctured the radiator. Forced to return to the Sivas control, they quickly debated the pros and cons of fitting a replacement radiator versus repairing the damaged item. Deciding on the latter, they plugged up the hole and continued on, arriving at Erzincan almost three hours down upon the allotted time.

Both cars crossed into Iran and arrived at the Teheran control within the allowed margin of time, although not without further trouble. Near the Turkish border Mike and Freddie began to notice a clunking noise coming from the rear of the Rover. Mike explained, "One of the big problems in the Rover was the rear suspension, the de Dion layout, trailing arm thing, and we thought we'd be very clever and we'd have Aeon rubbers on the chassis to limit the amount of up and down. Anyway Rover approved it so off we went and there was this noise. It got progressively worse, so we stopped, jacked the car up and the rear offside link had broken under the spring." Freddie flagged down a passing motorcyclist and took the broken link to a village they had passed in the hope of seeking repair. A few hours later he returned with the link newly welded, refitted it and No. 44 was able to carry on to Teheran where both Rovers were serviced and No. 54 had its errant electrics attended to. Then it was off on the 610-mile run to Mashhad and over the border into Afghanistan.

From the next service point at Herat, the Marathon followed the circular King's Highway south before turning northwards again at Kandahar. John and Frank pressed onwards, but up ahead, they saw a car jacked up on the side of the road and were dismayed to discover that it was No. 44, Mike and Freddie hard at work underneath. The Rover's de Dion tube suspension had failed again so John pulled over. Frustratingly, both teams realized there was nothing John and Frank could do to assist, so Mike told them to get back on the road before returning to the job at hand. However, the broken rear suspension required more work than they could achieve on the isolated Afghani roadside, so faced with no alternative and with darkness descending, they decided to try and redistribute the weight of their additional equipment, moving as much as possible into the interior of the car and strapping what they could onto the hood. Among the gear they were carrying were two sleeping bags, so the army-trained duo struck upon a clever plan to further reduce the weight-bearing stress on the Rover's rear end. Mike climbed into a sleeping bag and tucked himself in between the car's grille and 'roo bar and Freddie drove for 40-plus miles towards Kandahar while his teammate clung on up front! Shortly before reaching Kandahar itself, Freddie again pulled over to give Mike a break from his *al fresco* escapade. Moments later, a bus appeared so Mike flagged it down. "We had overalls on, racing overalls on, so we must have looked very strange to these people," he said. "Bus stops, the door opens, I look inside and the bus is full of men, Afghani men with their hats, standing, no seats, standing there—right through, up to the driver. So I said 'Kandahar?' He said 'uh,' so I thought—you know, when I think about it, I could have been murdered! Ignorance is bliss." Mike boarded the bus and, with Freddie coaxing the sagging Rover along behind, they arrived at a crossroads in central Kandahar, where Mike bade his fellow travelers farewell and Freddie guided No. 44 to the roadside.

An extraordinary sight lay before the two intrepid competitors—there in the middle of the junction stood a table, at which sat two local police officers, complete with a telephone. Mike explained how "I went over and said 'Excuse me, do you speak English?' He said 'Yes.' I said 'Car's broken down. I wonder if you can help me?' So he picks up this phone, and I thought this is sort of Noel Coward stuff, this is Whitehall Theatre, and he puts the phone down and he said, 'My driver will come up in a few minutes and he will escort you to the United States airbase about five miles out of town.'" Sure enough, the call was made and a few minutes later a car arrived, which led them to the United States base where they were able to have the broken links re-welded. Unfortunately, there is a difference between gas welding and electric welding as the pair would discover.

With their rear suspension holding up, John and Frank made it to Kabul in good time and were greeted by the British military attaché to Afghanistan, Colonel Timbrell, who had arranged for the pair to have a meal and a rest. Once the Lataband Pass was open, they were away again, losing only 24 points at Sarobi. Then, as John remembered, "We snatched a few vital minutes to make a photographic pilgrimage to Jalalabad, scene of the most glorious hour of the Regiment into which I was first commissioned, in order to send some pictorial records back to the regimental magazine." Sadly, a leaking water tank in the back of the Rover saw both camera and film destroyed some miles later.

Across Pakistan and India the crowds were unfathomable and agitated and, as well as the repeated attempts by onlookers to grab souvenirs from the Rover's exterior, John and Frank twice came face-to-face with the persistently chaotic behavior of road users. The first involved a "tuk-tuk," one of Pakistan's countless little motorized rickshaws, which, as John explained, "tried to cut across our path and we just caught it with the 'roo bar and we ripped open the side like a tin can and the whole side fell off. We didn't stop to find out, I'm afraid, we kept going." The second saw the Rover collide with a cyclist; John explained that this was as a consequence of the only time that he and Frank had a disagreement, with Frank complaining that John was using the car's air horn too much. John relinquished the wheel to Frank, who continued with greater stealth and thus failed to give a noisy warning to the wandering bicyclist. Despite the assorted wreckage left in their wake, they were fifth car into

Major Mike Bailey has a tea break in Afghanistan; others are unidentified (courtesy Mike Bailey).

Bombay and found themselves in 42nd place out of a field of 72 survivors. Any relief was tempered, however, by the fact that an ominous noise had begun to emanate from the Rover's rear suspension.

Far behind them, Mike and Freddie had struggled on, but between Delhi and Bombay, their suspension linkage went again. By now they were practiced in the drill, so the Rover was jacked up and the pair slid underneath. Presently, along came an Indian man who stopped and sprang into action, persuading them to follow him back up the road to a village through which they had just passed. The man led them to a garage workshop where, as Mike explained, "they knew exactly what to do. They had an electric welding kit and he didn't have a mask. He got his welding rod, he laid some strip metal between the earth [ground] point and the work piece and he set to. So it was about three quarters of an hour and we came out and he'd repaired this thing and off we went." They had learned the hard way that to repair the Rover's rather delicate de Dion tube suspension linkage, electric welding was the only choice. Thus, newly suspended, they arrived at Ballard's Pier in 58th place and immediately sent a message to Rover headquarters in England to highlight the car's weakness.

During the brief stop in Bombay, John and Frank had a lesson in the competitive rivalry between the different disciplines of the British Armed Forces. While their Rover was receiving its own welding repairs, John and Frank were invited to a party in their honor aboard an Indian Navy vessel moored next to the SS *Chusan*. John had previously been posted to the Indian Staff College and an Indian naval officer friend who was now commanding a destroyer had not only arranged for a celebration to take place, but had also facilitated the unexpected attendance of many of John's old colleagues from across India. One of the Marathon cars had been entered by the British Royal Navy and, as John explained, "We never met them because they were a little bit stand-offish to the Army, which was unusual, but they were looking down and apparently they were really upset because they were Royal Naval chaps and they hadn't been invited to anything and they saw this great party going on aboard this Indian naval vessel and they wouldn't speak to us again!"

After nine days of sun and mischief, the SS *Chusan* deposited competitors at Fremantle in Western Australia and, once the bureaucratic formalities of cleaning and inspecting the cars were complete, both teams joined the convoy to Gloucester Park in Perth, the plan being to take the two Rovers directly to a local dealership once they were flagged away to start the Australian leg of the Marathon. Arriving at the Perth Rover dealership, as Mike recounted, "There were these two crates broken open, ready for us to go in and there was everything in there. Rover knew what the problems were. They got these links out, jacked the car up, took the links off and we looked at these links from Rover and they were properly reinforced and made for the job and I thought, why the bloody hell didn't they fit those, they knew? So off we went. No more problems with the car." Refreshed and renewed, both teams and their Rovers set off to drive the 3,000 miles from Perth to Sydney. The journey would not be without incident.

"It was the bull dust, in texture like talcum powder, as fine and penetrating. Our nostrils filled with it, our throats were dry and rough, the air was hot and there was no wind. Through the dust clouds created by the previous car the sun disappeared into the brown red haze."[1] So wrote Mike Bailey of his experience of the Australian outback as he and Freddie Preston wrestled their Rover 2000TC across the rutted track and camouflaged craters. John Hemsley described the dust as "our main enemy in Australia. Bull dust filled up the worst holes so that they looked like smooth sand; rough tracks twisting through the eucalyptus bush, fit only for Land Rovers." These were the conditions that met both teams as they set off from the Youanmi checkpoint, both losing over half an hour as they thumped and bumped their way to the Marvel Loch control. However, on the Australian media-styled "horror stretch" to Lake King, both Rovers met obstacles that impacted progress, albeit for different reasons. John and Frank hit a mound at speed, which left the car's shock absorbers permanently compressed, and they were forced to drive over a thousand miles across the wretched Nullarbor Plain to Port Augusta "with only two inches ground clearance and every shock going straight up the steering column." This hindrance was nothing compared to that inflicted upon Mike and Freddie, however, as No. 44 whipped up dust and stones approximately 50 minutes behind.

Thirty miles short of Lake King, with Mike at the wheel on the seemingly deserted outback trail, they came across an orange tent erected just off the track. Mike wrote that "Standing alongside, taking pictures and cheering us on our way was a family—husband, wife and four children. Their green Holden estate [station wagon] had the back down and tea was being brewed."[2] The Rover skittered past and the cadence of the track ahead seemed to push the car first left and then right. Mike tried to correct the wheels, locking the brakes in the process, but it was too late. The car cannoned into the bush and rammed a tree, cutting out the engine. Mike and Freddie recovered themselves and climbed out to inspect the damage, their spirits sinking to discover that their 'roo bar had been forced into the front of the car and the hood wouldn't open. Leaving Freddie to pick over the damaged spotlights, Mike jogged back up

Major John Hemsley at Gloucester Park trotting track, Perth, December 14 (courtesy John Hemsley).

the trail to see whether the camping family could assist, which they were only too happy to do. A short while later, with the hood now prized open, Freddie watched as the green Holden wagon pulled up and out stepped Mike and their salvation in the form of the Orton family of Perth. With Mrs. Orton and the children watching, Mike, Freddie and Mr. Orton set about using the winch that Mike and Freddie had included in the car's spare equipment to drag the Rover out of its resting place. Next they used ropes and the winch to straighten the Rover's front end enough to remove the shattered radiator, quickly fitting the replacement they had almost decided not to carry. However, their trouble wasn't over yet as the battery was damaged. Somehow, with promises that the Rover's service crew would appear eventually carrying a replacement, Mike persuaded the Ortons to sacrifice their Holden's battery and after a quick cup of tea, the Rover resumed its scramble over the rocks and gullies towards Lake King. As Mike recalled, "When we got to Sydney, we had this guy's name, so we went to—it was either the radio station or *Sydney Telegraph*—and told them what had happened and they found this guy and we sent him a message thanking him." Despite the fact that there was no guarantee that the Rover service crew would have come along, the Ortons had eventually managed to get their family station wagon back to Perth.

No. 44's adventure on the way from Marvel Loch proved expensive, however, as Mike and Freddie hurtled into the Lake King control one minute and 54 seconds late, which earned them the maximum 1,440 point penalty. "'What the devil are we doing this for anyway, it's all so damned pointless if you ask me,' I [Mike] remarked. 'Nobody in their right senses does this unless he has to—we must be crazy.' 'All I can say is that there are 98 others, equally crazy, so I guess that's some sort of consolation,' he [Freddie] replied."[3] With this exchange lingering in the dusty air, the British Army pair carried on across the Nullarbor towards Ceduna.

At Port Augusta, John and Frank grabbed the chance to fix the Rover's paralyzed shock absorbers and both cars continued on towards the Flinders Ranges sections, but as John grappled the Rover's steering wheel over the relentless, rocky section between Menindee and Gunbar, an alarming clatter from underneath the car brought them to a halt. John recalled that "There were some lumbermen. We were in an area of forest and I thought, well the best thing to do, we'll tip the car on its side because we didn't have the things to jack it up. So we tipped the car on its side and put a couple of posts underneath. Frank got underneath and these Aussie lumberjacks were absolutely amazed, they hadn't seen anything like this before. I said no, no, this will work, we do this at home in the Scottish forests." The Rover's differential had come away from its mounting so Frank set about securing it back in place with some wire clipped from a nearby fence. Suddenly, a grating noise alerted John to impending danger so grabbing Frank's feet, he dragged him from underneath the car just as the supporting logs penetrated the Rover's floor pan, bringing the car crashing down, completely impaled. Once the lumberjacks had stopped laughing, they helped get the car free and John and Frank con-

tinued with two holes in the floor and a Rover that rapidly filled with bull dust! During the last 30 hours of the Marathon, Frank Webber made 22 further repairs to the Rover's differential.

By close of play on December 17, 1968, two dusty Rover 2000TCs and four dusty British army officers had rolled into Warwick Farm. John and Frank learned that they were 39th overall, with Mike and Freddie placed 44th. During the days that followed, the Australian Rover distributors for New South Wales looked after the four men and were very happy to put both cars on display in showrooms around the state, although Mike was left with a nagging question about the delicate de Dion tube suspension on the car. He explained that "When we got to the end, the chief for Rover in Australia said Rover knew all about this. When they had the prototypes trialed in Australia, this was one of the problems they had, so we told them what to do,

No. 44 at Warwick Farm Raceway, December 17 (courtesy Mike Bailey).

how to reinforce them and they had all the designs and everything but it was never taken up." Upon his return to England, Mike raised this with Rover, asking why they hadn't strengthened the suspension links for the Marathon. Mike was bemused to learn that Rover had never really believed the two cars would get to Sydney!

Finally, all that was left was for Mike Bailey, Freddie Preston, John Hemsley and Frank Webber to join up with David Harrison, Martin Proudlock, the Red Arrows team and the RAF Hunter crew, and take their seats on an RAF Hercules aircraft, which transported them back to England just in time for Christmas. As John explained, "It had been an unforgettable experience, but it had been a team effort all the way—from the people at home who were still manning their typewriters and telephones to keep the administrative back-up ticking over, to the service crews who waited long hours in the back of beyond to service the cars in biting cold or scorching heat and without whom we certainly should never have got through."

30

Can I Buy Your Axle Please?

Out of the little South Australian town of Mingary, only 31 points separated Bianchi and Ogier from the tenth-place car, another Citroën DS21 driven by French rally driver Robert Neyret and his regular co-driver Jacques Terramorsi, but while the professionals were jostling for position at the front, further down the field another battle was in full swing—the fight to be first-place private entry at Sydney. Across Australia, two entrants had been having their own private competition as first one and then the other car edged ahead on points. At Mingary, in their Porsche 911, German-born Kenyan Edgar Herrmann and German Hans Schüller held the advantage by 12 points over the MG Midget of British pair John Sprinzel and Roy Fidler. One hundred and sixteen miles later, Sprinzel and Fidler clocked into the Menindee control in New South Wales to claw back the lead by just one point.

Despite the relatively easy section along paved roads, 21 cars lost points at Menindee, including Zasada and Wachowski, who were piloting their Porsche at full throttle across Australia and beginning to challenge the leading five cars. Seven points down on Bianchi and Ogier, the German Ford 20MRS of Staepelaere and Lampinen arrived at the control without any shock absorption to their rear suspension and a back axle that was in danger of becoming completely dislocated. Their service team mobilized in lightning speed to strip the perished shocks and realign the axle and suspension, the entire German Ford team anxious to keep the third-place car in the competition. Gerry Lister and André Welinski roared into the control and Gerry quickly went in search of welding equipment, as their Volvo had damaged a track rod. For want of a welding rod Lister improvised, recalling that "I slipped underneath it, borrowed some Oxy from a bloke, a couple of coat hangers and did a bit of welding. The more I looked at it, this is just cracked everywhere, no point going any further so funnily enough, after we finished, I decided to pull the cross member off and it just fell apart, it just broke to pieces. I don't know why it held together."

The route from Mingary to Menindee took competitors through the isolated mining town of Broken Hill, where local police were again hard at work enforcing speed limits, with one newspaper reporting that "Russian Marathon drivers said N.S.W. [New South Wales] police were worse than Russian police. Mr. D. Tenishev, driver of car No. 19, a Moskvitch 408 said: 'In Russia police would help a rally like this.'"[1] Fellow Russian competitor Alexander Ipantenko claimed that he had been stopped at Broken Hill, reporting that "We lost 30 minutes while the police tried to find someone who could speak Russian to us. Finally the policeman gave up, but he still took our car number."[2] There would be more police intervention before the Marathon was over.

No. 52, the MG Midget of John Sprinzel and Roy Fidler, and No. 56, the SAAB 95 of Alister Percy and Jeremy Delmar-Morgan, at Gloucester Park trotting track, Perth, December 14 (courtesy Colin Cleaver).

From Menindee, the route took competitors southeast over 246 miles of mostly gravel roads to Gunbar. Lying in 17th place overall, Sprinzel and Fidler sped away from the control with everything to play for, not least because they had thus far defied all the skeptics back home to get the Midget this far. By 1968 Sprinzel already had quite a track record, combining rally and track racing to win both the 1959 British Rally Championship and a class victory in the 12 Hours of Sebring race in Florida in 1960. Together with established British rally driver Roy Fidler, he had spent four months preparing the Midget for the Marathon, replacing steel bodywork panels with fiberglass and fitting a rally-pedigree five speed gearbox. By the time the car was ready, Sprinzel wrote that it "looked like the highest and widest Spridget in the world."[3] The extremely compact cabin had meant being very economical with personal comforts, Sprinzel writing that "the total space allocated to personal effects allowed each person to have one toothbrush, one razor, a box of Kleenex, two extra sets of underwear and a rally jacket."[4] Determined to claim the $1,200 that accompanied the *Evening Standard* trophy for the best private entrant, they were one point ahead of their nearest rival when the wheels fell off their Marathon endeavor 14 miles into the section to Gunbar—quite literally. As Sprinzel wrote, "the front nearside wheel disappeared into the bush to join the 5,300 sheep on John Caskey's station of 45,000 acres."[5] The nearside front hub assembly had broken, so leaving Fidler to jack up the three-wheeled MG, Sprinzel hitched a ride back to Menindee from where he sent a message to the BMC service team at Broken Hill, some 70 miles back along the route. BMC personnel located a private Austin-Healey Sprite and obtained the relevant part, flying it out to Sprinzel and Fidler. However, the donated hub assembly was for the car's offside. Again, Sprinzel returned to Menindee and messaged ahead to Broken Hill. Again, BMC stripped the parts from the Sprite, this time sending them on with the *Sydney Telegraph* women's team. By the time the part was delivered and fitted, however, Sprinzel and Fidler had lost nine and a half hours and their chance of the amateur's prize.

To compound the recurrent problem of failing valves, Rosemary Smith and Lucette Pointet were now having to cope with suspension problems in their Cortina Lotus, but for other competitors, the section to the tiny settlement of Gunbar in southwestern New South Wales passed without event, with Rootes GB co-driver Colin Malkin suggesting that "these are better than the roads back home in Coventry."[6] Arriving at the control, the front runners were offered a few surprises. Usually populated by 30 or 40 people, on December 16, 1968, Gunbar was playing host to thousands of excited spectators who had traveled from miles around to see the Marathon pass through. Furthermore, local farmers' wives had organized a meal for early arriving competitors in a large shed decorated with a sign saying "The Gunbar Hilton." As Andrew Cowan wrote, "we all sat down at a big table with Lucien Bianchi and the BMC boys and had a fabulous meal. Obviously they were all farmers' wives and had cooked the meal themselves."[7] Once again an isolated rural village had been transformed by the Marathon into a bustling community, if only for a day or two, with many present cheering on local hero and Australian Ford team driver Bruce Hodgson, who ran a brake repair shop in Griffith, about 45 miles to the east. In front of the queue of well wishers was Hodgson's wife Alison, who had been sending messages to each control.

The next section from Gunbar to Edi would take competitors out of New South Wales to the foothills of the Victorian Alps. Twenty-two miles north of Edi is the city of Wangaratta, where once again competitors were faced with the force of the law as local police were focused on strict adherence to the city's speed limit of 35 mph. Frustrated drivers anxiously kept their speeds to the required limit and for the most part passed through without incident, but approaching the Edi control with minutes to spare, Gilbert Staepelaere and Simo Lampinen were pulled over by a traffic cop who advised them that they had been witnessed "travelling at 85 miles an hour over the Ovens Bridge and 75 miles an hour in the main street of Moyhu."[8] Local police divisional officer Inspector O'Sullivan was determined to treat the competitors like any other speeding motorist, but the language barrier led to an illogical exchange as the team had no English and the Australian police officer even less German or Finnish. The appearance of an increasing number of journalists eager to observe and record the farcical encounter eventually persuaded the law enforcement officer to allow the pair to continue. The delay cost them two minutes at a crucial stage of the event, placing BMC GB team driver Rauno Aaltonen and Rootes driver Andrew Cowan just one and two points behind the German Ford respectively. Bianchi and Ogier remained ahead with Clark and Andersson still four points adrift in second and just over 600 miles left to go.

The alpine section would take competitors from Edi up and over Mount Buffalo to Brookside and then around Mount Feathertop to Omeo before heading off via Murrindal across the Snowy Mountains to Ingebryra and Numeralla in New South Wales. Describing the difficult mountain roads, Nick Brittan wrote that "Some of the sheer drops were so severe that afterwards, even Roger Clark, who is not given to exaggeration, said, 'If you'd gone over the edge up there your clothes would have been out of fashion by the time you'd hit the bottom.'"[9] On the 48-mile forest section from Edi to Brookside, all 58 surviving cars lost points,

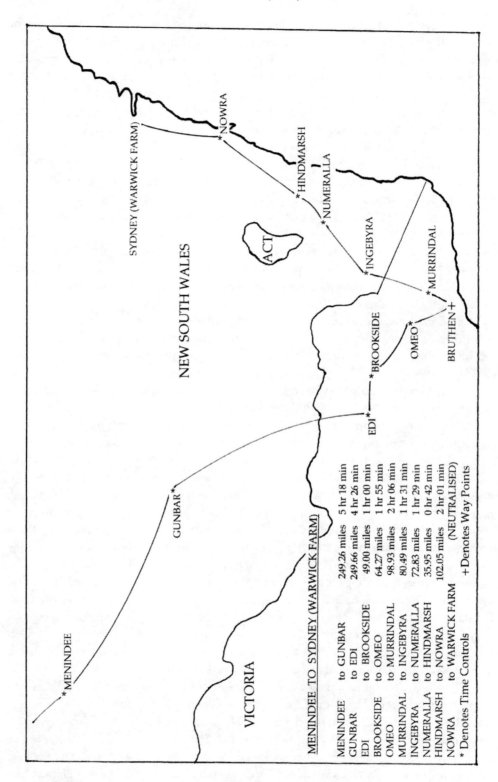

MENINDEE TO SYDNEY (WARWICK FARM)			
MENINDEE	to GUNBAR	249.26 miles	5 hr 18 min
GUNBAR	to EDI	249.66 miles	4 hr 26 min
EDI	to BROOKSIDE	49.00 miles	1 hr 00 min
BROOKSIDE	to OMEO	64.27 miles	1 hr 55 min
OMEO	to MURRINDAL	98.93 miles	2 hr 06 min
MURRINDAL	to INGEBYRA	80.49 miles	1 hr 31 min
INGEBYRA	to NUMERALLA	72.83 miles	1 hr 29 min
NUMERALLA	to HINDMARSH	35.95 miles	0 hr 42 min
HINDMARSH	to NOWRA	102.05 miles	2 hr 01 min
NOWRA	to WARWICK FARM	(NEUTRALISED)	

* Denotes Time Controls + Denotes Way Points

The final leg of the Marathon, from Menindee to Sydney (map by Martin Proudlock).

and although the leading competitors kept losses to a minimum, it was here that No. 58 came into its own as the Porsche of Zasada and Wachowski roared through the stage to lose just one minute, moving up to tenth place and only six behind Hodgson in the Australian Falcon. At the top, Clark was closing on Bianchi, just two minutes down on the leading Citroën.

Brookside to Omeo required competitors to traverse 92 miles of winding forest track in pitch darkness at an average speed of 51 mph, a target that not even the most experienced professionals were able to meet. David Benson wrote, "As Paddy Hopkirk checked in to the tiny mountain timber town ... just before dawn on Tuesday, he was rubbing his stiff arms after hundreds of gear changes over the Alps. He said: 'I want to meet the man who could get over those mountains without loss of points. No-one could ever do that.'"[10] Hopkirk was seventh fastest over this stage while again Polish rally driver and twice outright European Rally Champion Sobiesław Zasada was fastest, moving the Porsche up to eighth overall. Navigational mistakes cost No. 74, the French Citroën team headed by Robert Neyret, 48 minutes and 24 points for Aaltonen, Liddon and Easter, pushing the BMC GB Team back to ninth overall. Scotsmen Cowan, Malkin and Coyle remained in fourth place despite a close shave with the Victorian police. As Cowan wrote, "I had disconnected our rear lights as a safeguard against anyone following us in the dust or at night. I know that if you can see someone else's rear lights ahead, it is easier to follow and I didn't want this to happen. ...Colin took over as driver and was promptly booked by the police."[11]

From Omeo, the route continued to wind south across the Victorian Alps to Bruthen before turning northeast to Murrindal at the foot of the Snowy Mountains. So sudden and treacherous were these mountain roads that "one of the Aussie drivers announced his intention to keep his seat-belts undone and his door half-open ... in case he should have to jump for it."[12] In spite of this, only 14 cars lost points by the time the field had checked in at Murrindal, but among them was No. 48, the car and the crew that had dominated the Marathon all the way from England, the car that had seemingly escaped calamity back in Port Augusta. Fifty-six miles south of Omeo is the small town of Bruthen and it was here that the Cortina Lotus's differential perished. Once again people had come from miles around to watch the Marathon pass through, so Roger Clark began asking if anyone had a replacement part he could purloin. Blank faces met his anxious request until he spotted a Mark II Ford Cortina, the owner of which had paused to watch the cars pass through while on his way for a day's fishing. As David Benson wrote, "At first he refused Clark's offer to buy the back axle out of his car, but as Clark limped off up the road the fisherman chased after him in his own car. He called out: 'You're Roger Clark, the British driver, aren't you?'"[13] A deal was struck and an hour and a half later, Clark and Andersson were back on the road, promising to send payment once they got to Sydney. Despite the selfless generosity of the local man, however, Ford GB's star team lost 97 points at Murrindal, which pushed them down to 14th place overall. For 9,600 miles Roger Clark and Ove Andersson had been either leading or threatening. With 400 miles remaining, it would now be impossible for them to claim a podium position at Sydney.

The British Cortina's misfortune meant that there were a few changes to the leader board as competitors departed Murrindal at the southwestern tip of the Australian Great Dividing Range of which the Snowy Mountains forms its southerly section. Bianchi and Ogier were still leading, with Staepelaere and Lampinen six points behind in second and Cowan, Malkin and Coyle now in third. The BMC 1800 of Hopkirk, Nash and Poole was now running in fourth, while there was an intense struggle between the next five cars, with only eight points

Bianchi and Ogier between Numeralla and Hindmarsh—ten miles further on, disaster would strike (courtesy Bruce Thomas).

separating fifth and ninth. Perhaps surprisingly, despite the mountainous terrain, mud, rain and twisting roads through aptly named places such as Slippery Pinch and Dead Timber Hill, 58 cars remained in competition as they headed off on the rough, gravel covered route northwards over the Snowy Mountains to Ingebryra. Halfway along this section, they would pass back into New South Wales for the last time.

The leading positions remained unchanged at the next control, even though six of the ten leading cars lost time, including Bianchi and Ogier, who were forced to stop and repair a puncture. In total, only four cars made it to Ingebryra without penalty, which spotlighted the dexterity and sheer grit of Ian Vaughan, Sobiesław Zasada, Bruce Hodgson and Gilbert Staepelaere. Zasada was now having the time of his life after mixed fortunes across Europe and Asia, steering the red Porsche like a man possessed, while few had expected the German Ford 20MRS to be performing so superbly. Ahead lay the relatively easy, mostly paved section to Numeralla, taking in Jindabyne and Cooma, where once again, the police were waiting. As Nick Brittan wrote, "the drivers were 250 miles from the finish, they'd been on the go non-stop for three nights, they'd coped with 'roos, wombats, dust, creeks and potholes and they'd survived…. But the last thing they needed at six in the morning was a specially created police force laying traps though a town like Cooma…."[14] Need it or not, as each car entered the town a police vehicle fell in behind, escorting each competitor all the way out of town again. Nerves were fraying as each exhausted driver kept to the regulation 34.5 mph. Increasing irritation among the crews didn't boil over into any tickets, however, and all but 14 cars made it to Numeralla without incurring penalty. They would need every last drop of energy and

Cowan, Malkin and Coyle were in second place at Hindmarsh. Ten miles later, they would have to accept they had won (courtesy Bruce Thomas).

patience for this, the last special stage before Sydney. At 36 miles, the section from Numeralla to Hindmarsh Station would be the shortest of the entire Marathon, but also one of the trickiest. Drivers were required to complete it in 42 minutes with an average speed of 51 mph, and navigation notes stated, "The organizers say it is in the rally just to make sure no one gets in unpenalized."[15] To complicate matters further, Hindmarsh Station was just that—a sheep-farming station and homestead that wasn't on any map.

During the weekend of December 14 and 15, 1968, Australian journalist Bill Norman decided to explore the stage from Numeralla to the site of the Hindmarsh Station checkpoint, located alongside the Hindmarsh family's sheep and cattle station, "Jinden." Of his experience, Norman wrote that "With the safety harness pulled tight I hammered an EH Holden over the route at a speed, which seemed the maximum possible without actually bending something. My time of 62 minutes would have cost more points than the present Marathon leader, Roger Clark, has lost in the whole of the rally so far. ... At half distance there is a sign reading 'Cairo. A Good Rexona Town. Population Nil.' A few yards further on is a drab, galvanized iron woodcutter's shed, labeled 'Motel.' 100 yards and two bends later: 'Farewell Cairo. Population Still Nil.' Another sign points to a track leading to 'Hell Hole' and a fourth advises the use of 'five wheel drive.'"[16] For months, Marathon survey teams and organizers had been calling on the Hindmarsh family and now they were ready to watch the cars arrive and depart and offer any assistance they could, including the use of their own telephone to the many journalists that crowded around their isolated home. As Norman wrote, "Nothing quite so exciting has happened at 'Jinden' since the Clarke bush-ranger gang shot four policemen there in 1867."[17]

So difficult was this last special stage that no-one escaped without penalty, although most of the top ten careened into the control just two, three or four minutes down, with Paddy Hopkirk achieving the best performance—only one point lost. For one of the leaders, however, the road to Hindmarsh proved disastrous when Gilbert Staepelaere misjudged a gateway. The 20MRS bounced off a gate post and came to a skewed halt almost on its side. The impact had broken a track rod, and although Staepelaere and Lampinen were able to seek assistance from a local farm, Little Badger Station, and cannibalize yet another unlucky Cortina, the two hours needed to complete the necessary welding cost them 206 points and the top-three position they had held onto for so long. Another casualty before Hindmarsh was the privately entered British Cortina of Robin Clark, Martin Pearson and Peter Hall.

Lucien Bianchi and Jean-Claude Ogier now held an 11 point advantage over nearest rivals Cowan, Malkin and Coyle, with Hopkirk, Nash and Poole in third overall. With this unassailable lead, barring disaster the Franco-Belgian pair was home and dry, the clear winners of the 1968 London to Sydney Marathon. Ahead lay one last timed section to the town of Nowra, 111 miles south of the finish line, described in the Castrol navigation notes as "Not an easy section as there are only 14 miles of asphalt. The rest is gravel of which some is very rough. Do not spoil your chances by misjudging this section."[18]

Among the crowd that would be waiting at Warwick Farm in Sydney were two men who had shared their own 10,000-mile adventure in reverse, then experienced the Marathon in very different ways. Australian Bob Holden had driven his Volvo 142S all the way from Sydney to Gothenburg in Sweden and Australian filmmaker Rob McAuley had captured the entire journey on camera. Holden then joined the Amoco Volvo team at Crystal Palace, while McAuley crisscrossed the Marathon as part of the international press detail.

31

All the Way Back

Among the 98 competing cars arriving at London's Crystal Palace stadium on that bright November morning in 1968 were seven Volvos. Today, Volvos are a common sight on roads across the world, but before they became synonymous with Scandinavian reliability, before they became the byword for sensible, safety conscious motoring, middle class antique dealers and smart families, in the 1960s they were a rare commodity in the garages and on the drives of suburban British households. Considering the ruins of the British motor manufacturing industry today, it's astonishing to think that there wasn't a single imported vehicle in the British top 20 sales chart for 1968; best sellers of that year were the domestically produced BMC 1100/1300 and Ford's Mark II Cortina. Thus, any excited spectator jostling amid the throng of 80,000 people at Crystal Palace in November 1968 must have been fascinated to see the Porsches, Mercedes, Citroens and Simcas lined up in rows in the competitors' enclosure and even more excited to see these unusual automobiles bedecked with 'roo bars, replacement tires, sponsorship decals and other assorted paraphernalia. There among the Cortinas and BMCs were seven Volvos, a mix of privately entered and commercially sponsored cars and crews. Possibly attracting the most attention was the pale cream Volvo station wagon crewed by Elsie Gadd, Jenny Tudor-Owen, Sheila Kemp and Anthea Castell, but in serious contention for the actual Marathon prize was a group of four cars sponsored by the Australian oil company Amoco, each crewed by two well-established antipodean rally drivers and navigators. The four cars sat in the cold sunlight, conspicuous for their lack of 'roo bars and overly-laden roof racks—did these seasoned Australian competitors know something the other crews didn't?

As the minutes counted down to departure, the white car, No. 63, a two-door Volvo 142S, was undergoing final checks and inspection by its two-man crew, Tasmanian Laurie Graham and Melbourne-born Bob Holden. For Bob, this was the culmination of a long, event-filled journey that had begun some four months previously in Sydney. Not for him the comfort and convenience of a transcontinental flight from southern to northern hemisphere. Instead, Holden had made the necessary preparations to his Volvo and, together with photographer and filmmaker Rob McAuley, had set off to reconnoiter the 10,000-mile route "in reverse." As Bob said, "To allow for Rob to identify and set up shots of the car in motion often meant dropping Rob off, turning around, returning to a particular spot and then driving back again so he could capture the whole thing on film. We probably drove nearer 20,000 miles on that trip!" This Marathon prologue was designed to serve two purposes: to make detailed notes of the entire route, and thus build a comprehensive set of navigation instructions for Laurie, and to test the Volvo itself. What better way of making sure the car could withstand the challenge of thousands of miles of rough and unpredictable terrain than to complete the course beforehand? A serious challenge indeed, but his innate pragmatism and unassuming outlook on life weren't going to let any obstacles stand in Bob Holden's way.

Robin John Holden was born in suburban Melbourne in 1932 and, as he explained, "The story I used to believe was that I was a breech birth and my feet got twisted. I did some research and got some idea that it was a family hereditary thing." At age six, he was hospitalized for corrective surgery, but at this time, like other parts of the world, Australia was experiencing an outbreak of polio. Bob contracted the disease like so many other children and, as he explained, "Three or four years later I was still in plaster, hadn't walked, was never ever supposed to walk, but off I went and I was lucky. It's a big mind game, the whole thing, a big mind game. Children just work with what they've got." During his period of immobilization, Bob began to read books, constantly pestering his mother to bring more reading material home from the different libraries she had joined, which were keeping a list of books they thought he would like to see. The more he read, the more his imagination was fired up and, despite the damage caused by polio, Bob resolved to walk.

Into his teens, in order to try and build up his leg muscles, Bob decided to join a local cycling club, which eventually led him to compete successfully in long-distance events and even be considered for the prestigious *Tour de France* cycle race. Unfortunately, a cycling accident ended any hope of international competition, but, undaunted, Bob had already

Bob Holden with his Volvo 142S (courtesy Bob Holden).

begun to notice four-wheeled transportation and, in 1949, began rallying. His love of cars and competition saw him embrace both rally and track, and he explained, "I loved both rallying and circuit racing. The only reason I didn't rally much is because I couldn't afford it, it's more expensive than circuit racing. There was no hope of getting anything back on the rally driving, no prize money, no sponsorship, nothing." A highlight in Bob's career came in 1966 when, against the odds, he and Rauno Aaltonen won the Bathurst 500 in a Mini Cooper S, beating the second-place car by 11.5 seconds.

With the Marathon announced, Bob purchased a 142S from Max Winkless's Volvo dealership, secured backing from the Amoco Oil Company and decided to undertake his own reconnaissance of the 10,000-mile route. Through mutual friend Paul Bolton, Bob was introduced to independent filmmaker Rob McAuley, who had already shot a number of rallies for keen motorsports sponsor Rothmans. As Rob explained, "Bob was looking to consolidate his Amoco sponsorship by completing a survey trip, Sydney to London, prior to the event. Amoco wanted a film record of their involvement in the event and one thing led to another. I attended a meeting with Amoco's marketing manager, Lionel Barnes, who agreed to fund Bob's survey trip and agreed that I should go with him to film the trip. He assumed I was a cameraman, which I really wasn't, but as there was only room for one in the car, I instantly became a one-man production unit." Once their survey was complete, McAuley would then join Amoco and Dunlop Tires representatives and a journalist on an eight-seater Piper Navajo aircraft that would pursue the Marathon all the way back to Sydney. As Rob explained, "For a young bachelor, the whole adventure package was almost too good to be true!"

With the Volvo prepared by Bob and ready to go, the pair set off from Sydney, stopping at an Amoco gas station. McAuley recalled that "The attendant filled the tank and asked where we were heading. 'London,' said Bob. The attendant nodded his head and, with a blank look on his face, remarked, 'Don't think this one tank will get you there.'" As much as possible, the Volvo followed the proposed Marathon route and it wasn't long before McAuley had his first experience of motor rally, hanging on as Bob drifted the car through dirt-track corners at high speed. As they progressed across the continent, with a little trepidation Rob volunteered to drive from time to time, recalling that "After all, it was his precious racing car and there was a lot hanging on him getting there in one piece." Holden was all too happy to be given the chance to sleep so Rob got his first taste of driving the highly tuned Volvo, while Bob observed and then offered advice. According to McAuley, Bob told him, "You're doing okay, but two things you're doing wrong. First, when you took over, you immediately accelerated to 100 kph [62 mph] without first testing to see if the brakes worked. How did you know you had brakes, or how they felt, unless you tested them? From now on, take off, accelerate up a bit and then test the brakes. Always make a habit of doing that. The other thing is—you go into corners too fast and come out too slow. That's bad driving. The rule is, slow down going into corners and you speed up going out of them." Rob explained that he never forgot these two driving lessons.

Their trek across Australia was punctuated with pauses and setting up for filming. Bob recalled, "I think we worked out that I doubled the mileage from Bombay to London, backwards and forwards. We'd be going along at 100 mph and Rob would say, 'Oh that looks bloody interesting, stop!' So we'd have to stop and go back to what he'd seen, empty his gear out." Despite the stop-start journey, however, they were still able to visit Laurie Graham, Holden's soon-to-be Marathon co-driver and navigator who was working for a company that

Rob McAuley sets up a shot in Western Australia (courtesy Rob McAuley).

sold adhesive tape. Graham loaded the Volvo's trunk with assorted rolls of tape which, as they would discover, was highly fortuitous. By the time they reached Perth, both were exhausted. As arranged, the car was loaded onto a Dutch merchant vessel, the *Straat Singapore*. The two tired men found their cabin and the ship set sail for Bombay, via Malaysia, Singapore and Ceylon.

Serving aboard the *Straat Singapore* as fourth officer was a young Dutchman named Martin Bijeker who was due to take leave at Bombay. The two Australians and the Dutchman struck up a friendship on the voyage, which culminated in Bob agreeing to have Martin join them for the next leg across Asia and Europe. As Bob explained, "We picked him up out of desperation! We were both of us wiped out because we'd made the trip across Australia, up in the boonies and had come back down, special sections, all that sort of thing and poor old Rob was getting worn out. So was I! Rather than fly home, we threw him in the back. There was no back seat so we sat him on top of the luggage in the back and he did all the running around and gophering for Rob. He was a big strong lad too, younger than we were."

Docking in Singapore, Bob disembarked to meet up with a racing friend and Rob was left to oversea the Volvo's unloading at Bombay where they would meet up again. Once the ship docked, as Rob recalled, "In charge, or so it seemed, of unloading was a jovial man named Dr. Bomsi Wadia. He happened to be the only Indian entrant in the Marathon. Apparently

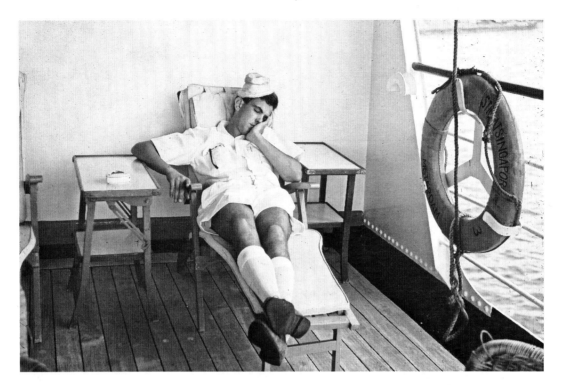

Martin Bijeker aboard the *Straat Singapore* (courtesy Rob McAuley).

he'd voluntarily put himself in charge of making sure our car was unloaded without mishap. Our car certainly got VIP treatment as it was swung out of the hold and onto the wharf. It was the first rally car most of the Indian workers had ever seen. They were in awe of this precious item of cargo and under Bomsi's meticulous and loudly vocal direction, the unloading was handled with extreme care and ceremony." Reunited with Bob, the trio set off across India, Rob astonished by the "humanity, color, sound and smell in such profusion. It was unbelievable. Vast crowds seemed to appear from nowhere every time the car appeared. It was very frightening. It was the most claustrophobic experience imaginable. Faces pressed to the windows looking in at us, myriads of hands beating a tattoo on the roof. No room to move, little room to breathe." Somehow, Rob and Martin managed to set up the camera to shoot footage, while Bob snapped away on his Bronica stills camera.

For the most part, the three men traveled in good humor, but, during Rob's attempt to film the Volvo at the Taj Mahal in Agra, Bob's patience was stretched a little thin. The plan was to try and get filming completed before the midday heat and then drive on to Delhi, so the team arranged for their hotel to make up packed lunches for them to eat as they drove. As Rob recalled, "For some reason, Bob was a bit grumpy this day. Maybe it was the heat. Come lunchtime, I was asked to hand over the lunch boxes—one to Martin, one to Bob, one for me. Inside there were sandwiches, a piece of fruit and a hard boiled egg. Martin eats his sandwich, then cracks his egg, peels it, eats it. Bob follows suit—sandwich and then cracks the egg on the bottom of the steering wheel. The problem was that this egg had missed being boiled. As Bob cracked it, the uncooked yolk and white cascaded down into Bob's trousers around the crotch area. Covered in raw egg, Bob exploded. He swung off the road and screamed to a halt. Martin and I were killing ourselves laughing—Bob was totally convinced we'd orchestrated the whole business!"

The team continued on into Pakistan with Rob covertly filming at the border, and, as they drove through empty countryside, they noticed a vehicle coming towards them. Rob remembered that "It was another rally car, a Hillman Hunter dressed to kill. We slowed down and the stranger slowed down. We stopped and got out, and were greeted in a broad Scottish accent by Andrew Cowan, closely followed by his co-driver—and brother in law—Brian Coyle. Bloody hell, what a strange place to meet and what a joy it was for

Lunch on the move—Bob Holden (courtesy Bob Holden).

all of us. Andrew was on a mission, surveying the course London to Bombay." After an evening of Marathon chatter over dinner, the two teams departed in opposite directions, aware that the next time they would meet would be at Crystal Palace in London.

At the entrance to the Khyber Pass, they were instructed not to film any of the passage and were told they had to be accompanied by an official guide. With the armed guide sitting in the front passenger seat and Martin and Rob crammed into the back, the Volvo set off over the Pass, but it wasn't long before Rob "wormed my way past his shoulder and sat on the open window, with my feet in his lap. I made it quite clear to him that he was to hold onto my legs firmly and not to let go. Martin passed me out my camera and, with the guide holding my legs, I filmed our entire trip through the Pass. I handed my camera back to Martin as we completed the journey, wriggled back into my seat and that was it. I have no idea what the guard thought I was doing looking out the window, but he made no attempt to stop me."

Over the Lataband Pass, with camera and tripod slung over their shoulders, Rob and Martin clambered up steep, rocky escarpments to film Bob throwing the Volvo into the Pass's many sharp turns, which at this point had still not been graded. As they made their way towards Kabul, the team encountered a local shepherd tending his flock. As Rob recalled, "We had a Polaroid still camera, which intrigued him, so I took his photo and he watched as the shot was developed and slowly rolled out of the camera. He didn't know what to make of it and reacted quite strangely when he saw the image of a man who I'm sure he didn't recognize as himself. By sign language we indicated that this was a photo of him. That completely confounded him. There was even a touch of anger and total disbelief in what he was seeing. Then we gave him the shot and, as we took off, he was still staring strangely at the photo. God only knows what the reaction of his family would have been when he arrived home with this strange gift from the three men in the strange car he had met."

Across Afghanistan and into Iran, the Volvo was beginning to suffer as first the differential began to fail and then cracks began to appear in the bodywork, particularly around the A-, B- and C-pillars. At one point, the cracks around the windshield became so exaggerated that the glass began to work loose. Bob and Rob remembered the rolls of tape Laurie had given them back in Australia and, with liberal use, the damage was mended. Bob explained that "When we got to Teheran, we arrived there in the very early morning and on the way through in the dark we saw

Rob McAuley catches up on sleep in the back of the Volvo 142S (courtesy Bob Holden).

Repairs are carried out to the Volvo 142S (courtesy Bob Holden).

this big Volvo sign. It turned out to be a truck assembly plant or something. There were three or four top engineers from Sweden there and they had a look at the car and nearly freaked and they spent one day at least welding things together so we could get as far as London. The back was folding, mainly at the back of the wheel arches, the back was falling off. Anyway, there were quite a few other things that were troublesome and the engineers were beautiful, they sent a telex three meters long with problems with the car, which they sent back to base." With the differential welded back in place and the bodywork patch-repaired, the Volvo headed on to Turkey.

During their overnight stay in Istanbul, they were forced to leave the car parked in the street outside the hotel and in the morning found that it had been broken into. Although they had taken most of their possessions out the night before, Rob had overlooked his extra 16mm camera, which was among the items now missing. Kicking himself, he filed a report with the local police, convinced it was gone for good, but to his surprise, some months later it was delivered to his brother who was working at Australia House in London!

Once in Italy the team made for the Amoco office in Milan, where they said farewell to Martin, who flew back to Holland with promises that he would be there for departure at Crystal Palace. Amoco made Rob and Bob extremely welcome, taking them to the Monza race track where they met up with New Zealand racing driver Chris Amon, an old friend of Bob's who was there to test a new Ferrari racing car. Coincidentally, some years later, Marathon competitor Tom Boyce would work with Amon to build a Formula One car. During the stay in Milan, Rob put a providential call in to a former girlfriend in London, only to find she was away. By chance, her roommate Anne answered the phone and, 48 years later, Rob and Anne are still happily married.

The pair finally made their way north and over to England, crossing the Channel by hovercraft to be met by Rob's brother. As Rob recalled, "We headed for their place in Reigate, following them and for the first time, not having to worry about the route we were taking. Or that's what we thought. My brother took a wrong turn and we were lost. After over 10,000 miles we were lost within a few short miles of 'home.'" Bob had called upon Rob's brother to act as an intermediary with Volvo in Sweden while they were on the road, and when he arrived in England, he was presented with a message saying, as Bob recalled, "'Am I happy to get me and the car up to Sweden absolutely immediately?' They wanted the car because they had the orders for these three other cars, and they needed to see mine to make sure these cars didn't fall to bits on the road." Leaving Rob to prepare for his job as photojournalist on the Marathon itself, Bob set off for the Volvo factory in Sweden.

32

And Half the Way There

After his drive from Sydney to London, and then from London to Gothenburg in Sweden, Bob Holden was tired. As he recalled, "When I got there, it was really funny. The Swedes in Gothenburg, they booked me into the hotel—Volvo was paying for this. I got there on a Sunday afternoon. Of course you couldn't contact anybody and I felt buggered anyway, it was the first time I'd stopped properly because I drove non-stop from London, which was a fair way. I was worn out and I was worried how I was going to get back to Australia with a ruddy dead car." The following day, he was able to speak to Volvo personnel, but instead of asking him to drive up to the factory, they came to the hotel and a long lunch followed, with Bob desperate to get started on the car. Eventually, he was taken to Volvo's headquarters and was pleasantly surprised to find that space had been made for him to work in the motorsports department where the other three Amoco Volvos were being prepared. Bob recalled that Elsie Gadd's Volvo station wagon was also being worked on while he was there. He was instructed to strip his 142S down and take everything he needed off the car. Next, Gunnar Anderson, Volvo's Competitions Team manager and hugely successful former rally driver, presented Bob with the solution. Bob explained, "There was another car there already parked in the shed where they put me, sitting there, another brand new car. He said that'll be your car. I said look, we can't do that, documentation and all that sort of stuff. They said it doesn't matter. They actually changed the body number and the whole bodywork of the car." Volvo was anxious to take the stripped out 142S, undertake a detailed inspection of the shell and analyze all the stress fractures that had occurred on the road from Sydney.

Bob spent a week working long hours on strengthening the donor car, while engineers looked on to learn what he was doing. Bob had concluded that certain parts of the car needed reinforcing, especially around the rear wheel arches, and knew that the best way of doing this was to utilize a particular kind of spot welding, whereby strengthened wheel arches could be welded on one side only. He raised this with the engineers who immediately left, returning a short while later. "There was a bloke in the factory selling that particular machine, that particular time I was there. You can't believe it. Coincidences follow me like there's no tomorrow. Well, he actually set up and he did the whole car with me, stayed the whole week." Eventually the car was ready, and once Bob's fellow Amoco team mates arrived, together with Rob McAuley, all four Marathon Volvos were driven over to London ready for the start of the Marathon.

During the days leading up to November 24, now accompanied by Anne Grundon, the future Mrs. McAuley, Rob was able to meet and socialize with some of the other Amoco

The 142S at Volvo's factory in Gothenburg (courtesy Bob Holden).

Volvo competitors, including Gerry Lister and André Welinski, and also observe the great mobilization of the media, with the BBC using some of his film footage for an introductory television program about the Marathon. On the day of departure, Rob suggested to Gerry and André that when it was their turn to drive up onto the starting ramp, he be allowed to climb onto their rear bumper and "hold onto their spare tire on the roof with one hand, movie camera filming with the other. I reckoned it would make a good shot and be a bit different than the newsreel boys." No. 43 was duly called to the start, with Rob balanced on the back, and at the agreed moment, Gerry Lister accelerated away. Unfortunately, Gerry forgot that Rob was aboard and Rob recalled how "I'm yelling—people are pointing and laughing, it's all happening for 100 yards or more. Then Gerry suddenly gets the message and slows to a walk. I jump off and we're off on our separate ways to Sydney." Half an hour later, with Martin Bijeker cheering them on, it was Bob Holden's turn to be flagged away. The Amoco Volvos were off on the first leg of the Marathon and Rob would be following them all the way by plane.

  Bob and Laurie made steady, uneventful progress through Europe and over into Turkey. After the first special stage between Sivas and Erzincan they were in 14th place, having picked up 25 points to achieve the best performance among the Amoco cars—Max Winkless and John Keran had by now fallen far behind as a result of their engine failure in Yugoslavia. The 142S performed perfectly across Iran and Afghanistan and over the now-graded Lataband

Anne Grundon and Gerry Lister at Crystal Palace, London, November 24 (courtesy Rob McAuley).

Pass, Holden drove superbly to be joint fifth fastest, sharing the honor with Ford Australia's Harry Firth, Ford GB's Eric Jackson and Bill Bengry in No. 1. At the Sarobi control, Bob and Laurie were sitting in tenth place overall, even though the Volvo's rear shocks had collapsed and needed repair. Bob remembered that "The Lataband Pass was beaut', but it was different from when we went through it a month before. After we'd been through there, they put a bloody grader through it, so it was nothing special at all. All of a sudden there was nothing to fight with. We weren't worried about anyone else."

Meanwhile, Anne dropped Rob off at London's Heathrow Airport and he took his seat in the Piper Navajo, joining Lionel Barnes from Amoco, Ross Dodson from Dunlop and Australian journalist Mike Kable. The Navajo took to the skies and wherever possible flew to airports and landing strips as near to the Marathon's key control points as possible so that Rob could film events both from the air and on the ground, although as he explained, "Great idea in theory, but of course there were some hiccups. Airports aren't usually close to off-road rally courses." During the flight between Italy and Turkey, the Navajo was pounded by bad weather, to the point that Rob began to wonder whether the small plane could survive. Nobody was comfortable, but Mike Kable was terrified and it was with audible relief that the skies cleared to reveal a landing strip.

As well as capturing footage of the Marathon action, Rob also wanted to film the Navajo itself from the air. Volvo had sent its own aircraft to carry service crews in support of both the Amoco cars and, where possible, the three other privately entered Volvos, so at a refueling stop in Afghanistan, Rob approached the Swedish pilots with the idea. Sure enough, when both planes took off again, Rob was sitting in the co-pilot seat of the Swedish plane, camera at the ready to shoot the Navajo at altitude. The pilots of both planes were in radio contact as they began a series of maneuvers with Rob aiming his camera through the window. Looking back, Rob recalled that "To this day I still don't know how close we were to a midair collision—was it the Navajo that rose sharply and unexpectedly, or did our plane dive down suddenly, to result in such, to me, a near miss. It couldn't have been too close as both pilots failed to seem concerned by the incident. One thing for sure, I'll never forget it."

Arriving at Kabul ahead of the competitors, Rob met up with Australian journalist John Smailes and together they drove up and over the Lataband Pass so that he could be in position to film the cars as they completed the much-feared 45-mile scramble to Sarobi. In sub-zero temperatures, the men manhandled the car over the Pass, helping themselves to liberal amounts of local whisky to keep out the chill. Arriving at Sarobi, Rob began to set up for the first cars' arrival amid the crowds of officials, service crews and the ever-present local police, who were attempting to impose their authority on the bustling scene. One particular police officer took against Rob as he grappled with his camera and tripod and attempted to push him out of the way. Rob recalled how "That did it for me. I thrust my handheld camera, with its large zoom lens, right into his face and told him 'If you don't get out of my f***ing road now, I'll knock your f***ing block off and then ram this camera right up your arse.' Poor old John Smailes saw a side of me that night that not even I knew I had. The guy causing the trouble didn't understand a word I was saying, but he sure understood the intent. He backed off and disappeared into the night—and I got my shots. My only excuse was, it was the whisky talking, not me. God it was cold that night—the coldest I've ever been in my life." Rob was there to see his friend Bob Holden roar into the control, obviously a serious contender for victory.

From Kabul, the Navajo flew on to New Delhi, crossing the Khyber Pass at low altitude, the pilots showing off their aerobatic skills by throwing the plane left and right so Rob could capture the dramatic scenery below. Not so happy was Kable, who hung on grimly, hurling abuse at anyone who would listen before becoming deathly quiet for the remainder of the trip to India.

Below them, the Marathon was progressing out of Afghanistan, across the congested heart of Pakistan and over into India, the final country before Australia. Once again, Bob and Laurie were performing well, determined that the professional crews would not have it all their own way. After Sarobi, the next checkpoint was at Delhi but with only 85 miles to go, disaster struck the 142S. Between Patiala and Delhi, a huge crowd had gathered at a large junction to watch the cars come by. Laurie was at the wheel as Bob caught a well-earned nap, but as they approached the junction in the late night darkness, it was clear that the last car through had done so some time before and the hordes of spectators had begun to surge forward during the lull in proceedings. As Bob explained, "Everybody started to move when nothing was happening for that 20 minutes and amongst other things that were moving was an army truck with a trainee driver on-board. He got it out of gear and couldn't get it back so he jumped out and let the truck go. So we actually hit the truck head on." The front of the Volvo was crushed under the weight of the truck and both Bob and Laurie received impact and glass injuries to their faces. Bouncing off the 142S, the truck careened off the road, finally coming to a halt and scattering onlookers. Amid the chaos, a witness to the crash was the daughter of the local maharaja and it didn't take long for the news of the accident to reach her father. Bleeding profusely, Bob and Laurie were helped from the wreckage and under the maharaja's instruction, were admitted to his own private wing at Patiala's hospital. Bob laughed as he recalled, "Their own suite at the hospital was big enough to have two four-poster beds in it, right? I woke up in one of these bloody four-poster beds, didn't I?"

In India, custom had it that during any hospital stay, it fell upon the patient's family to ensure they were fed, so again the maharaja intervened, sending food each day as well as arranging for a top plastic surgeon to treat Bob's badly damaged nose. Bob is convinced that this was all in gratitude for the fact that the maharaja's daughter had not been injured during the collision and resultant panic. As reported by Nick Brittan, Laurie described the man as "a delightful character, formerly an Oxford rowing blue who would come in and yarn with us every once in a while."[1]

Landing in New Delhi, Rob received the news of his friends' accident and immediately set off for the crash site in the hope of being able to find Bob and Laurie, recounting how "We found the smashed car, on the side of the road. The front of the car was a real mess and the windscreen smashed to smithereens. Armed police guarded the car and a huge assembly

Amoco Piper Navajo over Afghanistan (courtesy Rob McAuley).

The wreckage of No. 63 (courtesy Bob Holden).

of colorful locals surrounded the site. I made my way through the crowd, filmed the car and the site and then was taken to visit Bob and Laurie in a nearby hospital." With enormous relief he found them both sitting up and smiling, although as Rob explained, "For a while, their big problem was that all their personal papers, including passports, were missing. Apparently they'd been thrown out by the impact. But amazingly, in the dark, someone had picked up the entire package of papers and handed it in to the police. Even Bob's and Laurie's wallets had been handed in. Not a thing had been touched in either of them. Even the fairly substantial wad of money was intact. The honesty of these Indian villagers, thank God, was amazing." Thankful that his friends were okay, he bade them farewell and returned to Delhi. Laurie was discharged fairly quickly and made it to Bombay for the ship crossing home, but Bob needed to remain hospitalized for a week before he too was allowed to leave, flying back to Sydney. After all the meticulous preparation and planning, the thousands of miles spent testing the car and the route, Bob Holden's Marathon was over.

In Bombay, Rob joined the round of parties and receptions held for the Marathon competitors and recalled that during one particularly rowdy gathering, he and Volvo station wagon crew member Anthea Castell took their leave for a nighttime horse-drawn carriage ride through the city. As he recalled, "Off we jogged into the seething mass of traffic, people, smells and sounds all adding their own special magic to the moment. Then it happened, right smack in the middle of, what looked like the busiest of all the main roads. The back left hand wheel fell off! We recovered the wheel and assessed the situation. The old driver looked on in disbelief as I struggled to lift the left hand side up, while Anthea juggled the heavy wheel back into place on the axle. Not one person in the crowd offered us a hand. The driver couldn't believe that his two white, western passengers had taken over proceedings."

With the competitors and cars loaded onto the SS *Chusan*, the Navajo flew on to Darwen on the northern coast of Australia, via Burma, Malaysia and the island of Bali. Then it was onwards to Sydney and finally over to Perth in time to witness the arrival of the *Chusan* and the unloading of its Marathon cargo and passengers. Rob filmed the restart at Gloucester Park in Perth and then the Navajo leapfrogged the Australian leg back to Sydney, stopping at key points to allow Rob to capture the action on camera. On the approach to Sydney, news came over the radio that Bianchi and Ogier had crashed and that Cowan, Malkin and Coyle were on course to win. Getting to the Warwick Farm Raceway in time to see the Hillman Hunter arrive, Rob persuaded Cowan to let him climb on the back and film his triumphant entrance. Bob and Rob were reunited at Warwick Farm, Bob a little bruised but happy to watch the first cars crawl home and offer congratulations to the victors.

Of his Marathon experience, Rob said "What an event—what an experience and what an adventure the 1968 London to Sydney Marathon had been for me. I'd met the girl I was destined to marry, I had taken part in one of the world's great sporting events, I made a lot of friends, I had made a film, I had visited places far off the beaten track that today, you can no longer visit. What's more, I had a hell of a lot of fun along the way. You certainly can't beat that for one helluva six month adventure!"

Bob Holden continued to rally and race professionally, while also preparing cars for competition. As he explained, "I don't put airs on myself, I've got the numbers on the board, which is fortunate, but I've done it my way. I very rarely get in a car that I haven't prepared, I've got no confidence in a car that I haven't put together myself. I know I've done the best I can with what I've got and what I can afford, simple as that. There's a lot of other people who've done a lot more, but how much money has that cost them?"

Today Bob Holden is a celebrated figure in the history of Australian motorsports and, as recently as 2013, was still showing younger drivers how to do it by winning an event at the Philip Island race track off the coast of Victoria. As he remarked then, "I've got no money, never had any. As long as I've had enough to do the things I wanted to do and that's the way I work, that's quite different to most people. I'm 80 years old, would you believe? That's what f***ed the system down at Philip Island the other day when the boys suddenly realized they couldn't catch me!"

33

Meeting Triumph and Disaster

With only four miles to go before they reached the control at Nowra, No. 51, the BMC 1800 driven by Paddy Hopkirk, came upon a scene of devastation. There in the road was the tangled wreckage of two cars that had obviously collided head-on. One of the cars was a Mini, the other a blue Citroën DS21—the leading car, the clear winners. It was Ogier and Bianchi. Hopkirk wrote that "It was awful. Lucien was conscious, but there was a lot of blood streaming down his face. Alec [Poole] jumped out to try to get Lucien out of the car. Jean-Claude had already got out, but was staggering around in shock."[1] Leaving his teammates to tend to the apparently severely injured Belgian and the civilian occupants of the Mini, Hopkirk turned the 1800 around and hurtled back along the road to where he had seen a group of photographers. Someone had a two-way radio and immediately an ambulance was called for. Returning to the crash site, with enough people there to cut Bianchi free from the smashed Citroën and help the four injured and dazed men, No. 51 continued on, only just making the control.

Within moments of the tragedy unfolding, the Hillman Hunter of Cowan, Coyle and Malkin was flagged down by one of the group of photographers who warned them there was a crash up ahead. Cowan continued on and drew level with the mangled Citroën before being waved on with the message that everything was under control. As Cowan wrote, "After this we were all badly shaken…. Brian [Coyle] was particularly quiet and he said afterwards that he just couldn't keep control of his thoughts…. If the accident had given us a shake, the slow realization that we were now probably in the lead was almost horrifying."

In the years that have passed since the events of the morning of December 17, 1968, on a straight section of road on the way to Nowra, countless theories have been posed, shared and discussed. What was a civilian car doing on this section of the Marathon? Why hadn't the New South Wales police prevented the Mini from heading into the stage? How could the two cars have impacted when the road was wide enough for them to pass by each other? John Bryson reflected that Geoff Adams, vice-president of the North Shore Sporting Car Club, "had been manning the last significant control of the rally near Nowra. He asked the two young persons in the Mini to not travel towards the oncoming rally traffic. They knew what was going on and insisted it was a public road. There was little Geoff could do."[2]

It wasn't long after the crash that a number of completely unsubstantiated rumors began to spread—the Mini driver was intoxicated; the Mini's occupants were off-duty police officers; with Bianchi resting in the passenger seat, Ogier had momentarily forgotten on which side of the road he was meant to be driving; BMC had sent the Mini to intentionally crash into the leading Citroën as revenge for what had happened during the 1966 Monte Carlo Rally when the French organizers had disqualified the Mini Coopers, thus allowing a Citroën to win. John Smailes quoted Ogier as saying "We were winning. We had it won. We were going easy on time. We only had to get to the control and we would have been right from then. I saw the car coming. There was not enough room. I swerved, moved over—it came on. I tried to stop. It happened."[3] In 2009, Allan Chilcott, the passenger in the Mini, wrote, "I felt at the time and still believe that we were travelling on an open public road at a reasonable speed, in a safe manner when the accident happened. The road was narrow dirt with a crest in the center and no defined lanes for two-way traffic. The usual practice on these roads was to drive on the crest and move over when a car came the other way."[4]

Another myth that surfaced was that because Paddy Hopkirk, Tony Nash and Alec Poole stopped to help the Franco-Belgian team, it allowed No. 75 to continue on to victory. This is completely false, as when the BMC 1800 left the previous control at Hindmarsh, it was down six points on the Hillman Hunter. Both cars arrived at the Nowra control within the allowed margin of time, and thereafter to Warwick Farm, the final section was neutralized. In other words, provided a competitor managed to get their car to the finish line, the points they had accrued at Nowra would be their final tally for the entire Marathon. The Hunter rolled into Warwick Farm with a total of 50 penalty points, while the BMC 1800 finished with 56.

Whatever the cause of the crash, it robbed Lucien Bianchi, Jean-Claude Ogier and Citroën in France the victory they so deserved. As Max Stahl wrote, "Here was a stricken driver, who only minutes before was headed to victory in a history-making event. His skill and stamina had taken him to the top of the world's best and now he lay between life and death...."[5] In fact, although Bianchi sustained injuries they were serious not critical: a broken leg, a broken toe and cuts to his face. The driver of the Mini, 18 year old Gregory Stanton, suffered lacerations to his arms and a foot fracture, while 18-year-old Chilcott sustained a concussion and lacerations and contusions to his head, arms and legs. By nightfall, Stanton and Chilcott were discharged from hospital while Bianchi was transferred to the medical center at Mascot, before boarding a plane back to London and onwards to his home in Belgium. Speaking to journalists from his hospital bed, Bianchi was philosophical about the day's dramatic conclusion, the *Sydney Telegraph* reporting that "The two young occupants of the car which struck his were a little excited because of the rally. He said that while police could obviously help in such rallies, it was difficult to prevent non-rally cars from travelling on the route."[6] In the days that followed the conclusion of the Marathon, a fund was announced to raise money to cover any costs that Bianchi might have incurred as a result of his accident.

Others were not quite so sage about the conduct of the New South Wales police, however, with Hopkirk saying, "They were like a bunch of SS men; there were seven police cars following us from Nowra, but where were they when Lucien crashed? Don't talk to me about the Australian police!"[7] Max Stahl also questioned police tactics, writing that "The action of the NSW Police was strange right through the Marathon. Dire warnings were issued about penalties for speed limit infringements, or for causing inconvenience to the public. No offers of cooperation mark you, such as occurred throughout France, Italy and the Iron Curtain countries."[8] John Bryson reflected, "Legally the Perth cops were right, but as far as I am concerned they were stupid and only just outdone by the New South Wales constabulary. What I did not like was my country being rubbished around the globe when the rest of the world had been utterly helpful." However, there was also some praise for the beleaguered New South

Wales police force. Running towards the rear of the field across Australia, Rosemary Smith continued to be plagued with valve damage in her Cortina Lotus and towards the final stages was finding it very hard work to coax the Ford up any steep inclines. Not far from Warwick Farm she seized upon the opportunity to floor the gas pedal as the highway gradually descended, only to be stopped by a traffic cop. Having coped with thousands of miles of mechanical problems that deprived her of the Ladies' Prize, for which she had been the clear favorite, plus a less than cordial atmosphere inside the Cortina, Rosemary burst into tears. Instantly the officer took pity, disregarded the speeding violation, instructed her to switch on her hazard warning lights and gave her a police escort into Sydney.

The dreadful fate of the Citroën meant that as Andrew Cowan embarked on the last 100 miles to Warwick Farm, No. 75 was the victor, although as Cowan wrote, "This, to my mind, was the most frightening part of the entire rally because every time I pulled out to overtake a truck I had to pull back again because I was scared to put a wheel wrong."[9] The three Scots were silent as they entered Sydney's city limits and joined the Princess Highway towards the beltway that would take them to Warwick Farm. Up ahead, they saw two Chrysler signs by the roadside and realized Chrysler in Sydney had hastily set up a service point to receive the winning Hunter. Thus, led by a Valiant sedan, on December 17, 1968, the triumphant trio of Andrew Cowan, Colin Malkin and Brian Coyle covered the last few miles to the finish line. Outside the race track, Paddy Hopkirk had pulled over to allow the Hunter to be first in, so stopping momentarily to collect Rob McAuley, who clambered aboard the rear of the Hunter in order to film their arrival, at 12:35 pm No. 75 drove into Warwick Farm Raceway to be greeted by New South Wales Premier Robin Askin, Marathon organizer Jack Sears, *Express* and *Telegraph* newspaper proprietors Sir Max Aitken and Sir Frank Packer and a sea of press photographers, television news cameras and thousands and thousands of cheering spectators.

As other competitors steered their battered and dusty cars into the Raceway, Marathon organizers quickly totaled and posted the final results. With the Hunter first, Hopkirk, Poole and Nash were declared second in their BMC 1800 and, with a roar from the Australian crowd, Ian Vaughan, Bob Forsyth and Jack Ellis took third place on the winners' podium for Ford Australia, having successfully managed to hold off the ever-threatening Porsche 911 of Polish duo Zasada and Wachowski. Rounding off the top ten were BMC GB team Rauno Aaltonen, Henry Liddon and Paul Easter in fifth, the Australian Ford Falcon team of Bruce Hodgson and Doug Rutherford in sixth, Ford Germany's Herbert Kleint and Günther Klapproth in their Ford 20MRS in seventh, Firth, Hoinville and Chapman in eighth, Citroën duo Bob Neyret and Jacques Terramorsi in ninth and, with scant consolation for having led for so long, Roger Clark and Ove Andersson finished the Marathon in tenth place. An even bigger cheer went up when the winner of the team prize was made known—the Falcon crews had claimed the victory for Ford Australia. Champagne flowed under a blazing sun and the first-, second- and third-place crews clambered onto the roofs of their cars to be photographed and interviewed. Cowan recalled feeling "rather annoyed because, while I was answering questions, Brian and Colin were digging in at the champagne and getting pleasantly tiddly. I couldn't get drinking for speaking."[10]

Throughout the afternoon and into the evening, more tired crews and ragged cars came to a halt by the racing circuit. Edgar Herrmann and Hans Schüller took 15th position in their Porsche and thus claimed the private entry award, while at 8:00 p.m., a disintegrating Volvo station wagon finally came to rest and four tired but happy British women learned that they had won the Ladies' Prize. Jack Sears offered heartfelt congratulations to the winners and commiserations to the losers and, as the sun slowly faded from the sky, it was confirmed that of the 98 teams of competitors who had set off from London just over three weeks before, 56 cars were classified as finishers in Sydney, the last-place being the little DAF 55 of Dutch National Team crew David van Lennep and Peter Hissink. Despite amassing 13,790 points, they too had made it over the finish line. Late into the night, and for some the early hours of the morning, 139 men and nine women who had successfully run the gauntlet of 10,000 miles across 11 countries collapsed into bed to get whatever sleep they could as on December 18, they were expected to climb back into their Marathon cars and join a victory parade through the streets of Sydney.

In order of their final position, at 11:00 a.m. the following morning, 56 cars snaked their way from Warwick Farm through the streets of Sydney to Hyde Park. Thousands of people lined the route, waving, cheering and taking photographs as drivers negotiated press cars and the stop-start convoy. Such was the traffic jam that on the approach to Hyde Park the motorcade ground to a halt and, in the heat of the day in car No. 1, Arthur Brick went in search of cold drinks. Suddenly the convoy moved forward again, leaving Brick stranded until he was able to hitch a ride with another Marathon car further down the line. At last, the procession crawled into Hyde Park and took up positions near the Archibald Fountain. With some teams pinned inside their cars for a moment or two, excited spectators crowded around and asked for autographs and more photos, the crews bewildered and amused by their sudden celebrity

The victory parade in Sydney, December 18 (courtesy John Hemsley).

No. 45, the RAF Hillman Hunter, during the victory parade through Sydney (courtesy Mike Bailey).

status. Twelfth-place Australian Holden Monaro driver Barry Ferguson described the festivities as "bloody marvelous, mate. Somehow this makes it all seem worthwhile—all the tension and struggling and the times you asked yourself what you were doing in it at all."[11]

December 20 saw competitors attend a reception and prize-giving ceremony at Sydney's Trocadero dance and music hall on George Street, where New South Wales State Governor Sir Roden Cutler presided over the presentation of awards. Many thought the venue and ceremony were an anticlimax after their big adventure, with Tommy Sopwith recalling that "Part of the deal was that everything that happened in Sydney was their [*The Sydney Telegraph's*] side of ship and therefore they organized the prize giving and so forth and I can remember saying to Max [Aitken], I think they've got this wrong before it happened and afterwards saying I told you so." Jim Gavin remembered wishing Sir Frank Packer "hadn't said 'and of course we're going to have another one.' I thought, just let this be unique, a unique moment. Announce the other one in six months, but this is pretty unique. It's like getting to the top of Everest and immediately saying 'Oh we're going to do that again.'"

During the evening, Cowan, Malkin and Coyle received *The Daily Express* Trophy, a two-and-a-half-foot tall silver crescent engraved with gold images of London's Houses of Parliament, the Taj Mahal and Sydney's Harbor Bridge, mounted on a clear prism in which a golden globe was set, etched with the Marathon's route. To accompany the trophy, the three Scots received a check for $24,000 as well as free entry and air fares to compete in the 1969 East African Safari Rally. Further cash prizes were awarded to those competitors who made the top ten as well as the *Evening Standard* Trophy for best private entry, together with $200 for Herrmann and Schüller and the ladies' Cibie prize and $480 for Gadd, Tudor-Owen,

Kemp and Castell. The Ford Australia crews were awarded the team prize of $1,800, which was collected by their elder statesman Harry Firth, but there was another award which met with not a little controversy. Sir Frank Packer had decided that *The Sydney Telegraph* women's team of Eileen Westley, Minny Macdonald and Jenny Gates should be awarded with a check for $1,100, which many found baffling, given that in the final ranking they were very near the bottom. Forty-five years later, Minny Macdonald reflected on what the reaction might have been: "Hang on a minute, they came 50th! I think, yes, it was Sir Frank Packer—he sort of had a rush of blood to the head and thought he'd like to reward us. It would have been easier to have given us a Christmas bonus! I don't think we were at all aware that people resented us."

All too soon, the evening was over and while many continued to party into the night in some of the city's other hostelries, the London to Sydney Marathon was done. As *Daily Express* journalist David Benson was reported to have said during a radio interview, "There may be other events that will be longer, or faster, or tougher, but one thing you'll never take away from us. This was the first and it will always be the best."[12]

34

Waltzing Over the Khyber Pass

In 1968, Eileen Westley wrote that "The question that at first amused, and later annoyed us, was the suspected inability of three women to live in a car, in close confinement, for seven days. To us this was nonsense. Why should we disagree?"[1] Forty-five years later, reflecting upon her experience of the Marathon, Minny Macdonald said, "Well, we were offended at the notion that Jenny actually hit the donkey." Thus began the recollections of two of the three Australian women who drove a compact, pink and white Morris 1100 S on the 10,000-mile journey from London all the way home to Sydney.

Looking at the many written and filmed reports of the Marathon, it's easy to conclude that in 1968, the world of motorsports was very much a male domain and that female rally or racing drivers were perceived mostly as a decorative novelty. In the United States, although Donna Mae Mims was proving herself as a talented circuit racer, winning the Sports Car Club of America national championship in 1963, media focus was less on her skills behind the wheel and more on her trademark pink racing suit, pink crash helmet, pink sports cars and slogan "Think Pink." In Europe, Pat Moss, Gabriel Konig, Anita Taylor and Lucette Pointet were frequently scoring wins in rallies or on the track, but again the media highlighted their femininity over their achievements. Hugely successful Irish rally driver Rosemary Smith turned this to her advantage, always ensuring she looked immaculate for the cameras as she crossed the finish line, usually stopping just beforehand to apply makeup and brush her hair, while repeatedly winning *Coupe des Dames* prizes on the European rally circuit as well as triumphing outright on the 1965 Tulip Rally.

Press coverage of the forthcoming Marathon was no exception, with pages of nuanced copy devoted to the female competitors. *The Sydney Telegraph* reported on the MGB entered in the event, describing its crew as "attractive Jean Denton, 32-year-old racing driver and economist and Canadian engineer Tom Boyce."[2] In a feature about Nick and Jenny Brittan, the same newspaper reported that "Australian model Jenny Brittan doesn't look like the sort of girl who would compete in the longest and toughest race ever devised. She has a slight, willowy figure with long blonde hair and wide-set blue eyes … matched with a smile that suggests naivety rather than resourcefulness."[3] During the Marathon, Minny Macdonald continued her "Society Spy" column for *The Sydney Telegraph* and as she recalled, "I said in my column back before we started—I'm deeply ashamed—I was saying I'm not a bad driver for a woman. I mean, we were doing it to ourselves. But it didn't annoy us in the slightest—it was the way it was."

Stepping into the Marathon media spotlight, joining the nine other female competitors were three young Australian women, two of them journalists working for *The Sydney Telegraph*. Women's Editor Eileen Westley and columnist Marion "Minny" Macdonald were joined by Eileen's friend, financial secretary Jenny Gates, after Eileen had the idea to submit an entry form for the event. As Minny explained, "It was all down to Eileen. She was the one who saw that it was going to happen, that *The Telegraph* was sponsoring it, and she said she wanted to go. Why she asked me ... I suppose it was because she knew I could drive a car. Seemed to be a prerequisite! Initially, it was just going to be Eileen and me." *Telegraph* proprietor Sir Frank Packer was initially unconvinced by the idea, however, Jenny recalling that "Sir Frank had said to Eileen when she put this proposition to him, he thought he could sort of bluff her and he said okay, on condition that you find someone to provide the car in the first place and get it to England and find your airfares." Not one to be put off, Eileen set to work, finding a car and persuading Air India to cover the cost of transporting them to London. Turning the tables, she called Packer's bluff and so, presented with this *fait accompli*, he agreed to the *Telegraph* supporting them alongside the three Holden Monaro cars organized by fellow-journalist David McKay.

Eileen's chosen vehicle had already made the headlines in 1967 when, as a promotional stunt to launch BMC Australia's new Morris 1100 S model, rally drivers Evan Green and "Gelignite" Jack Murray had raced an 1100 S against a light aircraft from Sydney to Perth, the only rule being that the plane was not allowed to fly during the hours of darkness. The press referred to the event as "the tortoise and the hare" and so the car, complete with hot pink roof adorned with a large drawing of its namesake, became known as "The Galloping Tortoise."

In order to prepare Eileen and Minny for the Marathon, Peter Wherrett, racing driver and owner of an advanced drivers' school, took them and the 1100 S to the Warwick Farm Raceway in Sydney to put them through their paces. As each woman completed a circuit of the track, a touch of competitive rivalry began to emerge with each trying to outdo the other for fastest lap time. As Minny recalled, "They must have been mad to let us do this. Eileen had driven a very fast time on the last circuit and I thought I could do better. So I absolutely hit the accelerator and I obliterated about ten meters of the safety fence at Warwick Farm and my crash helmet came down and split my eyebrow open. So Peter Wherrett was a bit embarrassed by all this and the car they hastily towed away and they put a tarpaulin over it because they didn't want anyone to know this had happened." The car was in fact totaled by the crash, so maintaining a veil of secrecy, BMC Australia hastily prepared an identical car and plans continued as if nothing had happened!

While a new 1100 S was being prepared, discussion turned to the composition of its crew. As stated, the original plan had been to compete as a duo, but a visit from BMC GB team driver Henry Liddon persuaded them otherwise. Liddon was in Australia to undertake a survey of the route from Perth to Sydney and, as Jenny explained, told them that "We all have to have three drivers in the 1800s. David McNicoll, who was the Editor-In-Chief, said to him, 'Oh Lord!' We asked if we had to have three and did it have to be another journalist? David didn't care who we had! I think the thought of three women in a car, three girls in a car was horrendous—choose someone you think will get on with you and that was it."

Meeting friends for coffee, Eileen announced the plan and the need for a third driver. Jenny recalled that "We had all known what she wanted to do and we were all sitting there saying you're absolutely mad, God, don't do it! And this day she came along and said we need another driver in the car, are any of you interested? Anyway, I ended up being it." Minny added that "The others gave feeble excuses like they had flat feet!"

With agreement that Minny would continue writing her regular "Society Spy" column for the newspaper during the Marathon, on November 9, 1968, the three women boarded an Air India jet and, together with most of the Holden Monaro crews, set off for England. In her column written on the eve of departure, Minny wrote that "Ever since we announced that we were entering, Eileen, Jenny and I have been cornered by earnest-headed people who start: 'I don't know if they'd be of any use to you, but I just happen to have kept my notes on the 1929 Trans-Bulgaria Bicycle Trials...' It is kind of them to worry all the same."[4]

Although all three had been to Europe before, they were looking forward to spending time in fashionable London, but there was a surprise in store. No sooner had they landed than they were instructed to pick up a Morris Minor and drive over to France, down to the Mont Blanc Tunnel in Italy and back as a way of allowing them to grow accustomed to driving in continental Europe, all the while living on nothing but the food ration packs they would take on the Marathon. Ignoring the instruction not to drive into the center of Paris, their navigational skills were put to the test as they headed into the French capital, not helped by the fact that they also ran out of gas on the Champs-Elysées. On the return trip, they just missed the last ferry back to England and had to stay overnight at a hotel, which Minny described as looking like something out of an Alfred Hitchcock movie.

BMC took charge of the Morris 1100 S once it arrived in England and motorsports department engineers carried out further preparations on the little car at their base in Abingdon. As Jenny recalled, "Somewhere, someone set us a test to see how quickly we could change a tire. I think it was at Abingdon? That's where they did something to the fuel lines but yes, I remember this test to see how quickly we could change the tires. We never did have to change it anyway, because we knew we had the service crew somewhere coming behind!"

Twenty-four hours before departure at Crystal Palace, Jenny became ill and was confined to bed at *The Sydney Telegraph* team's base in North London. A doctor was summoned and, as Jenny recalled, "The doctor just said 'Well, you've got to stay in bed for at least three days' and I said 'But I can't, I'm driving to Sydney tomorrow!' He sort of choked. I don't remember Crystal Palace." Despite constant nausea, on Saturday, November 23, Jenny joined Eileen and Minny and took the car to Crystal Palace to be scrutinized by officials, a requirement for all Marathon entrants. In her column Minny wrote that during the inspection "There had been one trifling incident when a photographer asked us 'to pose doing something knowledgeable in the engine.' And we had been unable to open the bonnet."[5]

The 1100 S was drawn as No. 41 in the starting lineup and so, at 2:40 p.m. on November 24, they were flagged away with Eileen at the wheel. Through London and down to Dover, they were astonished at the number of people lining the roads, but made the ferry port at Dover in good time. Upon hearing the instruction not to drive on the main highway from Calais to Paris, Jenny explained that "We were being very dutiful, obeying the police and a lot of people just went on the *autoroute*, but we were obedient and took the back routes. I do remember trying to wind our way through, not having a clue, and we saw David McKay's car coming the other way, so we turned around and started following it, but then it turned around again!" The ever present fog that cut visibility to a minimum through the French countryside contributed to the fact that the 1100 S was one of only three cars to arrive late at the Le

Bourget control, although the car was also suffering from a faulty fuel pump, which forced them to rely on their six-gallon auxiliary gas tank.

Setting off from the French checkpoint, the three women struggled to find their way through the dark streets of Paris to the southerly *autoroute*, eventually seeking assistance from a passing Mercedes that led them in the right direction. By the time they reached Turin, not only did the fuel pump need fixing, but the car's odometer had also stopped working. Fortunately the BMC service team was on hand and had the car quickly repaired. So, dodging the crowds of young Italian men who had gathered to see their hero Baghetti speed through in his Lancia Fulvia but who were also very interested in the female occupants of No. 41, they pressed on to Belgrade in Yugoslavia, where the Hotel Metropole offered a brief respite. Gazing out of the hotel room window, Minny saw David McNicoll washing their car for the benefit of the many film and television cameras.

Once their road book was stamped, they were off across Yugoslavia towards the Bulgarian border, during which Jenny had "the trauma of the brakes failing in the mountains, with hairpin bends heading out that way. I was driving, Minny was navigating, Eileen was asleep and I didn't want to alarm Minny but I'd put my foot on the brake and it was going to the floor! I really clearly remember thinking, okay–I'm not going to say 'Ah, we've got no brakes!' I said, 'Minny, you did that course with Peter Wherrett, do you remember what he said about going through the gears because I think I'll have to do that, I've got no brakes. Can you teach me on the run?'" With Jenny being given a crash course in engine braking, they continued on carefully and eventually crawled up to border control where, sitting in the queue for Customs, they were nabbed by a Dutch television crew, eager to interview the three women. When they explained their depleted braking power, one of the Dutchmen volunteered to investigate while, as Minny wrote, "The other two, talking very fast in Jerry Lewis accents, set up arc lights, microphone and camera among the tool-kits and asked us to tell the viewers how it felt to lose your brakes mid–Marathon."[6]

Their impromptu interview complete, Minny realized they would need Bulgarian currency so went to the Yugoslavian customs official who pointed her toward the Bulgarian exchange office. The Bulgarian official gazed at her and asked for her passport, which she had left in the car. She turned to retrace her steps, but was then stopped by a Yugoslavian official who also demanded to see her passport. Minny wrote that "I pointed at the car, 20 yards away. But many's the secret agent who's pulled that old play-it-casual trick on the Slavs, obviously. 'You can't come into Yugoslavia without a passport,' he said."[7] After a few anxious moments, with Minny literally trapped in no-man's-land, she was finally allowed to retrieve her passport.

Fortified by cups of instant soup and with the brakes repaired enough to get them to Istanbul, they carried on to the next checkpoint where again, the BMC service crew overhauled the Morris's brake lines. Across the Bosporus, they were now in central Turkey where they encountered children at the roadside, apparently waving but in fact aiming carefully selected rocks to hurl at a passing Marathon competitor. Minny is convinced one even had a BB rifle as they later discovered a neat chip in the glass of one of the car's side windows. Aware they were running towards the rear of the field, they sped on as quickly as possible, lurching and thudding over the special stage from Sivas as best they could but still receiving 195 penalty points at the checkpoint at Erzincan.

Eileen, Minny and Jenny arrived at the next control at Teheran within the time allowed where once again, the car was checked over by the BMC service team, led this time by Bill Price. Stopping to rest and stretch their legs, because they were falling behind other competitors, Price suggested that perhaps they might want to get going, which they did, disappearing off towards the Iranian desert that would lead them up and over the mountains to the border with Afghanistan. At almost 1,500 miles, the section to Kabul would be long and difficult, especially for the 1100 S and its team. Approximately 125 miles out of Teheran, the odometer stopped working again, leaving the women without the ability to calculate either actual or average speeds. Then, as Minny wrote, they "hummed along for another 200 kilometers [125 miles] ... until Jenny didn't hit the donkey. We came into Bombay to find everyone chortling over the story of the Australian girls decimating a donkey. It is a rotten untruth, we love those donkeys."[8] In a bid to avoid hitting the wayward animal, Jenny swerved, skidded and jammed the car into a mud bank, the contents of the 1100 S shooting forward, including Eileen who was wrapped in a sleeping bag on the back seat. The three women got out to inspect the damage, discovering that the right front fender had been crumpled into the wheel. Eileen retrieved a set of wire cutters and began snipping away at the twisted metal to free it from the now deflated tire. Eventually a blue truck approached them and out stepped a local man who, as Minny wrote, "Scratched his belly, spat on his hands and pulled us out of the ditch."[9] The man proceeded to cut away the rest of the damaged fender, replace the tire and get the women back on the road again.

It wasn't long before a new problem began to manifest itself. It was apparent that the constant pounding from the dusty track hadn't agreed with the car's hydrolastic suspension setup and the car had begun to sag on one side. As Jenny recalled, "We stopped floating on fluid! We didn't get too concerned when we had to stop because we knew they [the BMC

"The BMC boys" work on No. 41 in Iran (courtesy Bill Price).

service mechanics] were behind, but they didn't turn up and it was two or three hours, and I bet he [Bill Price] didn't admit this—they had a problem with their suspension! That's why they were hours behind us and left us stuck in the desert without our guardian angels!" Sitting on the side of the road in the hot sun, the women attracted a group of small boys from the nearby settlement of mud houses and eventually the attention of a local police officer who appeared convinced that the 1100 S had hit another car, despite their attempts to explain what had happened via a series of theatrical gestures. By the time the sweeper car arrived, the sagging Morris and the three women had caused a small crowd to gather. Price repaired the drooping car, but would be called upon to pump up the Morris's hydrolastic suspension twice more before the women reached Kabul.

Crossing over into Afghanistan, with most other competitors running ahead of the women, just beyond Islam Qala they came upon what appeared to be a checkpoint that wasn't in their route notes. As Jenny explained, "Well, they put a log across the road. Well of course we had to stop and it was—not a bayonet, something that glittered, and it was a nasty looking implement and they were scary looking, Afghan tribesman. We were in no-man's land." Minny added that "Heaven only knows how we got through. As far as I remember, some of them were wearing semi-military bits and pieces, uniforms and guns and we really didn't know what they were. It was true, nobody did believe us, but it was true." Probably because the bandits were as surprised to see three women waving their passports and road book from inside a pink and white car as Eileen, Minny and Jenny were to see weaponry, they were able to swerve around the barrier and carry on to Herat, eventually making it to Kabul where their numerous stops across Iran and Afghanistan cost them 4,320 points.

The 1100 S was now severely hindered by its ailing suspension and restricted steering caused by the damage in Iran so Eileen, Minny and Jenny opted to take the alternative, easier route to Sarobi, avoiding the Lataband Pass altogether. Unfortunately, as Nick Brittan wrote, Sarobi was "the one and only control in the whole rally, which had to be approached from a specified direction and failure to comply with this regulation meant exclusion from the event."[10] Both the 1100 S and the valve-damaged Cortina Lotus of Rosemary Smith and Lucette Pointet were flagged down by frantic officials before they entered the 50 yard checkpoint zone as they were indeed coming in from the wrong direction. Their only alternative was to accept 1,440 points for a missed time control, turn around and head off for the Khyber Pass.

The Pass twists and winds for over 30 miles through the Spin Ghar Mountains from Afghanistan to Pakistan. At the border, Pakistani officials were astonished to learn that the occupants of this late-running Marathon car were insisting on being allowed to proceed over the Pass at night. Somehow the women persuaded them to agree and into the night they went. Each turn in the road brought a challenge for Eileen as she coaxed the 1100 S along, its limited steering severely restricting her ability to maneuver the car around the numerous corners. As Minny recalled, "We didn't have a turning circle. Peter Wherrett had taught us how to go through a corner, how you were supposed to go out to the outer edge and then you were supposed to carve through the corner and that kind of reduced your turning circle, so we put on a tape of Strauss waltzes and we danced through the Khyber Pass, going out to the edge."

Across Pakistan and into India, the three women carefully negotiated the crowds and unpredictable truck drivers and even managed to sidetrack for a little sight-seeing. As Jenny explained, "Now, Minny's conveniently forgotten this and no-one ever knew, but we actually diverted on the rally because Minny wanted to see the Taj Mahal by moonlight! We were so far behind anyway." Eileen, Minny and Jenny eventually made it to Bombay in 67th position, Minny barefoot and hopping up and down on the hot asphalt as Eileen answered questions for a television journalist.

With the 1100 S steam-cleaned and loaded into the belly of the *Chusan*, it was time to relax and catch up on other competitors' experiences, although boredom quickly set in on the nine-day voyage. As Minny mischievously wrote, "On a good day we get up in time for drinks before lunch, drink, swim, drink, lie in the sun, drink, dine, drink, dance, onwards into the early hours of the morning." [11]By the time the coast of Australia could be spotted, all three women were desperate to set foot on their home ground again.

Once unloaded, the obligatory police inspection of the pink and white car revealed a long list of defects that would need correcting for Eileen, Minny and Jenny to be allowed to continue. Consequently, as soon as Eileen had navigated the track at Gloucester Park in Perth, the women headed straight to the Guildford service point ten miles out of the city, where BMC mechanics worked down the list of "a complete tire change, rebuilding of suspension, fastening down of seats, which had come loose and replacement of a damaged mudguard [fender]."[12] It was obvious that the repairs would take many hours, so the women agreed to miss the Youanmi control and instead make for Southern Cross and the next control at Marvel Loch, by which time they felt confident that they would be able to join the Marathon again.

Across the outback, Eileen, Minny and Jenny continued their three-hour rotation of driving, navigating and resting, all the while trying to keep penalty points to a minimum. Eileen was reported as saying that "Our drive across Australia has been a succession of minor mechanical troubles overruled by a press-on-regardless spirit."[13] Somewhere between Lake

Jenny Gates and Minny Macdonald, December 1968 (courtesy Jennifer Bremner).

King and Quorn, the 1100 S developed a fuel leak, filling the cabin with fumes and forcing Minny and Jenny to quickly extinguish their cigarettes, and between Moralana Creek and Brachina Gorge they buckled the oil pan guard on a protruding rock. At Broken Hill they became involved in the frustrating events that befell John Sprinzel and Roy Fidler, delivering the correct hub axle part after an incorrect item had previously been supplied. During their dash across the isolated regions of central and southern Australia, they were often met with kindness from local people. At many of the control points, people presented them food and drink and one thoughtful woman even had buckets of water and shampoo for them to wash their hair. As Minny wrote, "It was lovely driving across Australia. The roads were vicious, but they were our own. The countryside was often desolate and dreary, but it was home."[14]

Finally, at 11:50 p.m. on December 17, 1968, Eileen Westley guided "The Galloping Tortoise" into the Warwick Farm Raceway to the cheers of those spectators who had chosen to remain long after most of the other competitors had arrived. They were met by family and friends, as well as David McNicoll and *Sunday Telegraph* editor John Moyes. Of the 56 cars to be classified as finishers at Sydney, No. 41, the battered and sagging Morris 1100 S, was placed 50th. At Warwick Farm, Eileen was reported to say "It's just great—this is fabulous. The old tortoise is still going sweetly and I'd like to drive her for the rest of my life."[15]

Forty-five years later, when asked what the highlight of her Marathon experience was, Jenny replied, "This is probably a very surface thing to say, but I just loved the fact that we were ... we liked to think we were the only women in history who had driven through the Khyber Pass at night." Minny added, "Yes, it's driving through the Khyber Pass and I remember the Strauss waltz and seeing the ravine as we went out to the edge and then danced away from it. Who says three women in a car can't get on?"

Remembering her mother Eileen, Lindsay Prehn said, "I was actually quite shocked that Mum did it, going into Iran and Afghanistan. I mean Iran in 1968 isn't like Iran now, but they were still very much male-dominated societies. Mum with her blonde hair and blue eyes, ordering men around about how to fix her car and get it back on the road. Quite fearless!"

Eileen Westley Prehn died in 2002.

Epilogue—After the Dust Had Settled

Nobody, least of all Chrysler, the giant multinational automobile manufacturer that by 1967 had acquired the British Rootes Group, expected the Hillman Hunter to win the Marathon. Former Rootes Group Competitions Manager Marcus Chambers wrote that "Rootes were in a state of shock. Their advertising people hadn't expected us to win and had no press handouts ready. The Australians coped much better in that they had a car called a Hillman Hunter GT ready and announced it two days before the event finished."[1] That said, Chrysler Australia was also ultimately caught off guard as pre-launch production quantities of the Hunter GT were nowhere near great enough to meet demand, and having to tell a performance-hungry customer that there would be a waiting list undoubtedly led some shoppers to go elsewhere. In Britain, Rootes was even less able to capitalize on Cowan's success, Chambers bitterly writing that recently appointed director of sales and marketing Geoffrey Ellison "said this was justified because there could be no confidence in the Competitions Department."[2] The fact that Rootes had been able to mobilize and prepare two Hunters for the Marathon at all was testimony to the tenacity of both Chambers and Rootes rally manager Des O'Dell in the face of overarching budget cuts imposed on Rootes by Chrysler and it's fascinating to consider that Rootes' total cost for competing in the event was just over $63,000, compared to *The Sydney Telegraph*'s Holden team, which chalked up $167,000. Surprising then that the result of the Marathon, which as David Benson wrote in 1968, "now rates as the largest live audience in history for a sporting event,"[3] was basically dismissed by the British Rootes Group under Chrysler's parentage.

Other manufacturers paid much closer attention, with Volvo studying the impact of 10,000 miles of endurance driving on its products in fine detail, while, as Max Stahl wrote, "Only three days after the Marathon began, the Mercedes factory 280SE test car hit a vee gutter and dislodged its radiator, hitting the fan! The appropriate changes have now been made on the production line."[4] General Motors Australia also sat up and took notice, after having previously enforced its strict "no motorsports" policy. As Holden competitor Barry Ferguson said, "Undoubtedly the braking systems will be improved on the next Holden. They've got to be. We ran out of them enough times."[5] Ford Australia was delighted with the success of the three Falcon GTs and their sales and marketing department quickly went to work producing promotional materials, commercials and even making sure the actual Marathon Falcons toured their dealership network around Australia.

For Citroën in France, during the closing hours of the Marathon they had quickly geared up to celebrate and extol the virtues of the DS21 and its revolutionary, albeit 15-year-old hydro-pneumatic self-leveling suspension system, even placing a triumphant advertisement in British newspapers. The ensuing crash that wiped out the Bianchi/Ogier car was therefore a bitterly disappointing loss of a great marketing opportunity for the French car producer.

For Ford GB there was disappointment and perhaps a little embarrassment for its own motorsports department. Having fielded two teams of three cars, it saw only three of its cars make it to Sydney and, under the international media spotlight, it watched three of its factory-prepared Cortina Lotuses suffer the same mechanical collapse. The high profile, highly experienced pairing of Bengt Söderström and Gunnar Palm had failed even to get out of Turkey when the Ford eight-valve, twin overhead camshaft engine blew a piston. The same problem plagued the car driven by Rosemary Smith and Lucette Pointet from Iran onwards and, worst of all, having led the Marathon right across Europe and Asia, and halfway across Australia, the bookies' favorites Roger Clark and Ove Andersson eventually had to accept tenth place when their car also suffered piston failure, forcing Ford GB to endure the double indignity of sacrificing a fourth team car in a bid to try and keep Clark and Andersson going. The fifth team car, that of Nick and Jenny Brittan, never got far enough to find out whether piston failure would defeat it and that left the sixth car, the ex-rally Cortina Lotus driven by British Army officers Captain David Harrison and Lieutenant Martin Proudlock, which finished in Sydney in 30th position. Martin Proudlock reflected, "I don't know why we didn't have the same mechanical problems as Rosemary, Roger and Bengt Söderström, except that the top three cars were bored out to 1800-cc. The last day or so we were beginning to get a problem and at the end of the event, David said I reckon if we'd driven our engine a bit harder, we'd have gone the same way." As Graham Robson wrote, Ford GB's Competitions Department "never really trusted the twin cam engine again for long-distance events. When the team came to prepare Escorts for the Daily Mirror World Cup in 1970, it chose to use enlarged Kent pushrod engines instead—and dominated the event!"[6]

Jack Sears and his committee had gone to great lengths to ensure the 10,000-mile route would be tough but not impossible, and initial predictions had been that at best, only 50 cars would survive the rigors of driving across Asia to Bombay. The fact that a total of 72 entrants qualified for the nine-day cruise to Perth, forcing a quick negotiation between Tommy Sopwith and the P&O shipping company, suggests that perhaps the route proved less challenging than intended. Certainly this was Roger Clark's view, expressed in a remark that "I had more sleep between London and Bombay than I normally get in England."[7] Many who contributed recollections to this book also competed in the London to Mexico World Cup Rally held two years later and an oft-reported view was that the drive to Mexico City was infinitely more difficult, with lessons having been learned from the Marathon. Yet for those competitors who broke down in the Iranian wilderness, got lost in the fog in Northern Europe, smashed into trucks, buses, horses, kangaroos and telephone poles, fended off bandits, spent the entire drive to Sydney suffering from constant car sickness or worse, suffering from profound and extremely stressful personality clashes inside their cramped cockpits, the Marathon was probably as challenging as it could get. American competitor Sid Dickson commented that "Well, there's something about adventure being the result of poor planning. I don't want adventure! A good, hard ride, a drink at night, a steak dinner. I don't want adventures!" But how could anyone have been prepared for the consequences of being pelted with rocks by gangs of Turkish kids or being obliterated by a runaway Indian Army truck?

Something the Marathon achieved with huge success was the facilitation of cooperation, whether it was at a grand, international level, or simply between individuals across the globe. Unthinkable today, Jack Sears managed to secure the goodwill and collaboration of countries that traditionally eyed each other with at best suspicion, at worst outright hostility, and all in the name of international motorsports. The fact that at the border, Indian and Pakistani officials worked together as a team, when only a few years before they had been at war, is a testimony not only to Jack but to the potential effect of a common, non-political goal. At the other end of the scale, despite the actions of the above mentioned youthful Turkish hoodlums and the almost theatrically officious attitude of the police in Western Australia and New South Wales, the Marathon resulted in countless acts of simple kindness in almost every country through which it passed, with local inhabitants often coming to the assistance of competitors broken down or crashed on the side of the road, doing all they could to help, usually without the benefit of a shared language. From the women who made sure there were refreshments for weary participants at controls across the outback to the Indians who cared for Bob Holden and Laurie Graham, or brooked no refusal—or offer of recompense—to fix a Volvo station wagon literally ripping at the seams, the collective excitement, enthusiasm and generosity on display across 10,000 miles were boundless. Among the competitors themselves, the spirit of camaraderie was also to the fore, with countless examples of one crew helping another at a time of crisis. Listening to some of those who contributed, from time to time there is a whiff of sabotage, but, repeatedly, the raw competitiveness of so many drivers, navigators and mechanics was suspended in the name of kindness and support. Consider American competitors Sid Dickson, John Saladin and Jerry Sims stopping to help a Soviet Moskvič stuck in a desert sand drift in Iran, or Volvo team Gerry Lister and André Welinski immediately pulling over to help when the British Vauxhall Ventora flipped over on the road to Belgrade. The fact that Australians John Bryson, Jack "Milko" Murray and Bert Madden carried the wounded British driver Doug Morris back to a medical center in Turkey started a chain of events that would eventually lead to their Holden almost being forced to retire from the Marathon before Bombay. Sometimes the hunger to win, or at least compete, was less important than giving a helping hand.

The Marathon was undertaken by two categories of competitor, the big manufacturer-backed teams and the determined "privateer," although even those who raised their own funds and prepared their own vehicles for the event stretched the definition of "private entry" to the limit. Max Stahl wrote, "Here is where the Marathon failed most. It was made for the 'big spender,' the factory that could afford to back its team with convoys of service vehicles and aircraft equipped with two-way radio, ready at a moment's notice to rush to a vehicle's aid."[8] Certainly a combination of professional drivers, professionally prepared cars and comprehensive backup meant that in Sydney, the first 14 places on the scoreboard were factory-backed and having a dedicated team of mechanics and managers focused on problem solving from England to Australia made life easier for the likes of Cowan, Clark, Hopkirk and Bianchi. Yet, as Bob Holden said," the Marathon was a few professionals and a whole lot of adventurers and that's what it's all about." Yes, British Navy competitor Captain James Hans Hamilton grumbled about the level of support offered to the professionals, but, for so many of those competing on a budget, the whole purpose of the Marathon was quite simply to be part of it and to get to Sydney. Irish competitor Jim Gavin's three objectives of getting to Calais, getting to Bombay and getting to the finish were his team's mantra and that was good enough for them, even if it meant being placed last, and while the factory team mechanics focused on their cars, for the most part they were more than happy to fix a damaged privately entered car if time allowed, as demonstrated by Bill Price in the BMC sweeper car.

Interest in the Marathon from both the public and the media was huge and, of all the countries that were represented in the competitors' enclosure at Crystal Palace in November 1968, perhaps the only one that had paid scant interest was the United States. Admittedly, only one team was waving the stars and stripes in their red, white and blue Rambler American, but other than some local newspaper coverage in the state of Maryland and a couple of items in *The New York Times* and *The Washington Post*, the Marathon mostly passed the United States by. The subsequent television broadcast of CBS's film *The Incredible Auto Race* in March 1970, as filmed by competitor Jerry Sims and narrated by Charles Kuralt, may have entertained, may even have inspired the average American "gearhead," but the fact that the movie's title refers to a "race" and the fact that it took 15 months to actually show the film suggests that the Marathon was considered an entertaining novelty rather than a serious international motorsports event. Certainly there wasn't a flurry of American applications for the 1970 London Mexico World Cup Rally. Rallying was and still remains a niche activity in the United States, where the focus continues to be directed towards NASCAR. As Sid Dickson commented, "If it hadn't been for the CBS movie, nobody would know about it. Rallying just isn't a big deal. Our racing is based on booze running—rum runners. NASCAR and stuff like that, that's all directly descended from booze running."

The 1968 London to Sydney Marathon probably occurred during a unique period in modern international political history, which allowed it to cross Iran, Afghanistan and Pakistan without threat of political upheaval or danger to life, notwithstanding the occasional bandit. Only five years later, Afghanistan experienced a coup, ending King Zahir Shah's 40-year reign and ushering in decades of political instability, while in neighboring Iran, rampant inflation and economic hardship during the early 1970s eventually led to the revolution that deposed the ruling dynasty. No coincidence that subsequent trans-global endurance motorsports events avoided the path followed in 1968, and although a second London to Sydney Marathon was announced as the first came to a close, scheduled to take place four years later, spiraling international gasoline prices and perhaps the changing face of international geopolitics meant that it never happened.

Returning to London in December 1968, Andrew Cowan, Colin Malkin and Brian Coyle were treated like heroes. British Prime Minister Harold Wilson dispatched Fred Peart, Lord President of the Council and Leader of the House of Commons, to receive the three Scotsmen at Heathrow Airport and the Duke of Edinburgh made a point of congratulating the winning team, Cowan writing that "he had obviously followed the Marathon with great interest."[9] The list of the ten highest placed Marathon teams highlights a group of rally drivers and navigators who were at the top of their game in 1968. Of these 25 professional rally competitors, 14 went on to compete in the London to Mexico event and, after the misfortune that befell Swedish professional driver and navigator Gunnar Palm in the Ford GB Cortina Lotus in 1968, compensation came in the form of an emphatic win alongside Hannu Mikkola at Mexico City in 1970.

Missing from the 1970 lineup, and indeed any international rally competitions after 1968, was Lucien Bianchi. Having vowed to return for the planned 1972 event, in March 1969, while driving an Alfa Romeo T33 on a test run at the Le Mans circuit in France, the man who was 11 points clear of his nearest rival as he headed to the Sydney finish line, the man who should have won the 1968 London to Sydney Marathon, crashed off the track. His car slammed into a telephone pole and Bianchi was killed instantly. He was 34 years old.

During the last 46 years there have been five subsequent motorsports marathons between England and Australia, most recently in 2014 with a reverse run from Sydney to London. There have also been countless international endurance rallies across many of the world's most physically demanding landscapes and terrains, but none has ever captured the public's imagination, has ever caused such global excitement, such fascination, as the 1968 London to Sydney Marathon.

Appendix 1: The Entrants

No.	Entrant	Car	Team	Country
1	RTS Motorway Remoulds	Ford Cortina GT	Bill Bengry Arthur Brick John Preddy	Great Britain
2	Ford Motor Co. (Aus)	Ford Falcon XT GT	Harry Firth Graham Hoinville Gary Chapman	Australia
3	Avon/RAF	Ford Cortina GT	First Officer Nigel Coleman Flight Lt. Allan Dalgleish Lt. Sean Moloney	Great Britain
4	British Leyland	BMC 1800	Tony Fall Mike Wood Brian Culcheth	Great Britain
5	R. Lewis	Chrysler Valiant Safari	Peter Lumsden Peter Sargent Redge Lewis John Fenton	Great Britain
6	Combined Insurance Company of America	Ford Fairmont XP	Clyde Hodgins Don Wait Brian Lawler	Australia
7	Avtoexport	Moskvič 408	Alexander Ipantenko Alexander Terekhin Eduard Baszhenov	USSR
8	AMOCO Australia Ltd.	Volvo 144S	Max Winkless John Keran	Australia
9	A. A. Bombelli	Ford Cortina Lotus	Alfredo "Freddy" Bombelli Tom Belsø	Switzerland
10	Royal Green Jackets	Porsche 911T	George Yannaghas Lt. Jack Dill	Great Britain
11	Blick Racing Team	Renault 16TS	Frizt Reust P. Grazter Axel Béguin	Switzerland
12	TVW-7, Daily News, Perth	Volvo 144S	Ken Tubman Jack Forrest	Australia
13	John Tallis	Volvo 123GT	John Tallis Paul Coltelloni	Great Britain

No.	Entrant	Car	Team	Country
14	Ford Deutschland	Ford 20MRS	Dieter Glemser Martin Braungart	West Germany
15	G.P. Franklin	Ford Cortina GT	Geoffrey Franklin Kim Brassington	Australia
16	D.A. Corbett	BMC 1800	David Corbett Geoffrey Mabbs Tom Fisk	Great Britain
17	Royal Navy	BMC 1800	Capt. James Hans Hamilton Capt. Ian Lees-Spalding Cmdr. Philip Stearns	Great Britain
18	M. A. Colvill	Ford Cortina	Mike Greenwood Dave Aldridge	Great Britain
19	Avtoexport	Moskvič 408	Sergej Tenishev Valentin Kislikh	U.S.S.R.
20	Avtoexport	Moskvič 408	Victor Schavelev Emmanuil "Misha" Lifshitz Valerij Shirotchenkov	U.S.S.R.
21	Hillcrest Motor Co.	BMC 1800	Berwyn Williams Martin Thomas Barry Hughes	Great Britain
22	G. Baghetti	Lancia Fulvia 1.3HF	Giancarlo Baghetti Giorgio Bassi	Italy
23	P. R. H. Wilson	Ford Corsair 2000E	Peter Wilson Ian Mackelden Keith Dwyer D. Maxwell	Great Britain
24	Ford Motor Co. (Aus)	Ford Falcon XT GT	Ian Vaughan Robert Forsyth Jack Ellis	Australia
25	Chesson Lydden Circuit La Trobe	Volvo 122S	John La Trobe William Chesson G. Warner	Great Britain
26	Michael Taylor	Mercedes-Benz 280SE	Michael Taylor Innes Ireland Andrew Hedges	Great Britain
27	F. Goulden	Triumph 2000	Frank Goulden Barry Goulden Geoffrey Goulden	Great Britain
28	A. Gorshenin	Mercedes-Benz 280SL	Alec Gorshenin Ian Bryson	Australia
29	Ford Motor Co. (Aus)	Ford Falcon XT GT	Bruce Hodgson Doug Rutherford	Australia
30	Dutch National Team	DAF 55	Rob Slotemaker Rob Janssen	Holland
31	BMC Australia	BMC 1800	Evan Green Jack Murray George Shepheard	Australia

No.	Entrant	Car	Team	Country
32	Captain F. Barker	Mercedes-Benz 280S	Capt. Fred Barker Capt. David Dollar Capt. John Lewis	Great Britain
33	Elsie Gadd	Volvo 145S	Elsie Gadd Jenny Tudor-Owen Sheila Kemp Anthea Castell	Great Britain
34	K. Brierley	Ford Cortina Lotus	Keith Brierley Dave Skittrall	Great Britain
35	R. A. Buchanan-Michaelson	Mercedes-Benz 280SE	Robert "Bobby" Buchanan-Michaelson David Seigle-Morris Max Stahl	Great Britain
36	Sydney Telegraph	Holden Monaro GTS	David McKay George Reynolds David Liddle	Australia
37	W.D. Cresdee	Austin 1300 Countryman	W. Dennis Cresdee Bob Freeborough Johnstone Syer	Great Britain
38	Ford Motor Co.	Ford Cortina Lotus	Bengt Söderström Gunnar Palm	Great Britain
39	Addison Motors	Alfa Romeo 1750 Berlina	Stewart McLeod Jack Lock Tony Theiler	Australia
40	Jim Russell I.R. Driving School	Vauxhall Ventora	David Walker Brian Jones Doug Morris	Great Britain
41	Sydney Telegraph	Morris 1100 S	Eileen Westley Marion "Minny" Macdonald Jenny Gates	Australia
42	P. G. Graham	Ford Cortina Savage V6	Peter Graham Leslie Morrish Michael Woolley	Great Britain
43	AMOCO Australia Ltd.	Volvo 144S	Gerry Lister André Welinski	Australia
44	British Army Motoring	Rover 2000TC	Maj. Mike Bailey Maj. Freddie Preston	Great Britain
45	RAF Motorsports Assoc.	Hillman Hunter	Flight Lt. David Carrington Squadron Ldr. Anthony King Flight Lt. John Jones	Great Britain
46	Simca Motors	Simca 1100	Bernard Heu Jean-Claude Syda	France
47	Nova Magazine	MGB	Jean Denton Tom Boyce	Great Britain
48	Ford Motor Co.	Ford Cortina Lotus	Roger Clark Ove Andersson	Great Britain

No.	Entrant	Car	Team	Country
49	Major P. S. Ekholdt	SAAB 96 V4	Maj. Per S. Ekholdt Maj. S. E. Haugen	Norway
50	Ford Motor Co.	Ford Cortina Lotus	Nick Brittan Jenny Brittan	Great Britain
51	British Leyland	BMC 1800	Paddy Hopkirk Tony Nash Alec Poole	Great Britain
52	John Sprinzel	MG Midget	John Sprinzel Roy Fidler	Great Britain
53	S.H. Dickson	Rambler American	Sidney Dickson John Saladin Jerry Sims	USA
54	British Army Motoring	Rover 2000TC	Maj. John Hemsley WO1 Frank Webber	Great Britain
55	E. G. Hermann	Porsche 911	Edgar Herrmann Hans Schüller	West Germany
56	A.J. Percy	SAAB 95 V4	Alister Percy Jeremy Delmar-Morgan	Great Britain
57	Ford Deutschland	Ford 20MRS	Gilbert Staepelaere Simo Lampinen	West Germany
58	Sobiesław Zasada	Porsche 911S	Sobiesław Zasada Marek Wachowski	Poland
59	Porsche Cars GB Ltd.	Porsche 911S	Terry Hunter John Davenport	Great Britain
60	Terry Thomas	Ford Cortina 1600E	Peter Capelin Antony Pargeter Tim Baker	Great Britain
61	British Leyland	BMC 1800	Rauno Aaltonen Henry Liddon Paul Easter	Great Britain
62	Desmond Praznovsky	Mercedes-Benz 280S	Desmond Praznovsky Stan Zovko Ian Inglis	Australia
63	AMOCO Australia Ltd.	Volvo 142S	Bob Holden Laurie Graham	Australia
64	Evan Cook	BMC 1800	Flight Lt. Terry Kingsley Flight Lt. Derek Bell Flight Lt. Peter Evans	Great Britain
65	Hydraulic Machinery Ltd.	BMC 1800	Graham White John Jeffcoat David Dunnell	Great Britain
66	T. E. Buckingham	Ford Cortina GT	T. Buckingham J. Lloyd D. Hackleton	Great Britain
67	C.J. Woodley	Vauxhall Ventora	Cecil Woodley Steven Green Richard Cullingford	Great Britain

No.	Entrant	Car	Team	Country
68	Sydney Telegraph	Holden Monaro GTS	Doug Whiteford Eddie Perkins Jim Hawker	Australia
69	Dutch National Team	DAF 55	David van Lennep Peter Hissink	Holland
70	Wilson's Motor Caravan Center	BMC 1800	Anthony Wilson Francis McDonald Colin Taylor	Great Britain
71	Vantona Eyeware Ltd	BMC 1800	Brian Field Des Tilley David Jones	Great Britain
72	Ernie McMillen	Ford Cortina Lotus	Ernie McMillen John L'Amie Ian Drysdale	Great Britain
73	Ford Motor Co.	Ford Cortina Lotus	Eric Jackson Ken Chambers	Great Britain
74	R. Neyret	Citroën DS21	Robert Neyret Jacques Terramorsi	France
75	Rootes Motors	Hillman Hunter	Andrew Cowan Colin Malkin Brian Coyle	Great Britain
76	Sydney Telegraph	Holden Monaro GTS	Barry Ferguson Doug Chivas Dave Johnson	Australia
77	Big 'N' Cash & Carry Group	BMC 1800	Robert Eaves John Vipond Frank Bainbridge	Great Britain
78	Super Sport Engines Ltd.	Ford Escort GT	Jim Gavin John Maclay Martin Maudling	Great Britain
79	P. A. Downs	Volkswagen 1200	Pat Downs Anthony Downs	Great Britain
80	I. M. Large	BMW 2000	Ian Large J. Langinger J. Dudley	Great Britain
81	Dr. B. Wadia	Ford Cortina Lotus	Bomsi Wadia K. Tarmaster F. Kaka	India
82	D. G. Bray	Ford Cortina Lotus	Duncan Bray Simon Sladen Peter Sugden	Great Britain
83	Kentredder (Ireland) Ltd.	Peugeot 404	John Cotton Sylvia Kay Paddy McClintock	Ireland
84	K. Schellenberg	Bentley Sports Tourer	Keith Schellenberg Norman Barclay Hon. Patrick Lindsay	Great Britain

No.	Entrant	Car	Team	Country
85	Tecalemit Ltd	Ford Cortina Lotus	Peter Harper David Pollard	Great Britain
86	Pan Australian Unit Trust	BMW 2000	Colin Forsyth Robbie Uniacke James Rich	Great Britain
87	Citroën Cars	Citroën DS21	Lucien Bianchi Jean-Claude Ogier	France
88	Simca Motors	Simca 1100	Roger Masson Jean Py	France
89	Longlife Group	Ford Cortina	Robin Clark Martin Pearson Peter Hall	Great Britain
90	British Army Motoring Association	Ford Cortina Lotus	Capt. David Harrison Lt. Martin Proudlock	Great Britain
91	Maitland Motors	Holden HK Belmont	Bert Madden Jack "Milko" Murray John Bryson	Australia
92	Ford Deutschland	Ford 20MRS	Herbert Kleint Günther Klapproth	West Germany
93	Henry Ford and Son	Ford Cortina Lotus	Rosemary Smith Lucette Pointet	Ireland
94	Automobile Club de France	Citroën DS21	Jean-Louis Lemerle Olivier Turact Patrick Vanson	France
95	N. Koga	Vauxhall Viva GT	Nobuo Koga Yojiro Terada Kazuhiko Mitsumoto	Japan
96	R. Rogers	Ford Cortina 1600E	Ronald Rogers Alec Sheppard	Great Britain
97	Lunwin Products Pty. Ltd.	Ford Falcon XT GT	Reg Lunn Clive Tippett Jack Hall	Australia
98	Avtoexport	Moskvič 408	Uno Aaava Jurij Lesovskij	U.S.S.R.
99	17/21st Lancers	Land Rover	Lt. Gavin Thompson Lt. C. Marriott Cpl. C. Skelton Tpr. Melvin Lewis	Great Britain
100	Simca Motors	Simca 1100	Pierre Boucher Georges Houel	France

Appendix 2: The Scoreboard

No.	Car	Points at Bombay	Position at Bombay	Final Points	Final Position
1	Ford Cortina GT	47	17th	360	23rd
2	Ford Falcon XT GT	29	7th	114	8th
3	Ford Cortina GT	801	57th	Retired	DNF
4	BMC 1800	344	50th	430	24th
5	Chrysler Valiant Safari	Retired	DNF		
6	Ford Fairmont XP	308	46th	Retired	DNF
7	Moskvič 408	776	40th	776	33rd
8	Volvo 144S	10,098	70th	13,350	55th
9	Ford Cortina Lotus	Retired	DNF		
10	Porsche 911T	249	39th	Retired	DNF
11	Renault 16TS	570	55th	2,491	43rd
12	Volvo 144S	47	18th	146	11th
13	Volvo 123GT	57	22nd	Retired	DNF
14	Ford 20MRS	Retired	DNF		
15	Ford Cortina GT	Retired	DNF		
16	BMC 1800	Retired	DNF		
17	BMC 1800	254	41st	656	31st
18	Ford Cortina	494	54th	1,075	39th
19	Moskvič 408	73	28th	269	20th
20	Moskvič 408	476	52nd	942	38th
21	BMC 1800	Retired	DNF		
22	Lancia Fulvia 1.3HF	Retired	DNF		
23	Ford Corsair 2000E	Retired	DNF		
24	Ford Falcon XT GT	37	11th	62	3rd
25	Volvo 122S	229	38th	Retired	DNF
26	Mercedes-Benz 280SE	50	19th	Retired	DNF
27	Triumph 2000	1,500	60th	Retired	DNF
28	Mercedes-Benz 280SL	89	31st	Retired	DNF
29	Ford Falcon XT GT	36	10th	70	6th
30	DAF 55	69	25th	208	17th
31	BMC 1800	30	8th	332	21st
32	Mercedes-Benz 280S	79	29th	264	18th
33	Volvo 145S	452	51st	2,399	41st
34	Ford Cortina Lotus	Retired	DNF		
35	Mercedes-Benz 280SE	Retired	DNF		
36	Holden Monaro GTS	86	30th	Retired	DNF
37	Austin 1300 Countryman	Retired	DNF		

No.	Car	Points at Bombay	Position at Bombay	Final Points	Final Position
38	Ford Cortina Lotus	Retired	DNF		
39	Alfa Romeo 1750 Berlina	Retired	DNF		
40	Vauxhall Ventora	9,255	69th	9,775	52nd
41	Morris 1100 S	6,154	67th	8,111	50th
42	Ford Cortina Savage V6	5,623	65th	5,925	47th
43	Volvo 144S	56	21st	171	13th
44	Rover 2000TC	804	58th	2,848	44th
45	Hillman Hunter	482	53rd	715	32nd
46	Simca 1100	1,101	59th	1,658	40th
47	MGB	319	49th	2,408	42nd
48	Ford Cortina Lotus	11	1st	144	10th
49	SAAB 96 V4	DNS			
50	Ford Cortina Lotus	Retired	DNF		
51	BMC 1800	22	4th	56	2nd
52	MG Midget	66	24th	Retired	DNF
53	Rambler American	1,782	61st	3,746	46th
54	Rover 2000TC	287	42nd	894	37th
55	Porsche 911	71	27th	195	15th
56	SAAB 95 V4	69	26th	438	25th
57	Ford 20MRS	20	2nd	206	16th
58	Porsche 911S	40	13th	63	4th
59	Porsche 911S	Retired	DNF		
60	Ford Cortina 1600E	309	47th	873	35th
61	BMC 1800	24	5th	68	5th
62	Mercedes-Benz 280S	59	23rd	455	26th
63	Volvo 142S	Retired	DNF		
64	BMC 1800	94	32nd	266	19th
65	BMC 1800	Retired	DNF		
66	Ford Cortina GT	Retired	DNF		
67	Vauxhall Ventora	Retired	DNF		
68	Holden Monaro GTS	53	20th	173	14th
69	DAF 55	10,719	71st	13,790	56th
70	BMC 1800	311	48th	816	34th
71	BMC 1800	215	37th	570	28th
72	Ford Cortina Lotus	289	43rd	587	29th
73	Ford Cortina Lotus	31	9th	Retired	DNF
74	Citroën DS21	42	14th	123	9th
75	**Hillman Hunter**	**27**	**6th**	**50**	**1st**
76	Holden Monaro GTS	37	12th	169	12th
77	BMC 1800	602	56th	873	36th
78	Ford Escort GT	295	44th	3,665	45th
79	Volkswagen 1200	5,992	66th	9,603	51st
80	BMW 2000	DNS			
81	Ford Cortina Lotus	Retired	DNF		
82	Ford Cortina Lotus	10,990	72nd	11,465	53rd
83	Peugeot 404	153	34th	470	27th
84	Bentley Sports Tourer	Retired	DNF		
85	Ford Cortina Lotus	Retired	DNF		
86	BMW 2000	Retired	DNF		
87	Citroën DS21	21	3rd	Retired	DNF
88	Simca 1100	Retired	DNF		

No.	Car	Points at Bombay	Position at Bombay	Final Points	Final Position
89	Ford Cortina	175	36th	Retired	DNF
90	Ford Cortina Lotus	299	45th	623	30th
91	Holden HK Belmont	8,657	68th	11,646	54th
92	Ford 20MRS	44	15th	91	7th
93	Ford Cortina Lotus	4,253	64th	6,139	48th
94	Citroën DS21	46	16th	Retired	DNF
95	Vauxhall Viva GT	2,042	62nd	Retired	DNF
96	Ford Cortina 1600E	Retired	DNF		
97	Ford Falcon XT GT	Retired	DNF		
98	Moskvič 408	151	33rd	358	22nd
99	Land Rover	3,382	63rd	6,787	49th
100	Simca 1100	162	35th	Retired	DNF

Chapter Notes

Chapter 1

1. "Aviation or Flying? Who flys [*sic*] what, where, how and why," *Queen Magazine*, July 5, 1967.

Chapter 2

1. David McKay and John Smailes, *The Bright Eyes of Danger* (Sydney: Shakespeare Head Press, 1970), 18.
2. Innes Ireland, *Marathon in the Dust* (London: William Kimber, 1970), 101.
3. "Pom" or "Pommie" is a derogatory term sometimes used in Australia to denote an English person.

Chapter 4

1. "Sydney, Here We Come," *Daily Express*, June 17, 1968.
2. "Easton Men to Drive in 10,000 Miler," *Washington Post*, October 25, 1968.
3. "Gelignite Gets in Gear on the Water," *Daily Express*, October 7, 1968.
4. "The Last Ditch Danger," *Daily Express*, October 7, 1968.
5. "Game Inspired by Marathon," *Sydney Daily Telegraph*, November 22, 1968.
6. "Ford's Down Blunder," *Classic Ford*, October 2004.

Chapter 5

1. *Cars and Car Conversions Magazine*, October 1968.
2. "Bring Another Drink, Steward—We've All Earned It," *Sunday Express*, December 8, 1968.

Chapter 6

1. "Landcrab Rally History," http://www.landcrab.net.
2. Andrew Cowan, *Why Finish Last?* (London: Queen Anne Press, 1969), 42–43.
3. Nick Brittan, *Marathon: Around the World in a Cloud of Dust* (London: Motor Racing Publications, 1969), 9–10.
4. "Marathon! Great Aussie Performances but Scotsman Takes Victory," *Racing Car News*, January 1969.

Chapter 8

1. Jack Kemsley, *Just Another Incident* (Petts Wood: Dunstonian Press, 1994), 71.
2. *Daily Express* London/Sydney Marathon Souvenir Booklet.

Chapter 9

1. "London to Sydney Can't Be Tougher Than This!" *Ford Bulletin*, November 29, 1968.

Chapter 10

1. McKay and Smailes, *The Bright Eyes of Danger*, 43.
2. Eric Jackson, *Petrol in My Blood* (Fort Lauderdale: Tropical Sun Design, 2012), 278–279.
3. McKay and Smailes, *The Bright Eyes of Danger*, 46.
4. "Marathon Round-up," *Motor*, December 7, 1968.
5. "Four Young Frenchman Showed Girls the Way," *Sydney Daily Telegraph*, November 27, 1968.
6. "Ford's Down Blunder."

Chapter 11

1. "Marathon! Great Aussie Performances but Scotsman Takes Victory."

Chapter 12

1. "Marathon! Great Aussie Performances but Scotsman Takes Victory."
2. Ibid.
3. Brittan, *Marathon: Around the World in a Cloud of Dust*, 42.
4. Cowan, *Why Finish Last?* 93.

Chapter 13

1. Brittan, *Marathon: Around the World in a Cloud of Dust*, 84.
2. Ireland, *Marathon in the Dust*, 161–162.

Chapter 14

1. "Dangerous Run for Rally Cars," *Daily Express*, November 29, 1968.
2. McKay and Smailes, *The Bright Eyes of Danger*, 81.

3. Ireland, *Marathon in the Dust*, 75.
4. "7000 Miles to Bombay: Clark Leads the Marathon," *Autosport*, December 6, 1968.

Chapter 16

1. "London-Sydney Progress," *Autosport*, December 13, 1968.
2. McKay and Smailes, *The Bright Eyes of Danger*, 87.
3. Kemsley, Just Another Incident, 73.
4. "Fuel Crisis—Cars Could Be Stranded," *Sydney Daily Telegraph*, November 29, 1968.

Chapter 17

1. "This Is Our Girl for the London-Sydney Car Race," *Nova*, November 1968.
2. "Now, Making Sure the Gas Is Turned Off, Mrs. Denton Will Drive 10,000 Miles to Sydney," *Nova*, December 1968.
3. "Early Arrival in Turin," *Sydney Daily Telegraph*, November 26, 1968.
4. The Great Race: The London-Sydney Marathon Sets Off from Crystal Palace," *Autosport*, November 29, 1968.
5. "This Is Jean Denton Reporting from Sydney," *Em*, February 1969.
6. Ibid.
7. Richard Ashton, *The First London to Sydney Car Rally November December 1968*, http://mgbsmadeinaustralia.org/wp-content/uploads/2012/07/The-First-London-to-Sydney-Marathon-Car-Rally.pdf.
8. "This Is Jean Denton Reporting from Sydney."

Chapter 18

1. Cowan, *Why Finish Last?* 100.
2. "Rally Record," *Autosport*, December 6, 1968.
3. Mackay and Smailes, *The Bright Eyes of Danger*, 101.
4. "What a Day for Kabul!" *Daily Express*, November 30, 1968.

Chapter 20

1. Ireland, *Marathon in the Dust*, 102.
2. Cowan, *Why Finish Last?* 113.
3. "Marathon! Teheran to Bombay (Well Most of the Way)," *Racing Car News*, February 1969.
4. Ireland, *Marathon in the Dust*, 109.
5. Arthur Brick, *Bill Bengry "Rally Driver,"* http://www.bengrymotors.co.uk/london-sydney-marathon.
6. "1968 London to Sydney Marathon," https://www.youtube.com/watch?v=9dkesttNOQE.
7. McKay and Smailes, *The Bright Eyes of Danger*, 117.
8. Kemsley, *Just Another Incident*, 75.
9. Brittan, *Marathon: Around the World in a Cloud of Dust*, 73.

Chapter 22

1. "India Opens Its Heart," *Daily Express*, December 1, 1968.
2. "The Mad Motorists—Half Way," *Autocar*, December 12, 1968.

3. "India Opens Its Heart."
4. "Marathon Ace May Be Ruled Out," *Daily Express*, December 2, 1968.
5. "Private Entrants Dissatisfied," *Times of India*, December 2, 1968.

Chapter 23

1. *The 1968 London to Sydney Marathon*, Castrol Australia Pty Ltd, 2006.
2. Australian term for a coupé utility or car-based pickup truck.

Chapter 24

1. Paddy Hopkirk and Bill Price, *The Paddy Hopkirk Story* (Yeovil: Haynes Publishing, 2005), 141.
2. Brittan, *Marathon: Around the World in a Cloud of Dust*, 81.
3. Kemsley, *Just Another Incident*, 79.
4. Brittan, *Marathon: Around the World in a Cloud of Dust*, 84.
5. "The Society Spy," *Sydney Sunday Telegraph*, December 15, 1968.
6. "Marathon," *Racing Car News*, March 1969.
7. MacKay and Smailes, *The Bright Eyes of Danger*, 130.
8. "Twenty Take Wrong Turn," *The Western Australian*, December 16, 1968.

Chapter 25

1. "Marathon! Great Aussie Performances but Scotsman Takes Victory."

Chapter 26

1. "2000 Greet Rally Cars and Drivers," *The Western Australian*, December 14, 1968.
2. "Police Car Run Off the Road," *The Sunday Times*, December 15, 1968.
3. Cowan, *Why Finish Last?* 122.
4. "Rally Leaders Make Light of W.A. Section," *The Daily News*, December 16, 1968.
5. McKay and Smailes, *The Bright Eyes of Danger*, 138.
6. Ibid.

Chapter 27

1. Alan Sawyer, *Marathon* (Melbourne: Horwitz Publications 1969), 61.

Chapter 28

1. Arthur Brick, *Bill Bengry "Rally Driver,"* http://www.bengrymotors.co.uk/london-sydney-marathon.
2. Cowan, *Why Finish Last?* 123.
3. Eric Jackson, *Petrol in My Blood*, 278–279.
4. "WA Entry a 1-Man Crew for 2 Hours," *The Western Australian*, December 16, 1968.
5. *Daily Express* London-Sydney Marathon Navigation Notes, Perth-Sydney Part 1.
6. Cowan, *Why Finish Last?* 124.
7. McKay and Smailes, *The Bright Eyes of Danger*, 152.

Chapter 29

1. "Marathon 68 Part 1," *The Craftsman*, April 1969.
2. Ibid.
3. Ibid.

Chapter 30

1. "Rally Men Angered by Police," *Sydney Daily Telegraph*, December 18, 1968.
2. Ibid.
3. "South to Sydney," *High Road*, March 1969.
4. Ibid.
5. Ibid.
6. "Cowan Wins," *Autosport*, December 27, 1968.
7. Cowan, *Why Finish Last?* 125.
8. "Police Question Rally Leader," *The Age*, December 17, 1968.
9. Brittan, *Marathon: Around the World in a Cloud of Dust*, 111.
10. "Day-by-Day," *The Daily Express London-Sydney Marathon*, 1968.
11. Cowan, *Why Finish Last?* 126.
12. "Cowan Wins."
13. "Day-by-Day."
14. Brittan, *Marathon: Around the World in a Cloud of Dust*, 114.
15. *Daily Express* London-Sydney Marathon Navigation Notes, Perth-Sydney Part 1.
16. "'Five-wheel drive' stage," *The Canberra Times*, December 16, 1968.
17. Ibid.
18. *Daily Express* London-Sydney Marathon Navigation Notes, Perth-Sydney Part 1.

Chapter 32

1. Brittan, *Marathon: Around the World in a Cloud of Dust*, 74.

Chapter 33

1. Hopkirk and Price, *The Paddy Hopkirk Story*, 142.
2. Cowan, *Why Finish Last?* 6.
3. McKay and Smailes, *The Bright Eyes of Danger*, 168.
4. "Globe Gallopers Pt 2: Shattered Dreams," *The Mini Experience*, October–December 2009.
5. "Marathon! Flinders Ranges to Sydney," *Racing Car News*, April 1969.
6. "Fabulous, Says Injured Bianchi," *Sydney Daily Telegraph*, December 19, 1968.
7. Hopkirk and Price, *The Paddy Hopkirk Story*, 144.

8. "Marathon! Flinders Ranges to Sydney."
9. Cowan, *Why Finish Last?* 6.
10. Ibid., 127.
11. "Glow for Rally Men," *Sydney Daily Telegraph*, December 19, 1968.
12. Brittan, *Marathon: Around the World in a Cloud of Dust*, 123.

Chapter 34

1. "Quite a Saga for the Women." *Daily Express London-Sydney Marathon*, 1968.
2. "Ready for Anything," *Sydney Daily Telegraph*, November 21, 1968.
3. "Model to Drive in Car Marathon," *Sydney Sunday Telegraph*, November 10, 1968.
4. "The Society Spy—Marathon Team Is on Its Way," *Sydney Daily Telegraph*, November 10, 1968.
5. "The Society Spy ... Leaves London in a Blaze of Glory," *Sydney Daily Telegraph*, November 24, 1968.
6. "The Society Spy," *Sydney Daily Telegraph*, December 1, 1968.
7. Ibid.
8. "The Society Spy ... Waiting to Go Aboard the Chusan," *Sydney Daily Telegraph*, December 5, 1968.
9. Ibid.
10. Brittan, *Marathon! Around the World in a Cloud of Dust*, 72.
11. "The Society Spy ... Finds Shipboard Life a Little Quiet," *Sydney Daily Telegraph*, December 12, 1968.
12. "'Tele' Girls Miss Control," *Sydney Sunday Telegraph*, December 15, 1968.
13. "3 Girls "Dusty, Tired"—Still Going," *Sydney Daily Telegraph*, December 17, 1968.
14. "The Society Spy ... Enters Sydney on a Wave of Triumph," *Sydney Daily Telegraph*, December 19, 1968.
15. "Tortoise Gets Greatest Cheer," *Sydney Daily Telegraph*, December 18, 1968.

Epilogue

1. "Bitter-Sweet," *Thoroughbred and Classic Cars*, July 1988.
2. Ibid.
3. "Summary," The Daily Express London-Sydney Marathon, 1968.
4. "Marathon! Flinders Ranges to Sydney."
5. McKay and Smailes, *The Bright Eyes of Danger*, 175.
6. "Ford's Down Blunder."
7. Brittan, *Marathon! Around the World in a Cloud of Dust*, 142.
8. "Marathon! Flinders Ranges to Sydney."
9. Cowan, *Why Finish Last?* Illustration 32.

Bibliography

"Ashton, Richard. *"The First London to Sydney Car Rally November December 1968."* http://mgbsmad einaustralia.org/wp-content/uploads/2012/07/ The-First-London-to-Sydney-Marathon-Car-Rally.pdf.

"Aviation or Flying? Who Flys [*sic*] What, Where, How and Why." *Queen Magazine*, July 5, 1967.

"Bitter-Sweet." *Thoroughbred and Classic Cars*, July 1988.

Brick, Arthur. *"Bill Bengry 'Rally Driver'"* http:// www.bengrymotors.co.uk/london-syndney-mara thon.

"Bring Another Drink, Steward—We've All Earned It." *Sunday Express*, December 8, 1968.

Brittan, Nick. *Marathon: Around the World in a Cloud of Dust*. London: Motor Racing Publications, 1969.

Cowan, Andrew. *Why Finish Last?* London: Queen Anne Press, 1969.

"Cowan Wins." *Autosport*, December 27, 1968.

Daily Express London-Sydney Marathon Navigation Notes, Perth-Sydney Part 1.

"Dangerous Run for Rally Cars." *Daily Express*, November 29, 1968.

"Day-by-Day." *The Daily Express London-Sydney Marathon*, 1968.

"Early Arrival in Turin." *Sydney Daily Telegraph*, November 26, 1968.

"Easton Men to Drive in 10,000 Miler." *Washington Post*, October 25, 1968.

"Fabulous, Says Injured Bianchi." *Sydney Daily Telegraph*, December 19, 1968.

"'Five-Wheel Drive' Stage." *The Canberra Times*, December 16, 1968.

"Ford's Down Blunder." *Classic Ford*, October 2004.

"Four Young Frenchmen Showed Girls the Way." *Sydney Daily Telegraph*, November 27, 1968.

"Fuel Crisis—Cars Could Be Stranded." *Sydney Daily Telegraph*, November 29, 1968.

"Game Inspired by Marathon." *Sydney Daily Telegraph*, November 22, 1968.

"Gelignite Gets in Gear on the Water." *Daily Express*, October 7, 1968.

"Globe Gallopers Pt 2: Shattered Dreams." *The Mini Experience*, October-November 2009.

"Glow for Rally Men." *Sydney Daily Telegraph*, December 19, 1968.

"The Great Race: The London-Sydney Marathon Sets Off from Crystal Palace." *Autosport*, November 29, 1968.

Hopkirk, Paddy, and Price, Bill. *The Paddy Hopkirk Story*. Yeovil, England: Haynes Publishing, 2005.

"India Opens Its Heart." *Daily Express*, December 1, 1968.

Ireland, Innes. *Marathon in the Dust*. London: William Kimber, 1970

Jackson, Eric. *Petrol in My Blood*. Fort Lauderdale, FL: Tropical Sun Design, 2012.

Kemsley, Jack. *Just Another Incident*. Petts Wood, England: Dunstonian Press, 1994.

"Landcrab Rally History." http://www.landcrab.net.

"The Last Ditch Danger." *Daily Express*, October 7, 1968.

"London-Sydney Progress." *Autosport*, December 13, 1968.

"London to Sydney Can't Be Tougher Than This!" *Ford Bulletin*, November 29, 1968.

"The Mad Motorists—Half Way." *Autocar*, December 12, 1968.

"Marathon." *Racing Car News*, March 1969.

"Marathon Ace May Be Ruled Out." *Daily Express*, December 2, 1968.

"Marathon! Flinders Ranges to Sydney." *Racing Car News*, April 1969.

"Marathon! Great Aussie Performances but Scotsman Takes Victory." *Racing Car News*, January 1969.

"Marathon Round-up." *Motor*, December 7, 1968.

"Marathon 68 Part 1." *The Craftsman*, April 1969.

"Marathon! Teheran to Bombay (Well Most of the Way)." *Racing Car News*, February 1969.

McKay, David, and John Smailes. *The Bright Eyes of Danger*. Sydney: Shakespeare Head Press, 1970

"Model to Drive in Car Marathon." *Sydney Sunday Telegraph*, November 10, 1968.

"1968 London to Sydney Marathon." https://www. youtube.com/watch?v=9dkesttNOQE.

The 1968 London to Sydney Marathon. Castrol Australia Pty Ltd, 2006.

"Now, Making Sure the Gas Is Turned Off, Mrs. Denton Will Drive 10,000 Miles to Sydney." *Nova,* December 1968.

"Police Car Run Off the Road," *The Sunday Times,* December 15, 1968.

"Police Question Rally Leader." *The Age,* December 17, 1968.

"Private Entrants Dissatisfied." *Times of India,* December 2, 1968.

"Quite a Saga for the Women." *Daily Express London-Sydney Marathon,* 1968

"Rally Leaders Make Light of W.A. Section." *The Daily News,* December 16, 1968.

"Rally Men Angered by Police." *Sydney Daily Telegraph,* December 18, 1968.

"Rally Record." *Autosport,* December 6, 1968.

"Ready for Anything." *Sydney Daily Telegraph,* November 21, 1968.

Sawyer, Alan. *Marathon.* Melbourne: Horwitz Publications 1969.

"7000 Miles to Bombay: Clark Leads the Marathon." *Autosport,* December 6, 1968.

"The Society Spy." *Sydney Daily Telegraph,* December 1, 1968.

"The Society Spy." *Sydney Sunday Telegraph,* December 15, 1968.

"The Society Spy ... Enters Sydney on a Wave of Triumph." *Sydney Daily Telegraph,* December 19, 1968.

"The Society Spy ... Finds Shipboard Life a Little Quiet." *Sydney Daily Telegraph,* December 12, 1968.

"The Society Spy ... Leaves London in a Blaze of Glory." *Sydney Daily Telegraph,* November 24, 1968.

"The Society Spy—Marathon Team Is on Its Way." *Sydney Daily Telegraph,* November 10, 1968.

"The Society Spy ... Waiting to Go Aboard the Chusan." *Sydney Daily Telegraph,* December 5, 1968.

"South to Sydney." *High Road,* March 1969.

"Summary." *The Daily Express London-Sydney Marathon,* 1968.

"Sydney, Here We Come." *Daily Express,* June 17, 1968.

"Tele' Girls Miss Control." *Sydney Sunday Telegraph,* December 15, 1968.

"This Is Jean Denton Reporting from Sydney." *Em,* February 1969.

"This Is Our Girl for the London-Sydney Car Race." *Nova,* November 1968.

"3 Girls 'Dusty, Tired'—Still Going." *Sydney Daily Telegraph,* December 17, 1968.

"Tortoise Gets Greatest Cheer." *Sydney Daily Telegraph,* December 18, 1968.

"Twenty Take Wrong Turn." *The Western Australian,* December 16, 1968.

"2000 Greet Rally Cars and Drivers." *The Western Australian,* December 14, 1968.

"WA Entry a 1-Man Crew for 2 Hours." *The Western Australian,* December 16, 1968.

"What a Day for Kabul!" *Daily Express,* November 30, 1968.

Index

*Numbers in **bold italics** indicate photographs*